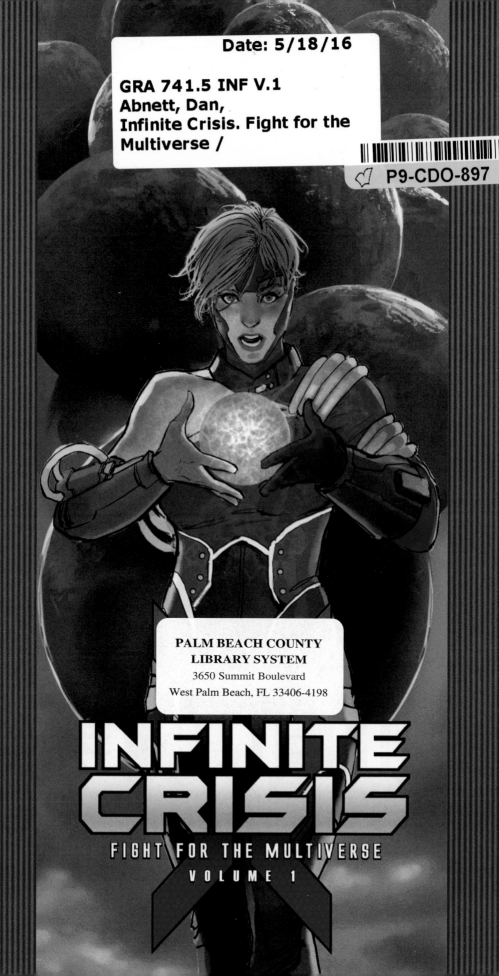

INFINITE CRISIS

FIGHT FOR THE MULTIVERSE

VOLUME 1

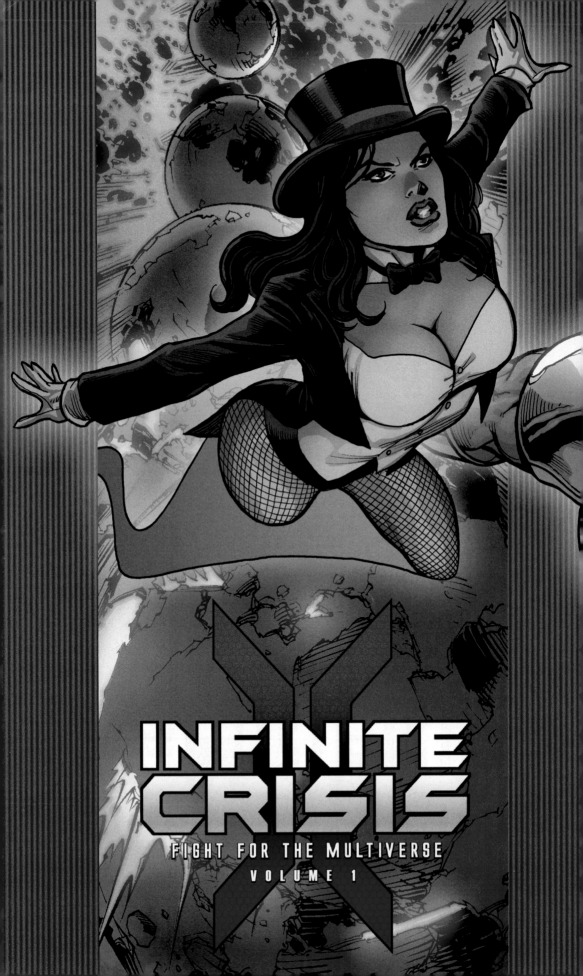

INFINITE CRISIS

FIGHT FOR THE MULTIVERSE

VOLUME 1

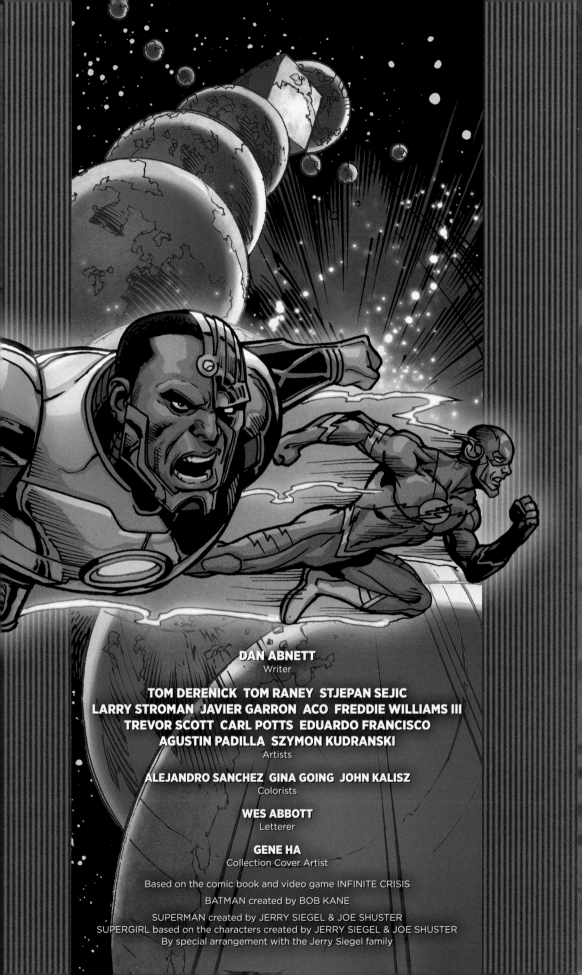

DAN ABNETT
Writer

**TOM DERENICK   TOM RANEY   STJEPAN SEJIC
LARRY STROMAN   JAVIER GARRON   ACO   FREDDIE WILLIAMS III
TREVOR SCOTT   CARL POTTS   EDUARDO FRANCISCO
AGUSTIN PADILLA   SZYMON KUDRANSKI**
Artists

ALEJANDRO SANCHEZ   GINA GOING   JOHN KALISZ
Colorists

WES ABBOTT
Letterer

GENE HA
Collection Cover Artist

Based on the comic book and video game INFINITE CRISIS

BATMAN created by BOB KANE

SUPERMAN created by JERRY SIEGEL & JOE SHUSTER
SUPERGIRL based on the characters created by JERRY SIEGEL & JOE SHUSTER
By special arrangement with the Jerry Siegel family

Jim Chadwick Editor – Original Series

Aniz Ansari Assistant Editor – Original Series

Paul Santos Editor

Robbin Brosterman Design Director – Books

Curtis King Jr. Publication Design

Hank Kanalz Senior VP – Vertigo & Integrated Publishing

Diane Nelson President

Dan DiDio and **Jim Lee** Co-Publishers

Geoff Johns Chief Creative Officer

Amit Desai Senior VP – Marketing & Franchise Management

Amy Genkins Senior VP – Business & Legal Affairs

Nairi Gardiner Senior VP – Finance

Jeff Boison VP – Publishing Planning

Mark Chiarello VP – Art Direction & Design

John Cunningham VP – Marketing

Terri Cunningham VP – Editorial Administration

Larry Ganem VP – Talent Relations & Services

Alison Gill Senior VP – Manufacturing & Operations

Jay Kogan VP – Business & Legal Affairs, Publishing

Jack Mahan VP – Business Affairs, Talent

Nick Napolitano VP – Manufacturing Administration

Sue Pohja VP – Book Sales

Fred Ruiz VP – Manufacturing Operations

Courtney Simmons Senior VP – Publicity

Bob Wayne Senior VP – Sales

INFINITE CRISIS: FIGHT FOR THE MULTIVERSE VOLUME 1

DC Comics, 4000 Warner Blvd., Burbank, CA 91522
A Warner Bros. Entertainment Company.
Printed by RR Donnelley, Owensville, MO, USA. 7/3/15.
First Printing. ISBN: 978-1-4012-5479-7

Library of Congress Cataloging-in-Publication Data

Abnett, Dan, author.
Infinite crisis : fight for the multiverse / Dan Abnett ; Tom Raney.
    pages cm
    ISBN 978-1-4012-5479-7 (paperback)
    1. Graphic novels. I. Raney, Tom, illustrator. II. Title. III. Title:
Fight for the multiverse.
PN6728.I469A33 2015
  741.5'973—dc23
                                              2015008042

**SUSTAINABLE
FORESTRY
INITIATIVE**

Certified Chain of Custody
20% Certified Forest Content,
80% Certified Sourcing

www.sfiprogram.org

SFI-01042

APPLIES TO TEXT STOCK ONLY

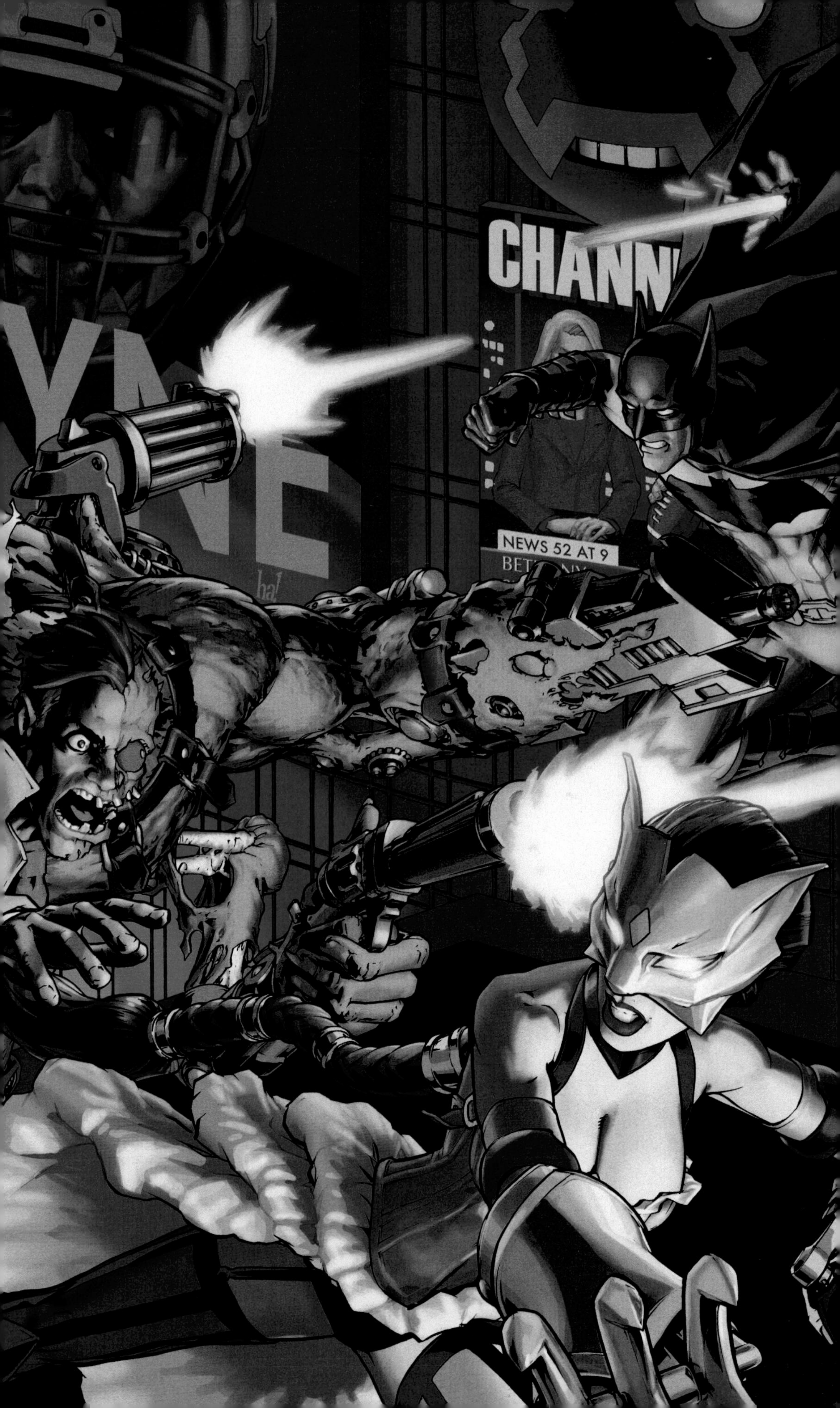

CHANN
YNE
ha!
NEWS 52 AT 9

PRELUDE

Carl Potts Larry Stroman Trevor Scott Szymon Kudranski Artists
Alejandro Sanchez John Kalisz Colorists
Cover Art by **Gene Ha**

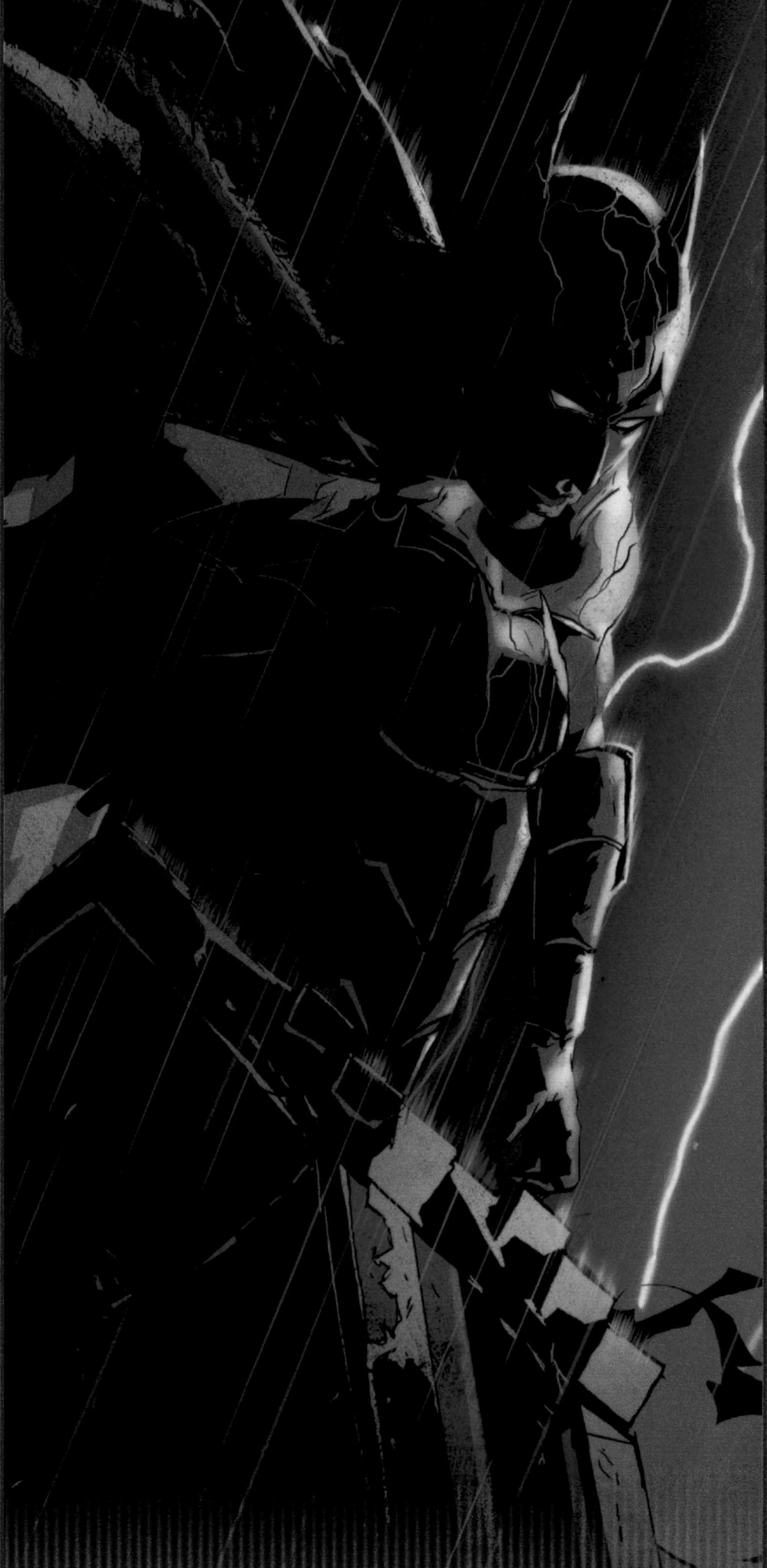

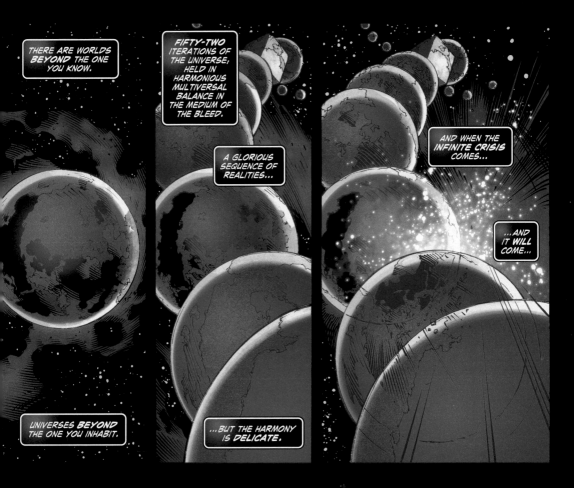

THERE ARE WORLDS *BEYOND* THE ONE YOU KNOW.

FIFTY-TWO *ITERATIONS* OF THE UNIVERSE, HELD IN *HARMONIOUS* MULTIVERSAL BALANCE IN THE MEDIUM OF THE BLEED.

A *GLORIOUS* SEQUENCE OF REALITIES...

AND WHEN THE *INFINITE CRISIS* COMES...

...AND IT *WILL* COME...

UNIVERSES *BEYOND* THE ONE YOU INHABIT.

...BUT THE HARMONY IS *DELICATE*.

...IT WILL TAKE SOMETHING *EXTRAORDINARY* TO STOP IT.

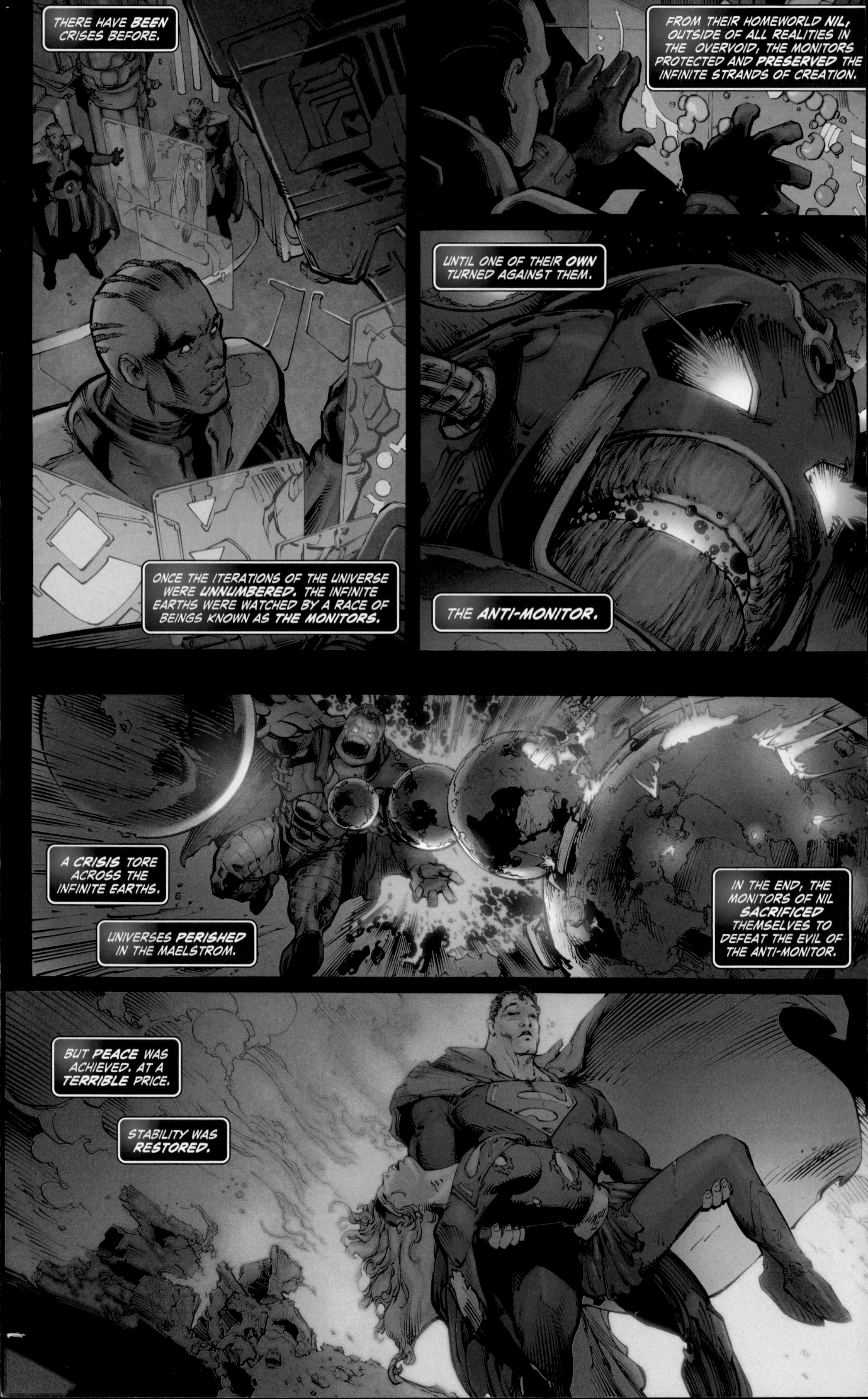
THERE HAVE BEEN CRISES BEFORE.
ONCE THE ITERATIONS OF THE UNIVERSE WERE UNNUMBERED. THE INFINITE EARTHS WERE WATCHED BY A RACE OF BEINGS KNOWN AS THE MONITORS.
FROM THEIR HOMEWORLD NIL, OUTSIDE OF ALL REALITIES IN THE OVERVOID, THE MONITORS PROTECTED AND PRESERVED THE INFINITE STRANDS OF CREATION.
UNTIL ONE OF THEIR OWN TURNED AGAINST THEM.
THE ANTI-MONITOR.
A CRISIS TORE ACROSS THE INFINITE EARTHS.
UNIVERSES PERISHED IN THE MAELSTROM.
IN THE END, THE MONITORS OF NIL SACRIFICED THEMSELVES TO DEFEAT THE EVIL OF THE ANTI-MONITOR.
BUT PEACE WAS ACHIEVED. AT A TERRIBLE PRICE.
STABILITY WAS RESTORED.

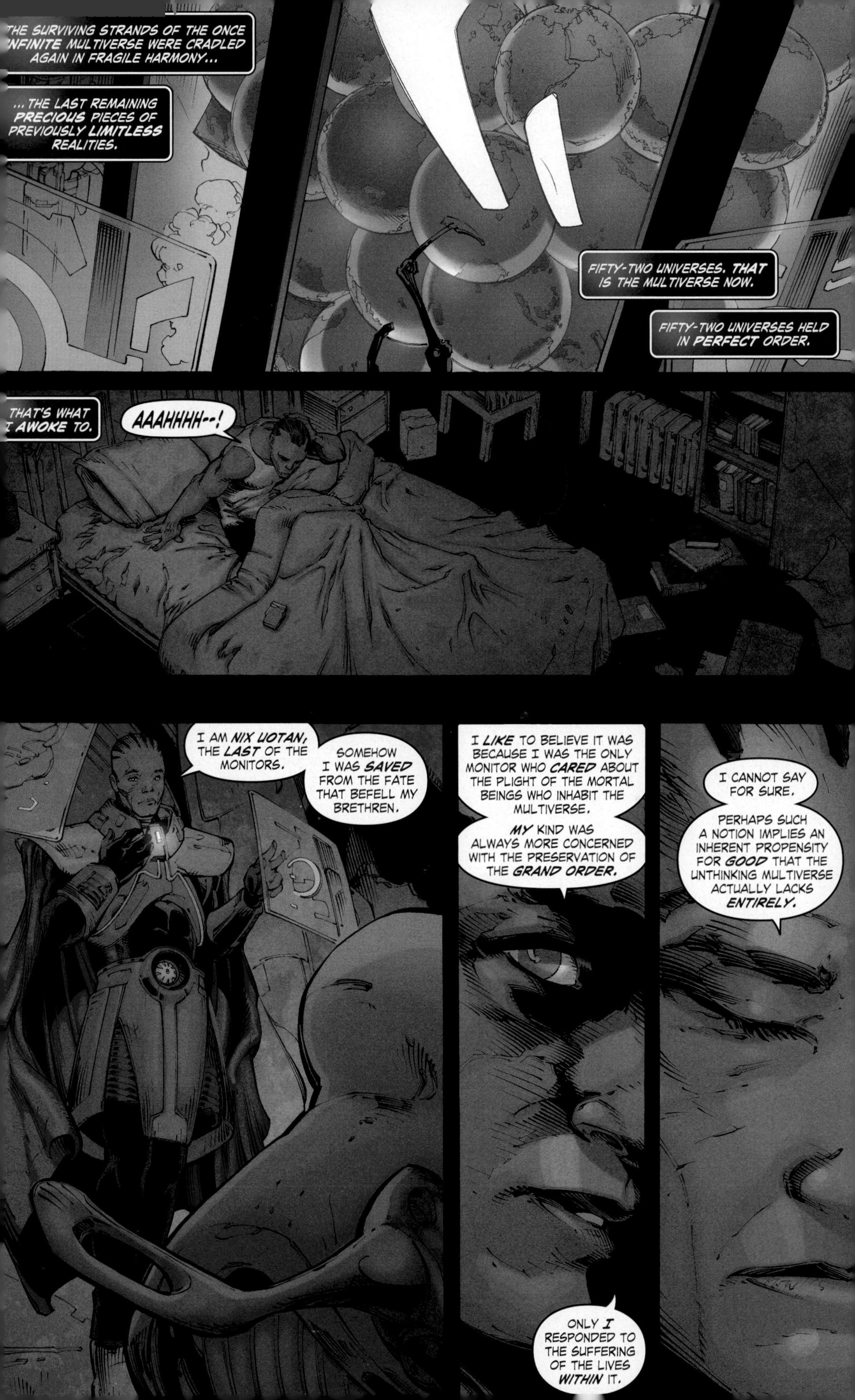

THE SURVIVING STRANDS OF THE ONCE INFINITE MULTIVERSE WERE CRADLED AGAIN IN FRAGILE HARMONY...
...THE LAST REMAINING PRECIOUS PIECES OF PREVIOUSLY LIMITLESS REALITIES.
FIFTY-TWO UNIVERSES. THAT IS THE MULTIVERSE NOW.
FIFTY-TWO UNIVERSES HELD IN PERFECT ORDER.
THAT'S WHAT I AWOKE TO.
AAAHHHH--!
I AM NIX UOTAN, THE LAST OF THE MONITORS.
SOMEHOW I WAS SAVED FROM THE FATE THAT BEFELL MY BRETHREN.
I LIKE TO BELIEVE IT WAS BECAUSE I WAS THE ONLY MONITOR WHO CARED ABOUT THE PLIGHT OF THE MORTAL BEINGS WHO INHABIT THE MULTIVERSE.
MY KIND WAS ALWAYS MORE CONCERNED WITH THE PRESERVATION OF THE GRAND ORDER.
ONLY I RESPONDED TO THE SUFFERING OF THE LIVES WITHIN IT.
I CANNOT SAY FOR SURE.
PERHAPS SUCH A NOTION IMPLIES AN INHERENT PROPENSITY FOR GOOD THAT THE UNTHINKING MULTIVERSE ACTUALLY LACKS ENTIRELY.

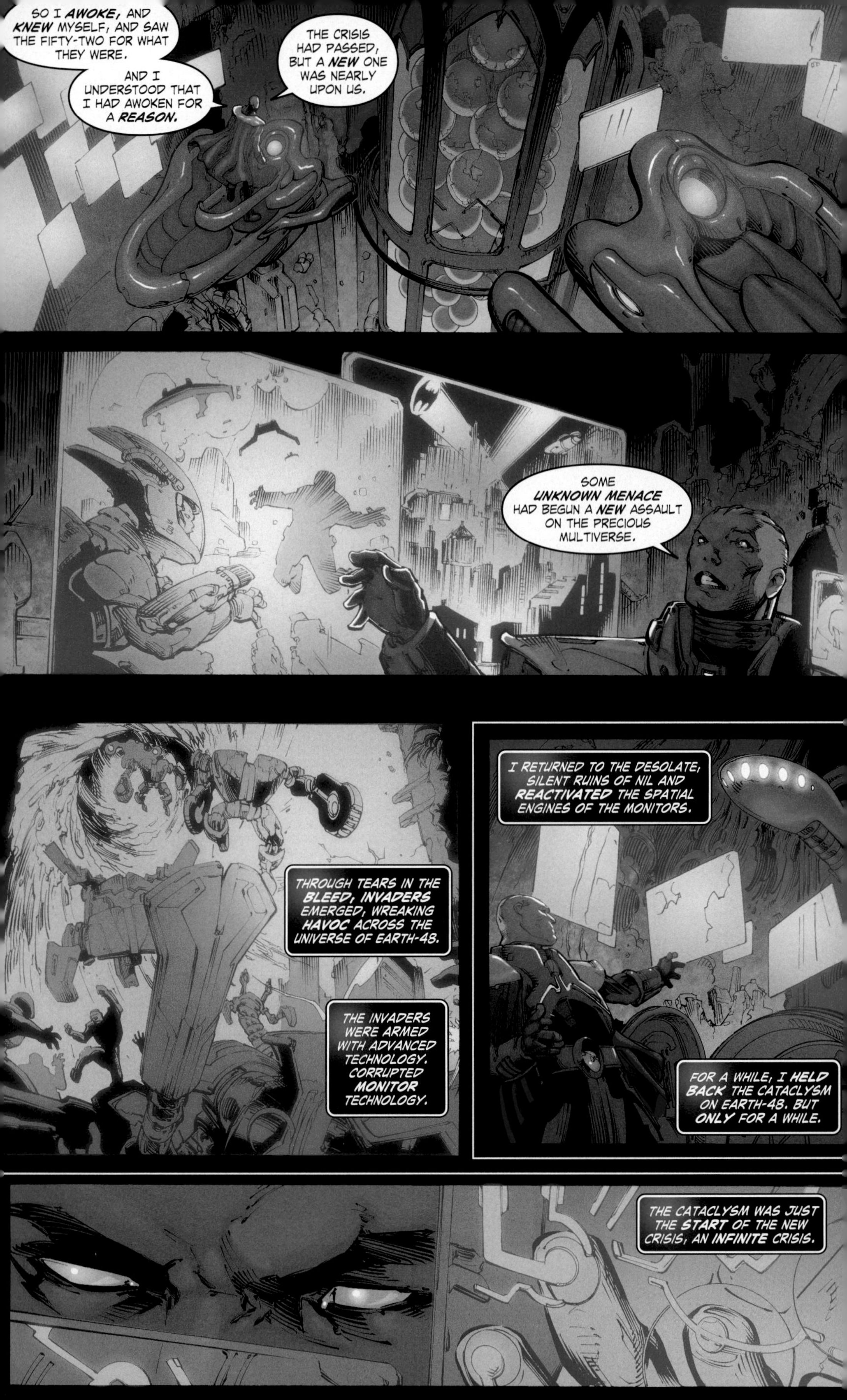
SO I AWOKE, AND KNEW MYSELF, AND SAW THE FIFTY-TWO FOR WHAT THEY WERE.
AND I UNDERSTOOD THAT I HAD AWOKEN FOR A REASON.
THE CRISIS HAD PASSED, BUT A NEW ONE WAS NEARLY UPON US.
SOME UNKNOWN MENACE HAD BEGUN A NEW ASSAULT ON THE PRECIOUS MULTIVERSE.
THROUGH TEARS IN THE BLEED, INVADERS EMERGED, WREAKING HAVOC ACROSS THE UNIVERSE OF EARTH-48.
THE INVADERS WERE ARMED WITH ADVANCED TECHNOLOGY. CORRUPTED MONITOR TECHNOLOGY.
I RETURNED TO THE DESOLATE, SILENT RUINS OF NIL AND REACTIVATED THE SPATIAL ENGINES OF THE MONITORS.
FOR A WHILE, I HELD BACK THE CATACLYSM ON EARTH-48. BUT ONLY FOR A WHILE.
THE CATACLYSM WAS JUST THE START OF THE NEW CRISIS, AN INFINITE CRISIS.

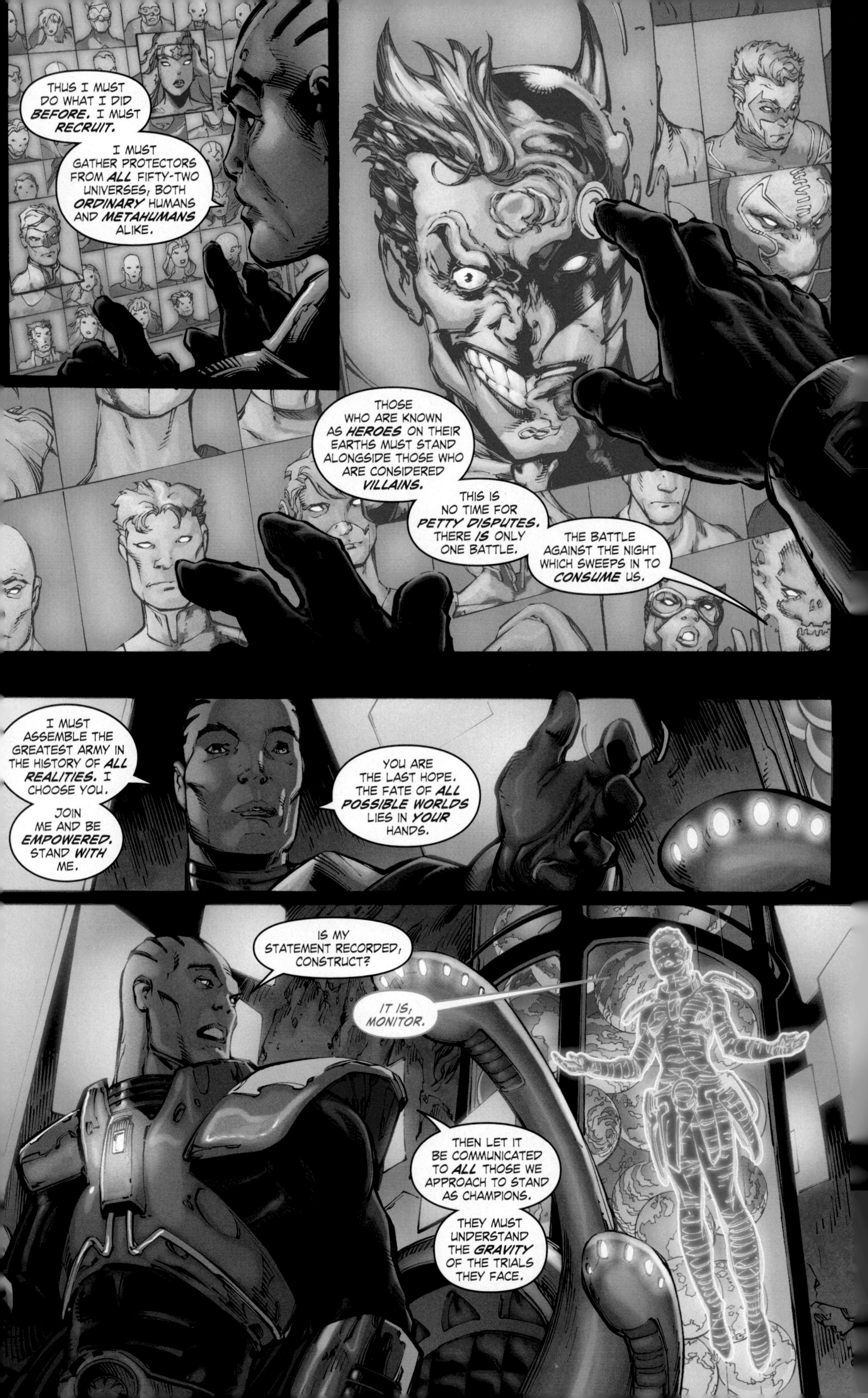
THUS I MUST DO WHAT I DID BEFORE. I MUST RECRUIT.
I MUST GATHER PROTECTORS FROM ALL FIFTY-TWO UNIVERSES, BOTH ORDINARY HUMANS AND METAHUMANS ALIKE.
THOSE WHO ARE KNOWN AS HEROES ON THEIR EARTHS MUST STAND ALONGSIDE THOSE WHO ARE CONSIDERED VILLAINS.
THIS IS NO TIME FOR PETTY DISPUTES. THERE IS ONLY ONE BATTLE.
THE BATTLE AGAINST THE NIGHT WHICH SWEEPS IN TO CONSUME US.
I MUST ASSEMBLE THE GREATEST ARMY IN THE HISTORY OF ALL REALITIES. I CHOOSE YOU.
JOIN ME AND BE EMPOWERED. STAND WITH ME.
YOU ARE THE LAST HOPE. THE FATE OF ALL POSSIBLE WORLDS LIES IN YOUR HANDS.
IS MY STATEMENT RECORDED, CONSTRUCT?
IT IS, MONITOR.
THEN LET IT BE COMMUNICATED TO ALL THOSE WE APPROACH TO STAND AS CHAMPIONS.
THEY MUST UNDERSTAND THE GRAVITY OF THE TRIALS THEY FACE.

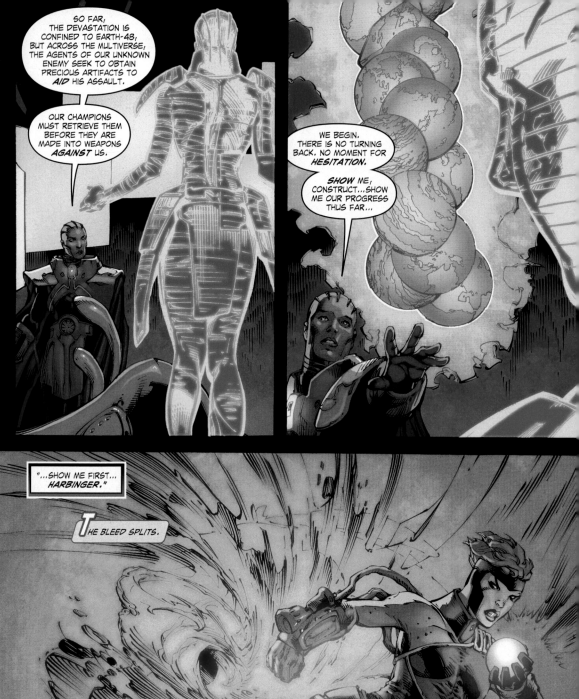

SO FAR, THE DEVASTATION IS CONFINED TO EARTH-48, BUT ACROSS THE MULTIVERSE, THE AGENTS OF OUR UNKNOWN ENEMY SEEK TO OBTAIN PRECIOUS ARTIFACTS TO *AID* HIS ASSAULT.

OUR CHAMPIONS MUST RETRIEVE THEM BEFORE THEY ARE MADE INTO WEAPONS *AGAINST* US.

WE BEGIN. THERE IS NO TURNING BACK. NO MOMENT FOR *HESITATION.*

SHOW ME, CONSTRUCT...SHOW ME OUR PROGRESS THUS FAR...

"...SHOW ME FIRST... *HARBINGER.*"

THE BLEED SPLITS.

SHE STEPS FROM WORLD TO WORLD.

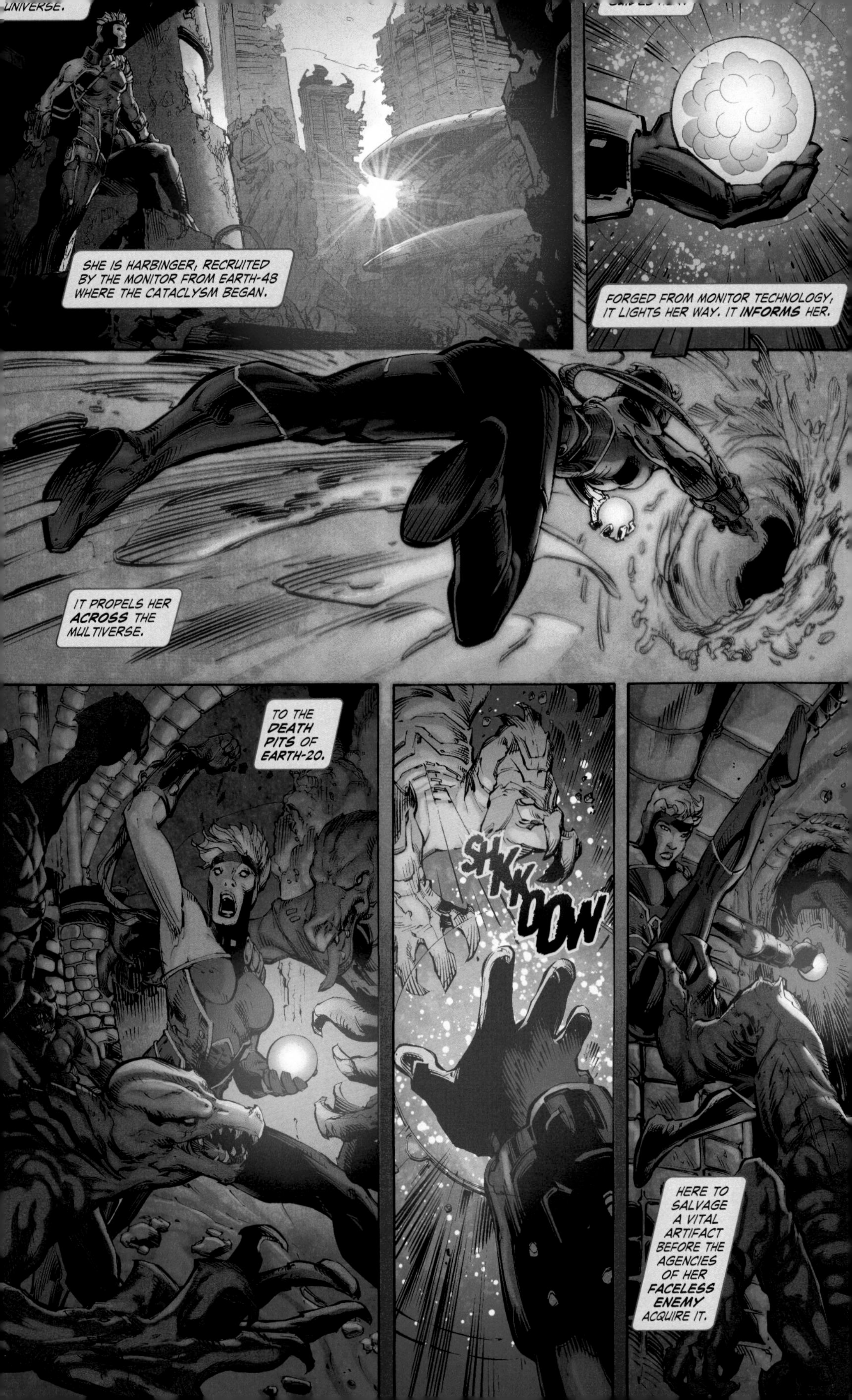
UNIVERSE.
SHE IS HARBINGER, RECRUITED BY THE MONITOR FROM EARTH-48 WHERE THE CATACLYSM BEGAN.
FORGED FROM MONITOR TECHNOLOGY, IT LIGHTS HER WAY. IT **INFORMS** HER.
IT PROPELS HER **ACROSS** THE MULTIVERSE.
TO THE **DEATH PITS** OF **EARTH-20.**
SHKKDOW
HERE TO SALVAGE A VITAL ARTIFACT BEFORE THE AGENCIES OF HER **FACELESS ENEMY** ACQUIRE IT.

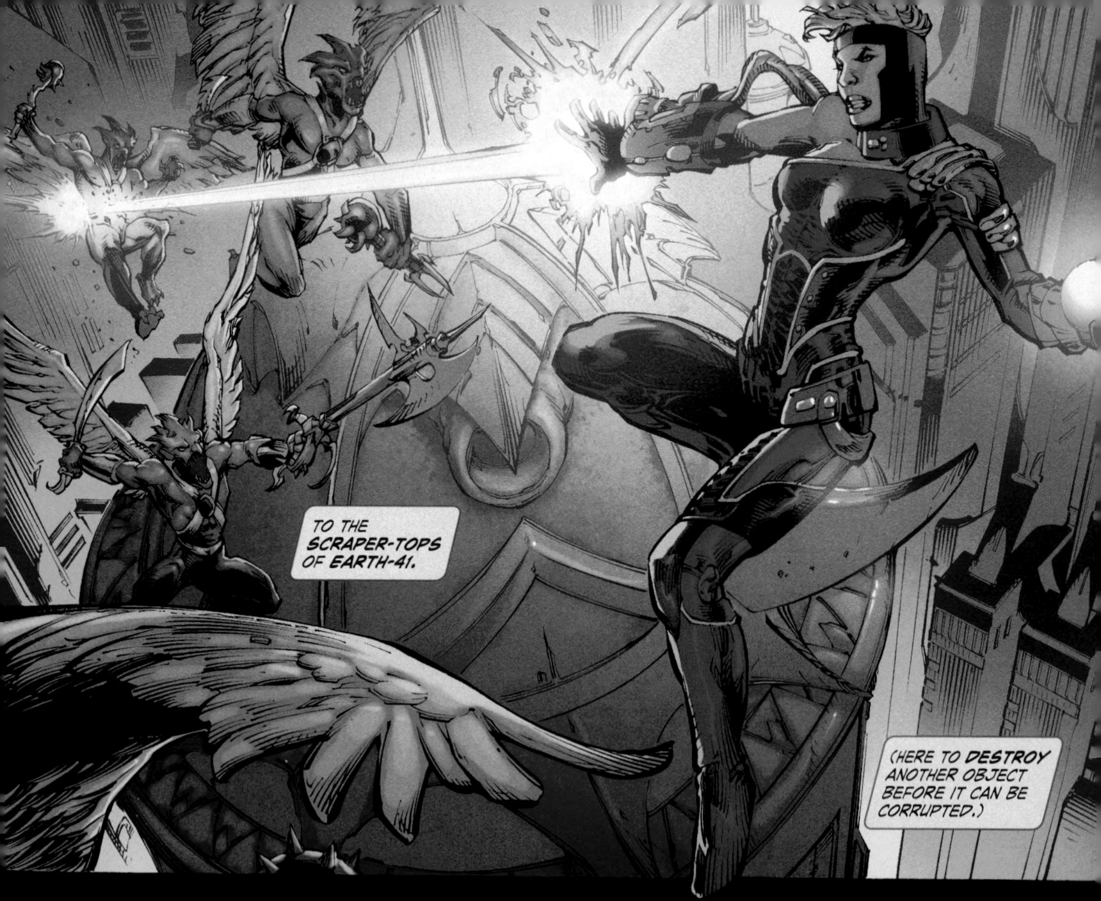
TO THE SCRAPER-TOPS OF EARTH-41.
(HERE TO DESTROY ANOTHER OBJECT BEFORE IT CAN BE CORRUPTED.)

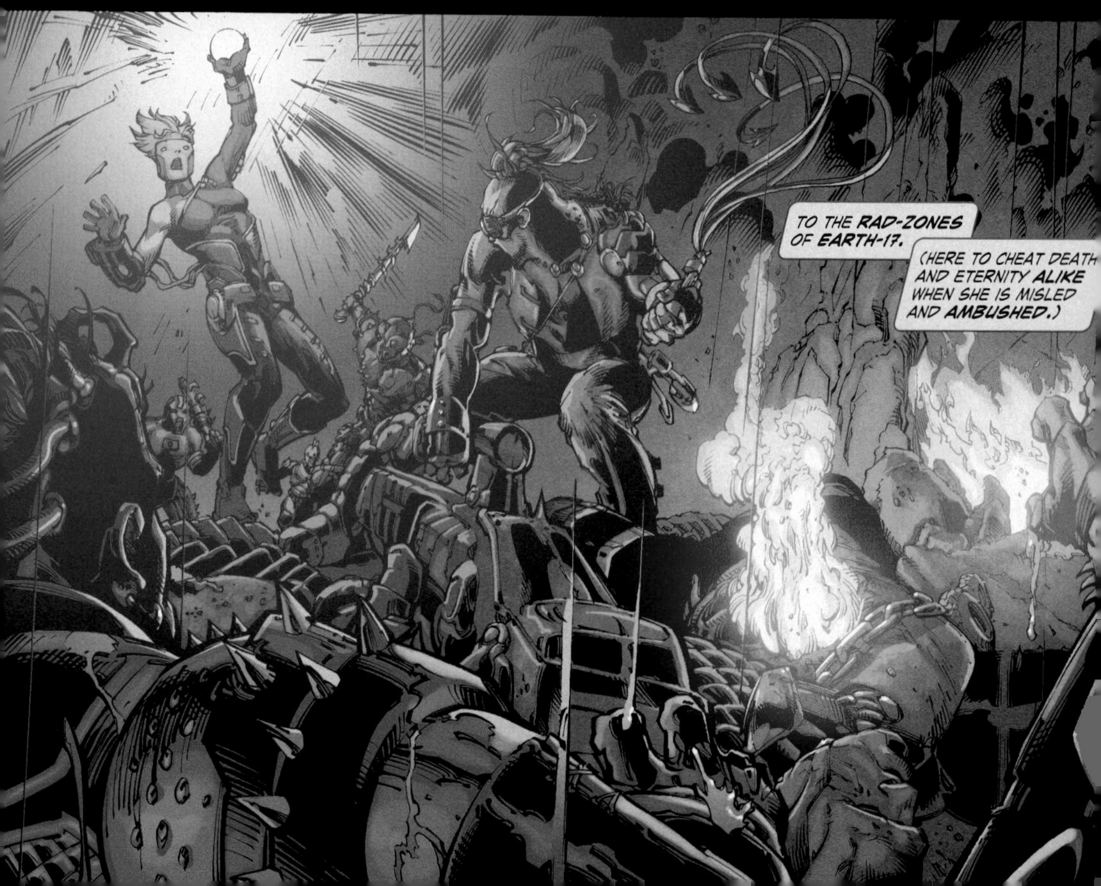
TO THE RAD-ZONES OF EARTH-17.
(HERE TO CHEAT DEATH AND ETERNITY ALIKE WHEN SHE IS MISLED AND AMBUSHED.)

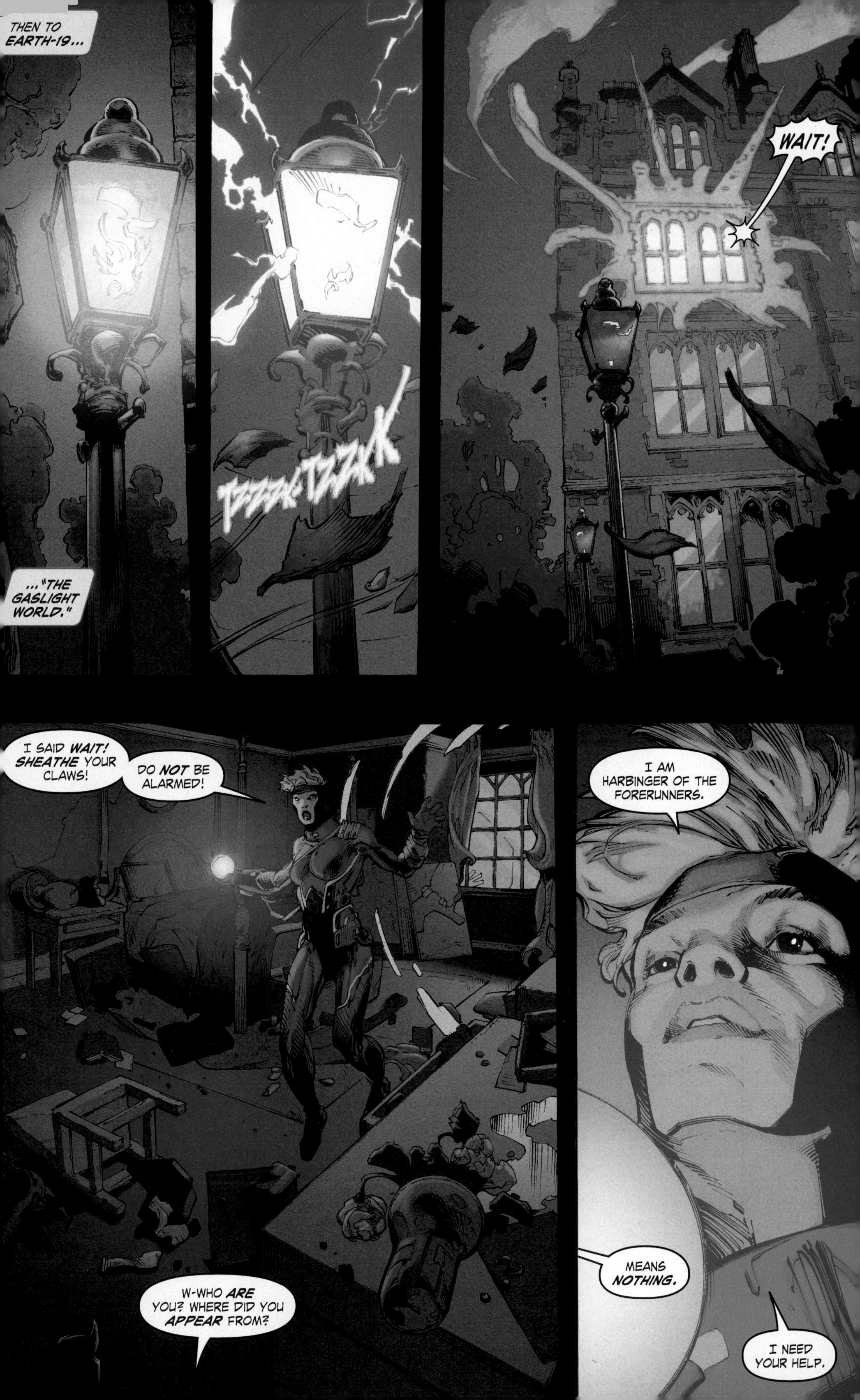
THEN TO EARTH-19...
..."THE GASLIGHT WORLD."
TZZZK! TZZK-K
WAIT!
I SAID WAIT! SHEATHE YOUR CLAWS!
DO NOT BE ALARMED!
W-WHO ARE YOU? WHERE DID YOU APPEAR FROM?
I AM HARBINGER OF THE FORERUNNERS.
MEANS NOTHING.
I NEED YOUR HELP.

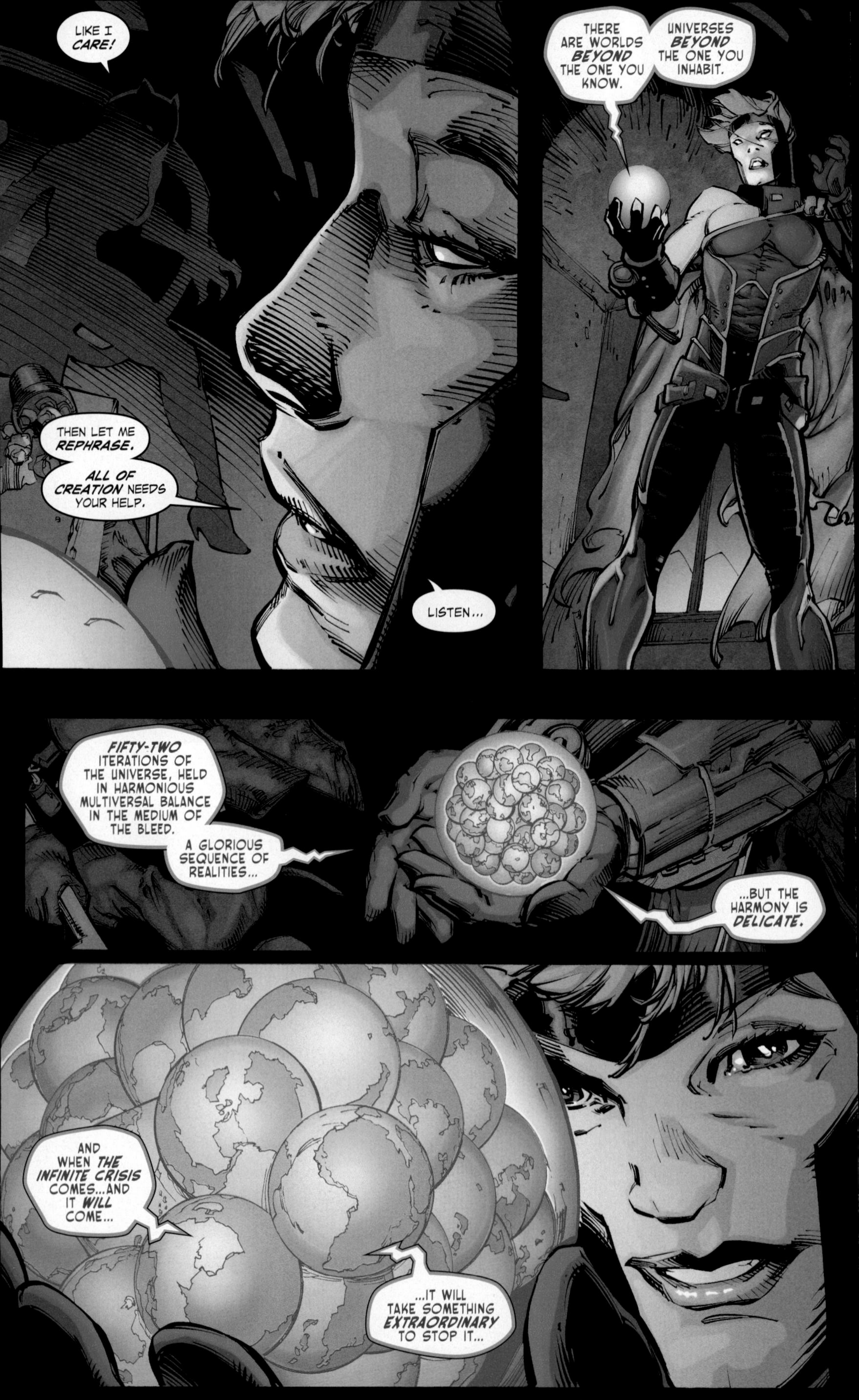
LIKE I CARE!
THEN LET ME REPHRASE.
ALL OF CREATION NEEDS YOUR HELP.
LISTEN...
THERE ARE WORLDS BEYOND THE ONE YOU KNOW.
UNIVERSES BEYOND THE ONE YOU INHABIT.
FIFTY-TWO ITERATIONS OF THE UNIVERSE, HELD IN HARMONIOUS MULTIVERSAL BALANCE IN THE MEDIUM OF THE BLEED.
A GLORIOUS SEQUENCE OF REALITIES...
...BUT THE HARMONY IS DELICATE.
AND WHEN THE INFINITE CRISIS COMES...AND IT WILL COME...
...IT WILL TAKE SOMETHING EXTRAORDINARY TO STOP IT...

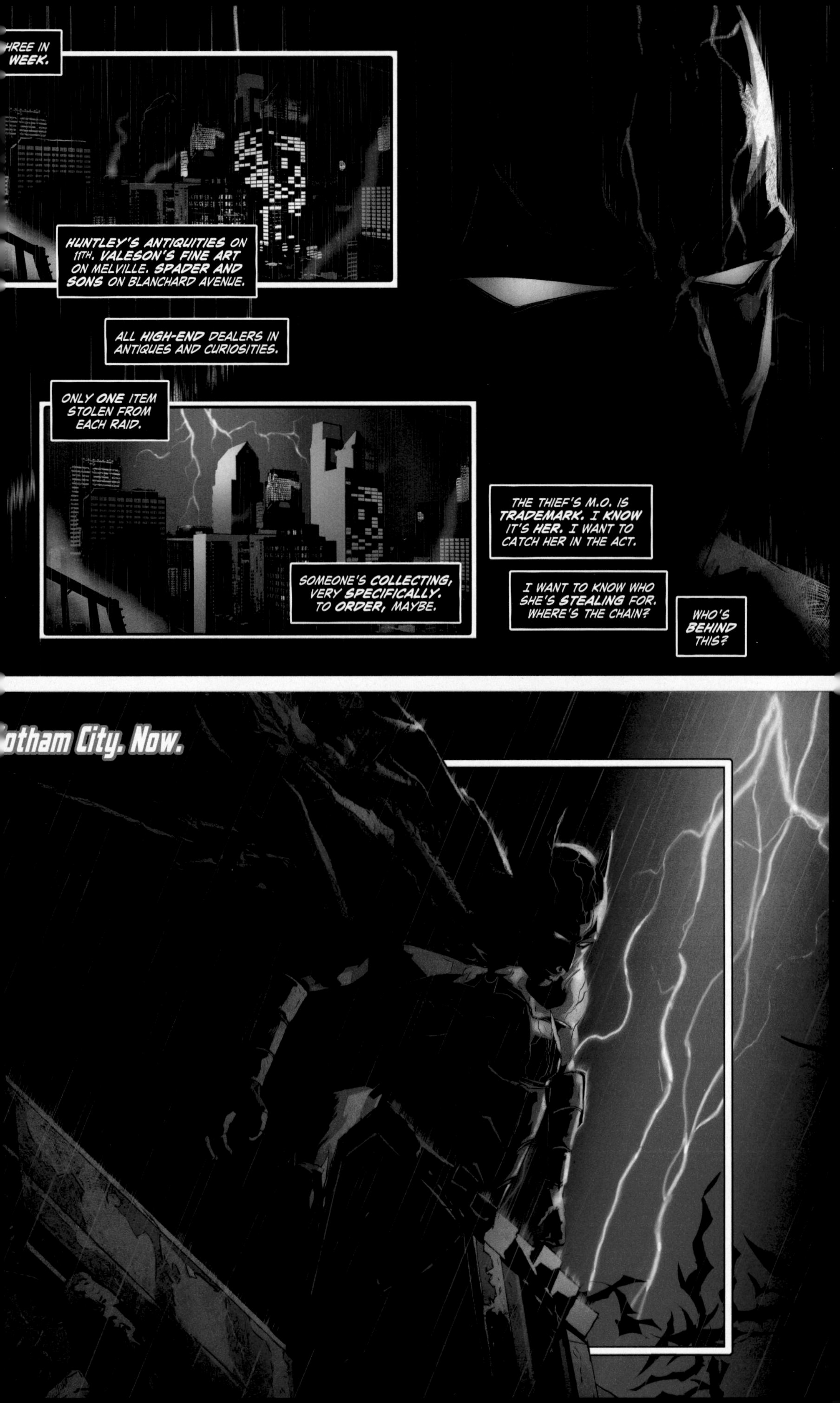

HREE IN
WEEK.
HUNTLEY'S ANTIQUITIES ON 11TH. VALESON'S FINE ART ON MELVILLE. SPADER AND SONS ON BLANCHARD AVENUE.
ALL HIGH-END DEALERS IN ANTIQUES AND CURIOSITIES.
ONLY ONE ITEM STOLEN FROM EACH RAID.
SOMEONE'S COLLECTING, VERY SPECIFICALLY. TO ORDER, MAYBE.
THE THIEF'S M.O. IS TRADEMARK. I KNOW IT'S HER. I WANT TO CATCH HER IN THE ACT.
I WANT TO KNOW WHO SHE'S STEALING FOR. WHERE'S THE CHAIN?
WHO'S BEHIND THIS?
otham City. Now.

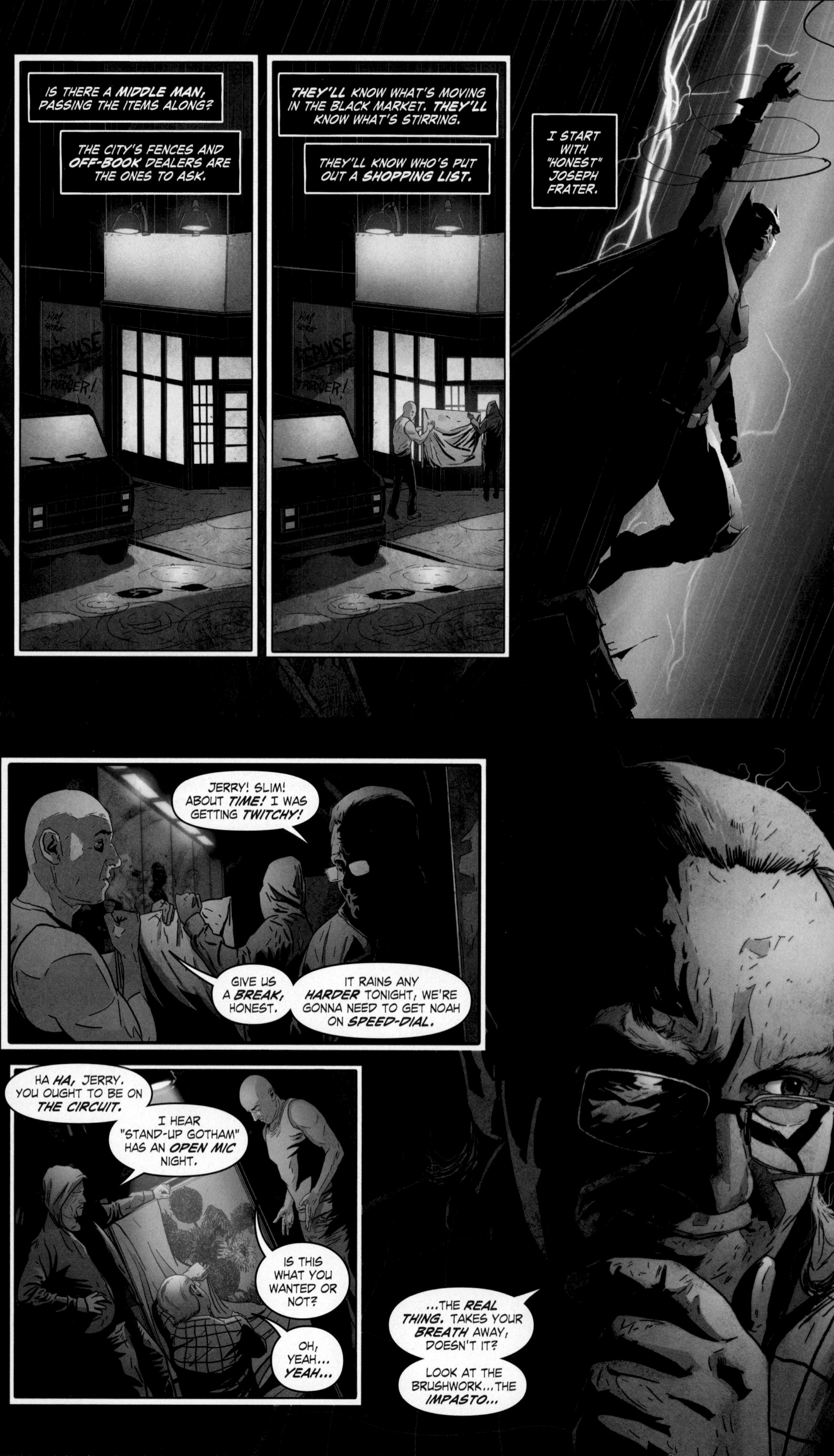
IS THERE A MIDDLE MAN, PASSING THE ITEMS ALONG?
THE CITY'S FENCES AND OFF-BOOK DEALERS ARE THE ONES TO ASK.
THEY'LL KNOW WHAT'S MOVING IN THE BLACK MARKET. THEY'LL KNOW WHAT'S STIRRING.
THEY'LL KNOW WHO'S PUT OUT A SHOPPING LIST.
I START WITH "HONEST" JOSEPH FRATER.
JERRY! SLIM! ABOUT TIME! I WAS GETTING TWITCHY!
GIVE US A BREAK, HONEST.
IT RAINS ANY HARDER TONIGHT, WE'RE GONNA NEED TO GET NOAH ON SPEED-DIAL.
HA HA, JERRY. YOU OUGHT TO BE ON THE CIRCUIT.
I HEAR "STAND-UP GOTHAM" HAS AN OPEN MIC NIGHT.
IS THIS WHAT YOU WANTED OR NOT?
OH, YEAH... YEAH...
...THE REAL THING. TAKES YOUR BREATH AWAY, DOESN'T IT?
LOOK AT THE BRUSHWORK...THE IMPASTO...

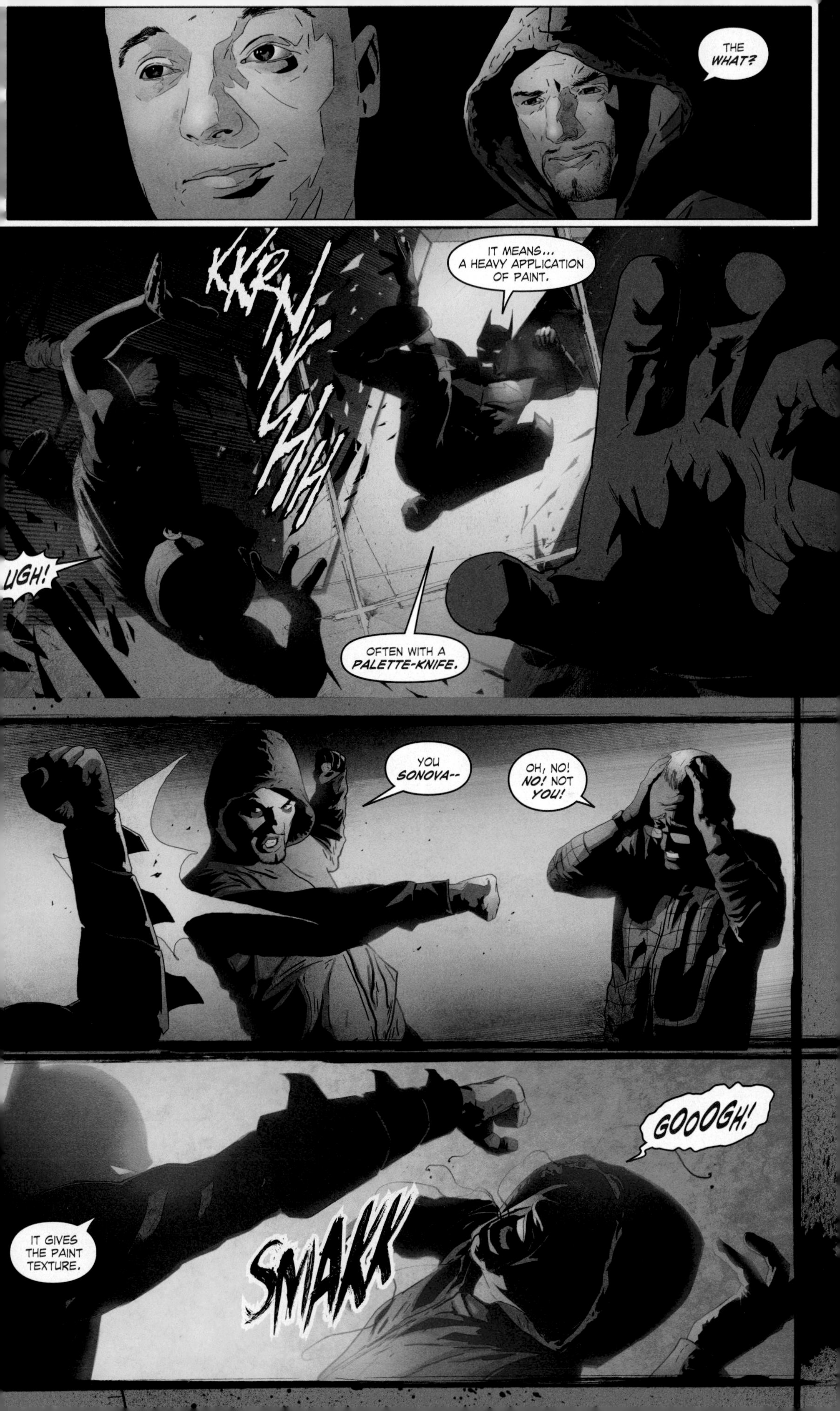

THE WHAT?
KKRNNNSHH
IT MEANS... A HEAVY APPLICATION OF PAINT.
UGH!
OFTEN WITH A PALETTE-KNIFE.
YOU SONOVA--
OH, NO! NO! NOT YOU!
GOOOGH!
IT GIVES THE PAINT TEXTURE.
SMAKK

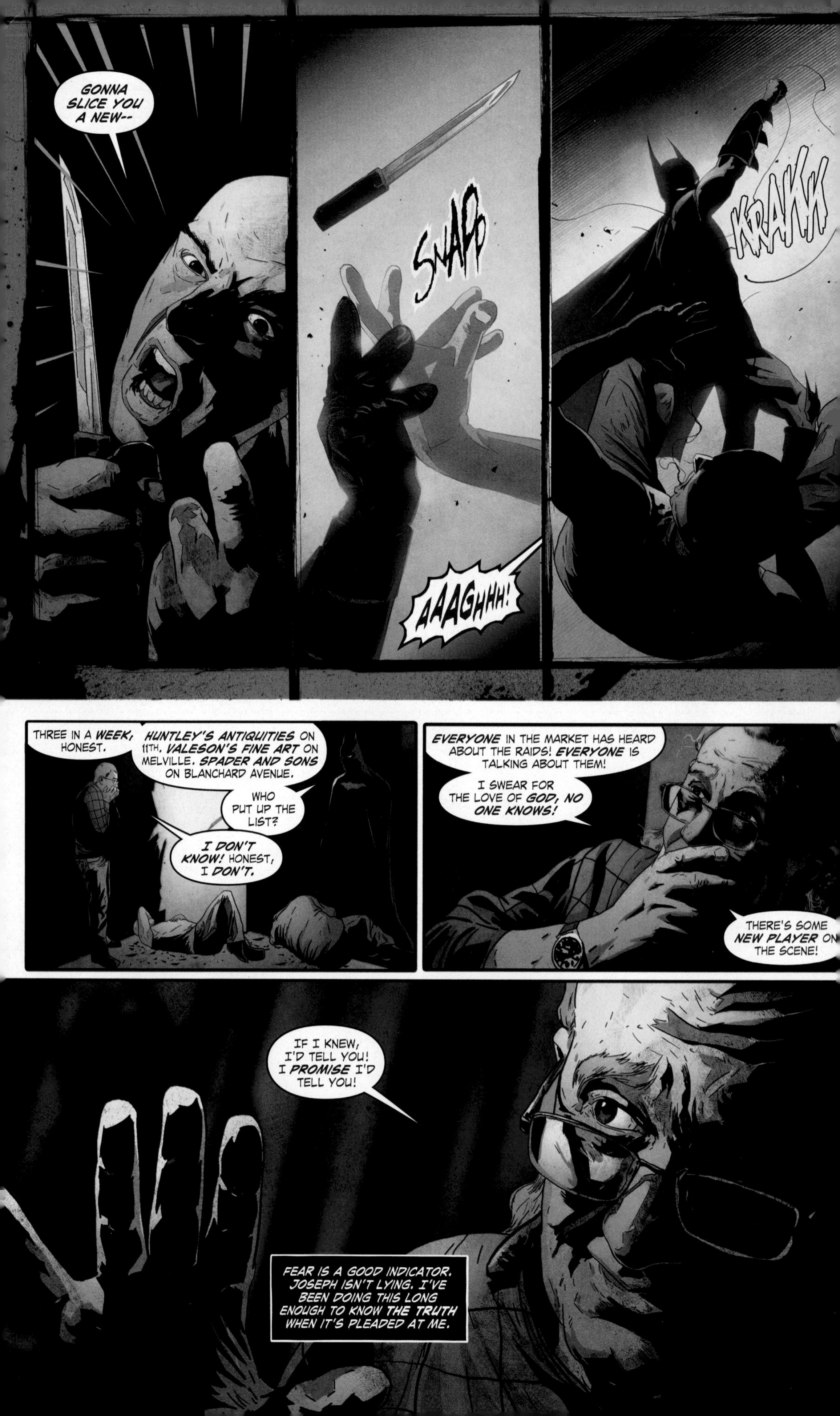
GONNA SLICE YOU A NEW--
SNAP
KRAKK
AAAGHHH!
THREE IN A WEEK, HONEST.
HUNTLEY'S ANTIQUITIES ON 11TH. VALESON'S FINE ART ON MELVILLE. SPADER AND SONS ON BLANCHARD AVENUE.
WHO PUT UP THE LIST?
I DON'T KNOW! HONEST, I DON'T.
EVERYONE IN THE MARKET HAS HEARD ABOUT THE RAIDS! EVERYONE IS TALKING ABOUT THEM!
I SWEAR FOR THE LOVE OF GOD, NO ONE KNOWS!
THERE'S SOME NEW PLAYER ON THE SCENE!
IF I KNEW, I'D TELL YOU! I PROMISE I'D TELL YOU!
FEAR IS A GOOD INDICATOR. JOSEPH ISN'T LYING. I'VE BEEN DOING THIS LONG ENOUGH TO KNOW THE TRUTH WHEN IT'S PLEADED AT ME.

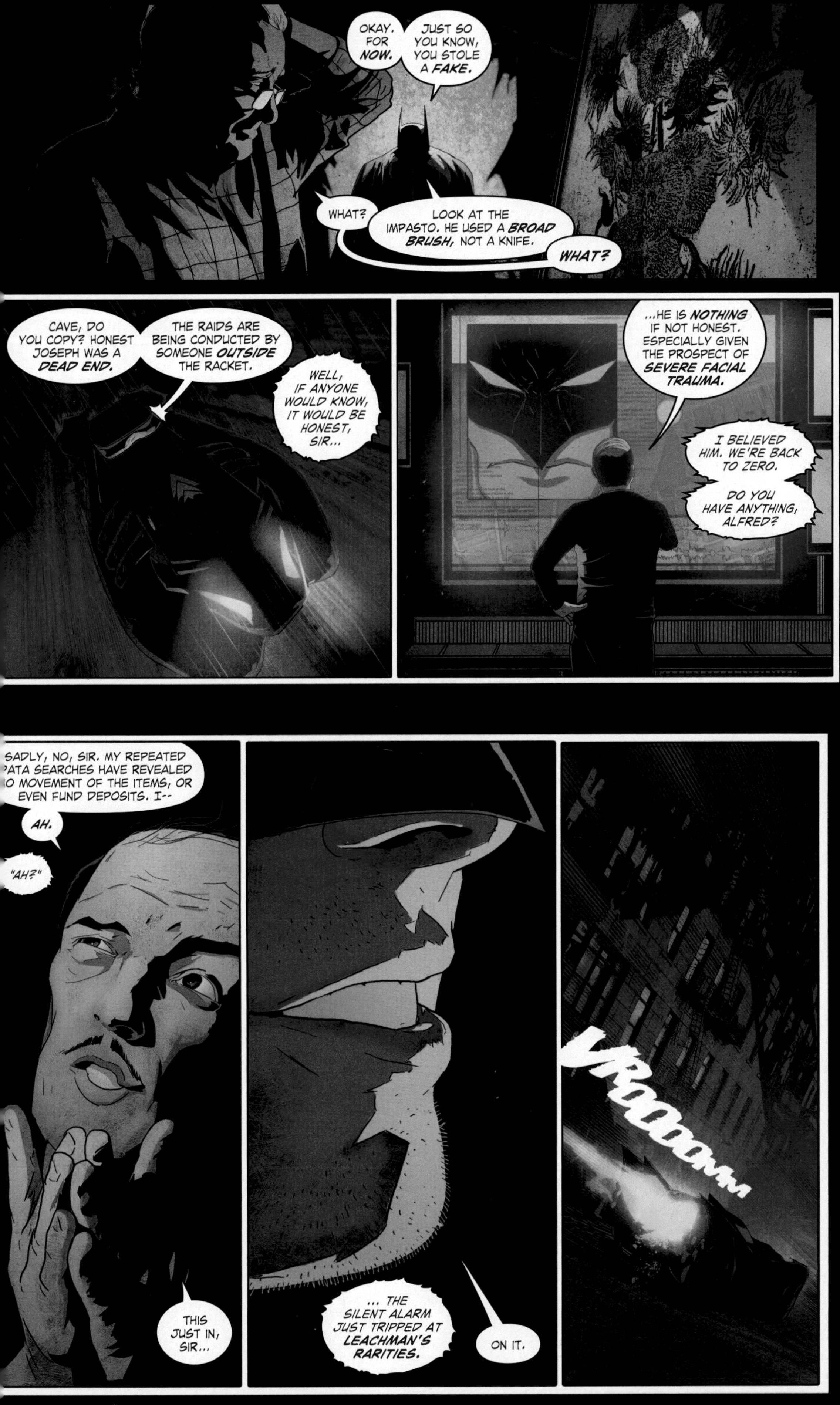
OKAY. FOR NOW.
JUST SO YOU KNOW, YOU STOLE A FAKE.
WHAT?
LOOK AT THE IMPASTO. HE USED A BROAD BRUSH, NOT A KNIFE.
WHAT?
CAVE, DO YOU COPY? HONEST JOSEPH WAS A DEAD END.
THE RAIDS ARE BEING CONDUCTED BY SOMEONE OUTSIDE THE RACKET.
WELL, IF ANYONE WOULD KNOW, IT WOULD BE HONEST, SIR...
...HE IS NOTHING IF NOT HONEST. ESPECIALLY GIVEN THE PROSPECT OF SEVERE FACIAL TRAUMA.
I BELIEVED HIM. WE'RE BACK TO ZERO.
DO YOU HAVE ANYTHING, ALFRED?
SADLY, NO, SIR. MY REPEATED DATA SEARCHES HAVE REVEALED NO MOVEMENT OF THE ITEMS, OR EVEN FUND DEPOSITS. I--
AH.
"AH?"
THIS JUST IN, SIR...
... THE SILENT ALARM JUST TRIPPED AT LEACHMAN'S RARITIES.
ON IT.
VROOOOMM

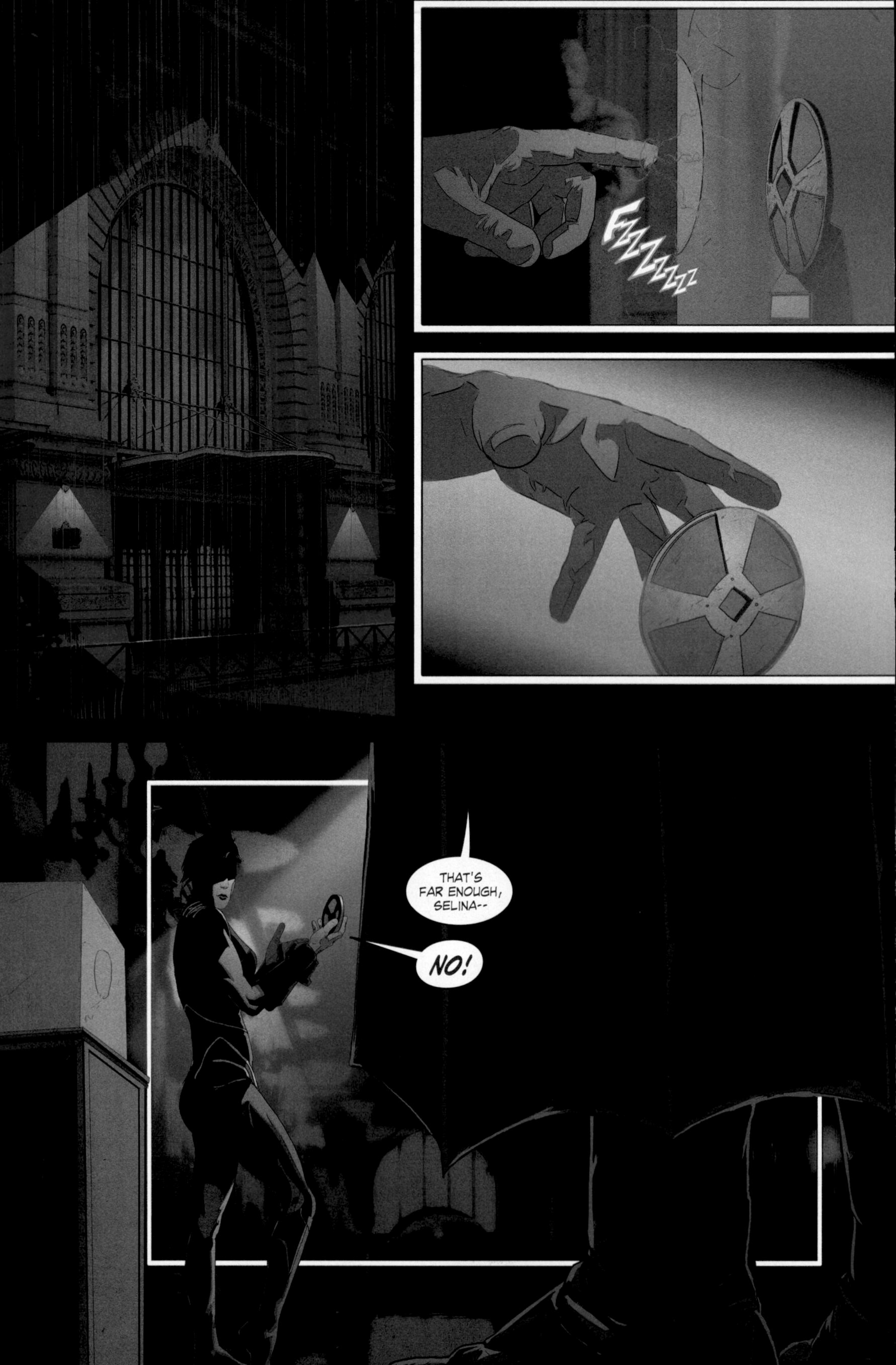
FZZZZZZZZ
THAT'S FAR ENOUGH, SELINA--
NO!

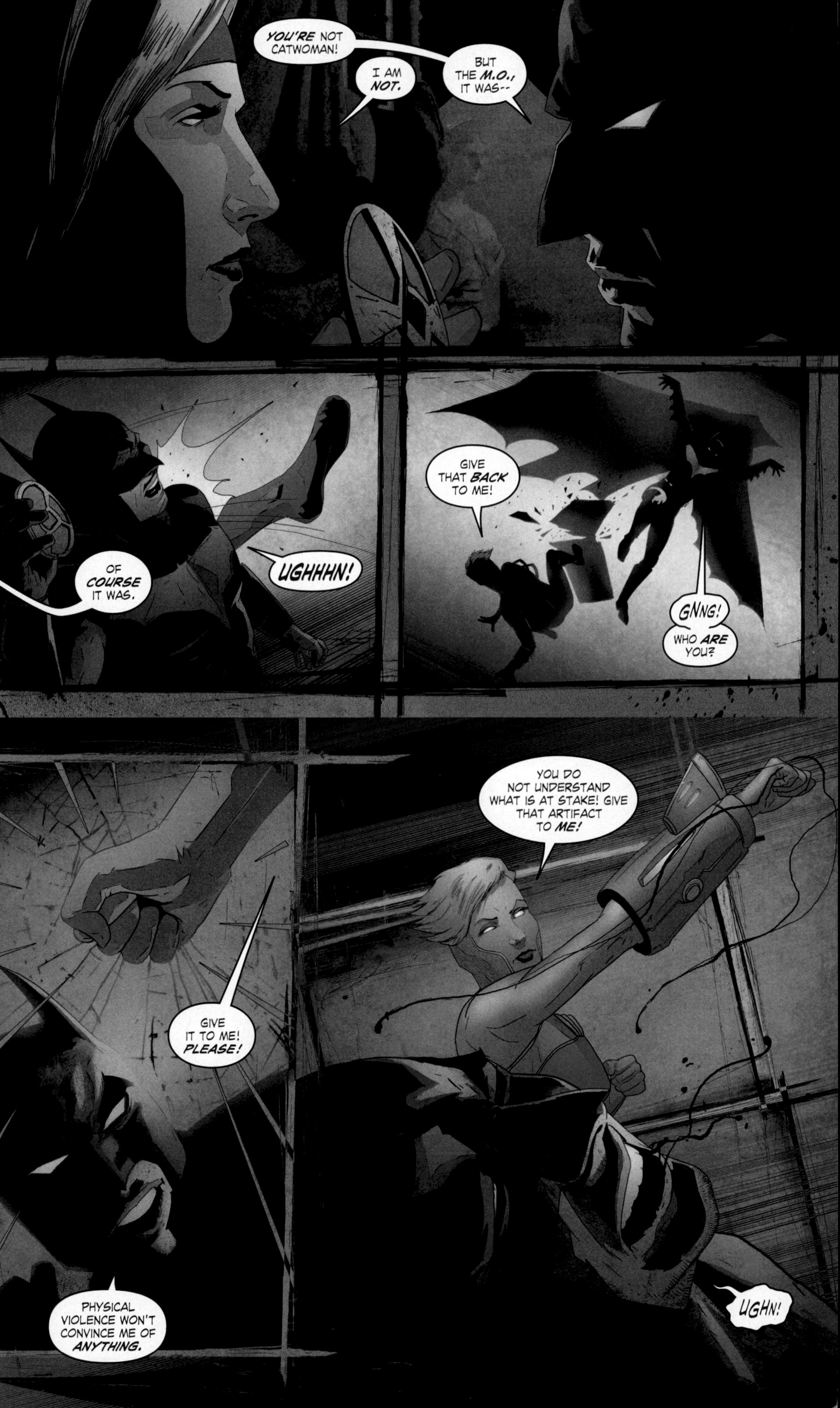
YOU'RE NOT CATWOMAN!
I AM NOT.
BUT THE M.O., IT WAS--
OF COURSE IT WAS.
UGHHHN!
GIVE THAT BACK TO ME!
GNNG!
WHO ARE YOU?
YOU DO NOT UNDERSTAND WHAT IS AT STAKE! GIVE THAT ARTIFACT TO ME!
GIVE IT TO ME! PLEASE!
PHYSICAL VIOLENCE WON'T CONVINCE ME OF ANYTHING.
UGHN!

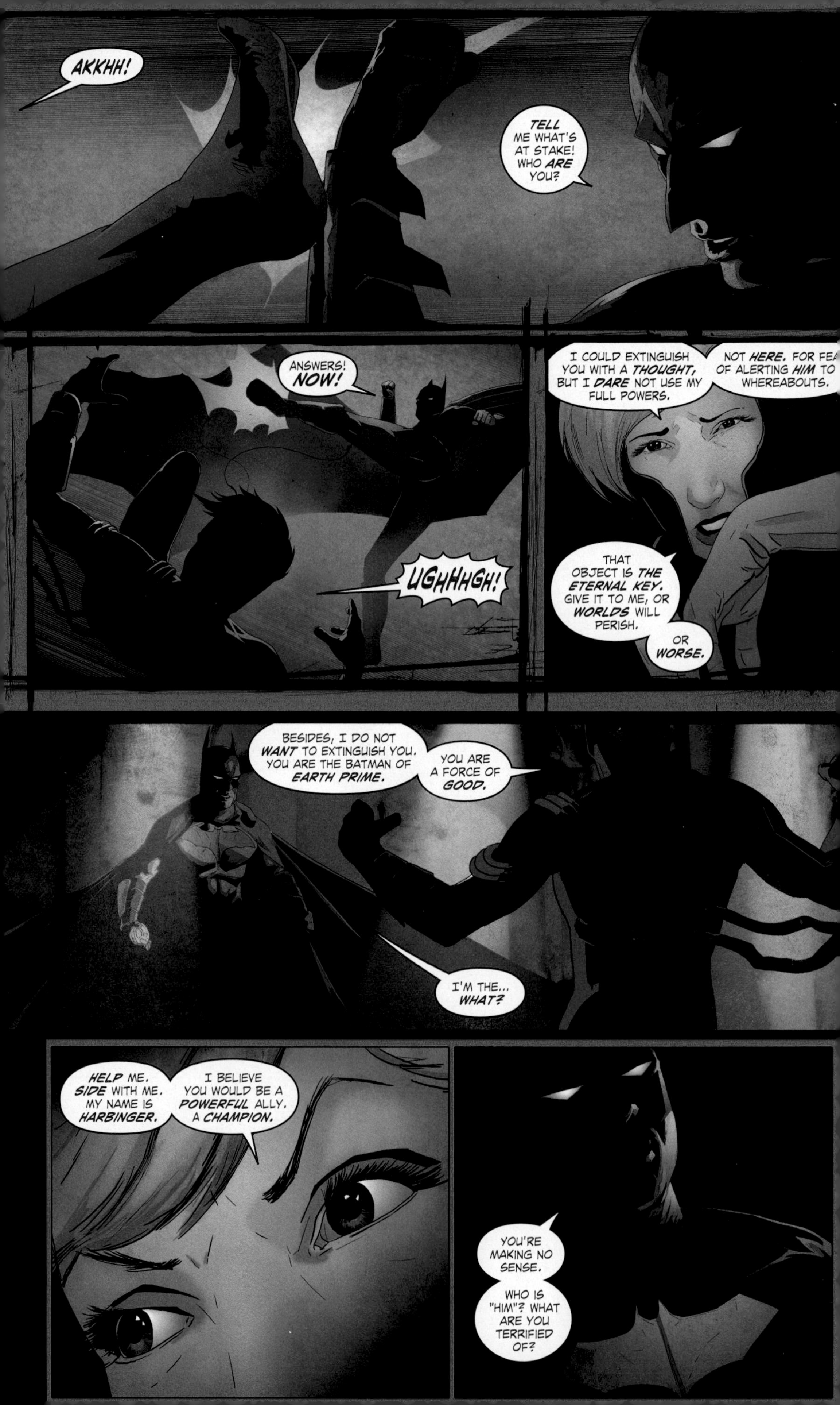

AKKHH!
TELL ME WHAT'S AT STAKE! WHO ARE YOU?
ANSWERS! NOW!
UGHHHGH!
I COULD EXTINGUISH YOU WITH A THOUGHT, BUT I DARE NOT USE MY FULL POWERS.
NOT HERE. FOR FEA OF ALERTING HIM TO WHEREABOUTS.
THAT OBJECT IS THE ETERNAL KEY. GIVE IT TO ME, OR WORLDS WILL PERISH.
OR WORSE.
BESIDES, I DO NOT WANT TO EXTINGUISH YOU. YOU ARE THE BATMAN OF EARTH PRIME.
YOU ARE A FORCE OF GOOD.
I'M THE... WHAT?
HELP ME. SIDE WITH ME. MY NAME IS HARBINGER.
I BELIEVE YOU WOULD BE A POWERFUL ALLY. A CHAMPION.
YOU'RE MAKING NO SENSE.
WHO IS "HIM"? WHAT ARE YOU TERRIFIED OF?

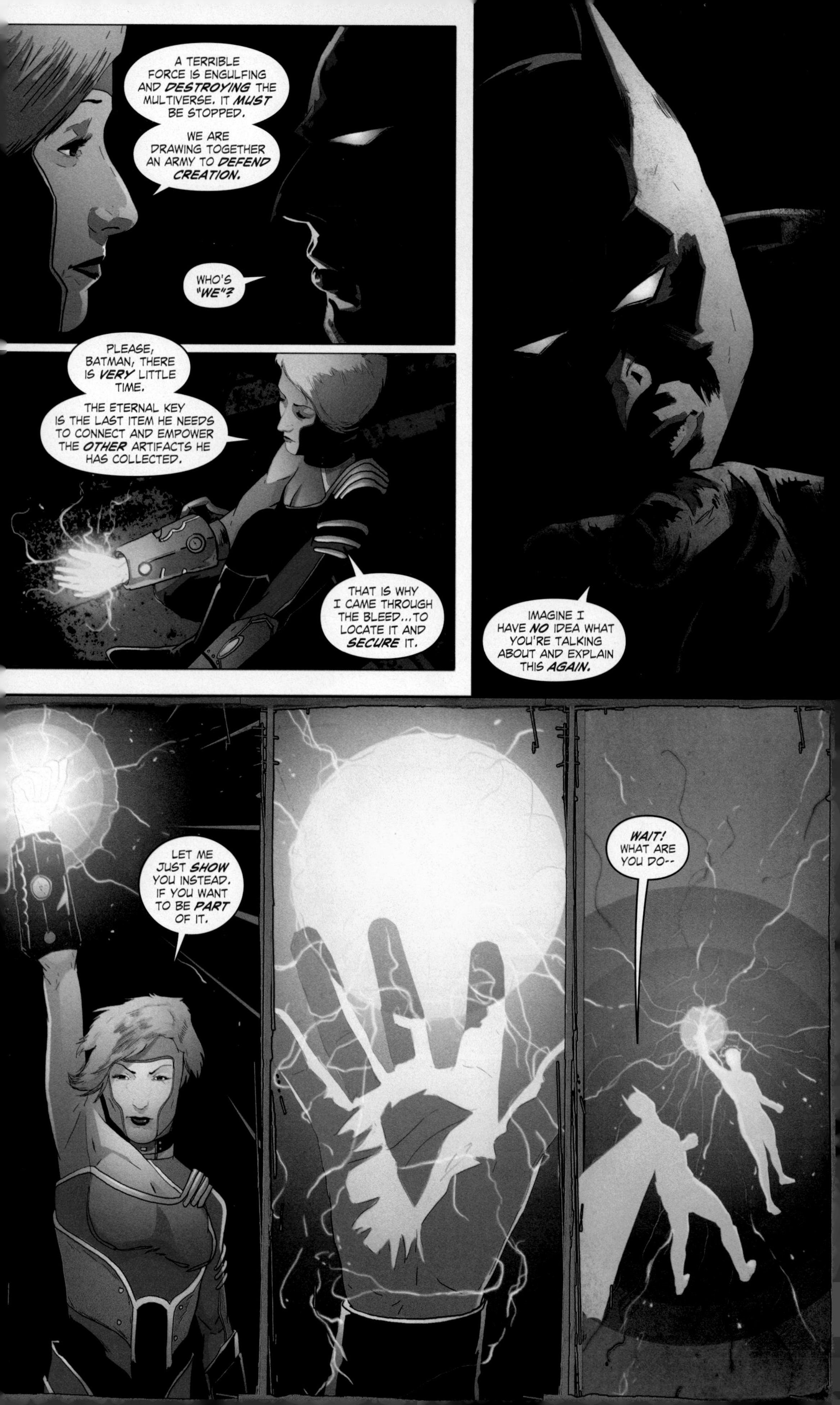

A TERRIBLE FORCE IS ENGULFING AND DESTROYING THE MULTIVERSE. IT MUST BE STOPPED.
WE ARE DRAWING TOGETHER AN ARMY TO DEFEND CREATION.
WHO'S "WE"?
PLEASE, BATMAN, THERE IS VERY LITTLE TIME.
THE ETERNAL KEY IS THE LAST ITEM HE NEEDS TO CONNECT AND EMPOWER THE OTHER ARTIFACTS HE HAS COLLECTED.
THAT IS WHY I CAME THROUGH THE BLEED...TO LOCATE IT AND SECURE IT.
IMAGINE I HAVE NO IDEA WHAT YOU'RE TALKING ABOUT AND EXPLAIN THIS AGAIN.
LET ME JUST SHOW YOU INSTEAD. IF YOU WANT TO BE PART OF IT.
WAIT! WHAT ARE YOU DO--

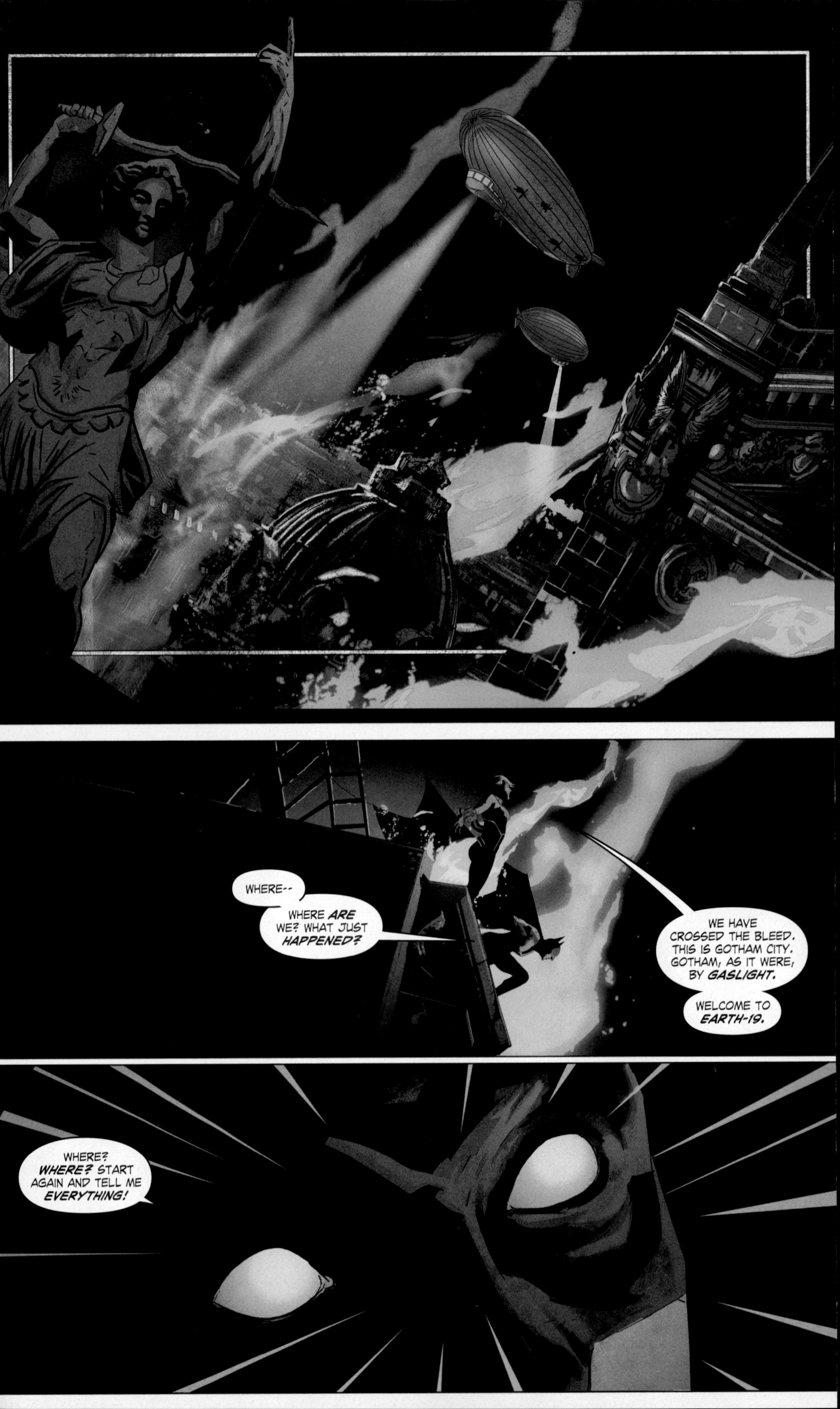
WHERE--
WHERE ARE WE? WHAT JUST HAPPENED?
WE HAVE CROSSED THE BLEED. THIS IS GOTHAM CITY. GOTHAM, AS IT WERE, BY GASLIGHT.
WELCOME TO EARTH-19.
WHERE? WHERE? START AGAIN AND TELL ME EVERYTHING!

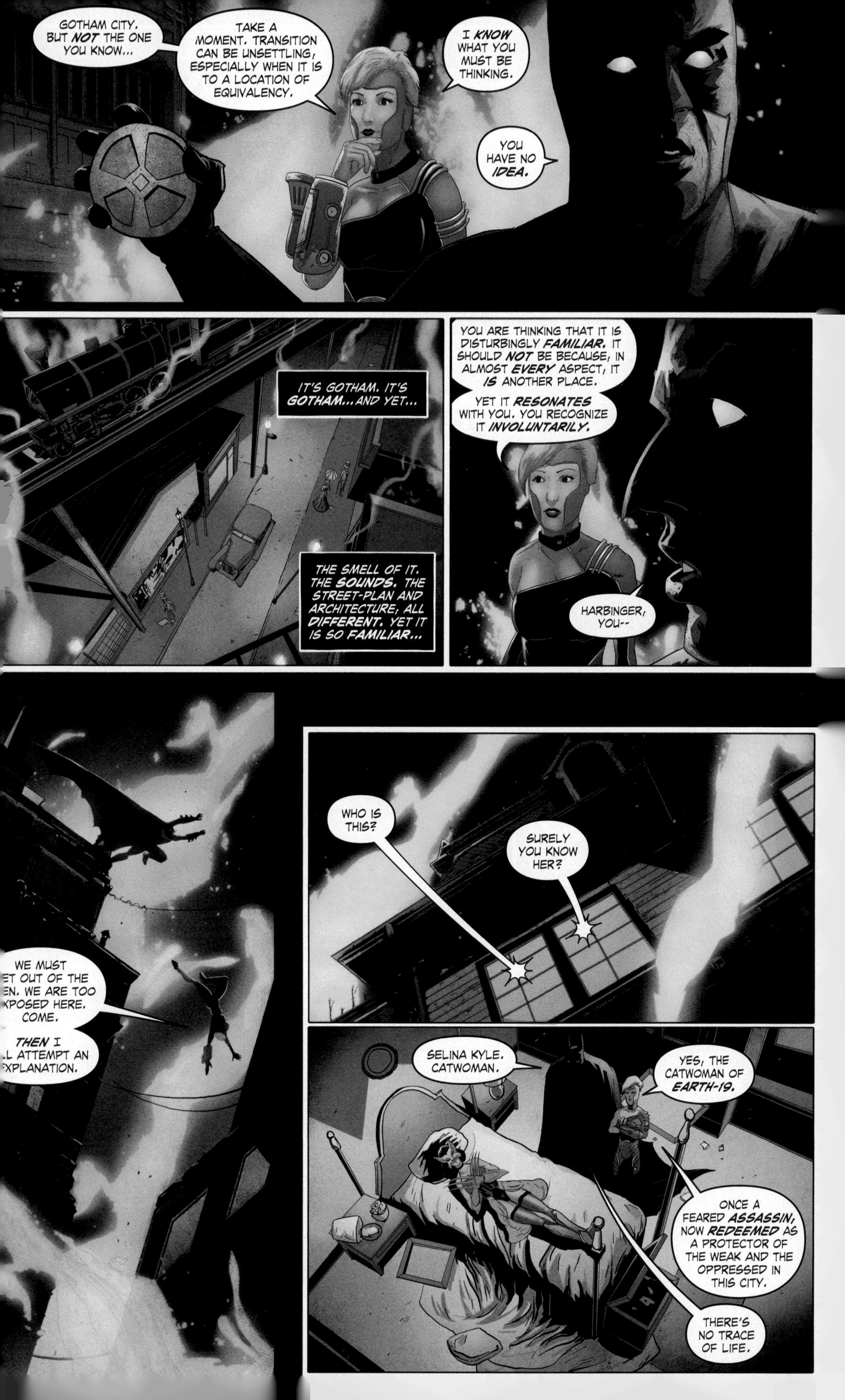
GOTHAM CITY. BUT NOT THE ONE YOU KNOW...
TAKE A MOMENT. TRANSITION CAN BE UNSETTLING, ESPECIALLY WHEN IT IS TO A LOCATION OF EQUIVALENCY.
I KNOW WHAT YOU MUST BE THINKING.
YOU HAVE NO IDEA.
IT'S GOTHAM. IT'S GOTHAM...AND YET...
THE SMELL OF IT. THE SOUNDS. THE STREET-PLAN AND ARCHITECTURE; ALL DIFFERENT. YET IT IS SO FAMILIAR...
YOU ARE THINKING THAT IT IS DISTURBINGLY FAMILIAR. IT SHOULD NOT BE BECAUSE, IN ALMOST EVERY ASPECT, IT IS ANOTHER PLACE.
YET IT RESONATES WITH YOU. YOU RECOGNIZE IT INVOLUNTARILY.
HARBINGER, YOU--
WE MUST
ET OUT OF THE
EN. WE ARE TOO
XPOSED HERE.
COME.
THEN I
L ATTEMPT AN
XPLANATION.
WHO IS THIS?
SURELY YOU KNOW HER?
SELINA KYLE. CATWOMAN.
YES, THE CATWOMAN OF EARTH-19.
ONCE A FEARED ASSASSIN, NOW REDEEMED AS A PROTECTOR OF THE WEAK AND THE OPPRESSED IN THIS CITY.
THERE'S NO TRACE OF LIFE.

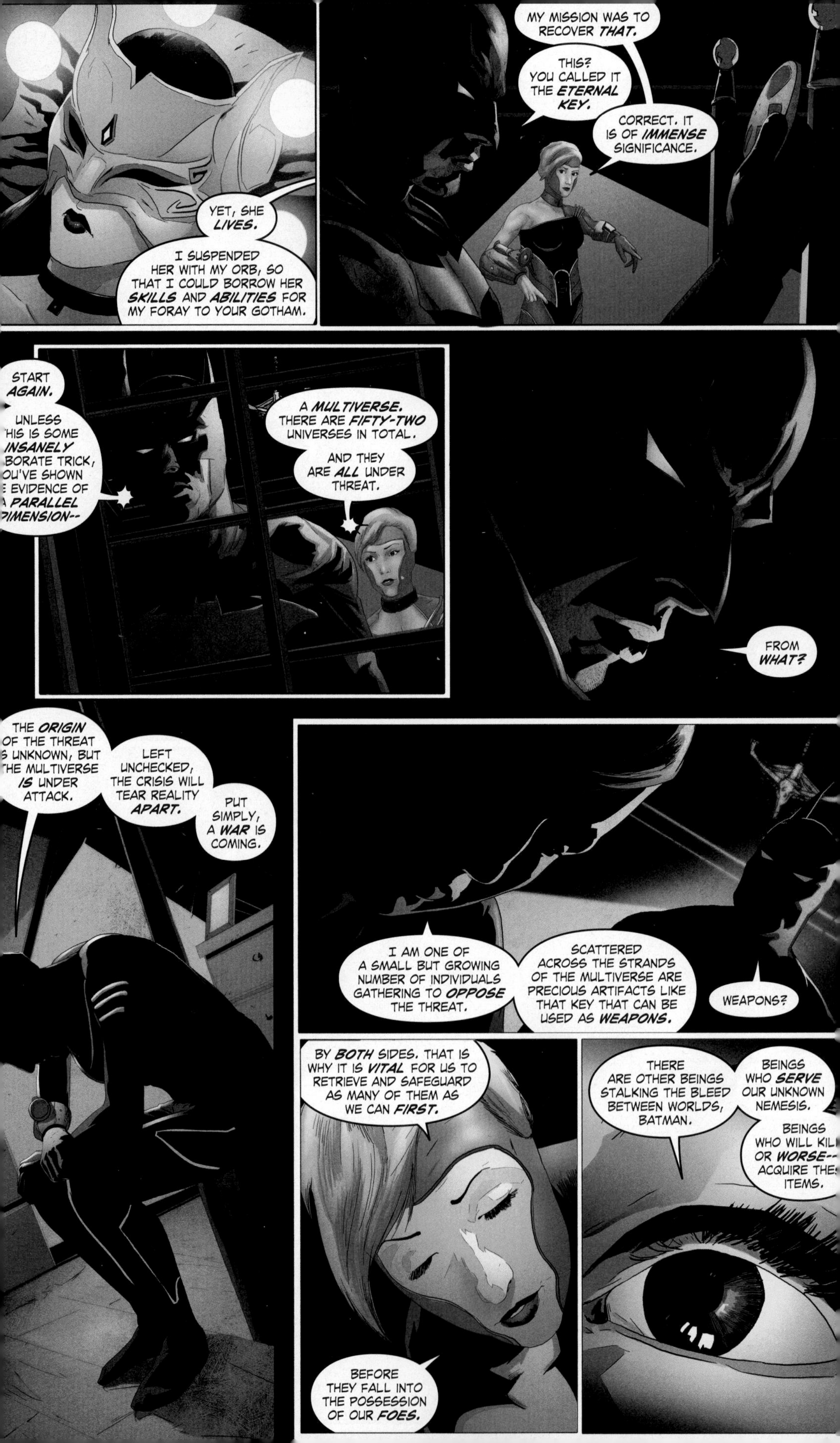

YET, SHE LIVES.
I SUSPENDED HER WITH MY ORB, SO THAT I COULD BORROW HER SKILLS AND ABILITIES FOR MY FORAY TO YOUR GOTHAM.
MY MISSION WAS TO RECOVER THAT.
THIS? YOU CALLED IT THE ETERNAL KEY.
CORRECT. IT IS OF IMMENSE SIGNIFICANCE.
START AGAIN.
UNLESS HIS IS SOME INSANELY BORATE TRICK, OU'VE SHOWN E EVIDENCE OF A PARALLEL DIMENSION--
A MULTIVERSE. THERE ARE FIFTY-TWO UNIVERSES IN TOTAL.
AND THEY ARE ALL UNDER THREAT.
FROM WHAT?
THE ORIGIN OF THE THREAT S UNKNOWN, BUT HE MULTIVERSE IS UNDER ATTACK.
LEFT UNCHECKED, THE CRISIS WILL TEAR REALITY APART.
PUT SIMPLY, A WAR IS COMING.
I AM ONE OF A SMALL BUT GROWING NUMBER OF INDIVIDUALS GATHERING TO OPPOSE THE THREAT.
SCATTERED ACROSS THE STRANDS OF THE MULTIVERSE ARE PRECIOUS ARTIFACTS LIKE THAT KEY THAT CAN BE USED AS WEAPONS.
WEAPONS?
BY BOTH SIDES. THAT IS WHY IT IS VITAL FOR US TO RETRIEVE AND SAFEGUARD AS MANY OF THEM AS WE CAN FIRST.
BEFORE THEY FALL INTO THE POSSESSION OF OUR FOES.
THERE ARE OTHER BEINGS STALKING THE BLEED BETWEEN WORLDS, BATMAN.
BEINGS WHO SERVE OUR UNKNOWN NEMESIS.
BEINGS WHO WILL KIL OR WORSE-- ACQUIRE THE ITEMS.

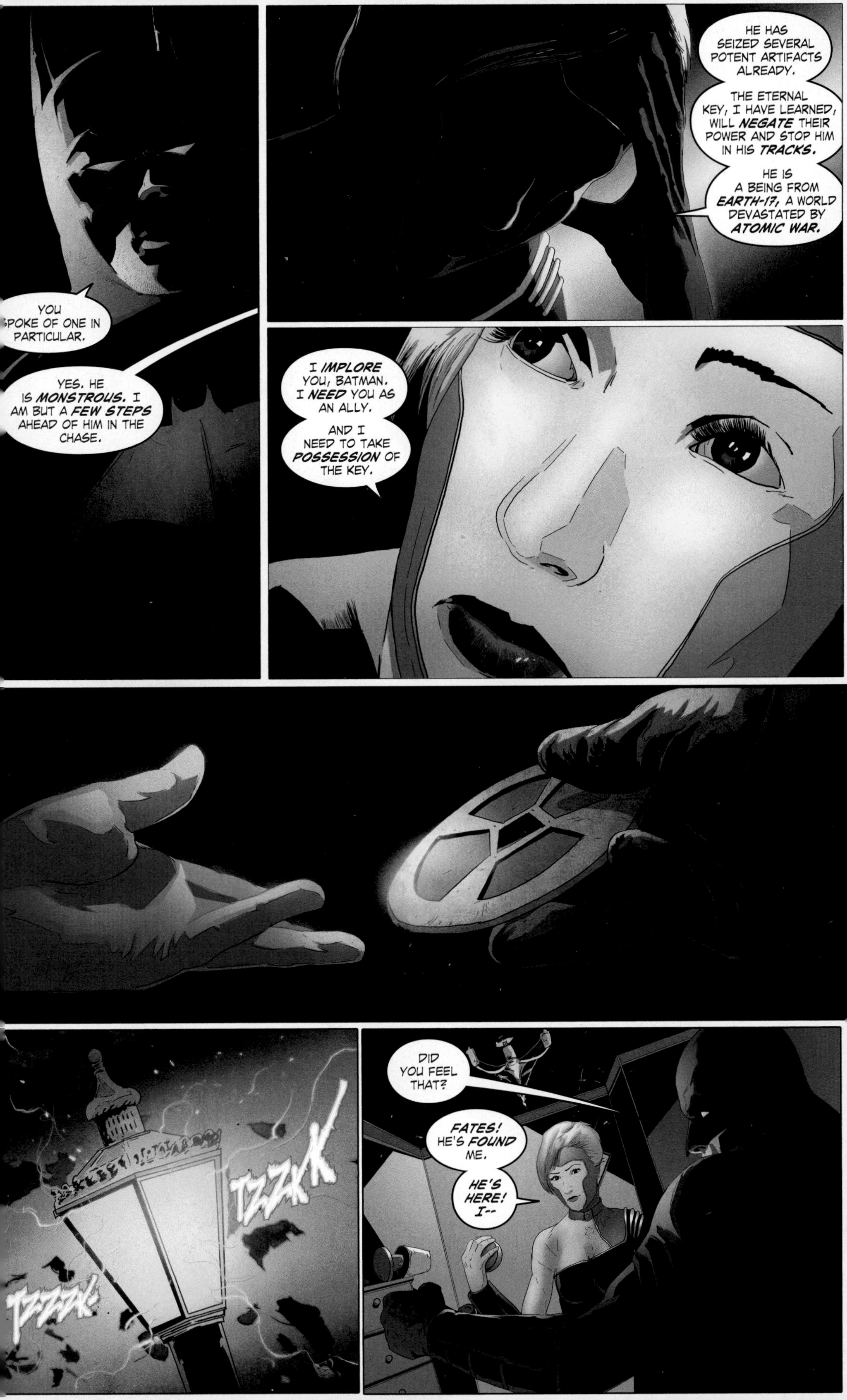
HE HAS SEIZED SEVERAL POTENT ARTIFACTS ALREADY.
THE ETERNAL KEY, I HAVE LEARNED, WILL NEGATE THEIR POWER AND STOP HIM IN HIS TRACKS.
HE IS A BEING FROM EARTH-17, A WORLD DEVASTATED BY ATOMIC WAR.
YOU SPOKE OF ONE IN PARTICULAR.
YES. HE IS MONSTROUS. I AM BUT A FEW STEPS AHEAD OF HIM IN THE CHASE.
I IMPLORE YOU, BATMAN. I NEED YOU AS AN ALLY.
AND I NEED TO TAKE POSSESSION OF THE KEY.
TZZKK
TZZZK
DID YOU FEEL THAT?
FATES! HE'S FOUND ME.
HE'S HERE! I--

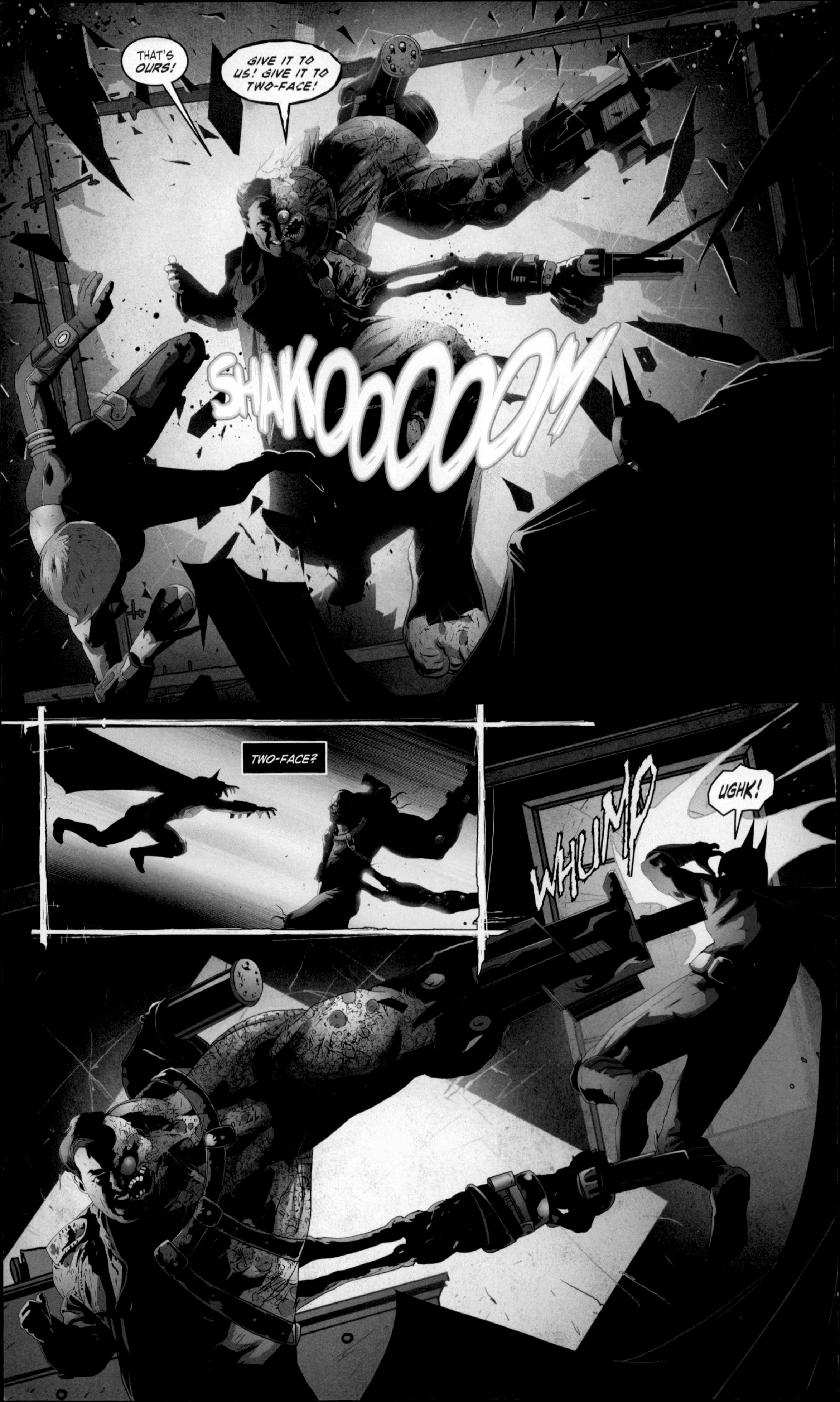
THAT'S OURS!
GIVE IT TO US! GIVE IT TO TWO-FACE!
SHAKOOOOOOM
TWO-FACE?
WHUMP
UGHK!

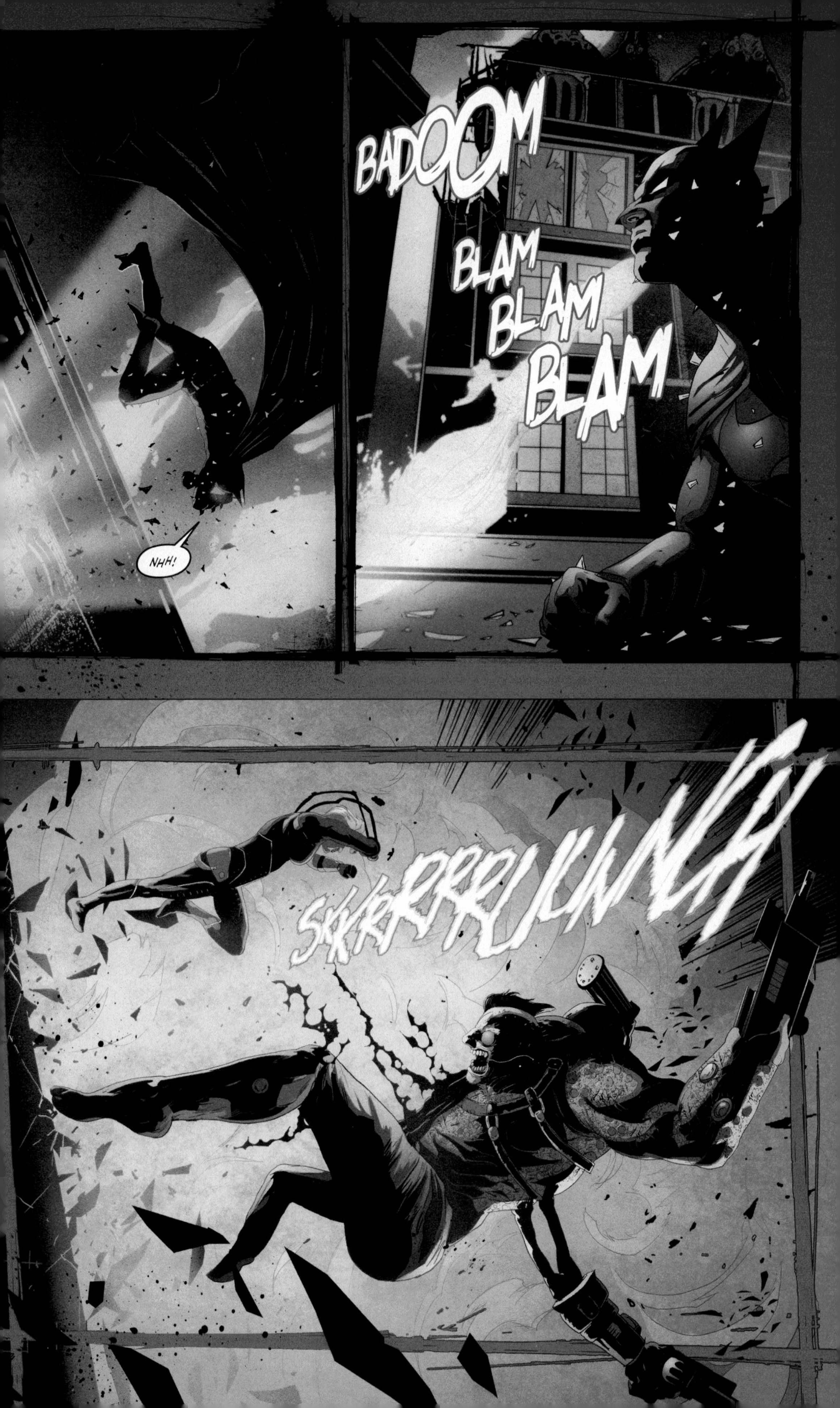
NHH!
BADOOM
BLAM
BLAM
BLAM
SKKRRRRUUNCH

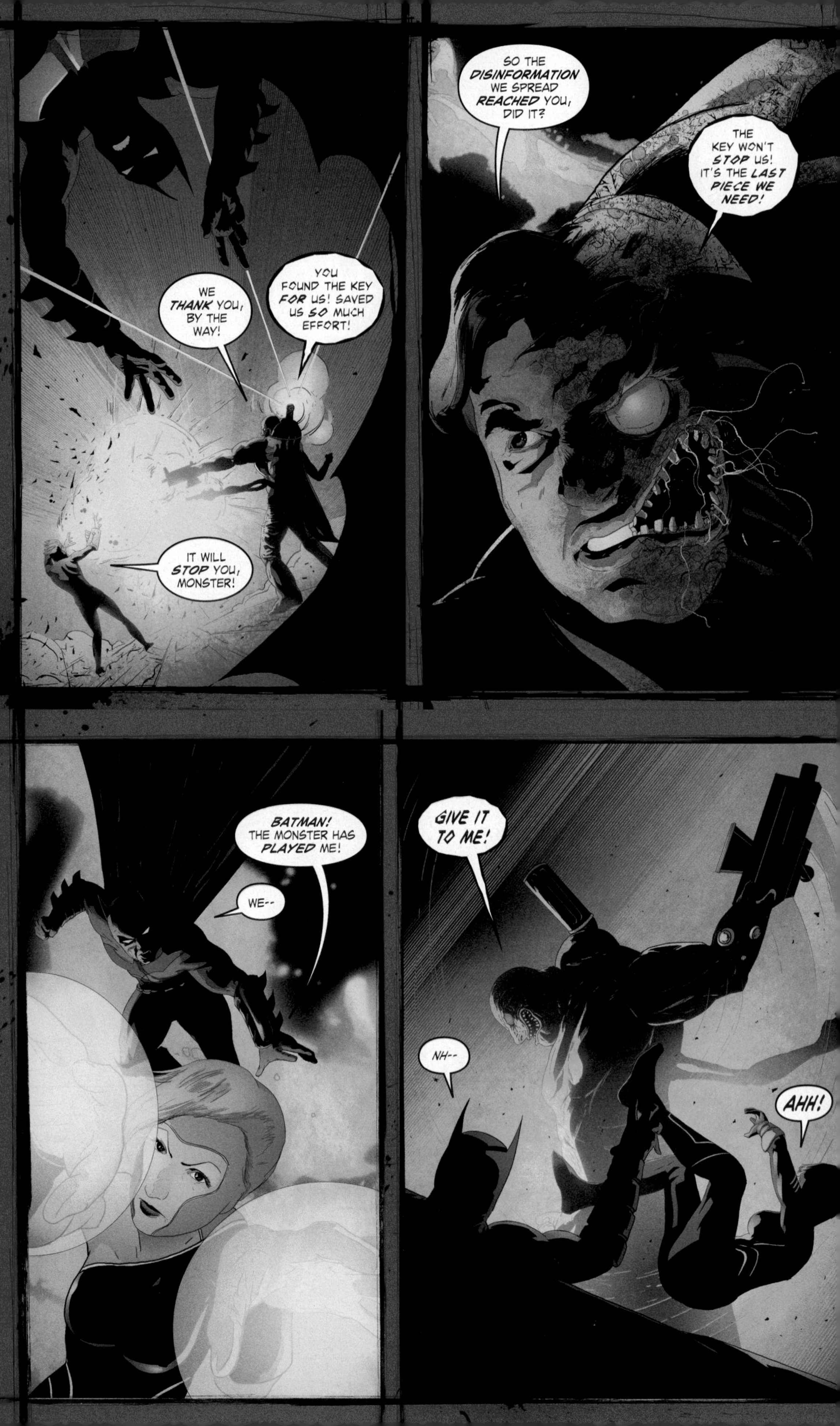

WE *THANK* YOU, BY THE WAY!
YOU FOUND THE KEY *FOR* US! SAVED US *SO* MUCH EFFORT!
IT WILL *STOP* YOU, MONSTER!
SO THE *DISINFORMATION* WE SPREAD *REACHED* YOU, DID IT?
THE KEY WON'T *STOP* US! IT'S THE *LAST PIECE WE NEED!*
BATMAN! THE MONSTER HAS *PLAYED* ME!
WE--
GIVE IT TO ME!
NH--
AHH!

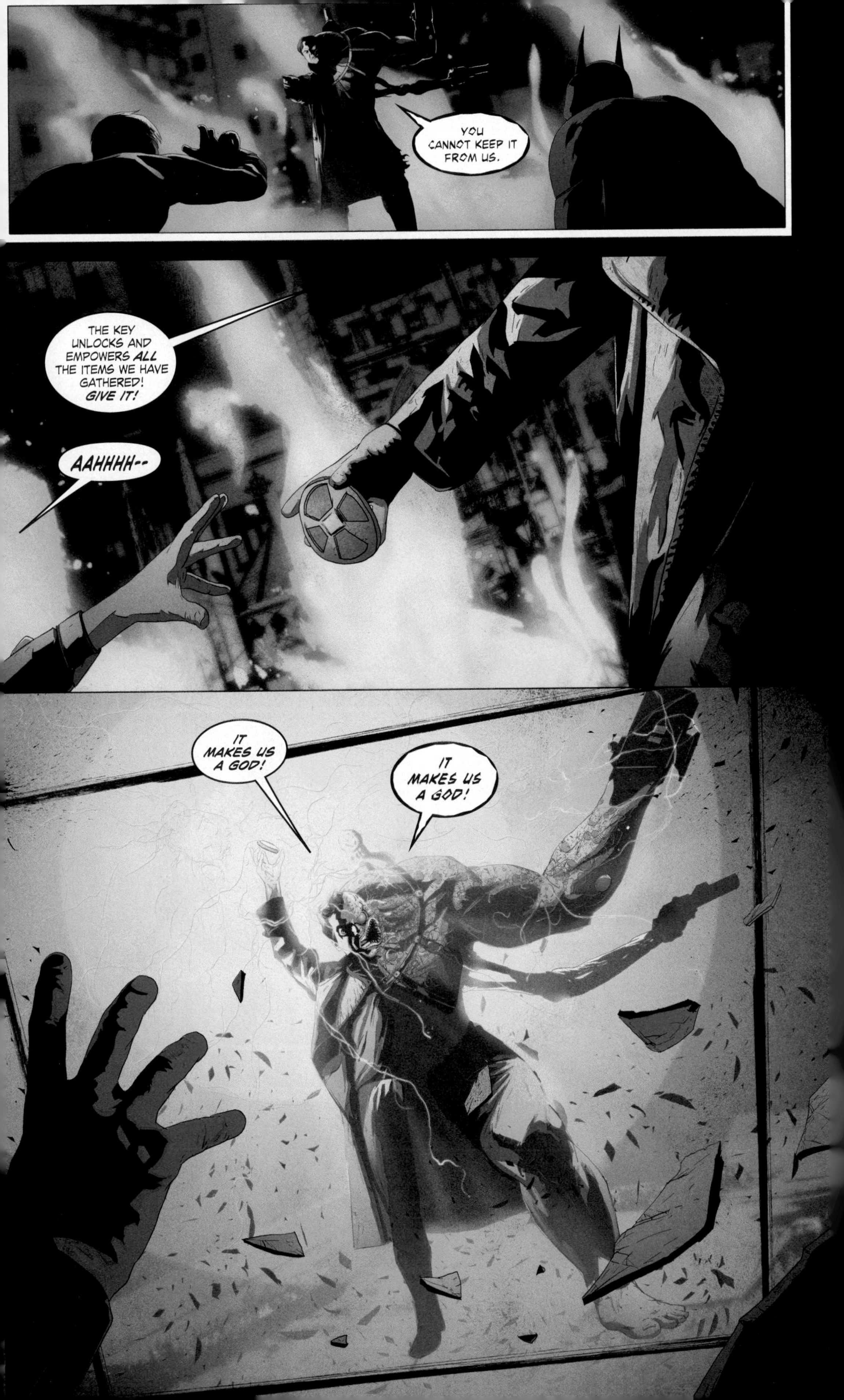
YOU CANNOT KEEP IT FROM US.
THE KEY UNLOCKS AND EMPOWERS *ALL* THE ITEMS WE HAVE GATHERED! *GIVE IT!*
AAHHHH--
IT MAKES US A GOD!
IT MAKES US A GOD!

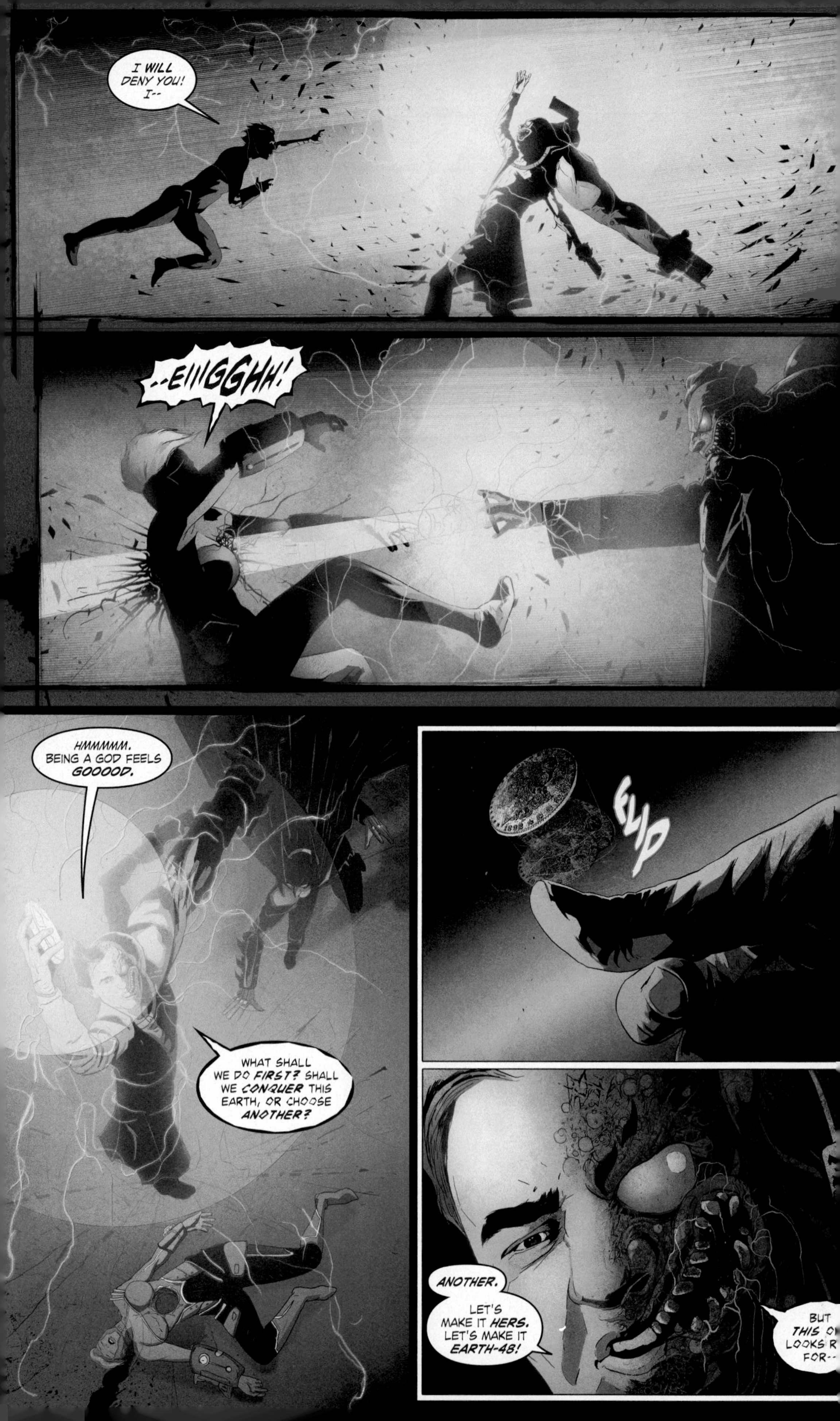
I WILL DENY YOU! I--
--EIIIGGHH!
HMMMMM. BEING A GOD FEELS GOOOOD.
WHAT SHALL WE DO FIRST? SHALL WE CONQUER THIS EARTH, OR CHOOSE ANOTHER?
FLIP
ANOTHER.
LET'S MAKE IT HERS. LET'S MAKE IT EARTH-48!
BUT THIS O LOOKS R FOR--

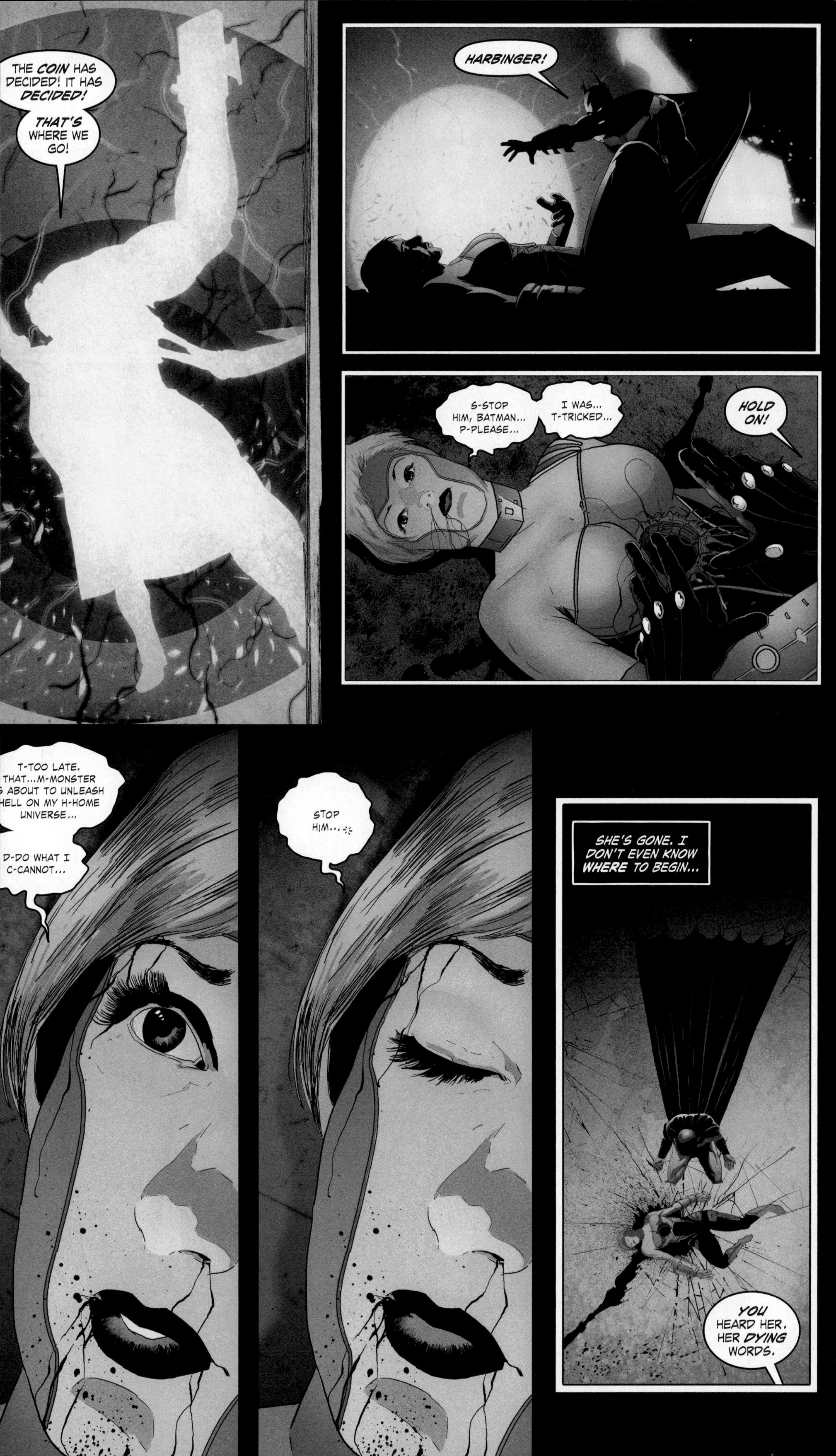
THE COIN HAS DECIDED! IT HAS DECIDED!
THAT'S WHERE WE GO!
HARBINGER!
S-STOP HIM, BATMAN... P-PLEASE...
I WAS... T-TRICKED...
HOLD ON!
T-TOO LATE. THAT...M-MONSTER IS ABOUT TO UNLEASH HELL ON MY H-HOME UNIVERSE...
D-DO WHAT I C-CANNOT...
STOP HIM...
SHE'S GONE. I DON'T EVEN KNOW WHERE TO BEGIN...
YOU HEARD HER. HER DYING WORDS.

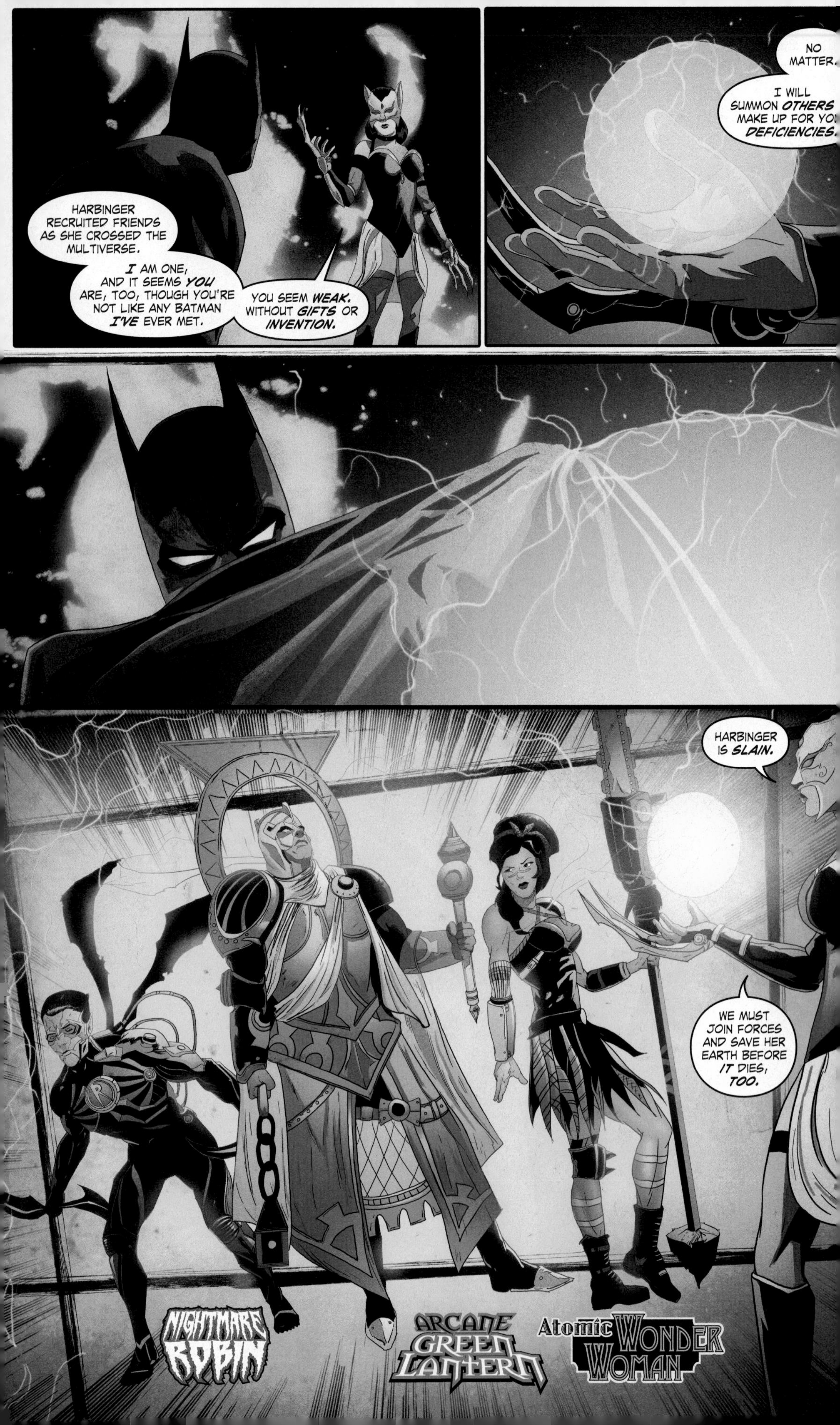

HARBINGER RECRUITED FRIENDS AS SHE CROSSED THE MULTIVERSE.
I AM ONE, AND IT SEEMS YOU ARE, TOO, THOUGH YOU'RE NOT LIKE ANY BATMAN I'VE EVER MET.
YOU SEEM WEAK. WITHOUT GIFTS OR INVENTION.
NO MATTER.
I WILL SUMMON OTHERS MAKE UP FOR YO DEFICIENCIES.
HARBINGER IS SLAIN.
WE MUST JOIN FORCES AND SAVE HER EARTH BEFORE IT DIES, TOO.
NIGHTMARE ROBIN
ARCANE GREEN LANTERN
Atomic WONDER WOMAN

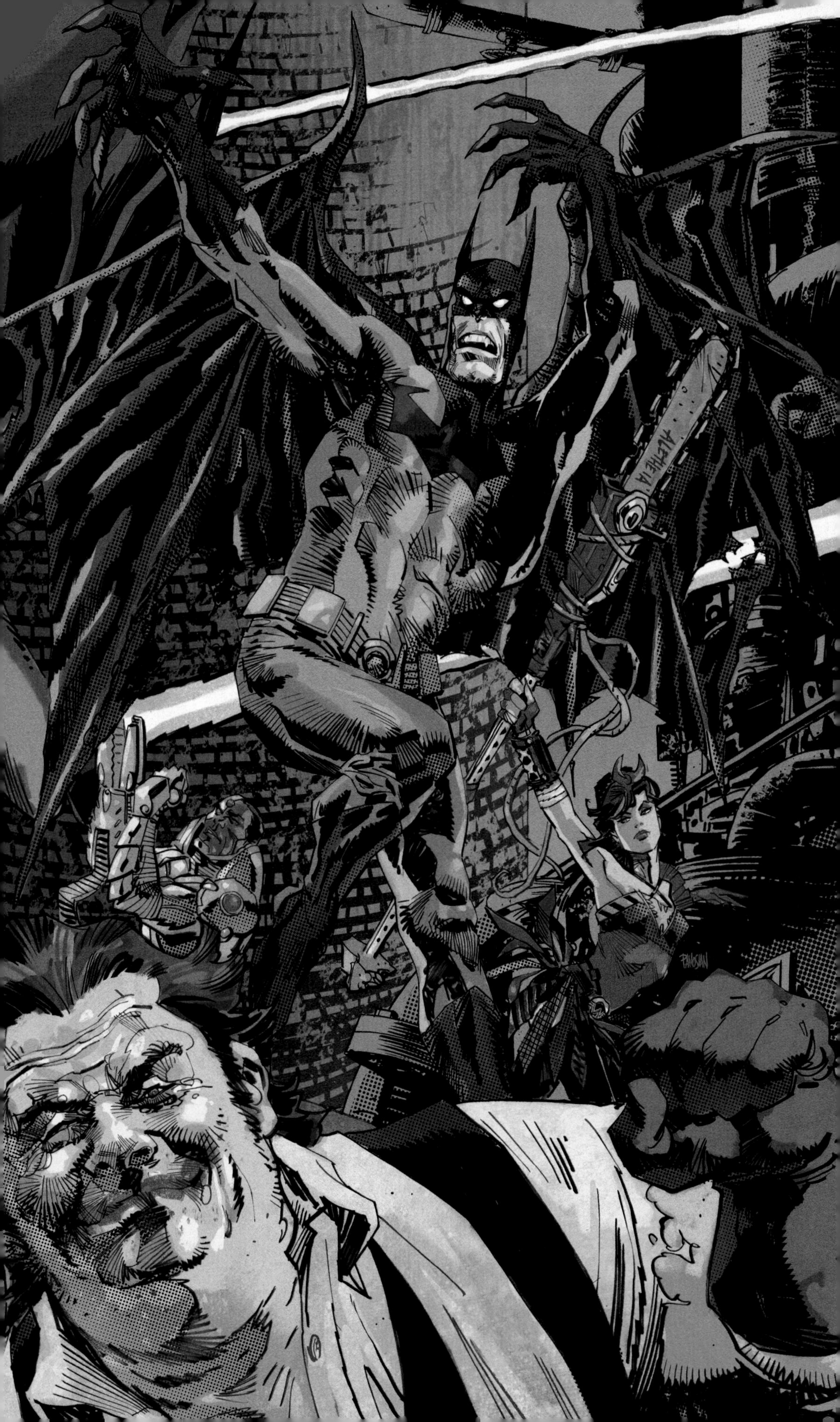
ALETHEIA
PANOSIAN

NIGHTMARE

Tom Raney Stjepan Sejic Artists **Gina Going** Colorist
Cover Art by **Dan Panosian**

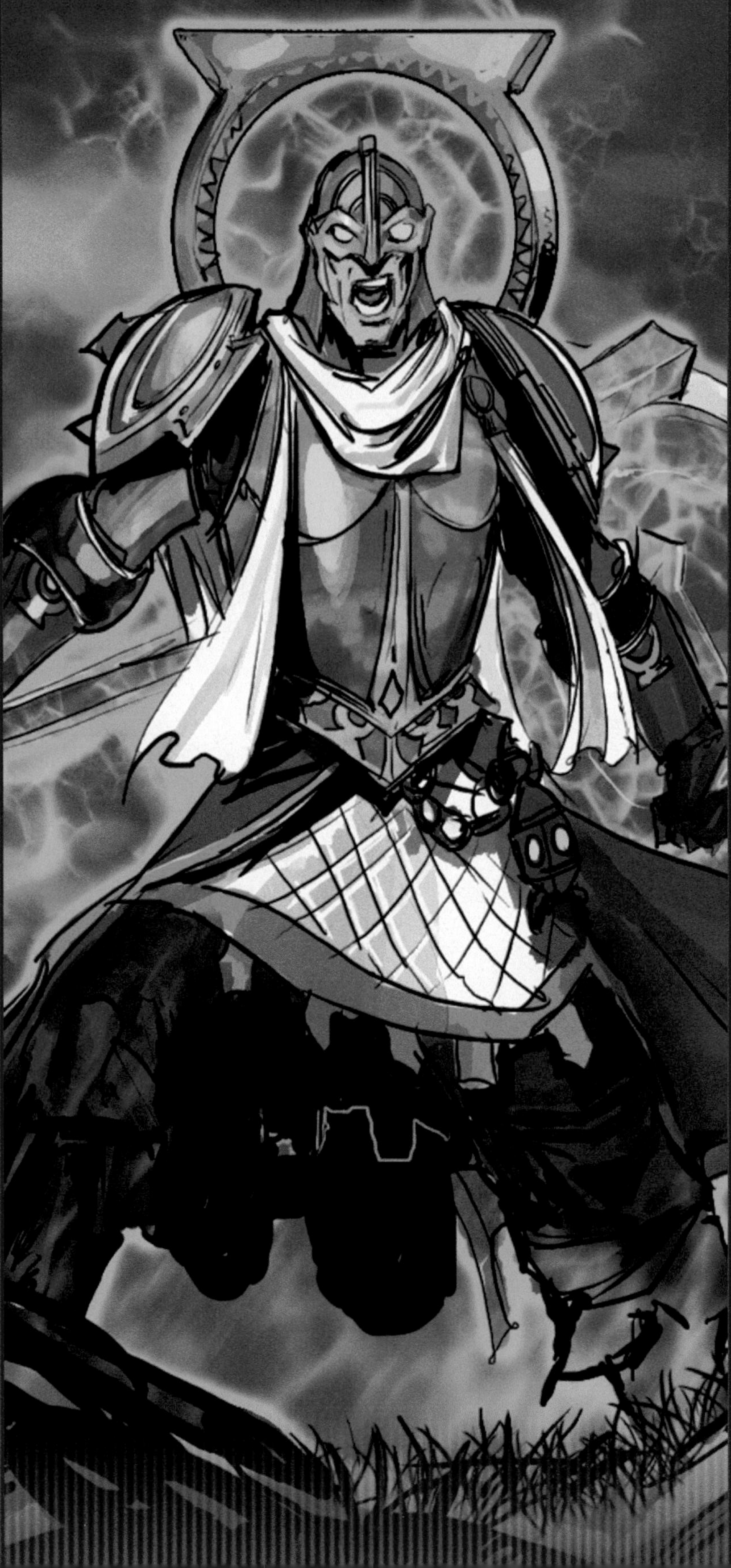

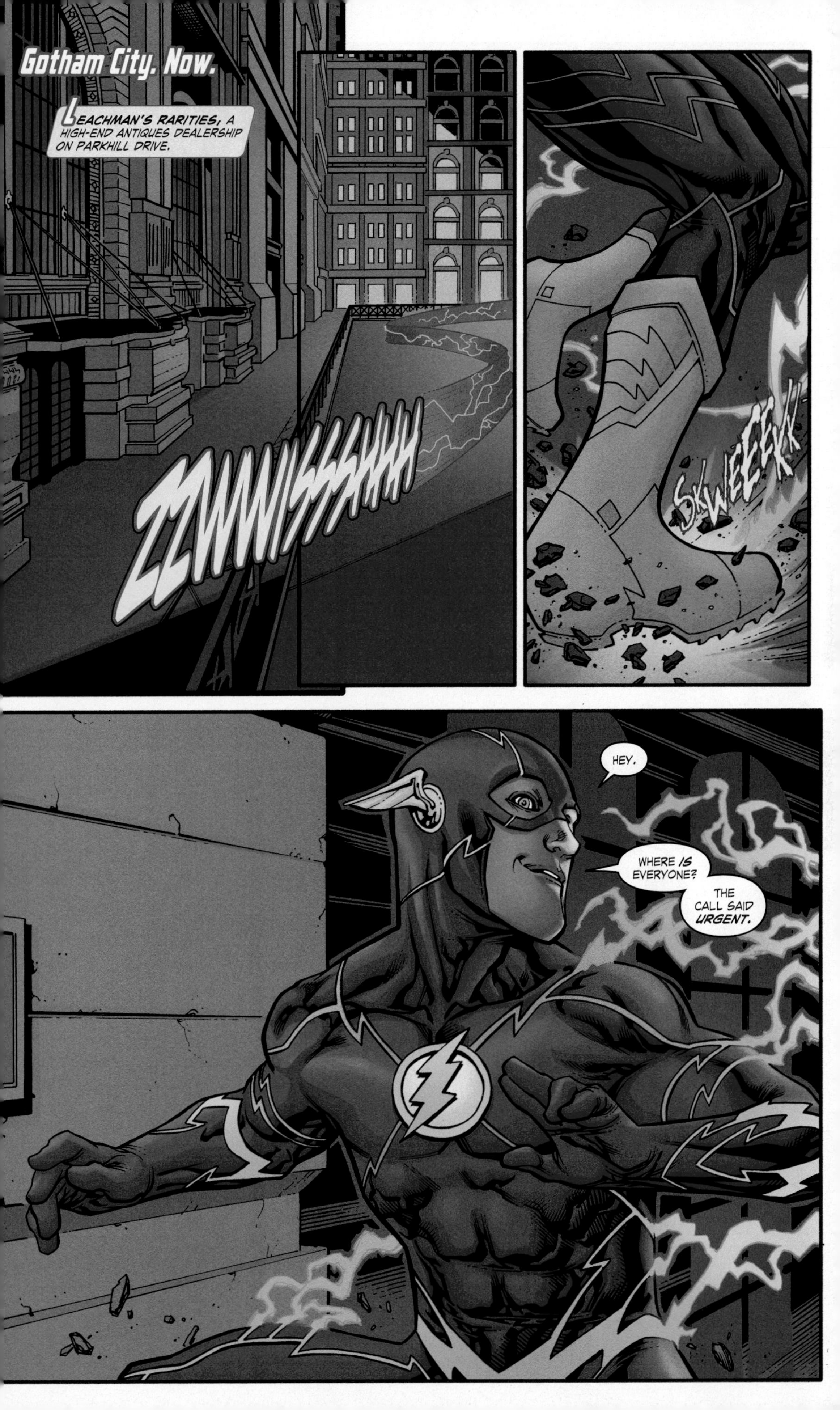
Gotham City. Now.
LEACHMAN'S RARITIES, A HIGH-END ANTIQUES DEALERSHIP ON PARKHILL DRIVE.
ZZWWISSSHHH
SKWEEEKK
HEY.
WHERE IS EVERYONE?
THE CALL SAID URGENT.

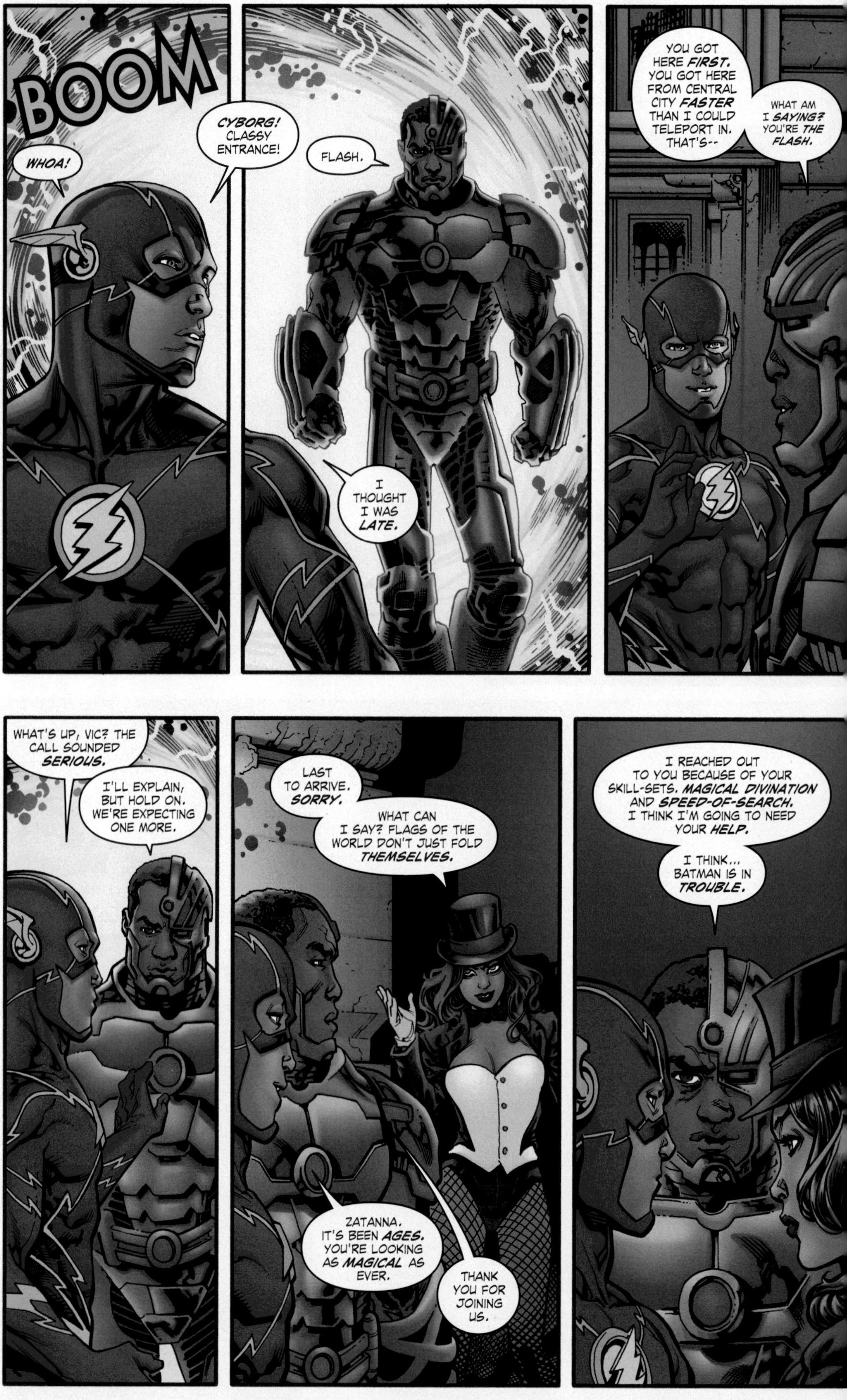
BOOM
WHOA!
CYBORG! CLASSY ENTRANCE!
FLASH.
I THOUGHT I WAS LATE.
YOU GOT HERE FIRST. YOU GOT HERE FROM CENTRAL CITY FASTER THAN I COULD TELEPORT IN. THAT'S--
WHAT AM I SAYING? YOU'RE THE FLASH.
WHAT'S UP, VIC? THE CALL SOUNDED SERIOUS.
I'LL EXPLAIN, BUT HOLD ON. WE'RE EXPECTING ONE MORE.
LAST TO ARRIVE. SORRY.
WHAT CAN I SAY? FLAGS OF THE WORLD DON'T JUST FOLD THEMSELVES.
ZATANNA. IT'S BEEN AGES. YOU'RE LOOKING AS MAGICAL AS EVER.
THANK YOU FOR JOINING US.
I REACHED OUT TO YOU BECAUSE OF YOUR SKILL-SETS. MAGICAL DIVINATION AND SPEED-OF-SEARCH. I THINK I'M GOING TO NEED YOUR HELP.
I THINK... BATMAN IS IN TROUBLE.

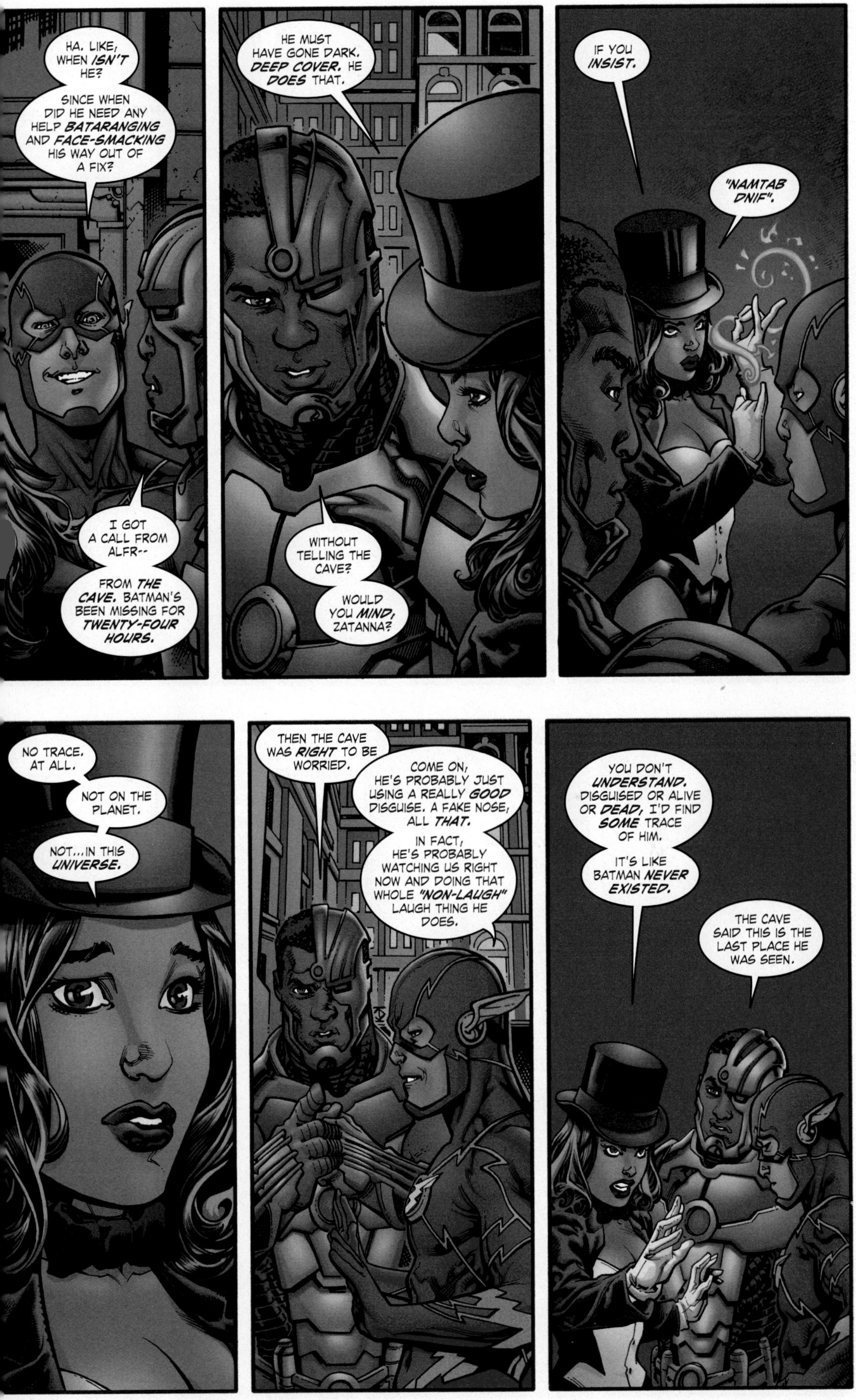
HA. LIKE, WHEN ISN'T HE?
SINCE WHEN DID HE NEED ANY HELP BATARANGING AND FACE-SMACKING HIS WAY OUT OF A FIX?
I GOT A CALL FROM ALFR--
FROM THE CAVE. BATMAN'S BEEN MISSING FOR TWENTY-FOUR HOURS.
HE MUST HAVE GONE DARK. DEEP COVER. HE DOES THAT.
WITHOUT TELLING THE CAVE?
WOULD YOU MIND, ZATANNA?
IF YOU INSIST.
"NAMTAB DNIF".
NO TRACE. AT ALL.
NOT ON THE PLANET.
NOT...IN THIS UNIVERSE.
THEN THE CAVE WAS RIGHT TO BE WORRIED.
COME ON, HE'S PROBABLY JUST USING A REALLY GOOD DISGUISE. A FAKE NOSE, ALL THAT.
IN FACT, HE'S PROBABLY WATCHING US RIGHT NOW AND DOING THAT WHOLE "NON-LAUGH" LAUGH THING HE DOES.
YOU DON'T UNDERSTAND. DISGUISED OR ALIVE OR DEAD, I'D FIND SOME TRACE OF HIM.
IT'S LIKE BATMAN NEVER EXISTED.
THE CAVE SAID THIS IS THE LAST PLACE HE WAS SEEN.

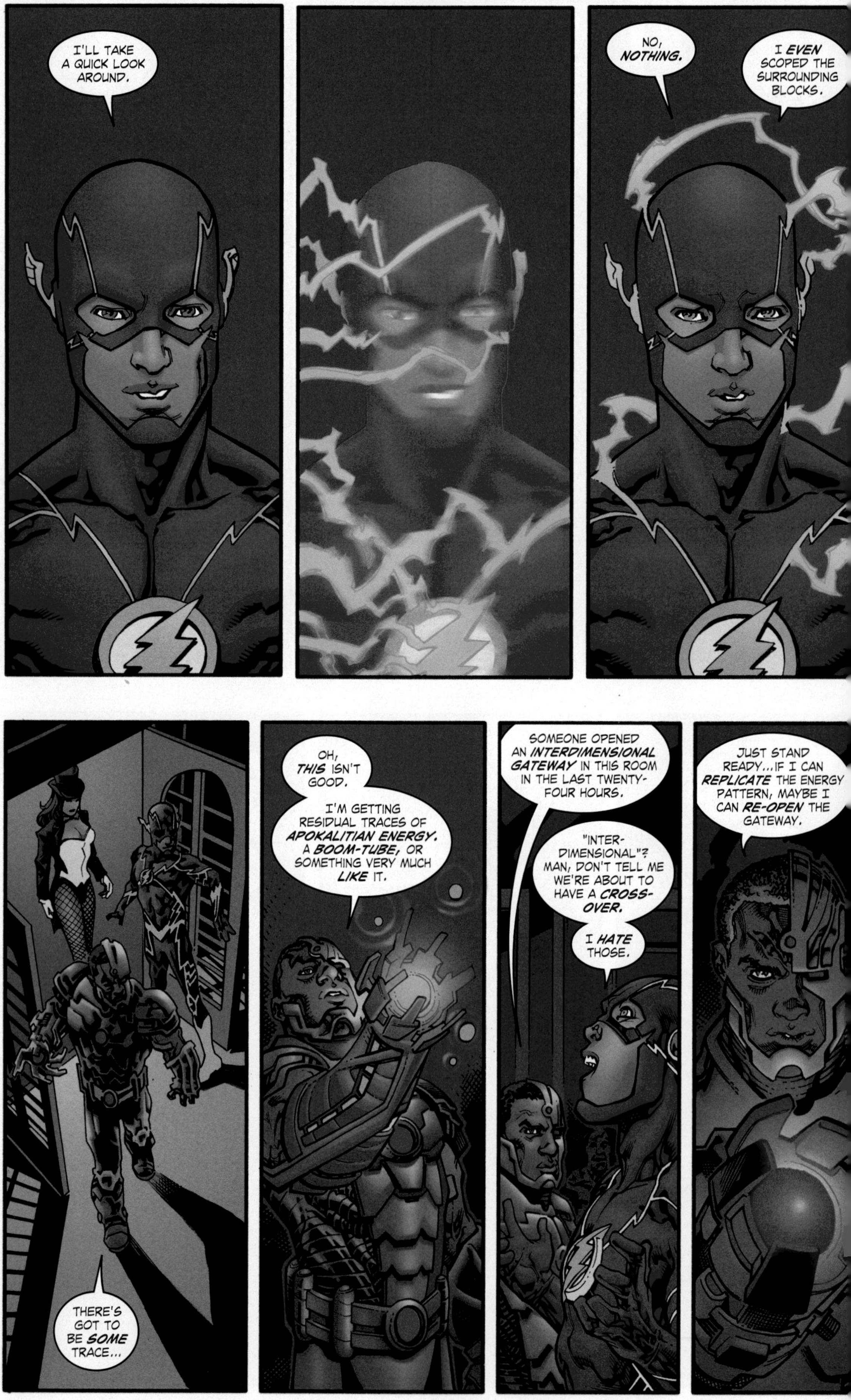
I'LL TAKE A QUICK LOOK AROUND.
NO, NOTHING.
I EVEN SCOPED THE SURROUNDING BLOCKS.
THERE'S GOT TO BE SOME TRACE...
OH, THIS ISN'T GOOD.
I'M GETTING RESIDUAL TRACES OF APOKALITIAN ENERGY. A BOOM-TUBE, OR SOMETHING VERY MUCH LIKE IT.
SOMEONE OPENED AN INTERDIMENSIONAL GATEWAY IN THIS ROOM IN THE LAST TWENTY-FOUR HOURS.
"INTER-DIMENSIONAL"? MAN, DON'T TELL ME WE'RE ABOUT TO HAVE A CROSS-OVER.
I HATE THOSE.
JUST STAND READY...IF I CAN REPLICATE THE ENERGY PATTERN, MAYBE I CAN RE-OPEN THE GATEWAY.

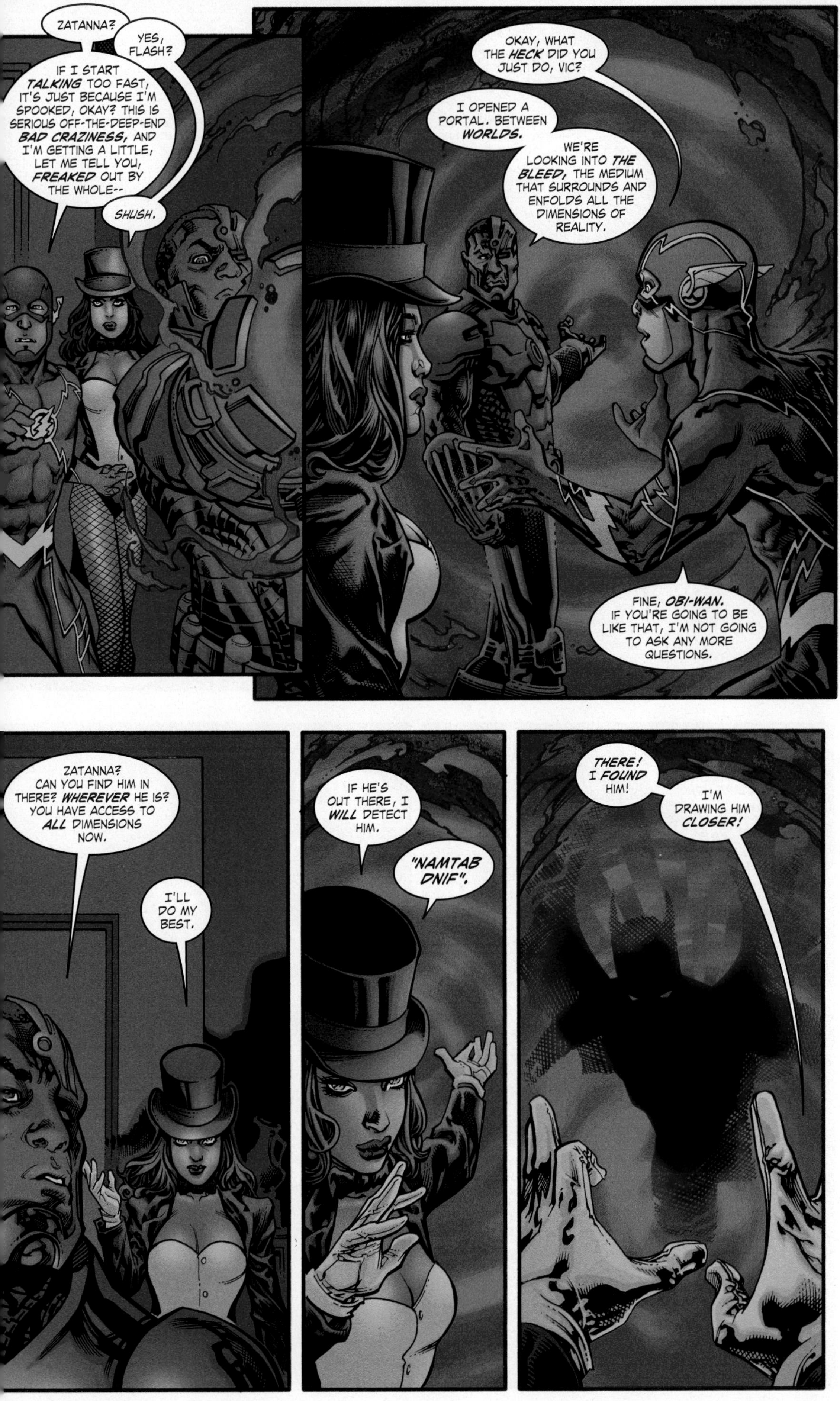
ZATANNA?
YES, FLASH?
IF I START TALKING TOO FAST, IT'S JUST BECAUSE I'M SPOOKED, OKAY? THIS IS SERIOUS OFF-THE-DEEP-END BAD CRAZINESS, AND I'M GETTING A LITTLE, LET ME TELL YOU, FREAKED OUT BY THE WHOLE--
SHUSH.
OKAY, WHAT THE HECK DID YOU JUST DO, VIC?
I OPENED A PORTAL. BETWEEN WORLDS.
WE'RE LOOKING INTO THE BLEED, THE MEDIUM THAT SURROUNDS AND ENFOLDS ALL THE DIMENSIONS OF REALITY.
FINE, OBI-WAN. IF YOU'RE GOING TO BE LIKE THAT, I'M NOT GOING TO ASK ANY MORE QUESTIONS.
ZATANNA? CAN YOU FIND HIM IN THERE? WHEREVER HE IS? YOU HAVE ACCESS TO ALL DIMENSIONS NOW.
I'LL DO MY BEST.
IF HE'S OUT THERE, I WILL DETECT HIM.
"NAMTAB DNIF".
THERE! I FOUND HIM!
I'M DRAWING HIM CLOSER!

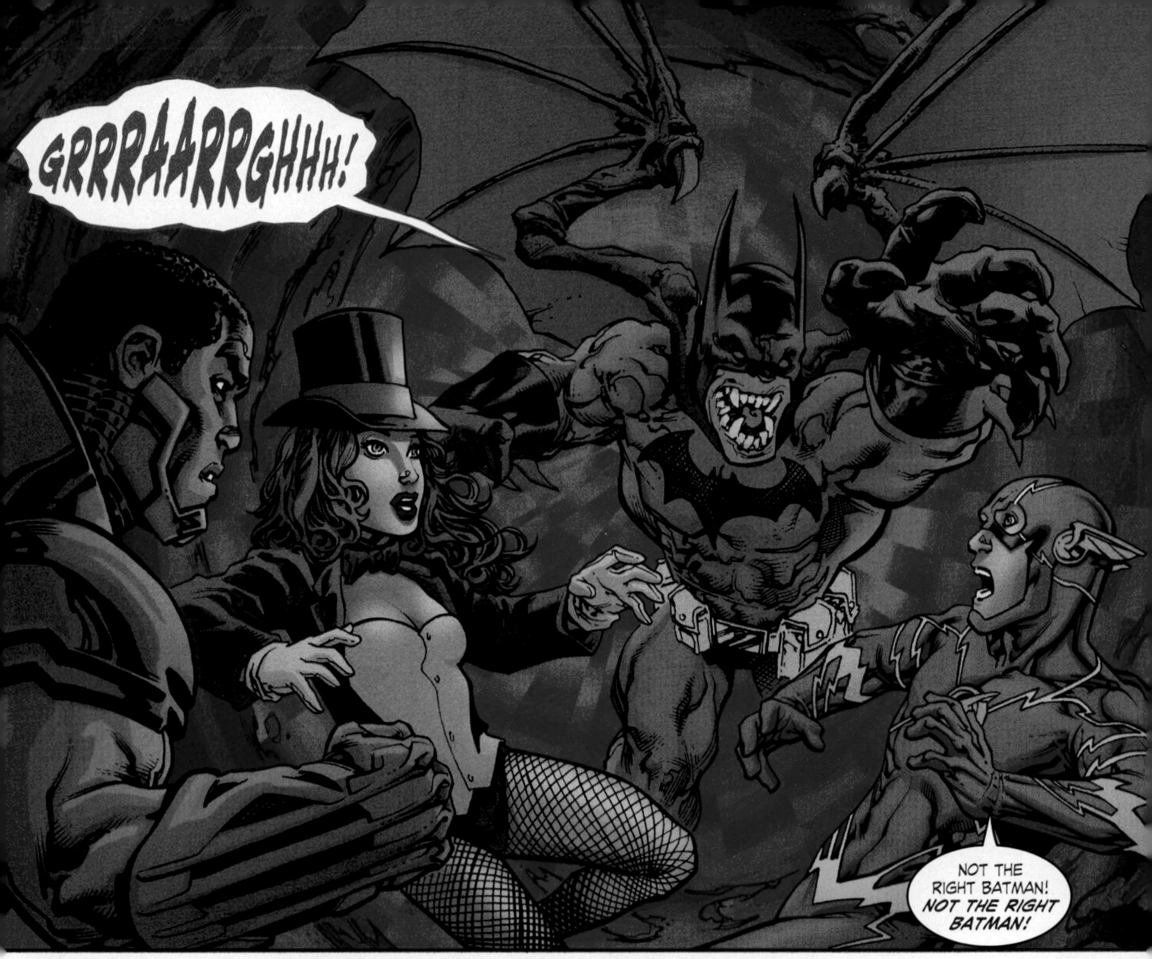
GRRRAARRGHHH!
NOT THE RIGHT BATMAN! *NOT THE RIGHT BATMAN!*

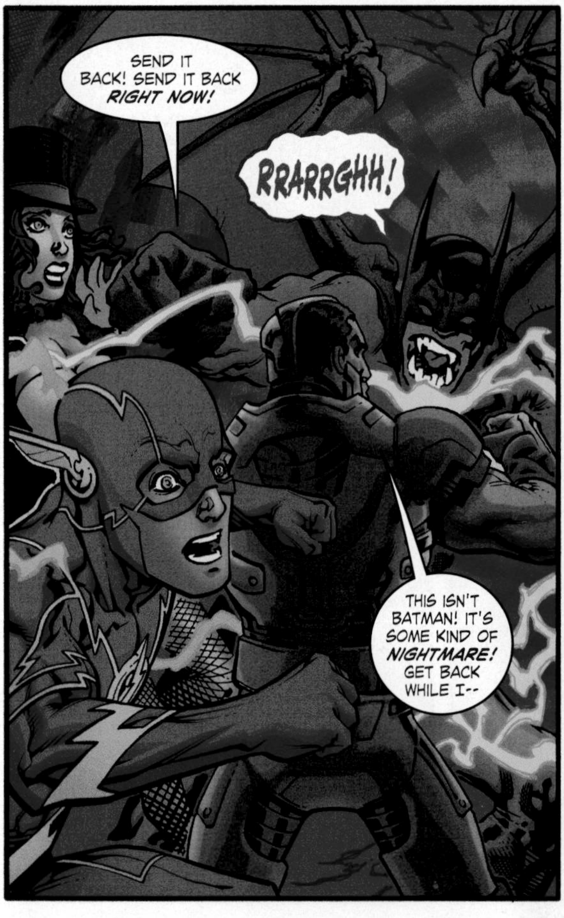
SEND IT BACK! SEND IT BACK *RIGHT NOW!*
RRARRGHH!
THIS ISN'T BATMAN! IT'S SOME KIND OF *NIGHTMARE!* GET BACK WHILE I--

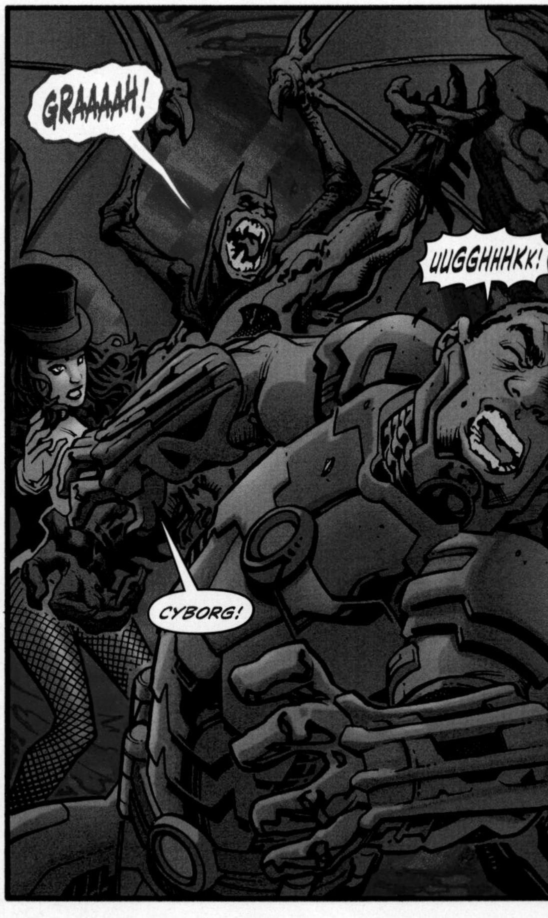
GRAAAAH!
UUGGHHHKK!
CYBORG!

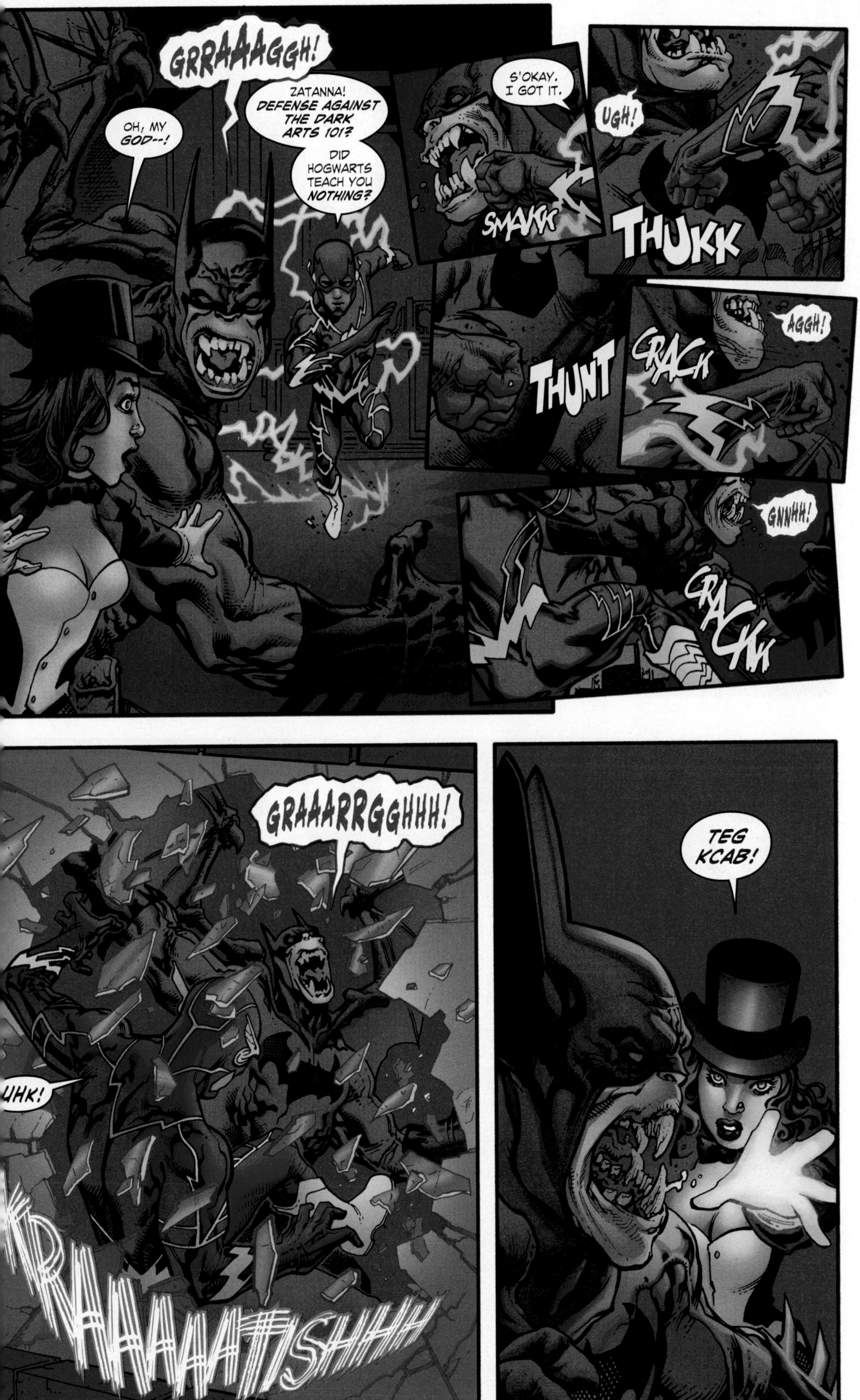
GRRAAAGGH!
OH, MY GOD--!
ZATANNA! DEFENSE AGAINST THE DARK ARTS 101?
DID HOGWARTS TEACH YOU NOTHING?
S'OKAY. I GOT IT.
SMAKK
UGH!
THUKK
THUNT
CRACK
AGGH!
GNNHH!
CRACKK
GRAAARRGHHH!
UHK!
KRAAAAATSHHH
TEG KCAB!

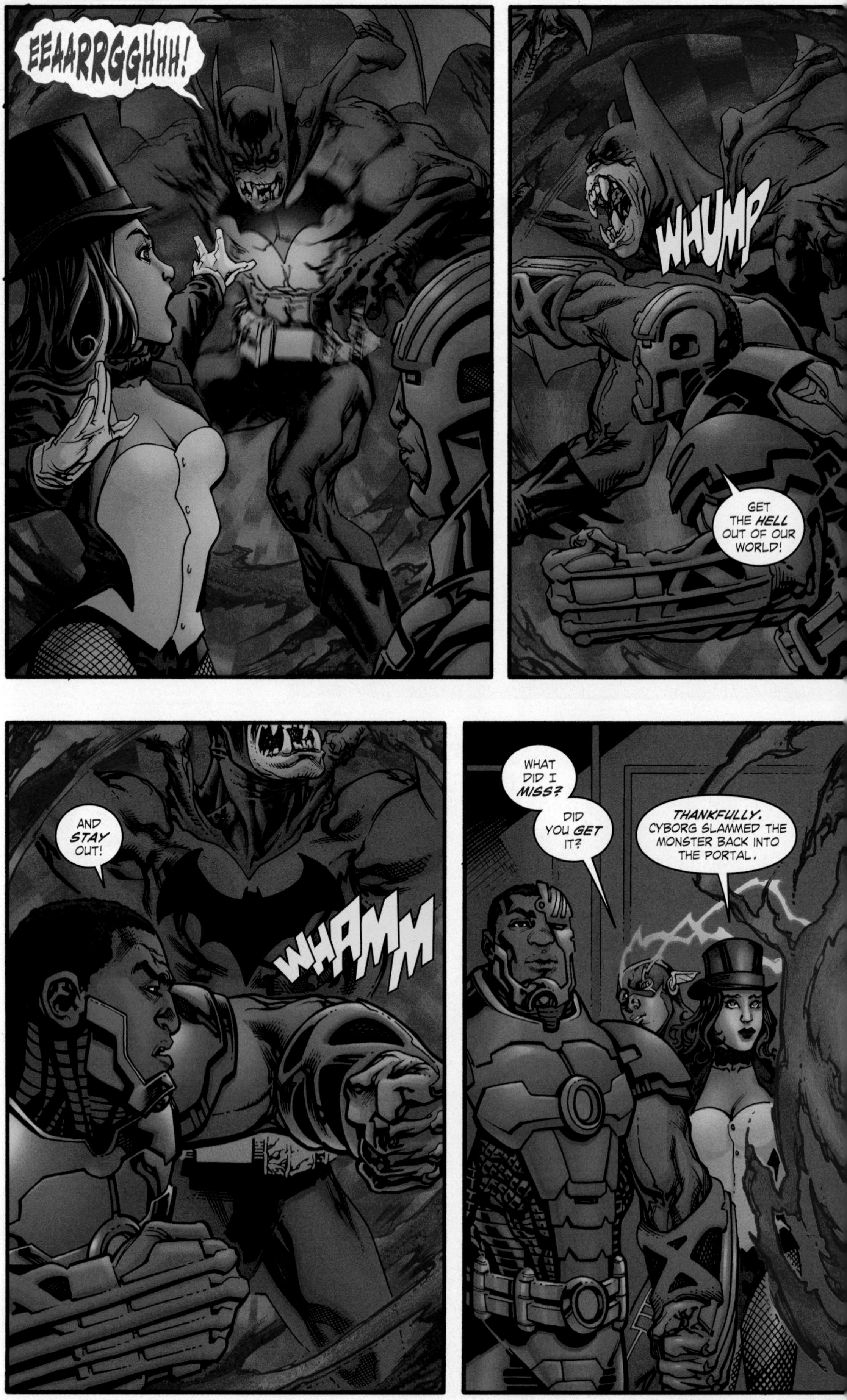
EEAARRGGHHH!
WHUMP
GET THE HELL OUT OF OUR WORLD!
AND STAY OUT!
WHAMM
WHAT DID I MISS?
DID YOU GET IT?
THANKFULLY. CYBORG SLAMMED THE MONSTER BACK INTO THE PORTAL.

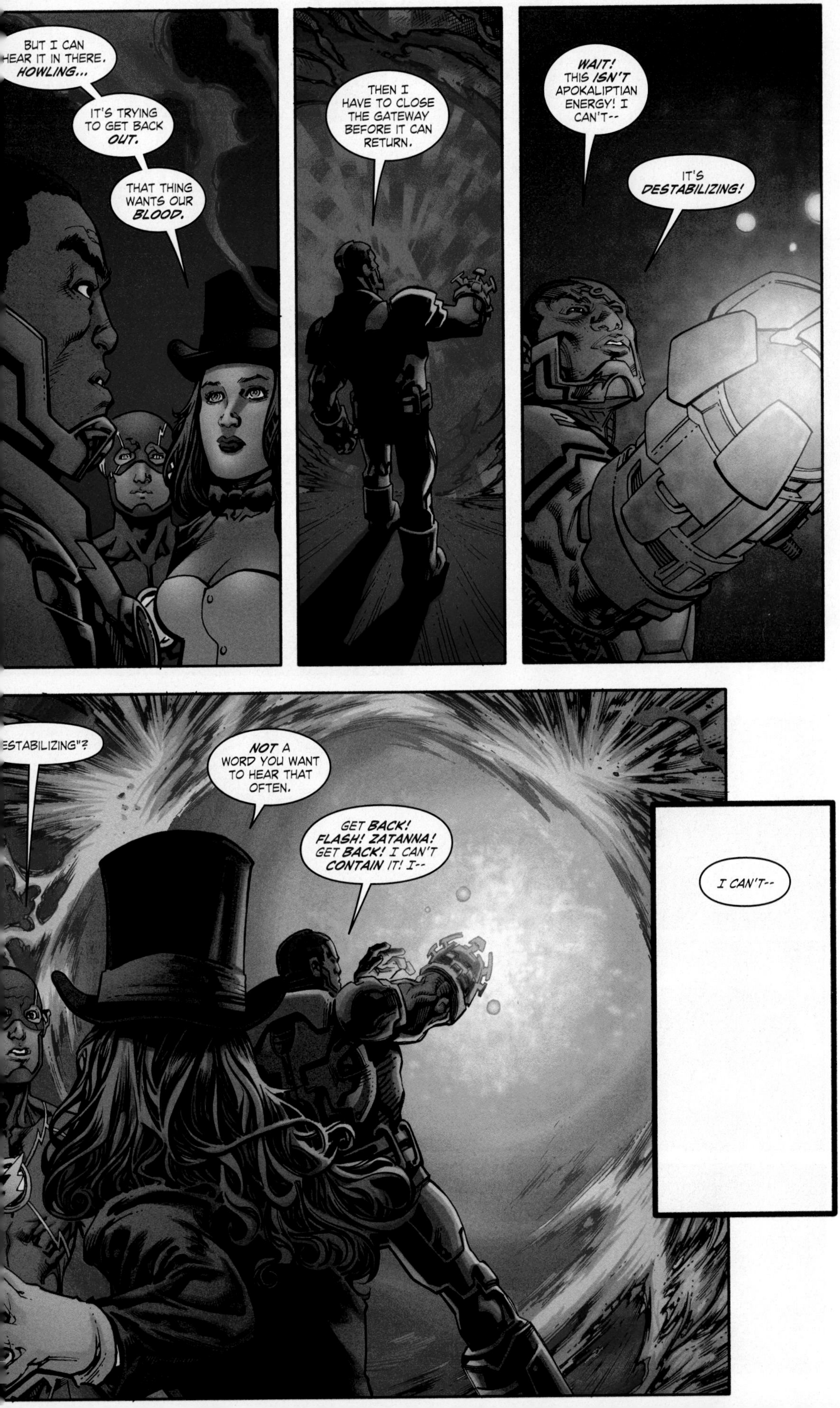

BUT I CAN HEAR IT IN THERE. HOWLING...
IT'S TRYING TO GET BACK OUT.
THAT THING WANTS OUR BLOOD.
THEN I HAVE TO CLOSE THE GATEWAY BEFORE IT CAN RETURN.
WAIT! THIS ISN'T APOKALIPTIAN ENERGY! I CAN'T--
IT'S DESTABILIZING!
ESTABILIZING"?
NOT A WORD YOU WANT TO HEAR THAT OFTEN.
GET BACK! FLASH! ZATANNA! GET BACK! I CAN'T CONTAIN IT! I--
I CAN'T--

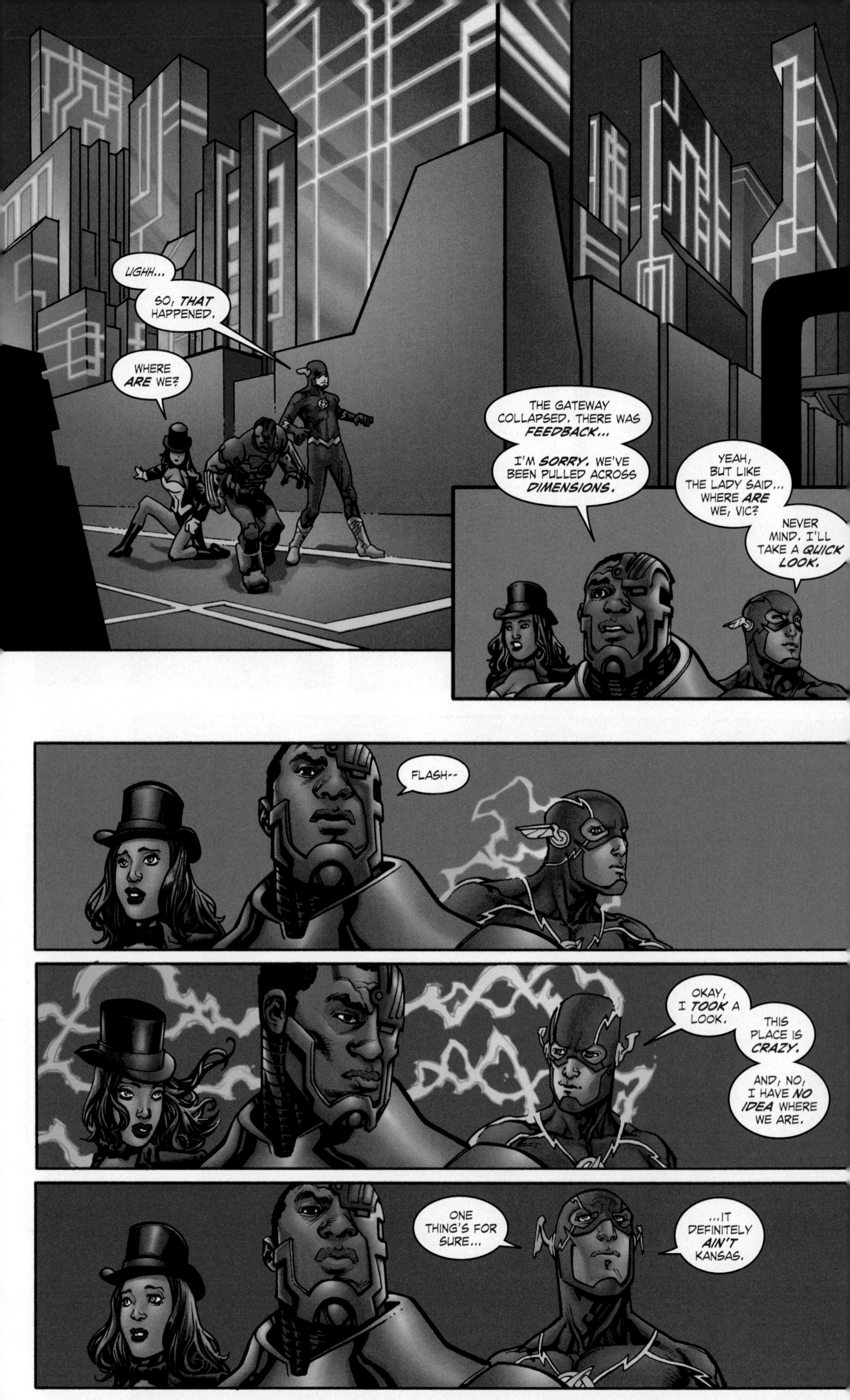
UGHH...
SO, THAT HAPPENED.
WHERE ARE WE?
THE GATEWAY COLLAPSED. THERE WAS FEEDBACK...
I'M SORRY. WE'VE BEEN PULLED ACROSS DIMENSIONS.
YEAH, BUT LIKE THE LADY SAID... WHERE ARE WE, VIC?
NEVER MIND. I'LL TAKE A QUICK LOOK.
FLASH--
OKAY, I TOOK A LOOK.
THIS PLACE IS CRAZY.
AND, NO, I HAVE NO IDEA WHERE WE ARE.
ONE THING'S FOR SURE...
...IT DEFINITELY AIN'T KANSAS.

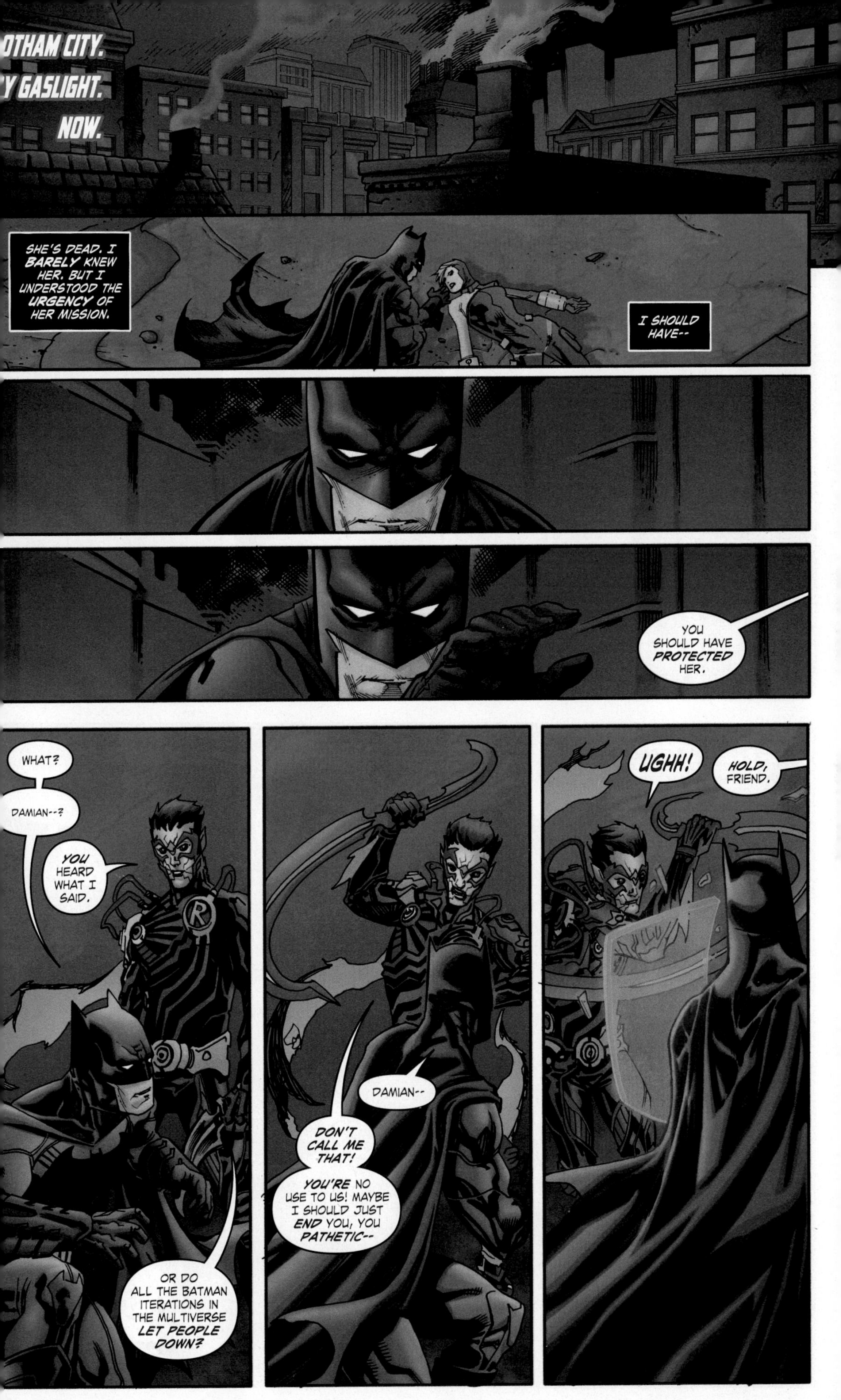

OTHAM CITY.
Y GASLIGHT.
NOW.
SHE'S DEAD. I BARELY KNEW HER. BUT I UNDERSTOOD THE URGENCY OF HER MISSION.
I SHOULD HAVE--
YOU SHOULD HAVE PROTECTED HER.
WHAT?
DAMIAN--?
YOU HEARD WHAT I SAID.
OR DO ALL THE BATMAN ITERATIONS IN THE MULTIVERSE LET PEOPLE DOWN?
DAMIAN--
DON'T CALL ME THAT!
YOU'RE NO USE TO US! MAYBE I SHOULD JUST END YOU, YOU PATHETIC--
UGHH!
HOLD, FRIEND.

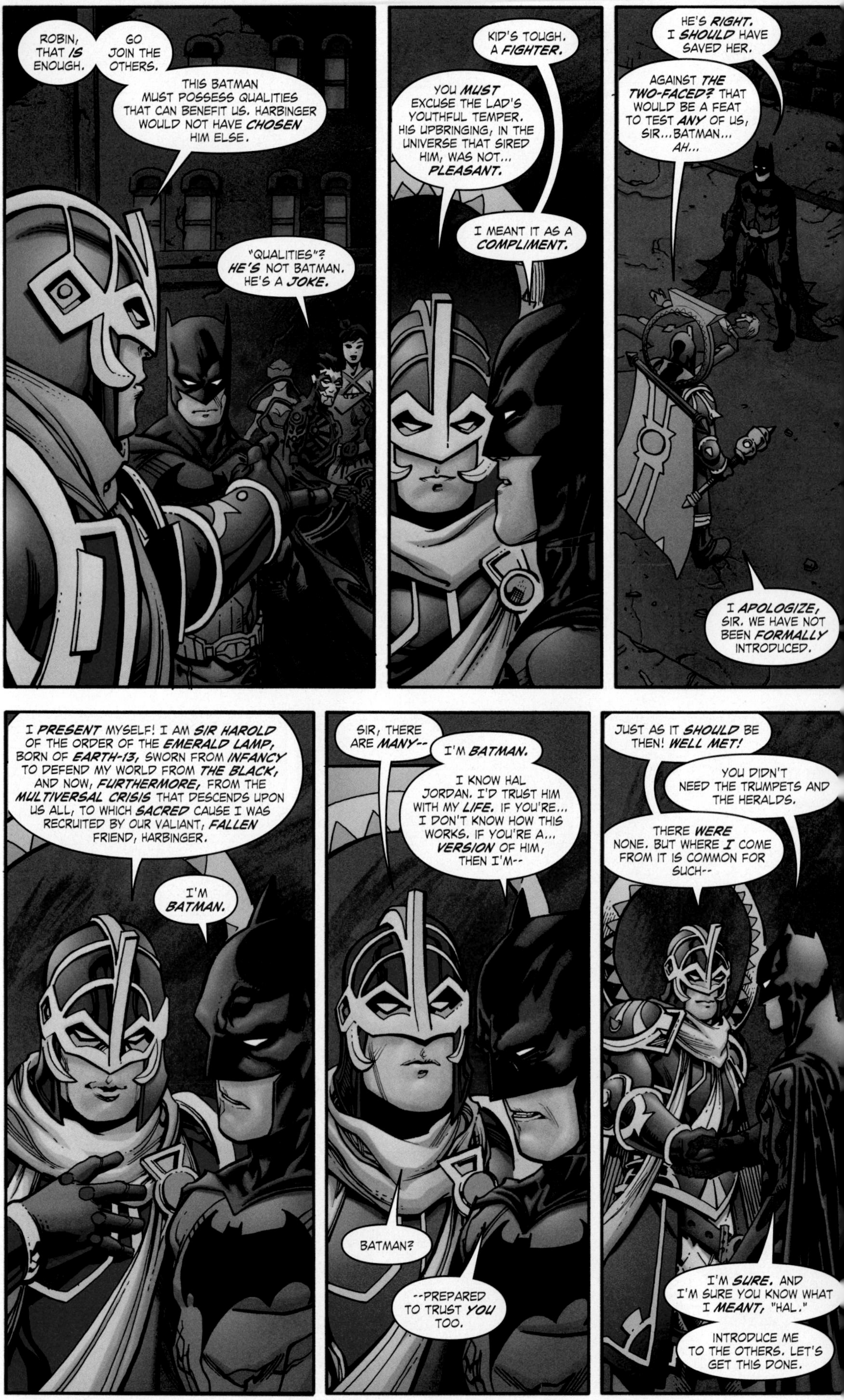
ROBIN, THAT IS ENOUGH.
GO JOIN THE OTHERS.
THIS BATMAN MUST POSSESS QUALITIES THAT CAN BENEFIT US. HARBINGER WOULD NOT HAVE CHOSEN HIM ELSE.
"QUALITIES"? HE'S NOT BATMAN. HE'S A JOKE.
YOU MUST EXCUSE THE LAD'S YOUTHFUL TEMPER. HIS UPBRINGING, IN THE UNIVERSE THAT SIRED HIM, WAS NOT... PLEASANT.
KID'S TOUGH. A FIGHTER.
I MEANT IT AS A COMPLIMENT.
AGAINST THE TWO-FACED? THAT WOULD BE A FEAT TO TEST ANY OF US, SIR...BATMAN... AH...
HE'S RIGHT. I SHOULD HAVE SAVED HER.
I APOLOGIZE, SIR. WE HAVE NOT BEEN FORMALLY INTRODUCED.
I PRESENT MYSELF! I AM SIR HAROLD OF THE ORDER OF THE EMERALD LAMP, BORN OF EARTH-13, SWORN FROM INFANCY TO DEFEND MY WORLD FROM THE BLACK, AND NOW, FURTHERMORE, FROM THE MULTIVERSAL CRISIS THAT DESCENDS UPON US ALL, TO WHICH SACRED CAUSE I WAS RECRUITED BY OUR VALIANT, FALLEN FRIEND, HARBINGER.
I'M BATMAN.
SIR, THERE ARE MANY--
I'M BATMAN.
I KNOW HAL JORDAN. I'D TRUST HIM WITH MY LIFE. IF YOU'RE... I DON'T KNOW HOW THIS WORKS. IF YOU'RE A... VERSION OF HIM, THEN I'M--
BATMAN?
--PREPARED TO TRUST YOU TOO.
JUST AS IT SHOULD BE THEN! WELL MET!
YOU DIDN'T NEED THE TRUMPETS AND THE HERALDS.
THERE WERE NONE. BUT WHERE I COME FROM IT IS COMMON FOR SUCH--
I'M SURE. AND I'M SURE YOU KNOW WHAT I MEANT, "HAL."
INTRODUCE ME TO THE OTHERS. LET'S GET THIS DONE.

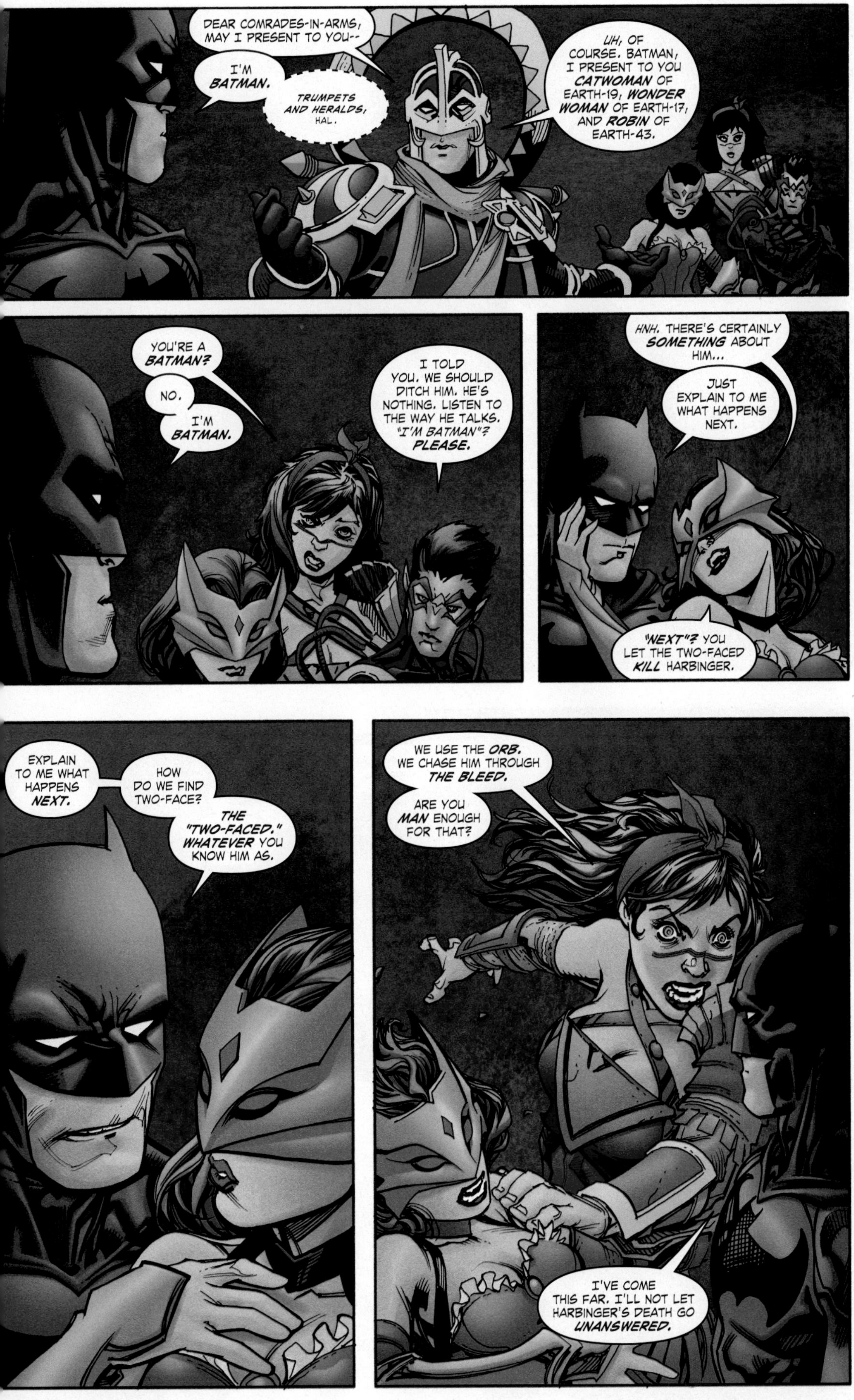
DEAR COMRADES-IN-ARMS, MAY I PRESENT TO YOU--
I'M BATMAN.
TRUMPETS AND HERALDS, HAL.
UH, OF COURSE. BATMAN, I PRESENT TO YOU CATWOMAN OF EARTH-19, WONDER WOMAN OF EARTH-17, AND ROBIN OF EARTH-43.
YOU'RE A BATMAN?
NO.
I'M BATMAN.
I TOLD YOU. WE SHOULD DITCH HIM. HE'S NOTHING. LISTEN TO THE WAY HE TALKS. "I'M BATMAN"? PLEASE.
HNH. THERE'S CERTAINLY SOMETHING ABOUT HIM...
JUST EXPLAIN TO ME WHAT HAPPENS NEXT.
"NEXT"? YOU LET THE TWO-FACED KILL HARBINGER.
EXPLAIN TO ME WHAT HAPPENS NEXT.
HOW DO WE FIND TWO-FACE?
THE "TWO-FACED." WHATEVER YOU KNOW HIM AS.
WE USE THE ORB. WE CHASE HIM THROUGH THE BLEED.
ARE YOU MAN ENOUGH FOR THAT?
I'VE COME THIS FAR. I'LL NOT LET HARBINGER'S DEATH GO UNANSWERED.

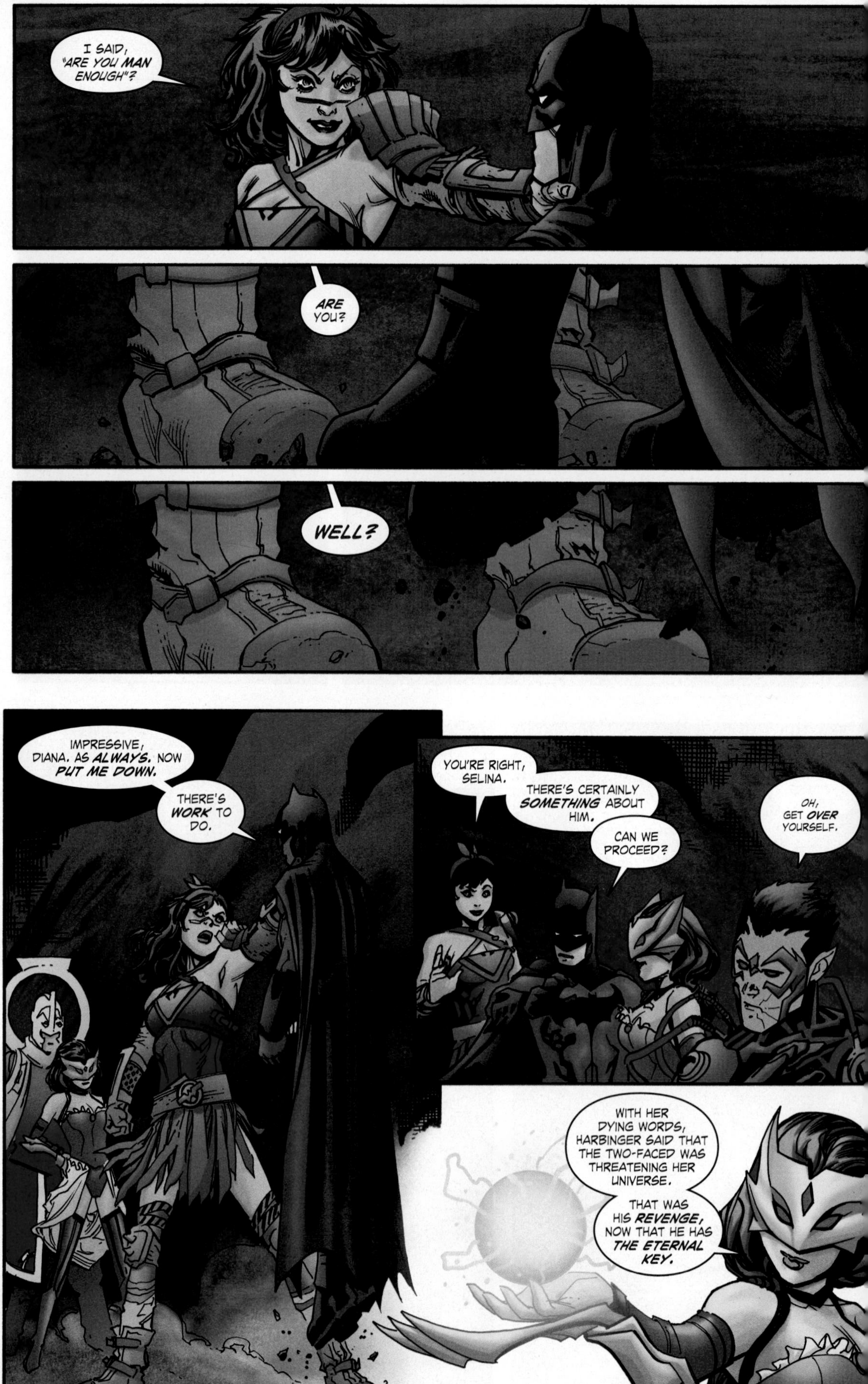
I SAID, "ARE YOU MAN ENOUGH"?
ARE YOU?
WELL?
IMPRESSIVE, DIANA. AS ALWAYS. NOW PUT ME DOWN.
THERE'S WORK TO DO.
YOU'RE RIGHT, SELINA.
THERE'S CERTAINLY SOMETHING ABOUT HIM.
CAN WE PROCEED?
OH, GET OVER YOURSELF.
WITH HER DYING WORDS, HARBINGER SAID THAT THE TWO-FACED WAS THREATENING HER UNIVERSE.
THAT WAS HIS REVENGE, NOW THAT HE HAS THE ETERNAL KEY.

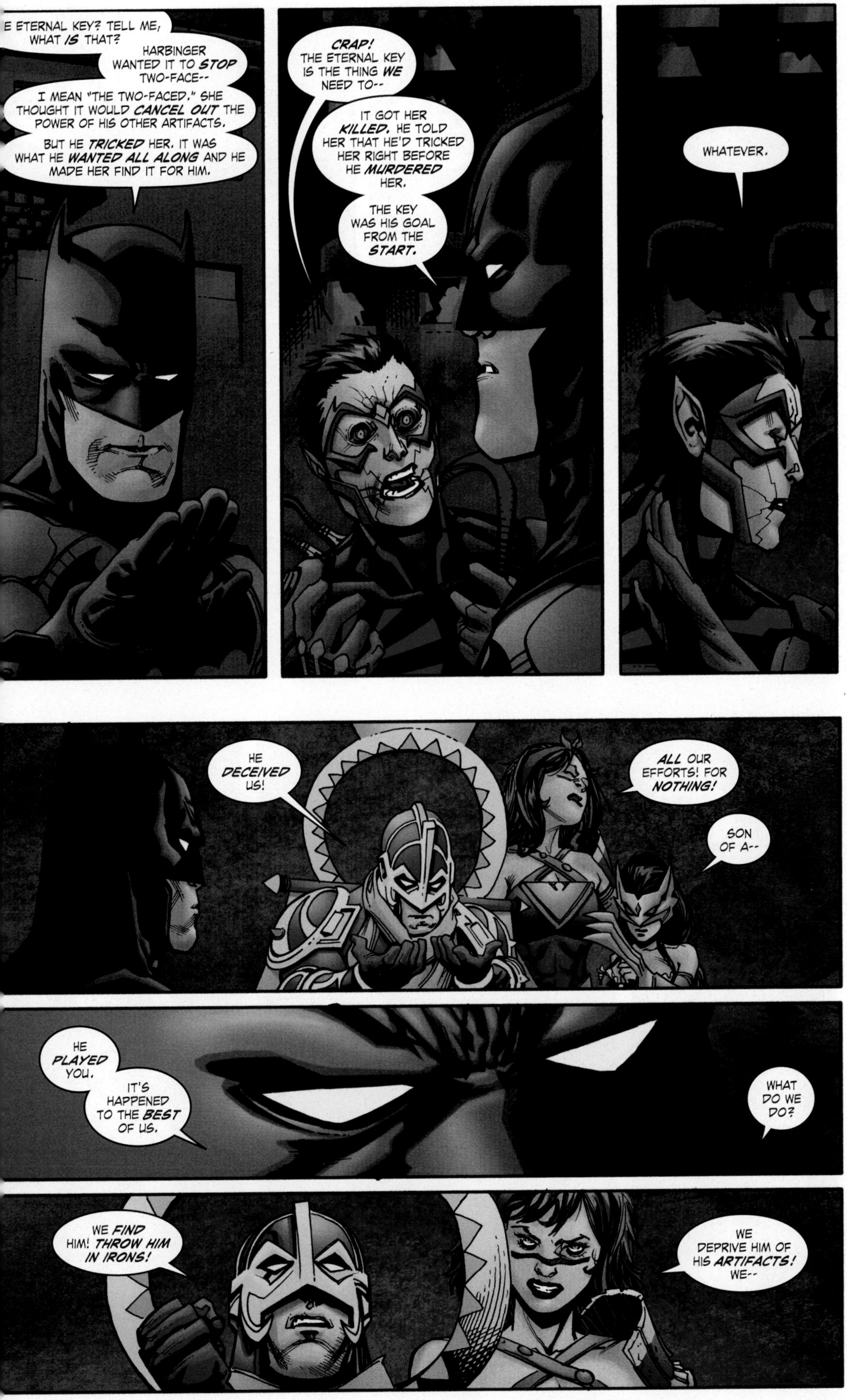
E ETERNAL KEY? TELL ME, WHAT *IS* THAT?
HARBINGER WANTED IT TO *STOP* TWO-FACE--
I MEAN "THE TWO-FACED." SHE THOUGHT IT WOULD *CANCEL OUT* THE POWER OF HIS OTHER ARTIFACTS.
BUT HE *TRICKED* HER. IT WAS WHAT HE *WANTED ALL ALONG* AND HE MADE HER FIND IT FOR HIM.
CRAP! THE ETERNAL KEY IS THE THING *WE* NEED TO--
IT GOT HER *KILLED.* HE TOLD HER THAT HE'D TRICKED HER RIGHT BEFORE HE *MURDERED* HER.
THE KEY WAS HIS GOAL FROM THE *START.*
WHATEVER.
HE *DECEIVED* US!
ALL OUR EFFORTS! FOR *NOTHING!*
SON OF A--
HE *PLAYED* YOU.
IT'S HAPPENED TO THE *BEST* OF US.
WHAT DO WE DO?
WE *FIND* HIM! *THROW HIM IN IRONS!*
WE DEPRIVE HIM OF HIS *ARTIFACTS!* WE--

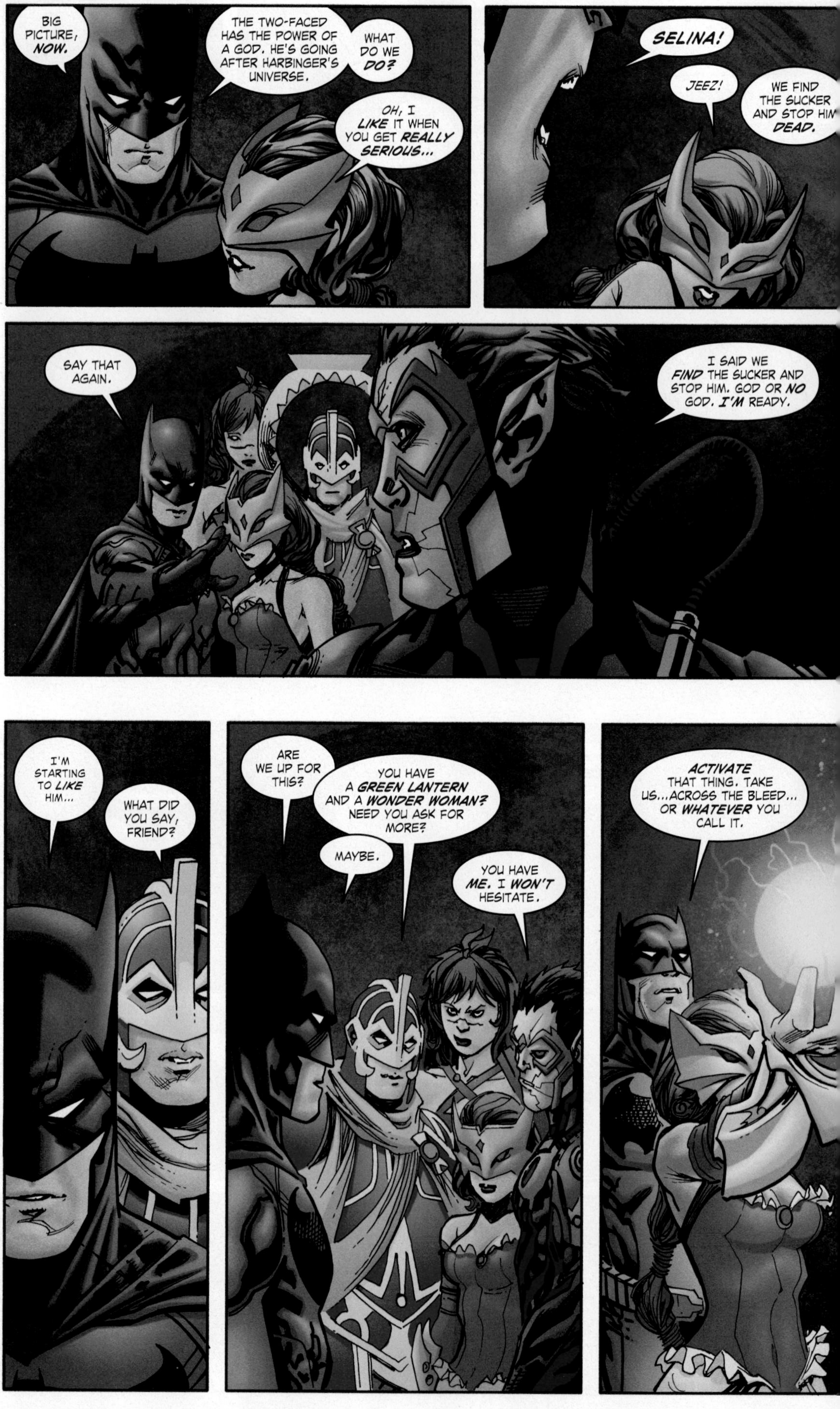
BIG PICTURE, NOW.
THE TWO-FACED HAS THE POWER OF A GOD. HE'S GOING AFTER HARBINGER'S UNIVERSE.
WHAT DO WE DO?
OH, I LIKE IT WHEN YOU GET REALLY SERIOUS...
SELINA!
JEEZ!
WE FIND THE SUCKER AND STOP HIM DEAD.
SAY THAT AGAIN.
I SAID WE FIND THE SUCKER AND STOP HIM. GOD OR NO GOD. I'M READY.
I'M STARTING TO LIKE HIM...
WHAT DID YOU SAY, FRIEND?
ARE WE UP FOR THIS?
YOU HAVE A GREEN LANTERN AND A WONDER WOMAN? NEED YOU ASK FOR MORE?
MAYBE.
YOU HAVE ME. I WON'T HESITATE.
ACTIVATE THAT THING. TAKE US...ACROSS THE BLEED... OR WHATEVER YOU CALL IT.

IS THIS...

ARE WE *THERE*?

DEFINITELY.

THE ORB READS THAT THIS IS EARTH-48.

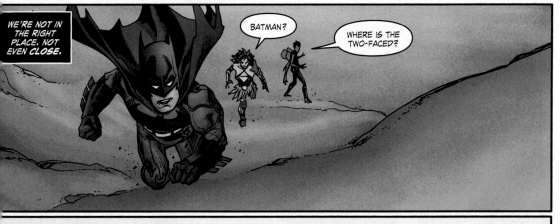

WE'RE NOT IN THE RIGHT PLACE. NOT EVEN *CLOSE*.

BATMAN?

WHERE IS THE TWO-FACED?

HE'S *THERE*.

WE'RE NOT CLOSE *ENOUGH*.

SO WE--

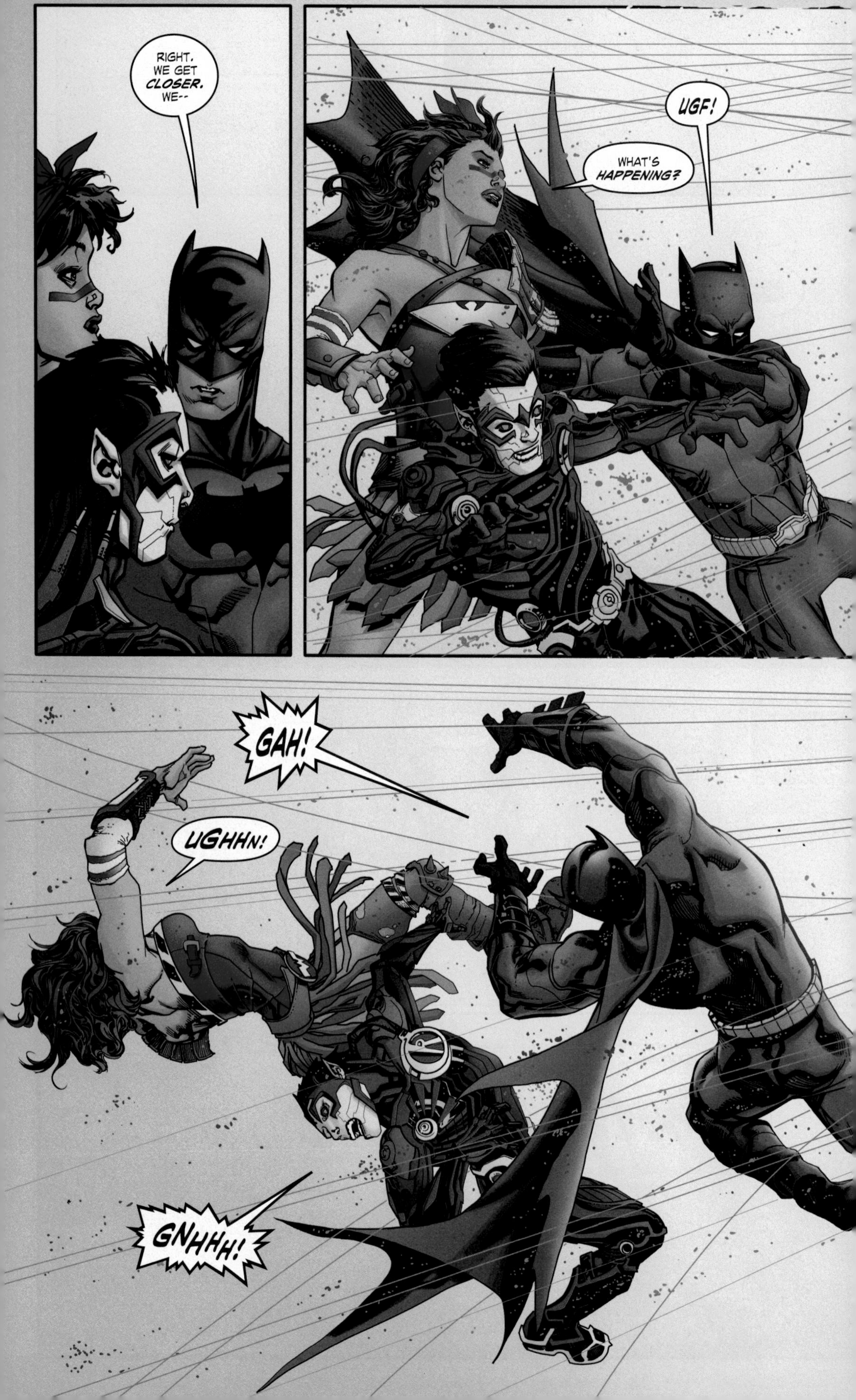
RIGHT. WE GET CLOSER. WE--
WHAT'S HAPPENING?
UGF!
GAH!
UGHHN!
GNHHH!

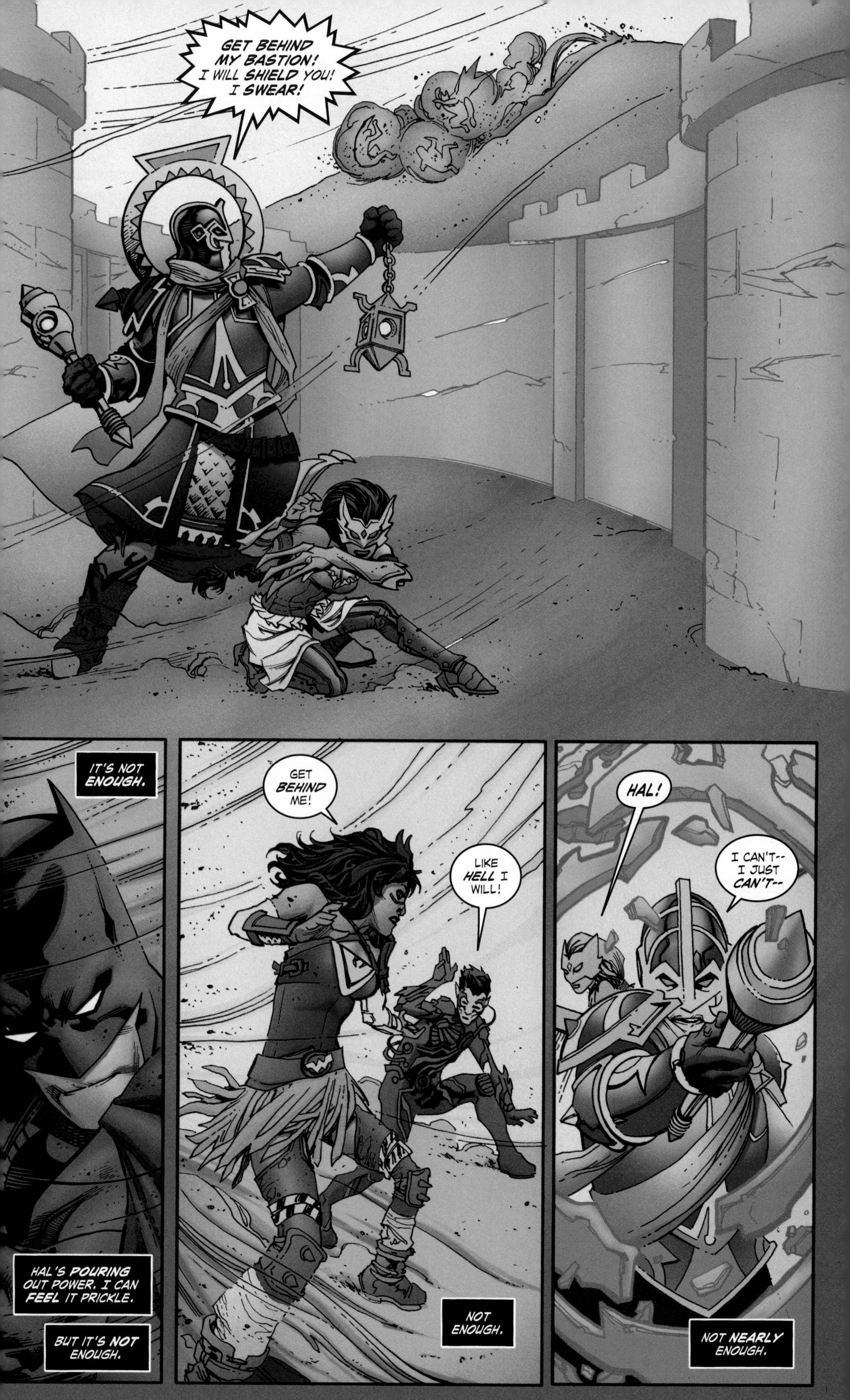
GET BEHIND MY BASTION! I WILL SHIELD YOU! I SWEAR!
IT'S NOT ENOUGH.
HAL'S POURING OUT POWER. I CAN FEEL IT PRICKLE.
BUT IT'S NOT ENOUGH.
GET BEHIND ME!
LIKE HELL I WILL!
NOT ENOUGH.
HAL!
I CAN'T-- I JUST CAN'T--
NOT NEARLY ENOUGH.

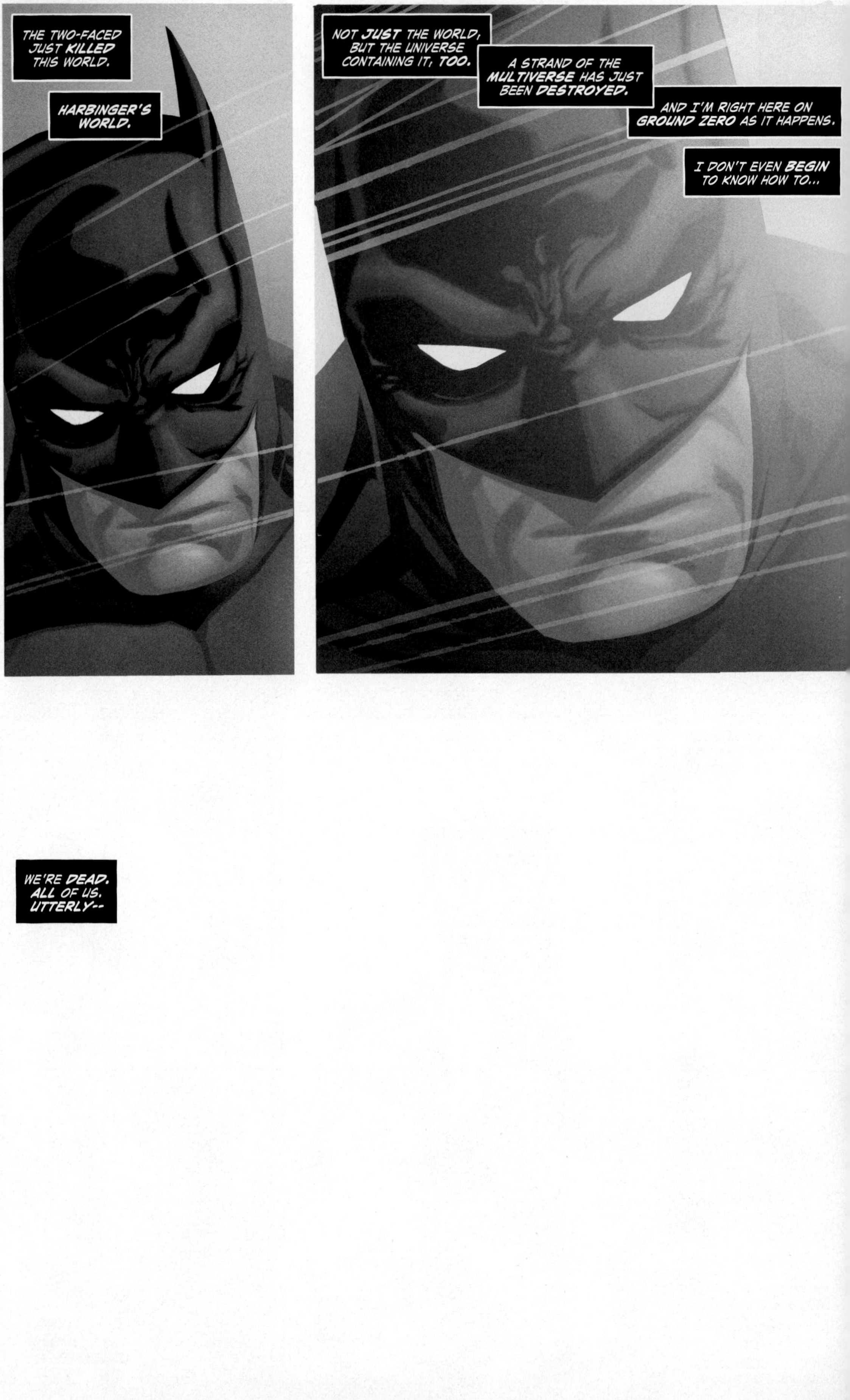
THE TWO-FACED JUST KILLED THIS WORLD.
HARBINGER'S WORLD.
NOT JUST THE WORLD, BUT THE UNIVERSE CONTAINING IT, TOO.
A STRAND OF THE MULTIVERSE HAS JUST BEEN DESTROYED.
AND I'M RIGHT HERE ON GROUND ZERO AS IT HAPPENS.
I DON'T EVEN BEGIN TO KNOW HOW TO...
WE'RE DEAD. ALL OF US. UTTERLY--

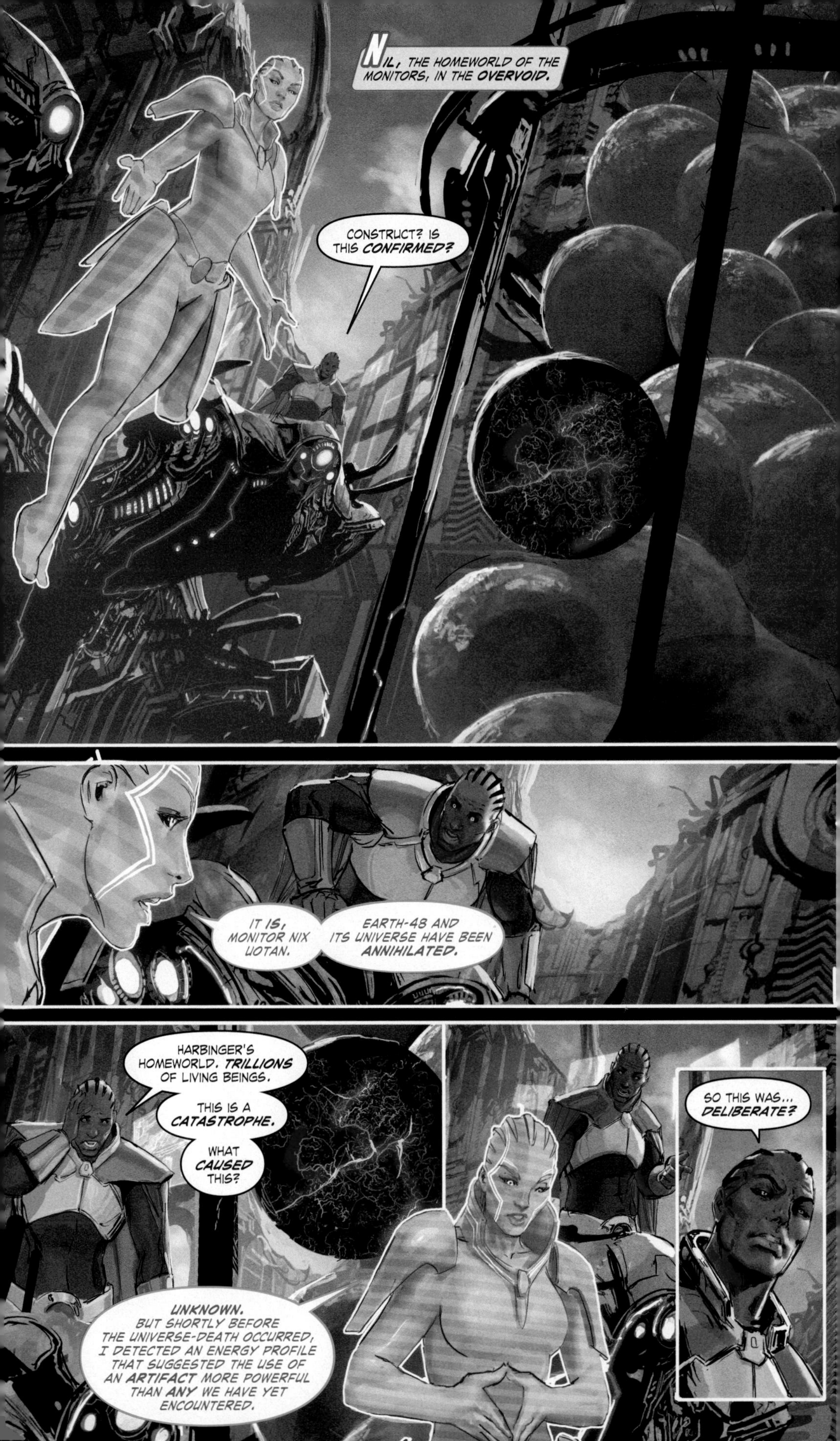
NIL, THE HOMEWORLD OF THE MONITORS, IN THE OVERVOID.
CONSTRUCT? IS THIS CONFIRMED?
IT IS, MONITOR NIX UOTAN.
EARTH-48 AND ITS UNIVERSE HAVE BEEN ANNIHILATED.
HARBINGER'S HOMEWORLD. TRILLIONS OF LIVING BEINGS.
THIS IS A CATASTROPHE.
WHAT CAUSED THIS?
UNKNOWN. BUT SHORTLY BEFORE THE UNIVERSE-DEATH OCCURRED, I DETECTED AN ENERGY PROFILE THAT SUGGESTED THE USE OF AN ARTIFACT MORE POWERFUL THAN ANY WE HAVE YET ENCOUNTERED.
SO THIS WAS... DELIBERATE?

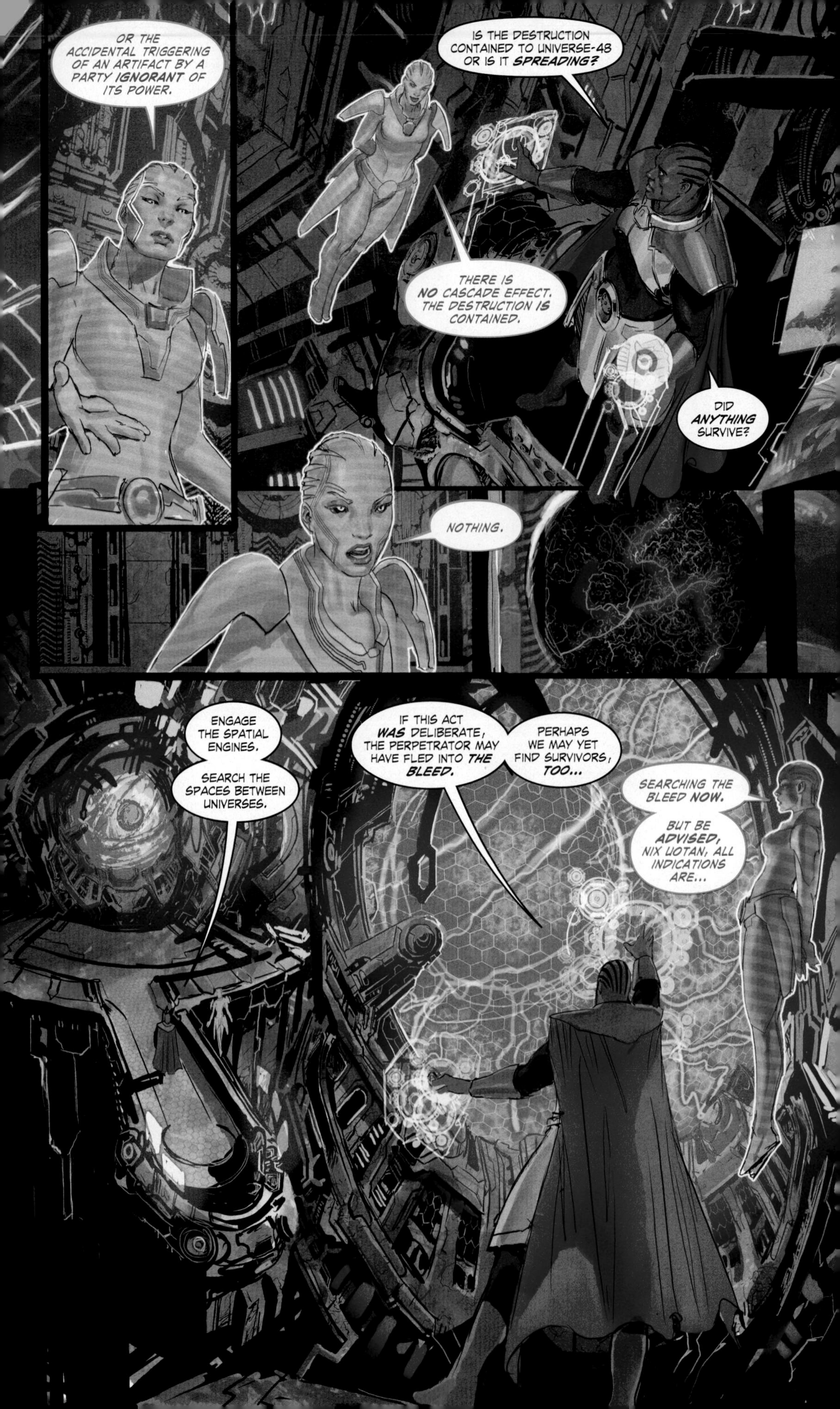

OR THE ACCIDENTAL TRIGGERING OF AN ARTIFACT BY A PARTY IGNORANT OF ITS POWER.
IS THE DESTRUCTION CONTAINED TO UNIVERSE-48 OR IS IT SPREADING?
THERE IS NO CASCADE EFFECT. THE DESTRUCTION IS CONTAINED.
DID ANYTHING SURVIVE?
NOTHING.
ENGAGE THE SPATIAL ENGINES.
SEARCH THE SPACES BETWEEN UNIVERSES.
IF THIS ACT WAS DELIBERATE, THE PERPETRATOR MAY HAVE FLED INTO THE BLEED.
PERHAPS WE MAY YET FIND SURVIVORS, TOO...
SEARCHING THE BLEED NOW.
BUT BE ADVISED, NIX UOTAN, ALL INDICATIONS ARE...

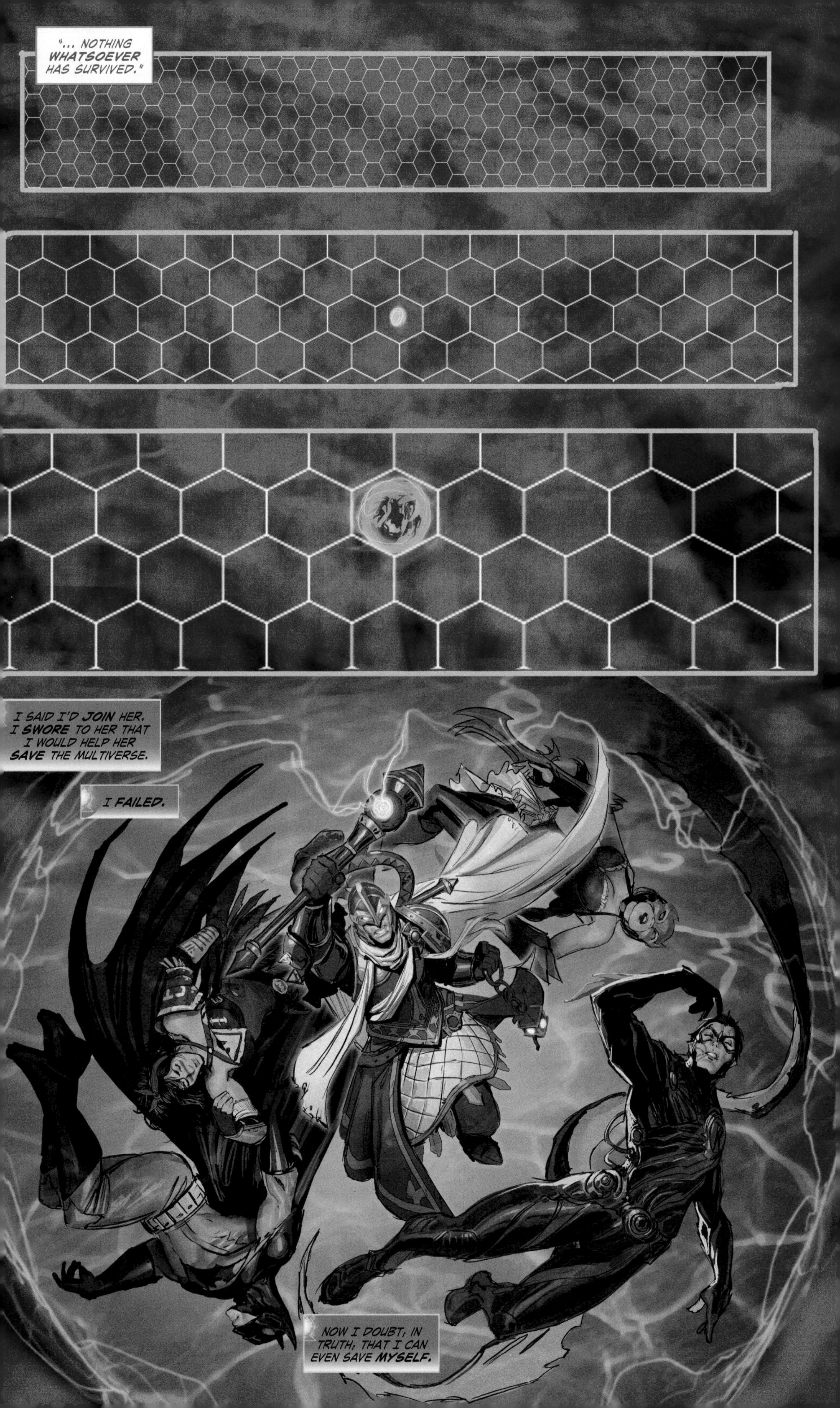
"... NOTHING WHATSOEVER HAS SURVIVED."
I SAID I'D JOIN HER. I SWORE TO HER THAT I WOULD HELP HER SAVE THE MULTIVERSE.
I FAILED.
NOW I DOUBT, IN TRUTH, THAT I CAN EVEN SAVE MYSELF.

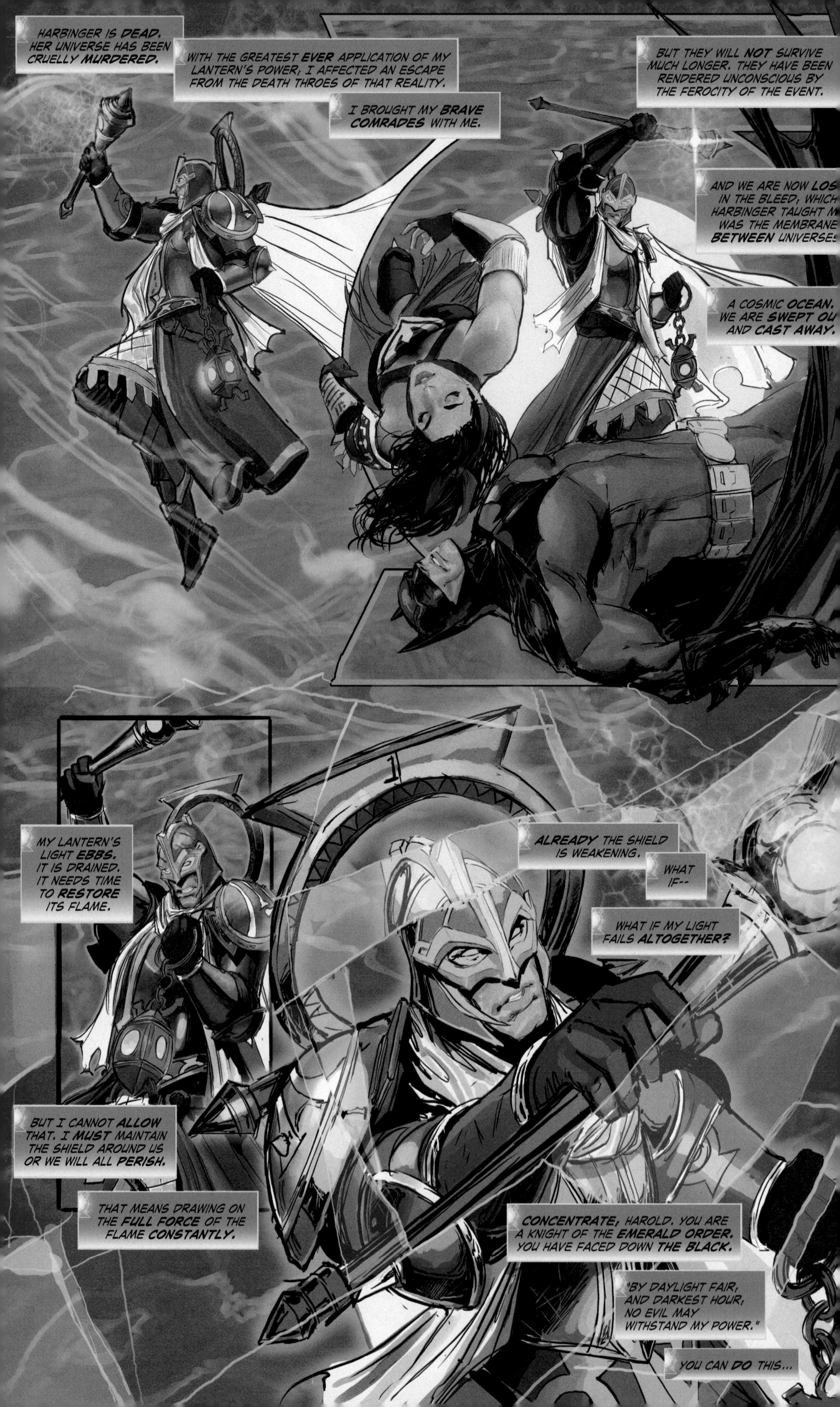

HARBINGER IS DEAD. HER UNIVERSE HAS BEEN CRUELLY MURDERED.
WITH THE GREATEST EVER APPLICATION OF MY LANTERN'S POWER, I AFFECTED AN ESCAPE FROM THE DEATH THROES OF THAT REALITY.
I BROUGHT MY BRAVE COMRADES WITH ME.
BUT THEY WILL NOT SURVIVE MUCH LONGER. THEY HAVE BEEN RENDERED UNCONSCIOUS BY THE FEROCITY OF THE EVENT.
AND WE ARE NOW LOS IN THE BLEED, WHICH HARBINGER TAUGHT M WAS THE MEMBRANE BETWEEN UNIVERSES
A COSMIC OCEAN. WE ARE SWEPT OU AND CAST AWAY.
MY LANTERN'S LIGHT EBBS. IT IS DRAINED. IT NEEDS TIME TO RESTORE ITS FLAME.
ALREADY THE SHIELD IS WEAKENING.
WHAT IF--
WHAT IF MY LIGHT FAILS ALTOGETHER?
BUT I CANNOT ALLOW THAT. I MUST MAINTAIN THE SHIELD AROUND US OR WE WILL ALL PERISH.
THAT MEANS DRAWING ON THE FULL FORCE OF THE FLAME CONSTANTLY.
CONCENTRATE, HAROLD. YOU ARE A KNIGHT OF THE EMERALD ORDER. YOU HAVE FACED DOWN THE BLACK.
"BY DAYLIGHT FAIR, AND DARKEST HOUR, NO EVIL MAY WITHSTAND MY POWER."
YOU CAN DO THIS...

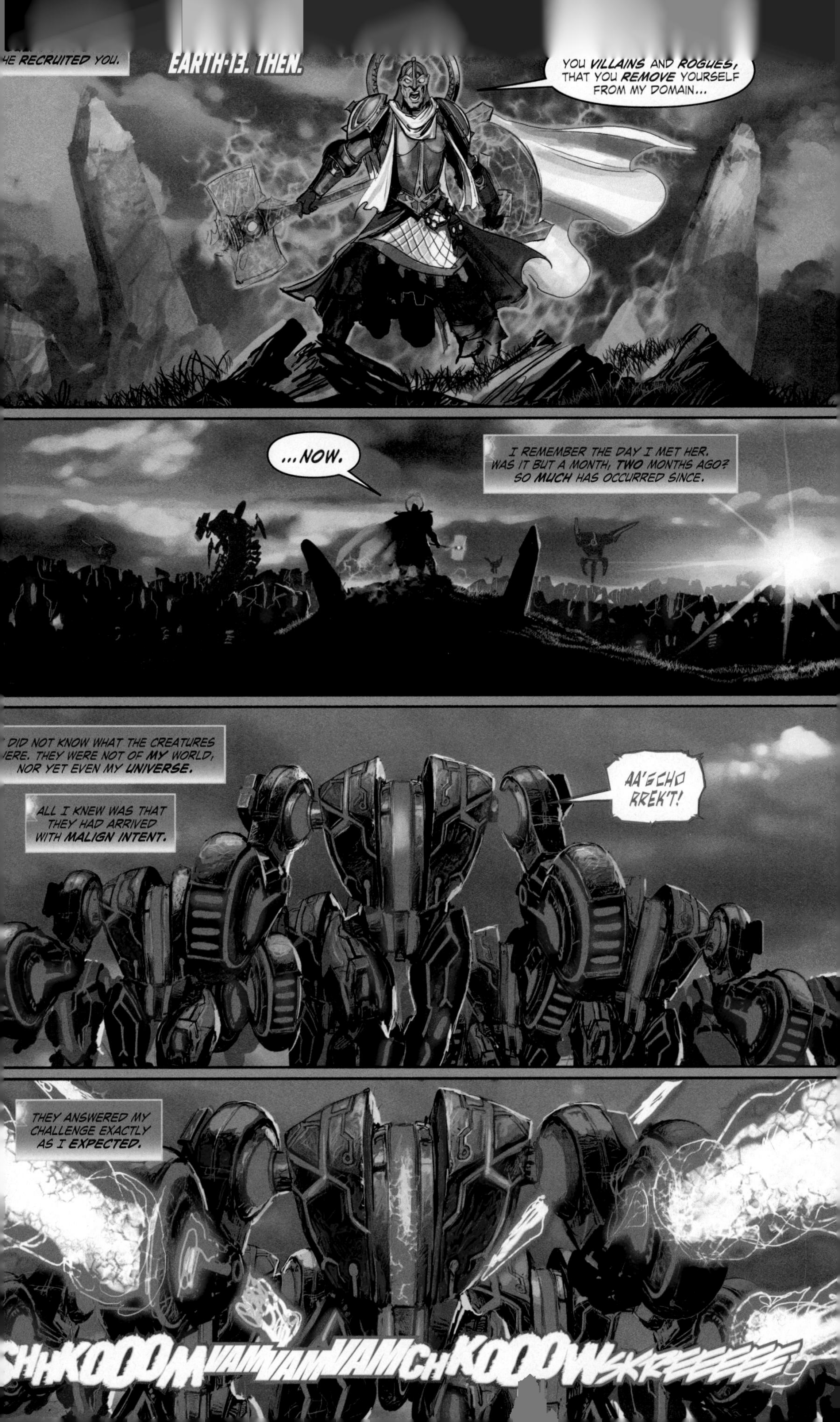

HE RECRUITED YOU.
EARTH-13. THEN.
YOU VILLAINS AND ROGUES, THAT YOU REMOVE YOURSELF FROM MY DOMAIN...
...NOW.
I REMEMBER THE DAY I MET HER. WAS IT BUT A MONTH, TWO MONTHS AGO? SO MUCH HAS OCCURRED SINCE.
DID NOT KNOW WHAT THE CREATURES WERE. THEY WERE NOT OF MY WORLD, NOR YET EVEN MY UNIVERSE.
ALL I KNEW WAS THAT THEY HAD ARRIVED WITH MALIGN INTENT.
AA'ECHO RREK'T!
THEY ANSWERED MY CHALLENGE EXACTLY AS I EXPECTED.
SHHKOOOM VAM VAM VAM CH KOOOW SKREEEEEE

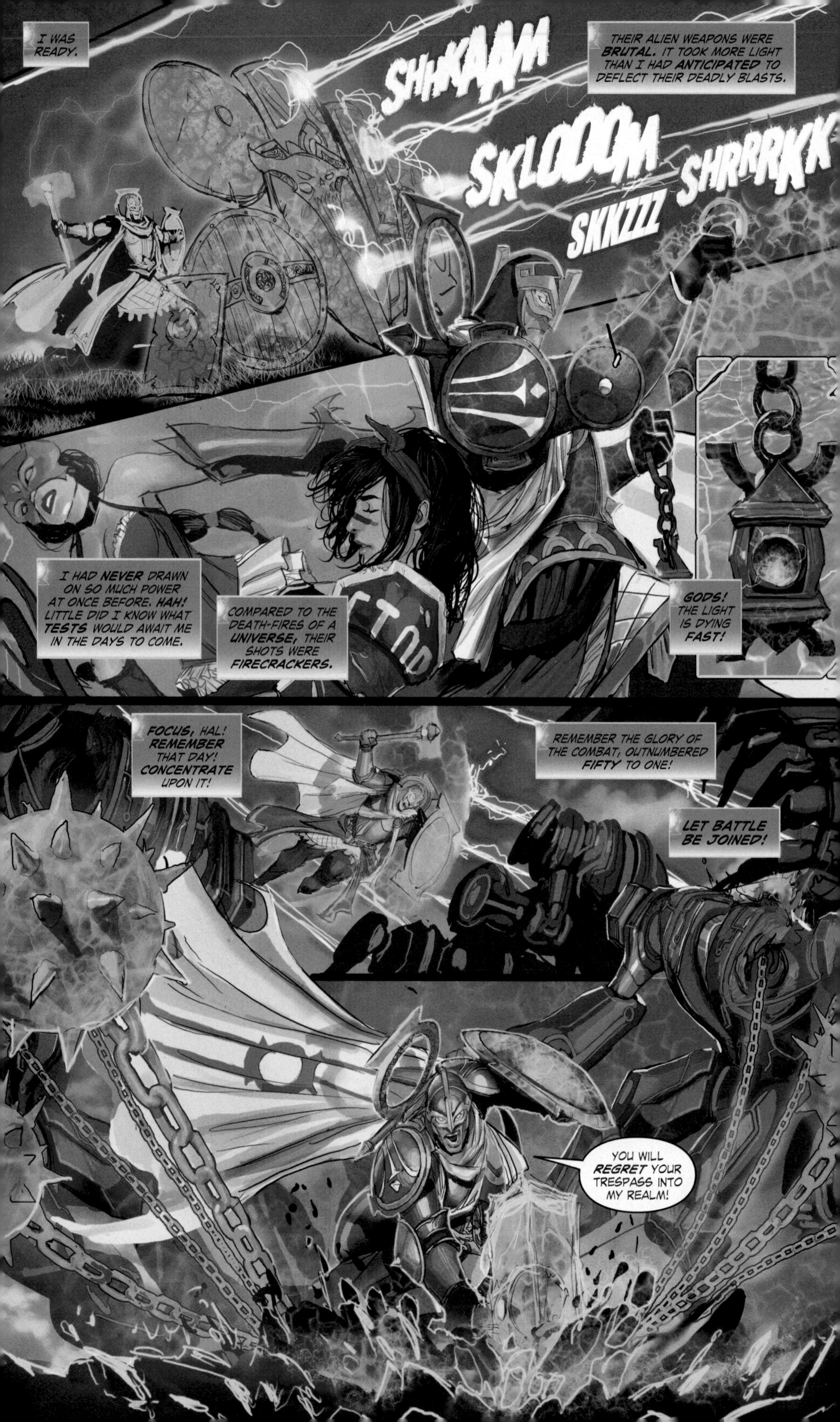
I WAS READY.
THEIR ALIEN WEAPONS WERE BRUTAL. IT TOOK MORE LIGHT THAN I HAD ANTICIPATED TO DEFLECT THEIR DEADLY BLASTS.
SHHKAAM
SKLOOOM
SKKZZZ
SHRRRKK
I HAD NEVER DRAWN ON SO MUCH POWER AT ONCE BEFORE. HAH! LITTLE DID I KNOW WHAT TESTS WOULD AWAIT ME IN THE DAYS TO COME.
COMPARED TO THE DEATH-FIRES OF A UNIVERSE, THEIR SHOTS WERE FIRECRACKERS.
GODS! THE LIGHT IS DYING FAST!
FOCUS, HAL! REMEMBER THAT DAY! CONCENTRATE UPON IT!
REMEMBER THE GLORY OF THE COMBAT, OUTNUMBERED FIFTY TO ONE!
LET BATTLE BE JOINED!
YOU WILL REGRET YOUR TRESPASS INTO MY REALM!

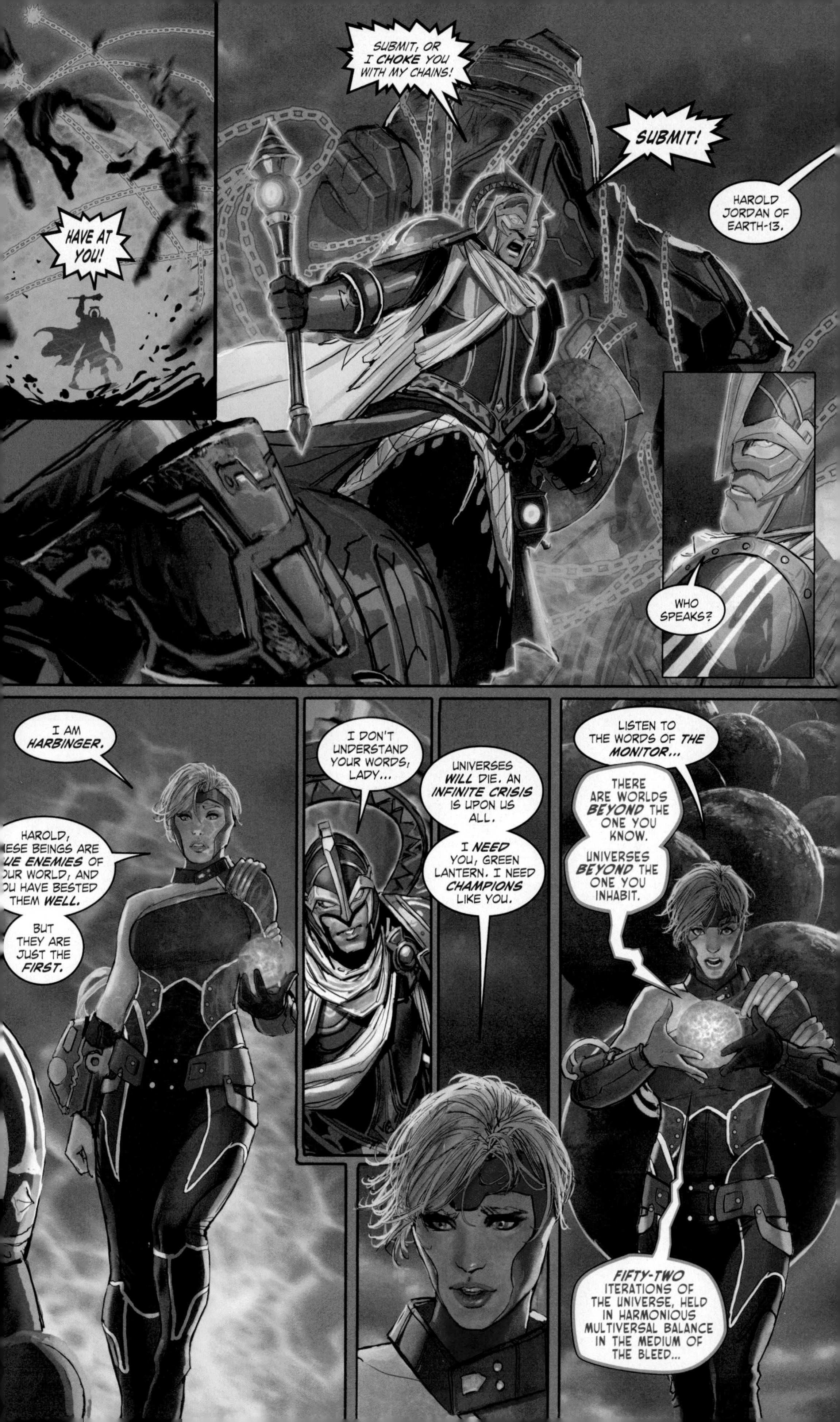
HAVE AT YOU!
SUBMIT, OR I CHOKE YOU WITH MY CHAINS!
SUBMIT!
HAROLD JORDAN OF EARTH-13.
WHO SPEAKS?
I AM HARBINGER.
HAROLD, ESE BEINGS ARE UE ENEMIES OF OUR WORLD, AND OU HAVE BESTED THEM WELL.
BUT THEY ARE JUST THE FIRST.
I DON'T UNDERSTAND YOUR WORDS, LADY...
UNIVERSES WILL DIE. AN INFINITE CRISIS IS UPON US ALL.
I NEED YOU, GREEN LANTERN. I NEED CHAMPIONS LIKE YOU.
LISTEN TO THE WORDS OF THE MONITOR...
THERE ARE WORLDS BEYOND THE ONE YOU KNOW.
UNIVERSES BEYOND THE ONE YOU INHABIT.
FIFTY-TWO ITERATIONS OF THE UNIVERSE, HELD IN HARMONIOUS MULTIVERSAL BALANCE IN THE MEDIUM OF THE BLEED...

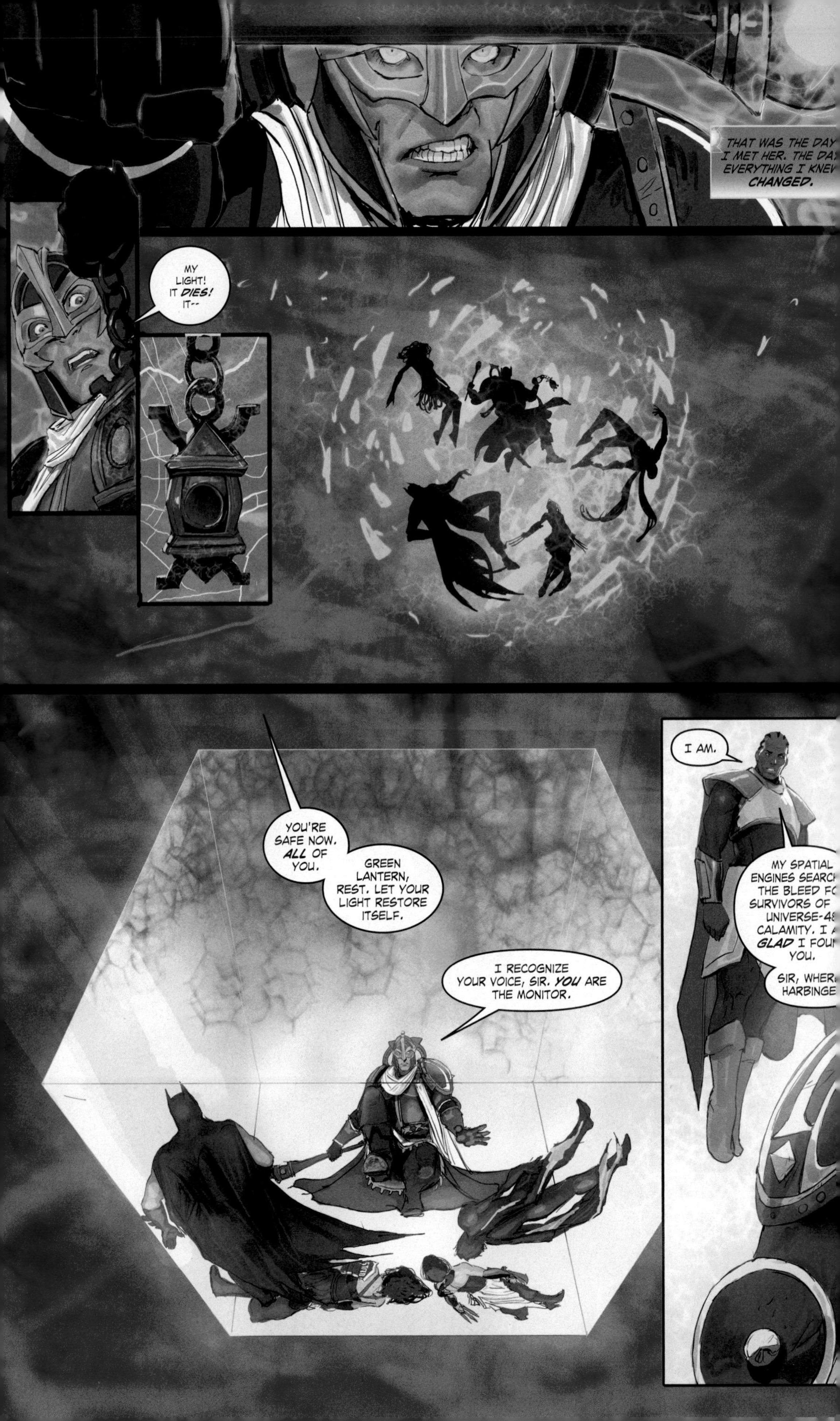

THAT WAS THE DAY I MET HER. THE DAY EVERYTHING I KNEW CHANGED.
MY LIGHT! IT DIES! IT--
YOU'RE SAFE NOW. ALL OF YOU.
GREEN LANTERN, REST. LET YOUR LIGHT RESTORE ITSELF.
I RECOGNIZE YOUR VOICE, SIR. YOU ARE THE MONITOR.
I AM.
MY SPATIAL ENGINES SEARCH THE BLEED FO SURVIVORS OF UNIVERSE-48 CALAMITY. I A GLAD I FOUN YOU.
SIR, WHER HARBINGE

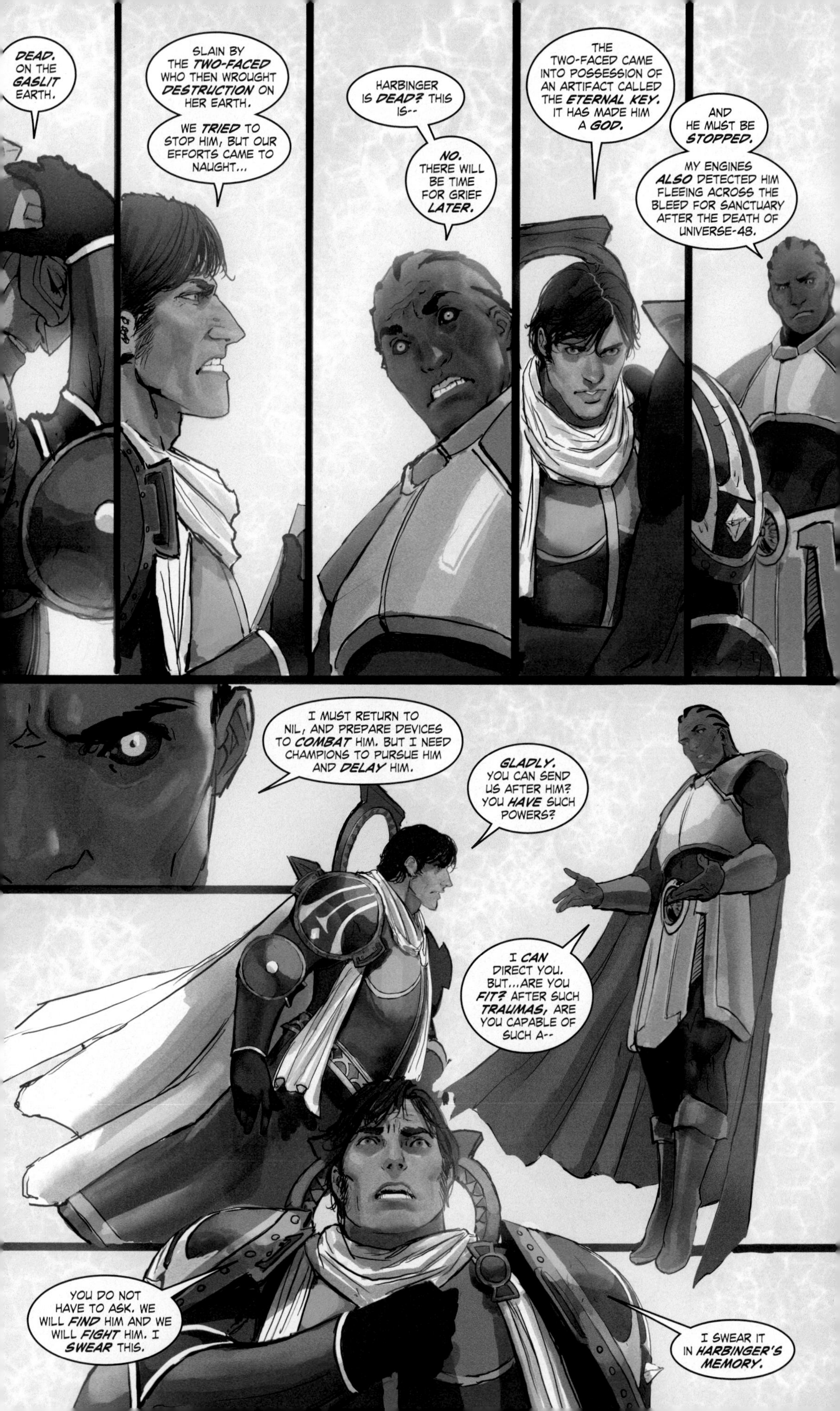
DEAD. ON THE GASLIT EARTH.
SLAIN BY THE TWO-FACED WHO THEN WROUGHT DESTRUCTION ON HER EARTH.
WE TRIED TO STOP HIM, BUT OUR EFFORTS CAME TO NAUGHT...
HARBINGER IS DEAD? THIS IS--
NO. THERE WILL BE TIME FOR GRIEF LATER.
THE TWO-FACED CAME INTO POSSESSION OF AN ARTIFACT CALLED THE ETERNAL KEY. IT HAS MADE HIM A GOD.
AND HE MUST BE STOPPED.
MY ENGINES ALSO DETECTED HIM FLEEING ACROSS THE BLEED FOR SANCTUARY AFTER THE DEATH OF UNIVERSE-48.
I MUST RETURN TO NIL, AND PREPARE DEVICES TO COMBAT HIM. BUT I NEED CHAMPIONS TO PURSUE HIM AND DELAY HIM.
GLADLY. YOU CAN SEND US AFTER HIM? YOU HAVE SUCH POWERS?
I CAN DIRECT YOU. BUT...ARE YOU FIT? AFTER SUCH TRAUMAS, ARE YOU CAPABLE OF SUCH A--
YOU DO NOT HAVE TO ASK. WE WILL FIND HIM AND WE WILL FIGHT HIM. I SWEAR THIS.
I SWEAR IT IN HARBINGER'S MEMORY.

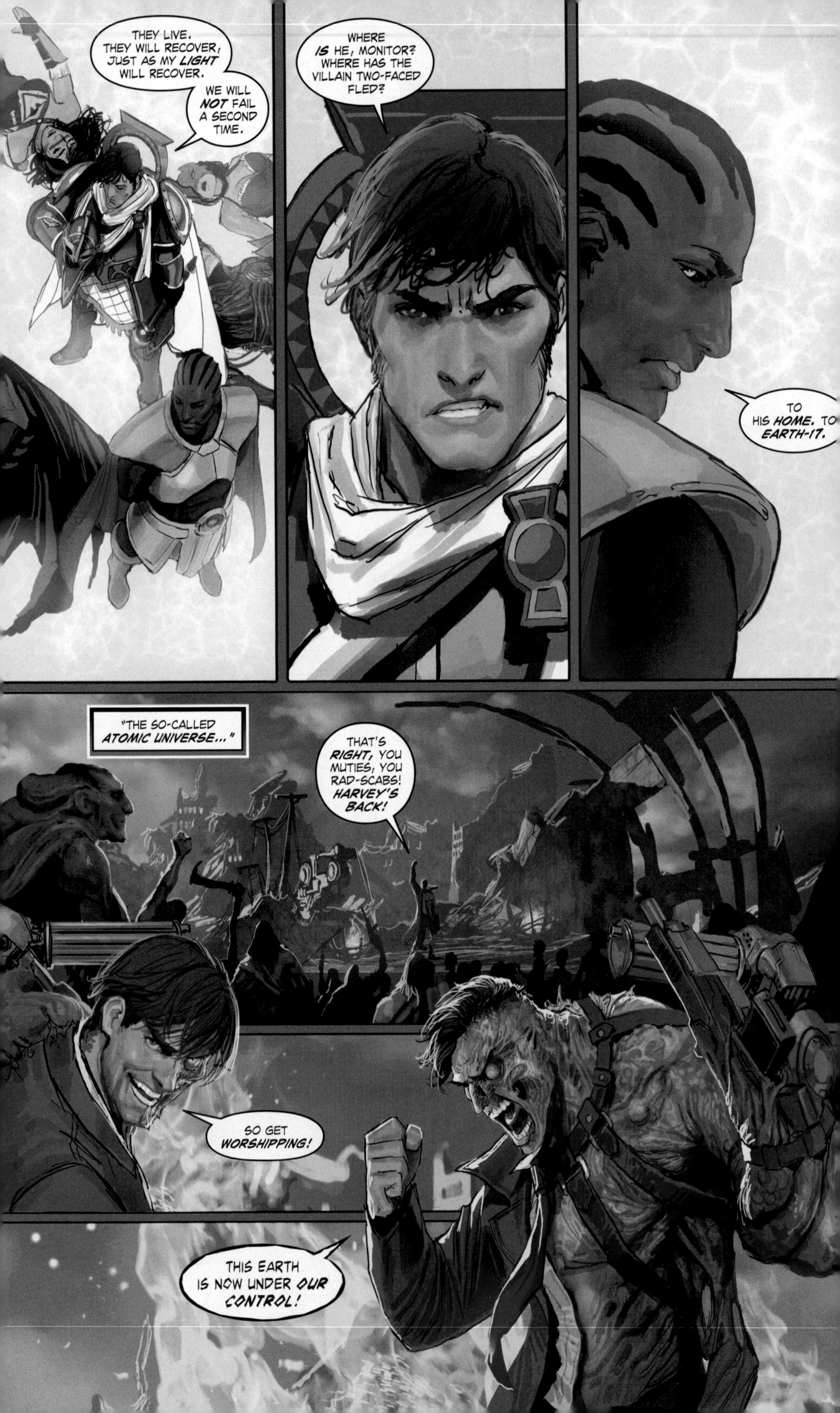
THEY LIVE. THEY WILL RECOVER, JUST AS MY *LIGHT* WILL RECOVER.
WE WILL *NOT* FAIL A SECOND TIME.
WHERE *IS* HE, MONITOR? WHERE HAS THE VILLAIN TWO-FACED FLED?
TO HIS *HOME.* TO *EARTH-17.*
"THE SO-CALLED *ATOMIC UNIVERSE...*"
THAT'S *RIGHT,* YOU MUTIES, YOU RAD-SCABS! *HARVEY'S BACK!*
SO GET *WORSHIPPING!*
THIS EARTH IS NOW UNDER *OUR CONTROL!*

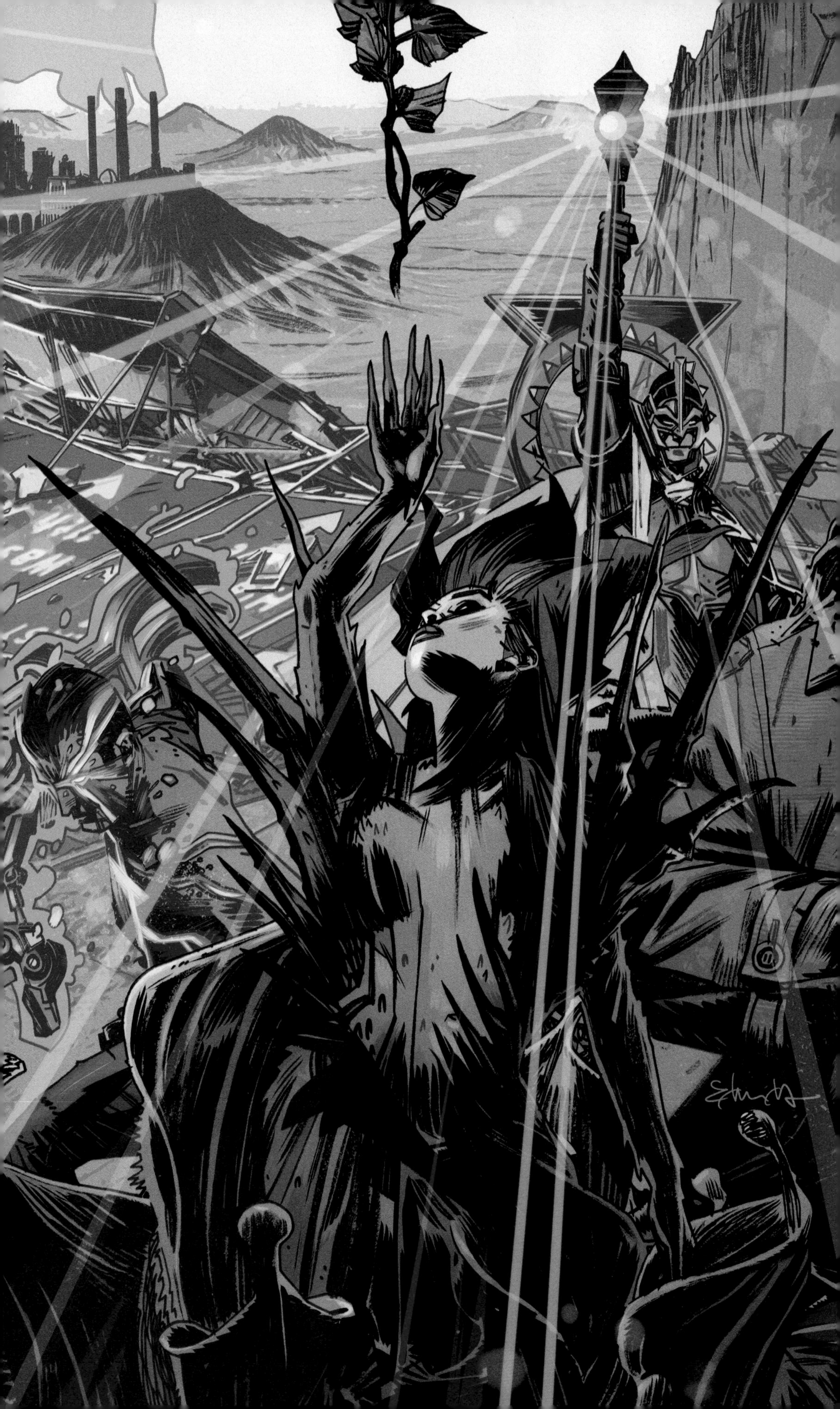

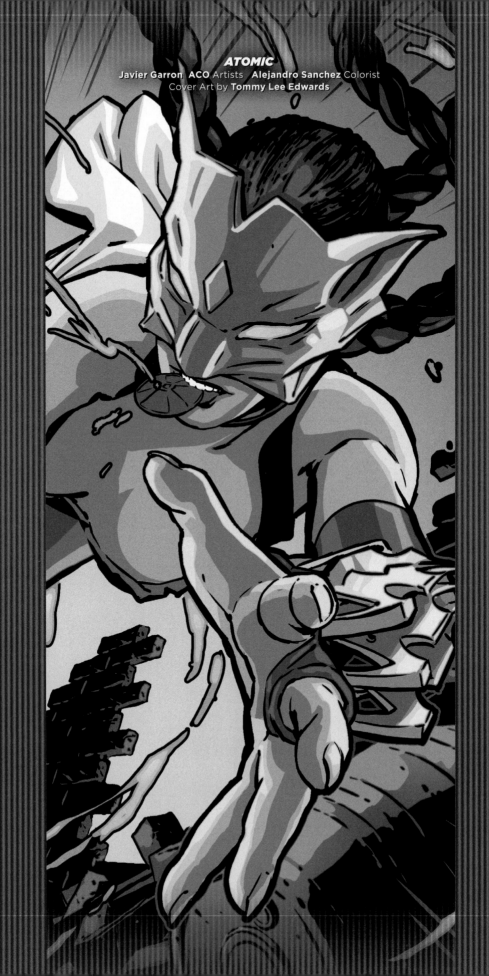

ATOMIC
Javier Garron **ACO** Artists **Alejandro Sanchez** Colorist
Cover Art by **Tommy Lee Edwards**

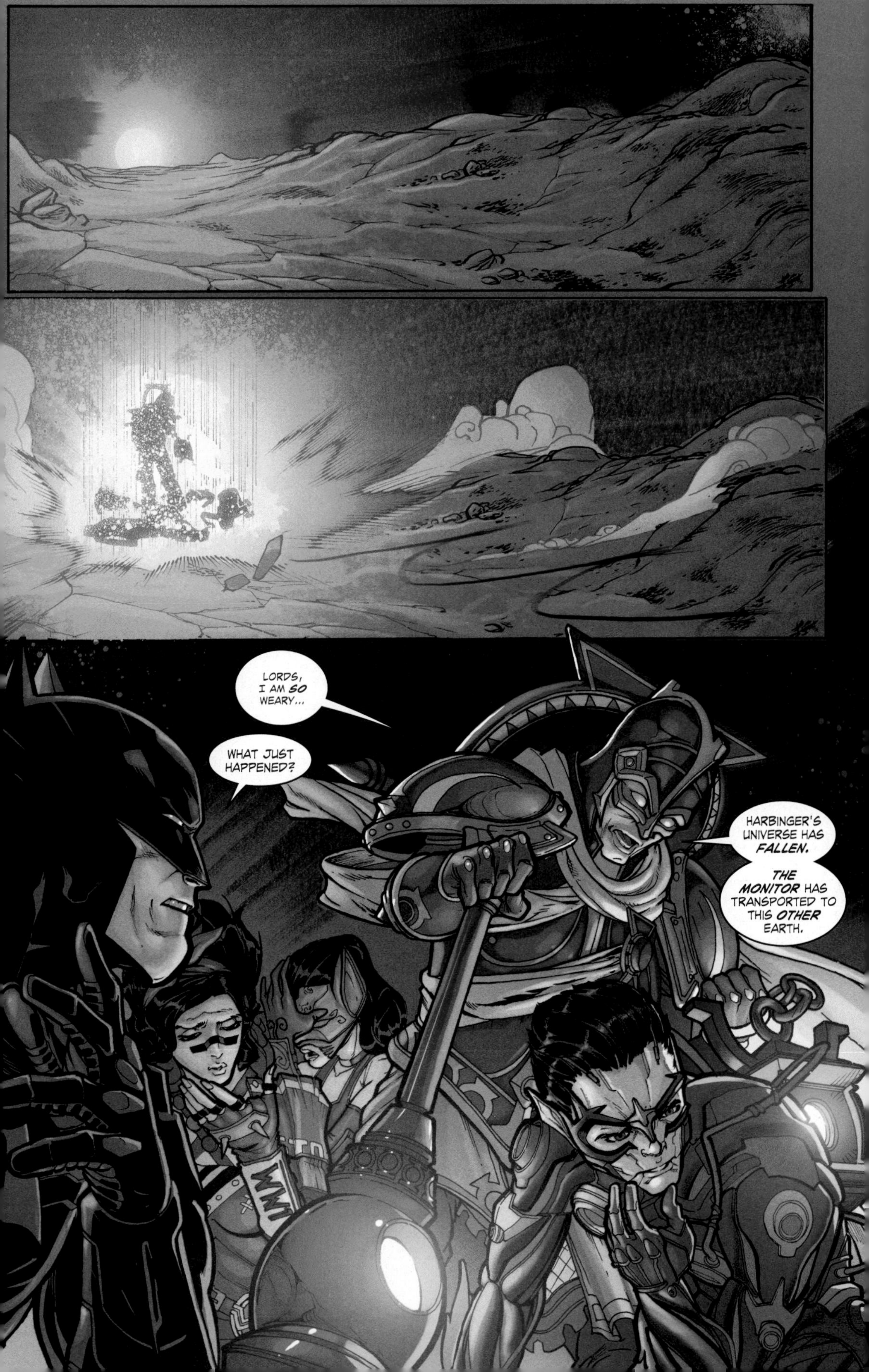
LORDS, I AM SO WEARY...
WHAT JUST HAPPENED?
HARBINGER'S UNIVERSE HAS FALLEN.
THE MONITOR HAS TRANSPORTED TO THIS OTHER EARTH.

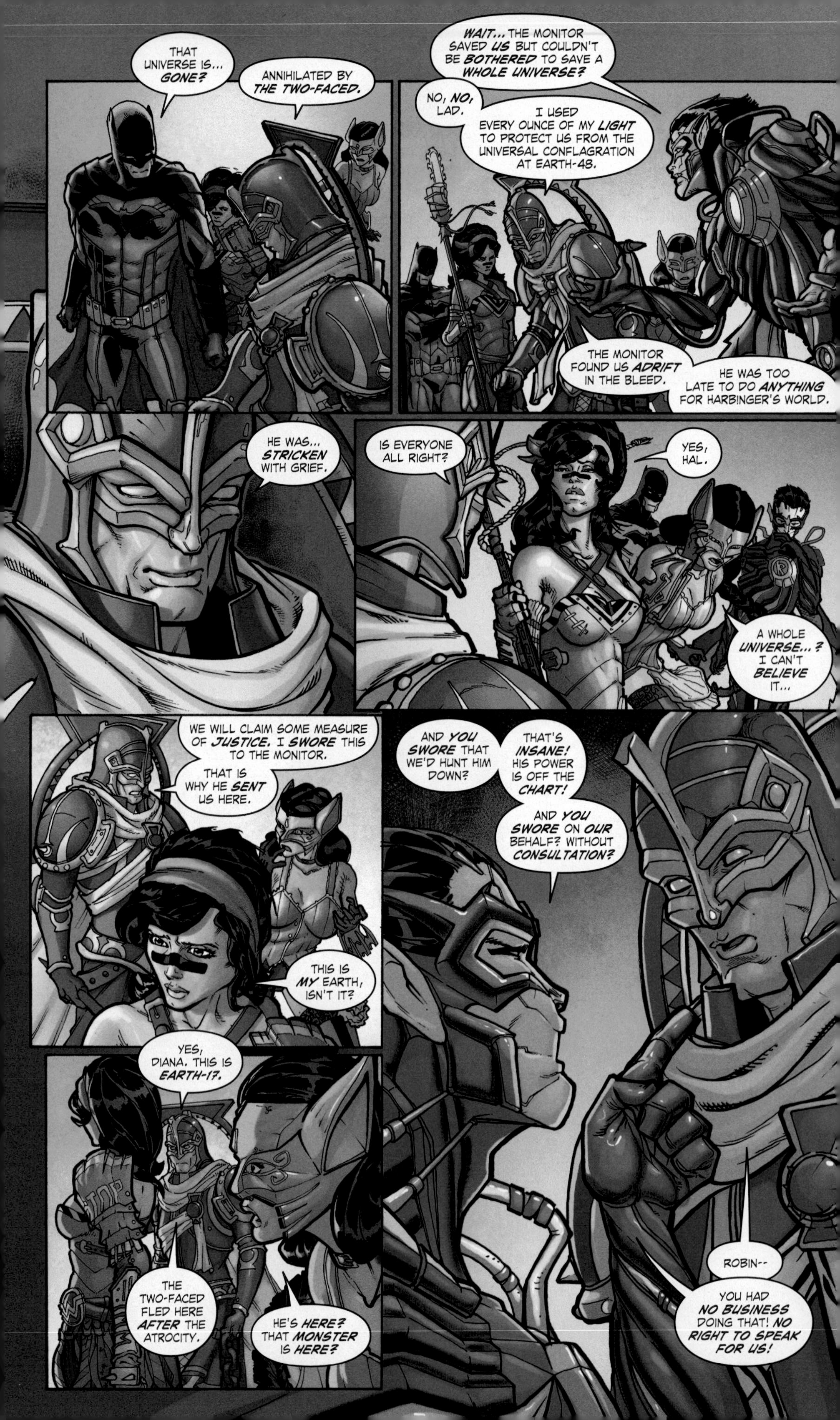

THAT UNIVERSE IS... GONE?
ANNIHILATED BY THE TWO-FACED.
WAIT... THE MONITOR SAVED US BUT COULDN'T BE BOTHERED TO SAVE A WHOLE UNIVERSE?
NO, NO, LAD.
I USED EVERY OUNCE OF MY LIGHT TO PROTECT US FROM THE UNIVERSAL CONFLAGRATION AT EARTH-48.
THE MONITOR FOUND US ADRIFT IN THE BLEED.
HE WAS TOO LATE TO DO ANYTHING FOR HARBINGER'S WORLD.
HE WAS... STRICKEN WITH GRIEF.
IS EVERYONE ALL RIGHT?
YES, HAL.
A WHOLE UNIVERSE...? I CAN'T BELIEVE IT...
WE WILL CLAIM SOME MEASURE OF JUSTICE. I SWORE THIS TO THE MONITOR.
THAT IS WHY HE SENT US HERE.
THIS IS MY EARTH, ISN'T IT?
YES, DIANA. THIS IS EARTH-17.
THE TWO-FACED FLED HERE AFTER THE ATROCITY.
HE'S HERE? THAT MONSTER IS HERE?
AND YOU SWORE THAT WE'D HUNT HIM DOWN?
THAT'S INSANE! HIS POWER IS OFF THE CHART!
AND YOU SWORE ON OUR BEHALF? WITHOUT CONSULTATION?
ROBIN--
YOU HAD NO BUSINESS DOING THAT! NO RIGHT TO SPEAK FOR US!

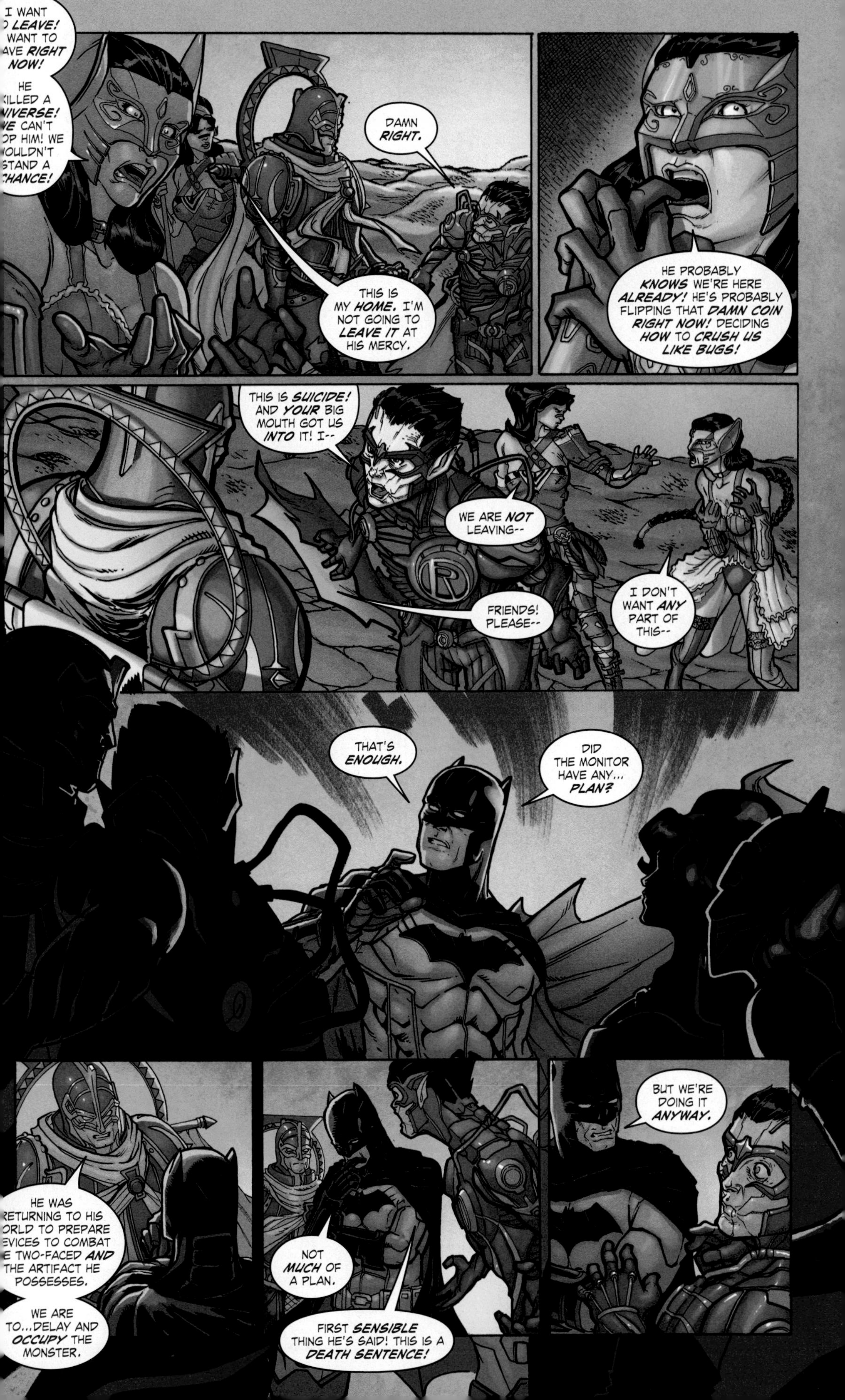

I WANT LEAVE! WANT TO AVE RIGHT NOW!
HE KILLED A NIVERSE! E CAN'T P HIM! WE OULDN'T STAND A HANCE!
DAMN RIGHT.
THIS IS MY HOME. I'M NOT GOING TO LEAVE IT AT HIS MERCY.
HE PROBABLY KNOWS WE'RE HERE ALREADY! HE'S PROBABLY FLIPPING THAT DAMN COIN RIGHT NOW! DECIDING HOW TO CRUSH US LIKE BUGS!
THIS IS SUICIDE! AND YOUR BIG MOUTH GOT US INTO IT! I--
WE ARE NOT LEAVING--
FRIENDS! PLEASE--
I DON'T WANT ANY PART OF THIS--
THAT'S ENOUGH.
DID THE MONITOR HAVE ANY... PLAN?
HE WAS RETURNING TO HIS ORLD TO PREPARE EVICES TO COMBAT E TWO-FACED AND THE ARTIFACT HE POSSESSES.
WE ARE TO...DELAY AND OCCUPY THE MONSTER.
NOT MUCH OF A PLAN.
FIRST SENSIBLE THING HE'S SAID! THIS IS A DEATH SENTENCE!
BUT WE'RE DOING IT ANYWAY.

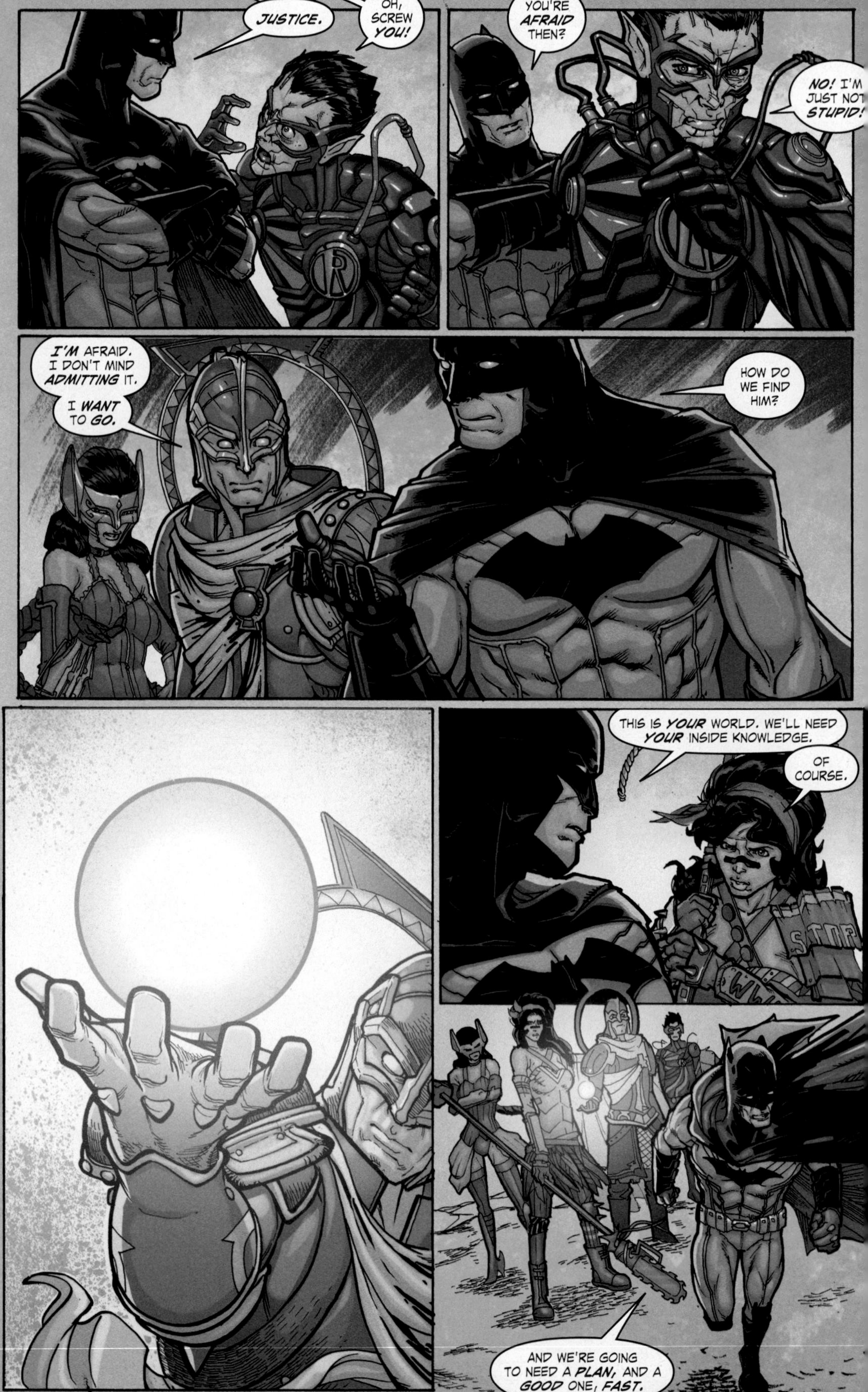
WHAT? WHAT? WHY?
GIVE ME ONE GOOD REASON?
JUSTICE.
OH, SCREW YOU!
YOU'RE AFRAID THEN?
NO! I'M JUST NOT STUPID!
I'M AFRAID. I DON'T MIND ADMITTING IT.
I WANT TO GO.
HOW DO WE FIND HIM?
THIS IS YOUR WORLD. WE'LL NEED YOUR INSIDE KNOWLEDGE.
OF COURSE.
AND WE'RE GOING TO NEED A PLAN, AND A GOOD ONE, FAST.

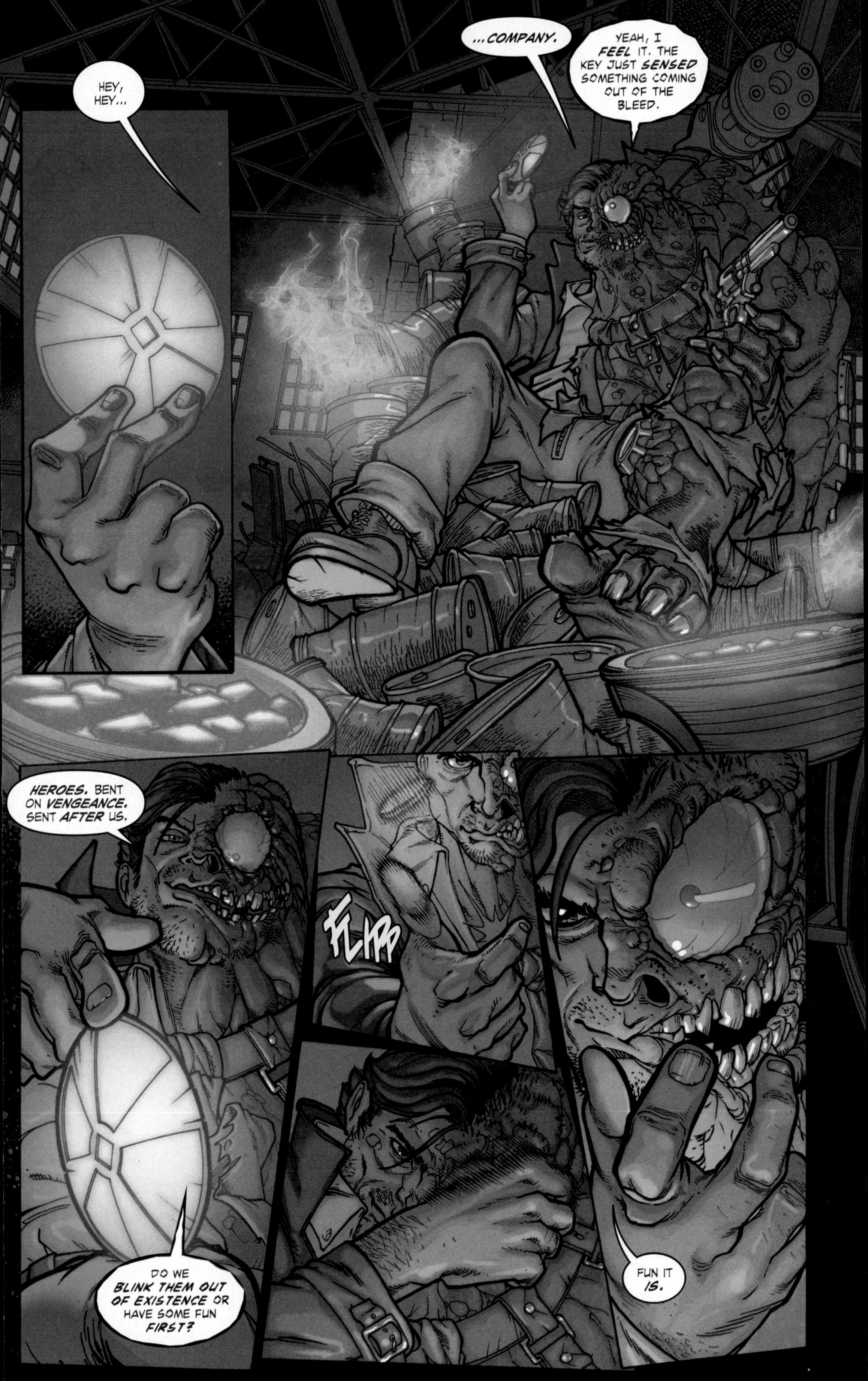
HEY, HEY...
...COMPANY.
YEAH, I FEEL IT. THE KEY JUST SENSED SOMETHING COMING OUT OF THE BLEED.
HEROES. BENT ON VENGEANCE. SENT AFTER US.
FLIPP
DO WE BLINK THEM OUT OF EXISTENCE OR HAVE SOME FUN FIRST?
FUN IT IS.

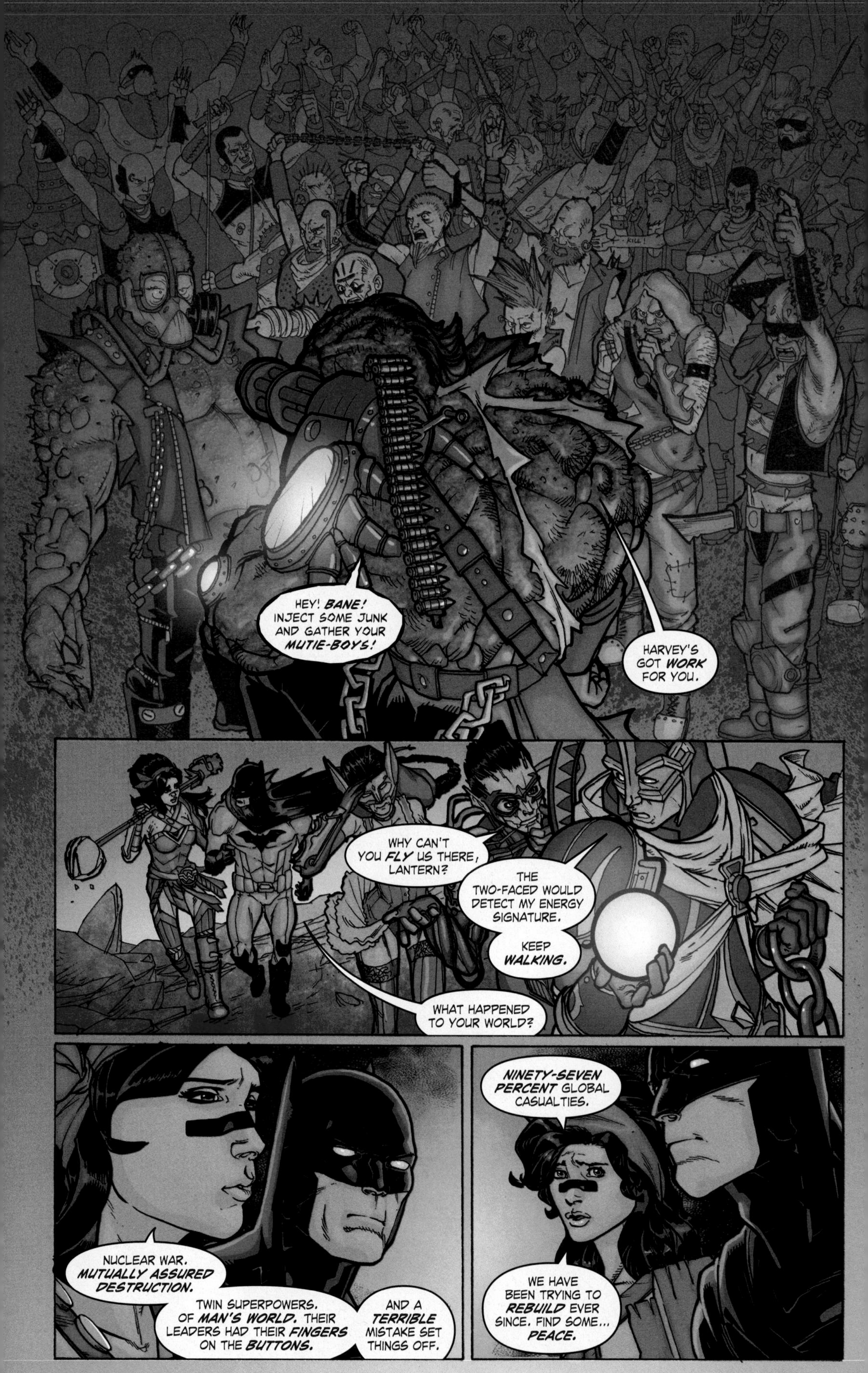
HEY! BANE! INJECT SOME JUNK AND GATHER YOUR MUTIE-BOYS!
HARVEY'S GOT WORK FOR YOU.
KILL!
WHY CAN'T YOU FLY US THERE, LANTERN?
THE TWO-FACED WOULD DETECT MY ENERGY SIGNATURE.
KEEP WALKING.
WHAT HAPPENED TO YOUR WORLD?
NUCLEAR WAR. MUTUALLY ASSURED DESTRUCTION.
TWIN SUPERPOWERS. OF MAN'S WORLD. THEIR LEADERS HAD THEIR FINGERS ON THE BUTTONS.
AND A TERRIBLE MISTAKE SET THINGS OFF.
NINETY-SEVEN PERCENT GLOBAL CASUALTIES.
WE HAVE BEEN TRYING TO REBUILD EVER SINCE. FIND SOME... PEACE.

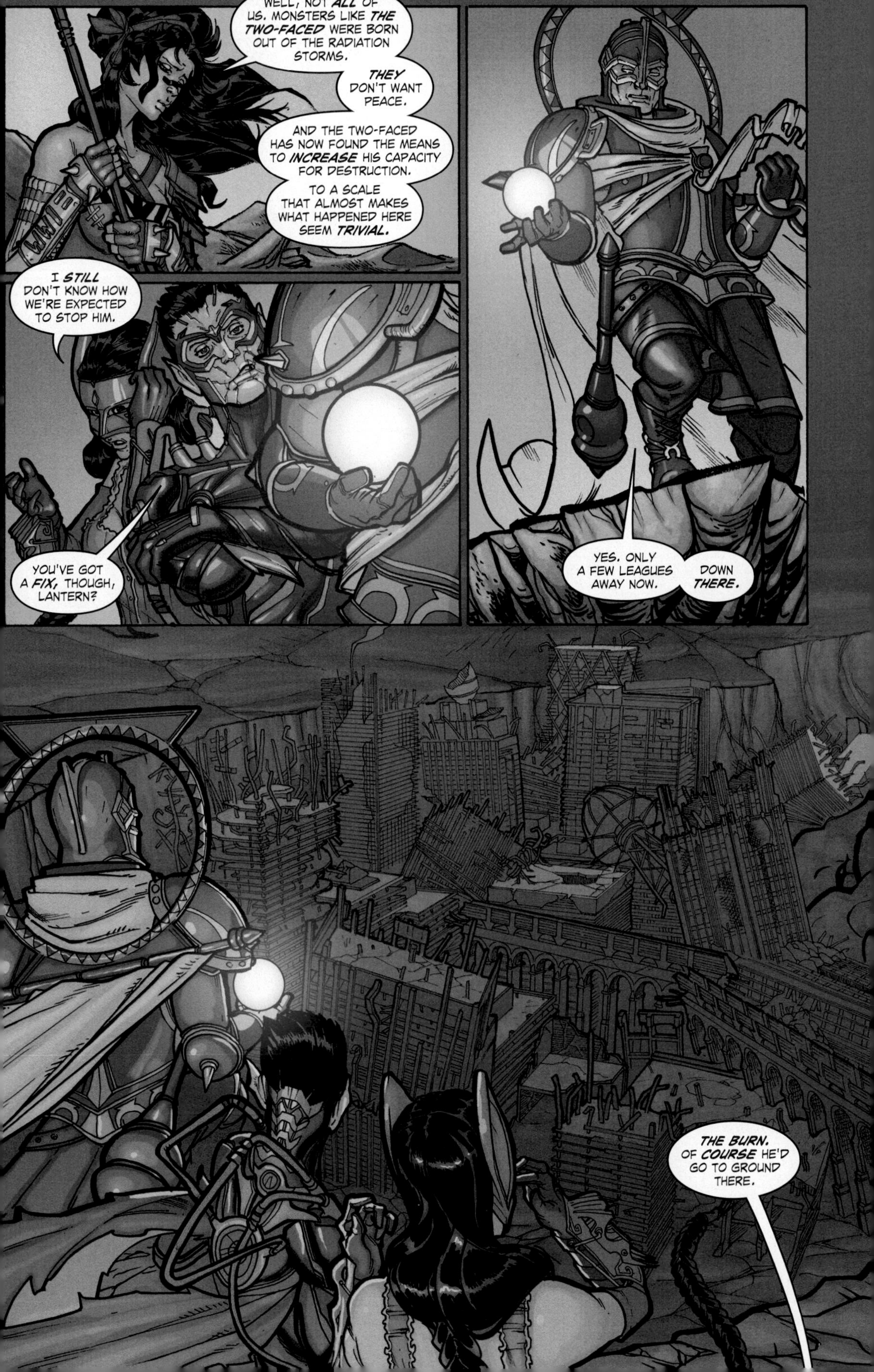

WELL, NOT ALL OF US. MONSTERS LIKE THE TWO-FACED WERE BORN OUT OF THE RADIATION STORMS.
THEY DON'T WANT PEACE.
AND THE TWO-FACED HAS NOW FOUND THE MEANS TO INCREASE HIS CAPACITY FOR DESTRUCTION.
TO A SCALE THAT ALMOST MAKES WHAT HAPPENED HERE SEEM TRIVIAL.
I STILL DON'T KNOW HOW WE'RE EXPECTED TO STOP HIM.
YOU'VE GOT A FIX, THOUGH, LANTERN?
YES. ONLY A FEW LEAGUES AWAY NOW.
DOWN THERE.
THE BURN. OF COURSE HE'D GO TO GROUND THERE.

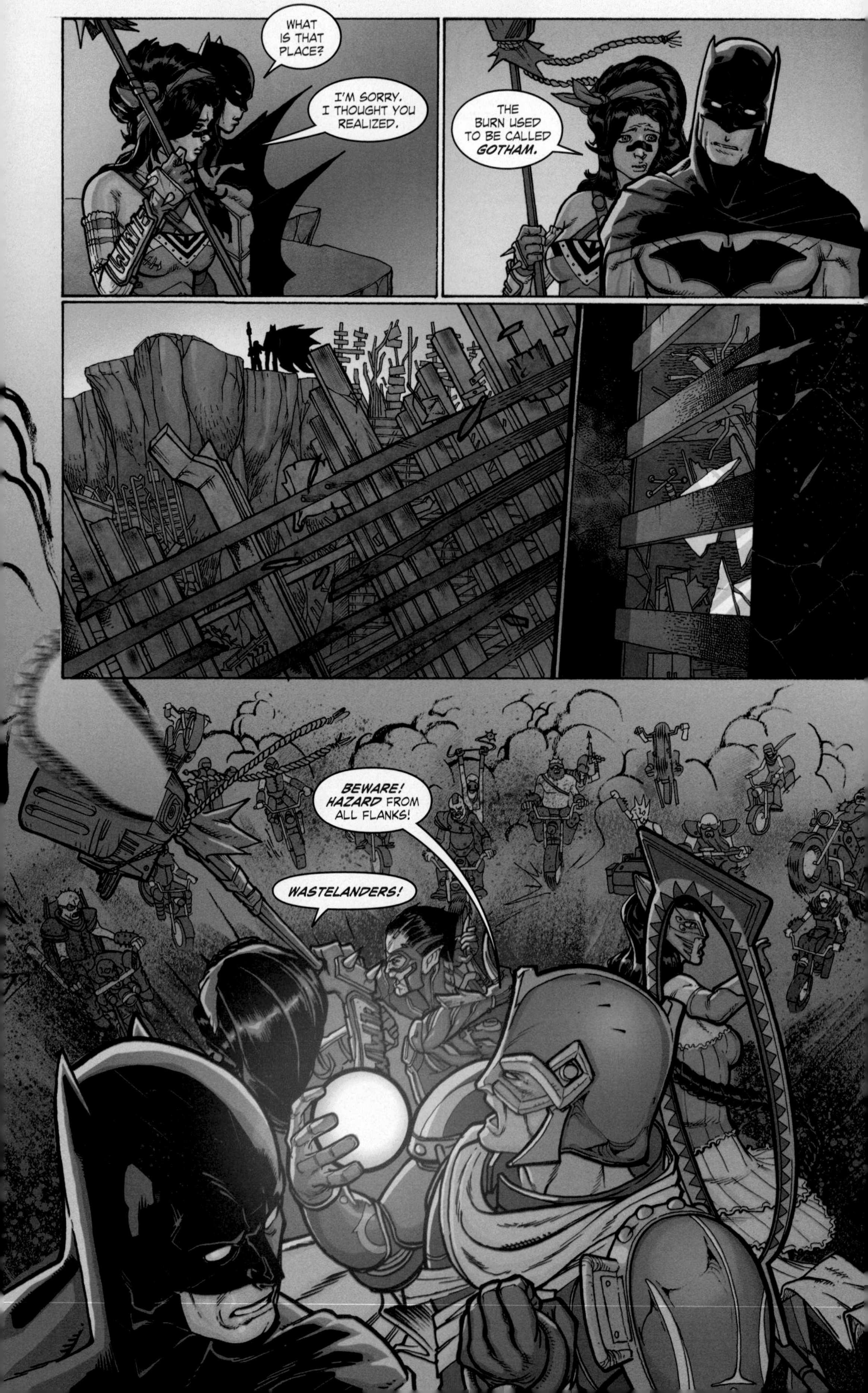
WHAT IS THAT PLACE?
I'M SORRY. I THOUGHT YOU REALIZED.
THE BURN USED TO BE CALLED GOTHAM.
BEWARE! HAZARD FROM ALL FLANKS!
WASTELANDERS!

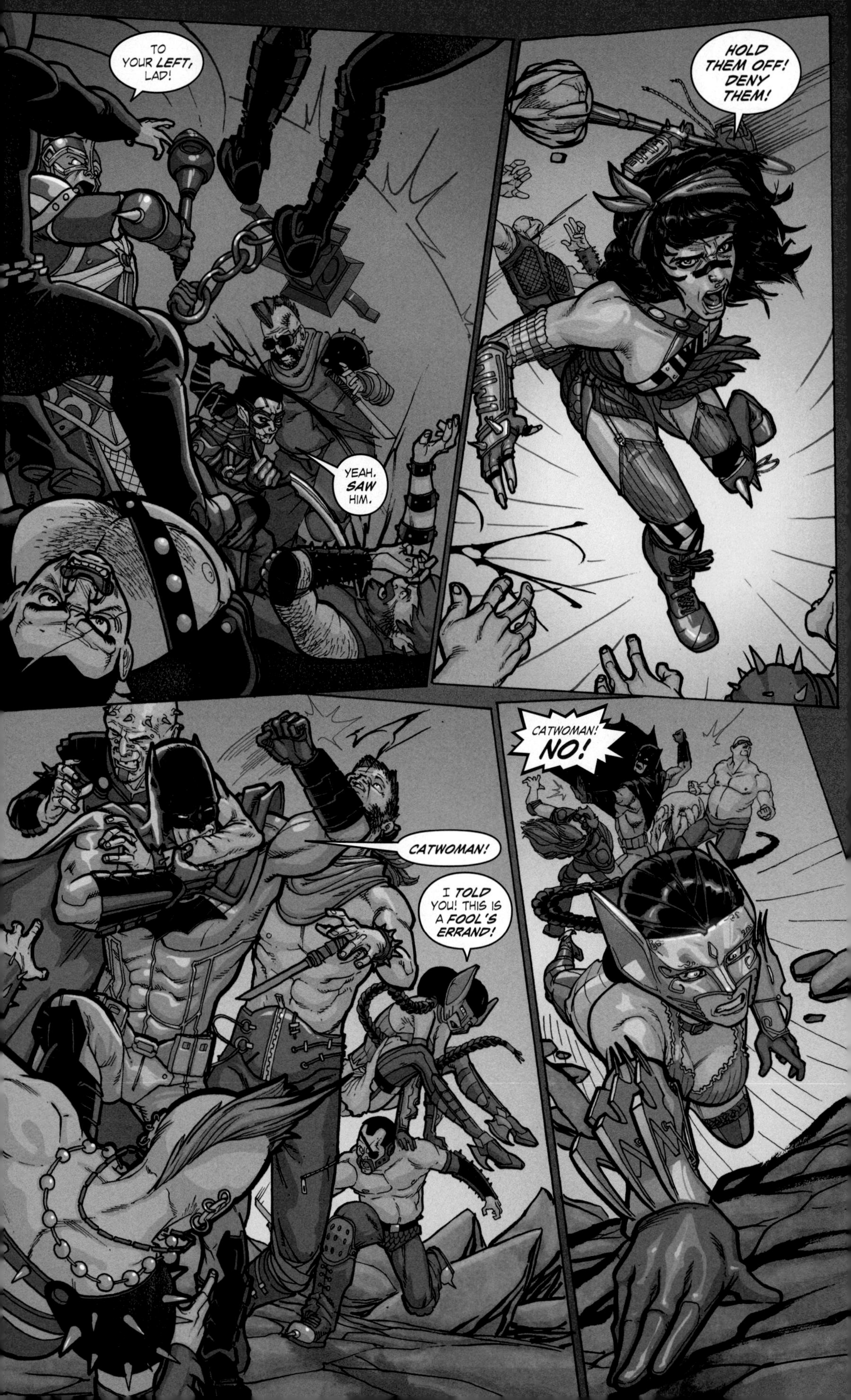
TO YOUR LEFT, LAD!
YEAH. SAW HIM.
HOLD THEM OFF! DENY THEM!
CATWOMAN!
I TOLD YOU! THIS IS A FOOL'S ERRAND!
CATWOMAN! NO!

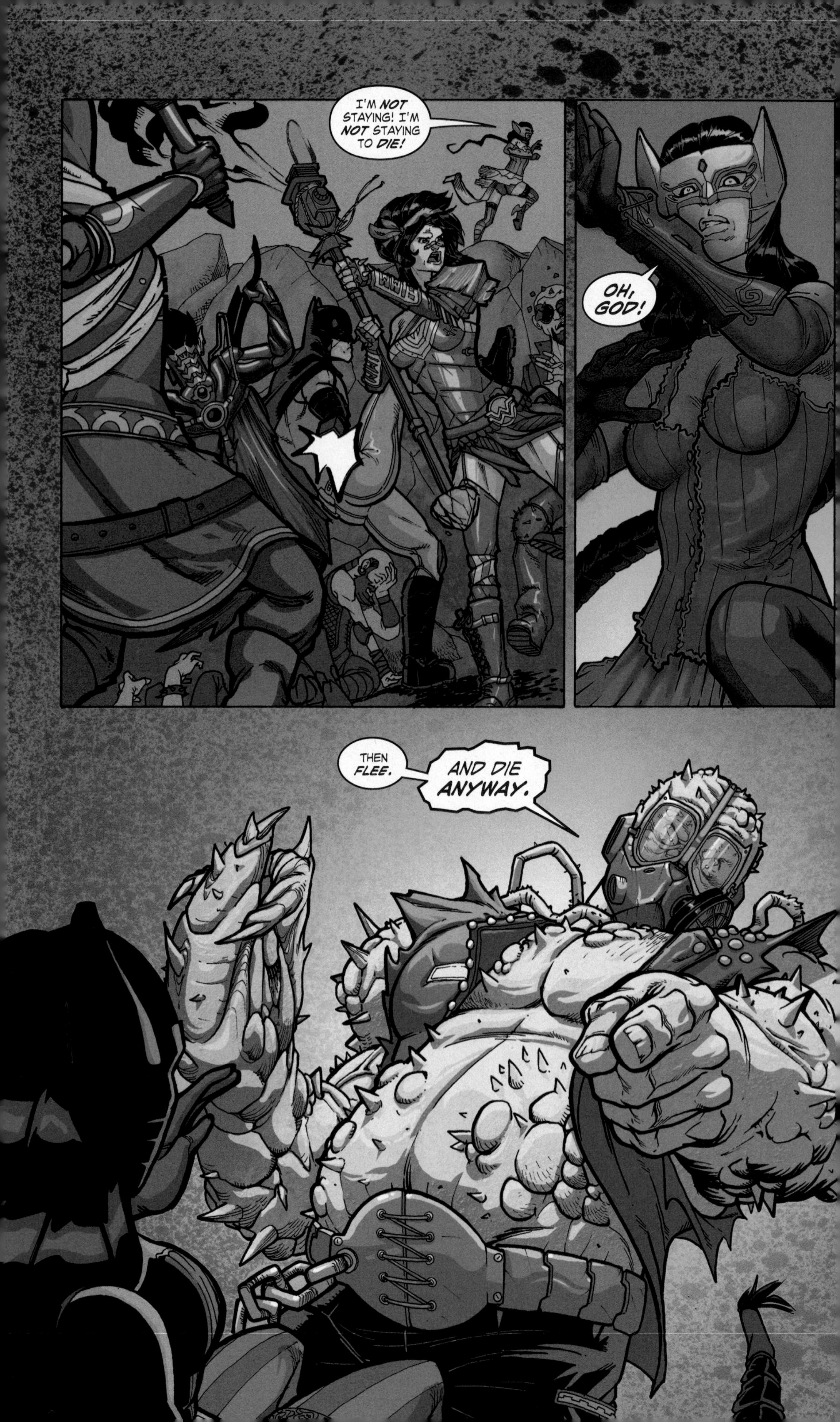

I'M NOT STAYING! I'M NOT STAYING TO DIE!
OH, GOD!
THEN FLEE.
AND DIE ANYWAY.

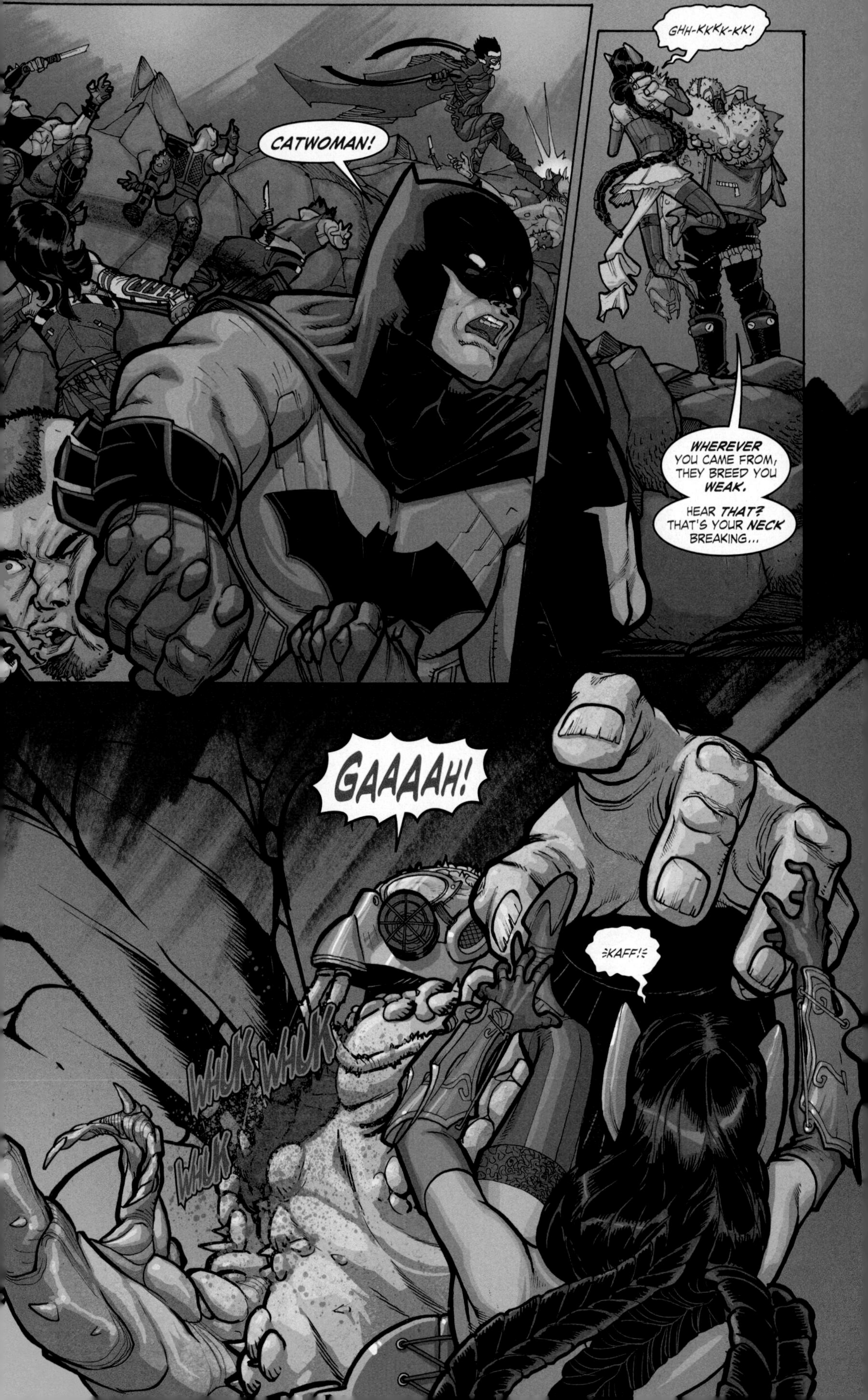
CATWOMAN!
GHH-KKKK-KK!
WHEREVER YOU CAME FROM, THEY BREED YOU WEAK.
HEAR THAT? THAT'S YOUR NECK BREAKING...
GAAAAH!
KAFF!
WHUK WHUK
WHUK

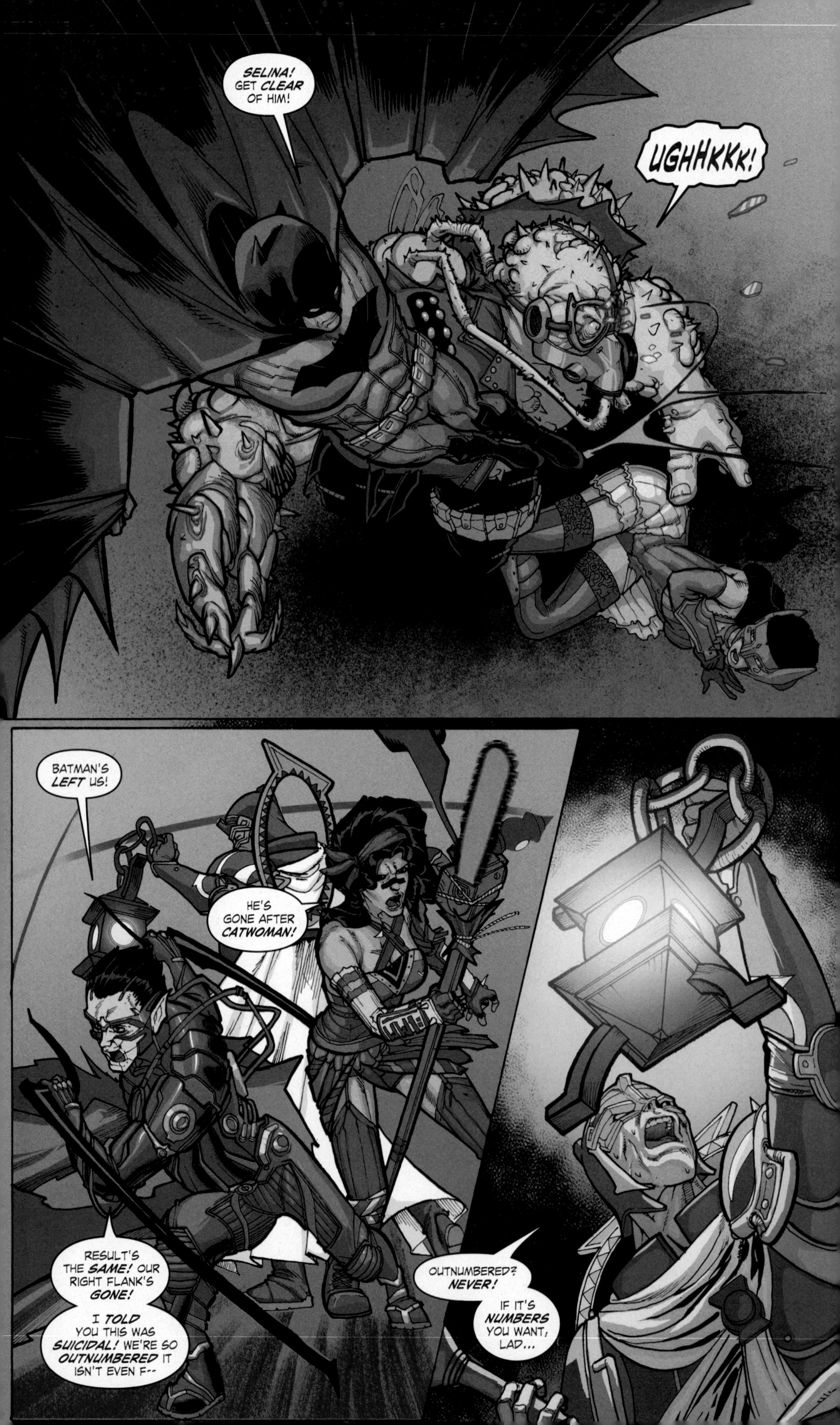
SELINA! GET CLEAR OF HIM!
UGHHKKK!
BATMAN'S LEFT US!
HE'S GONE AFTER CATWOMAN!
RESULT'S THE SAME! OUR RIGHT FLANK'S GONE!
I TOLD YOU THIS WAS SUICIDAL! WE'RE SO OUTNUMBERED IT ISN'T EVEN F--
OUTNUMBERED? NEVER!
IF IT'S NUMBERS YOU WANT, LAD...

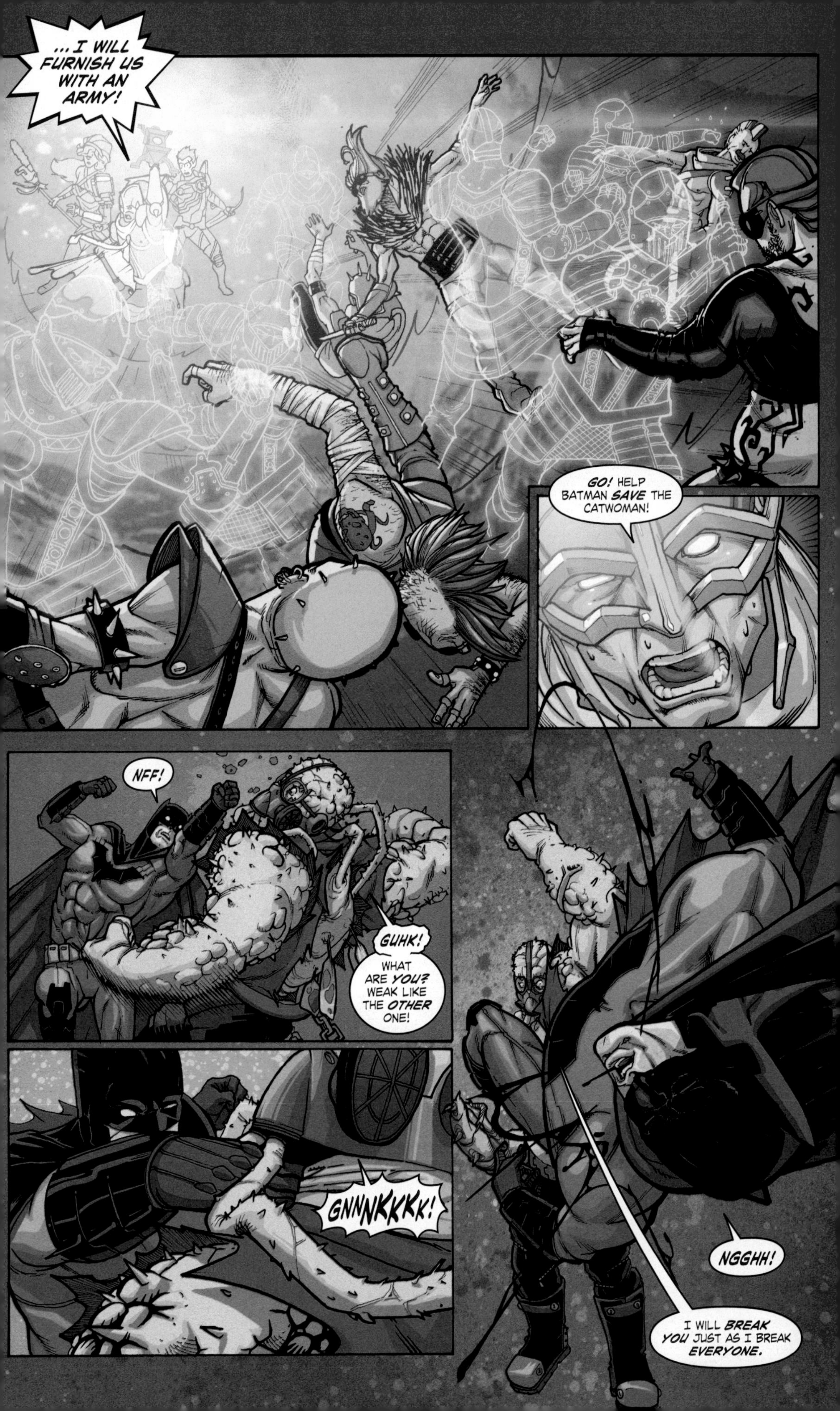
...I WILL FURNISH US WITH AN ARMY!
GO! HELP BATMAN SAVE THE CATWOMAN!
NFF!
GUHK!
WHAT ARE YOU? WEAK LIKE THE OTHER ONE!
GNNNKKKK!
NGGHH!
I WILL BREAK YOU JUST AS I BREAK EVERYONE.

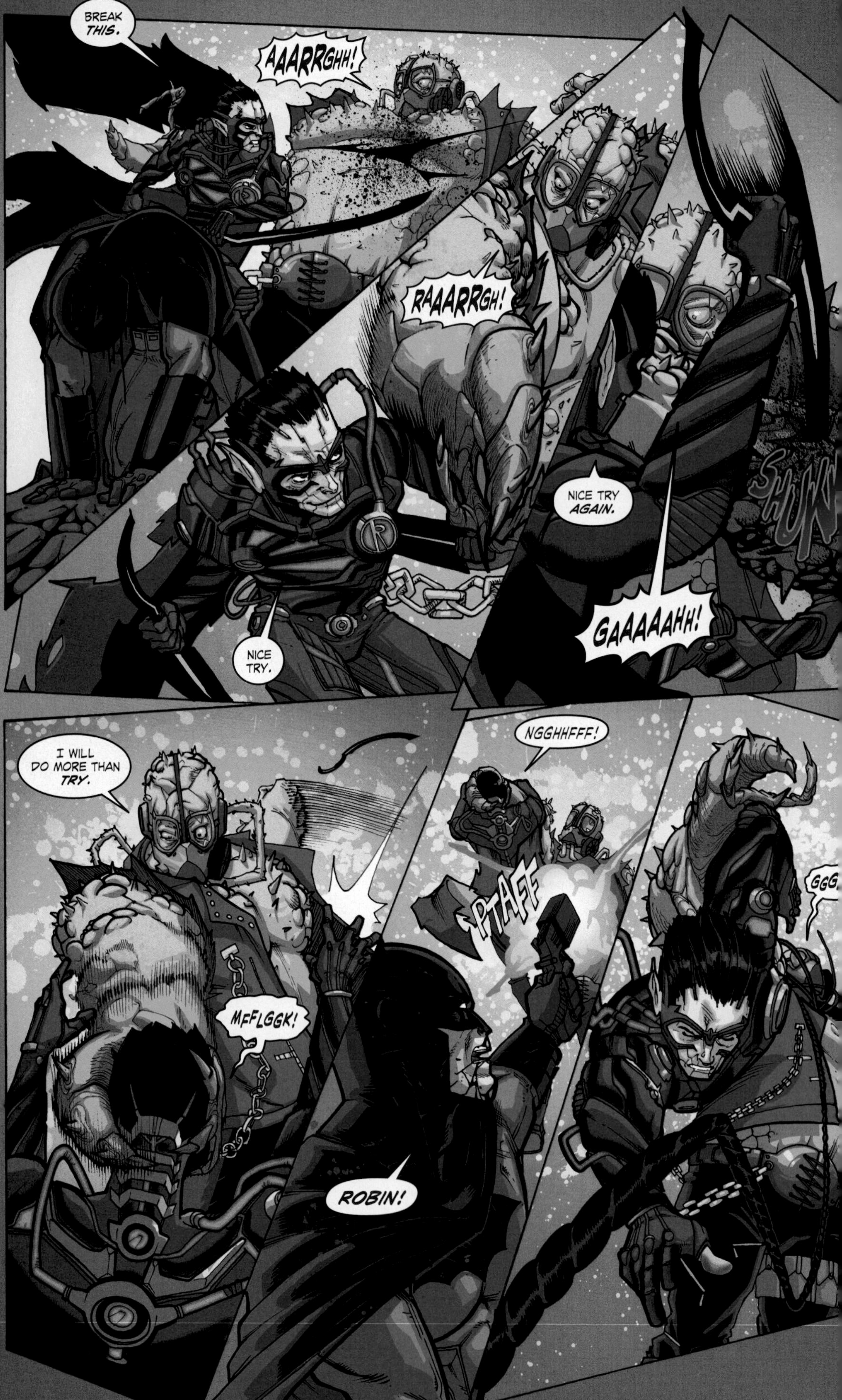
BREAK *THIS.*
AAARRGHH!
RAAARRGH!
NICE TRY.
NICE TRY *AGAIN.*
SHUK
GAAAAAHH!
I WILL DO MORE THAN *TRY.*
MFFLGGK!
ROBIN!
NGGHHFFF!
PTAFF
GGG

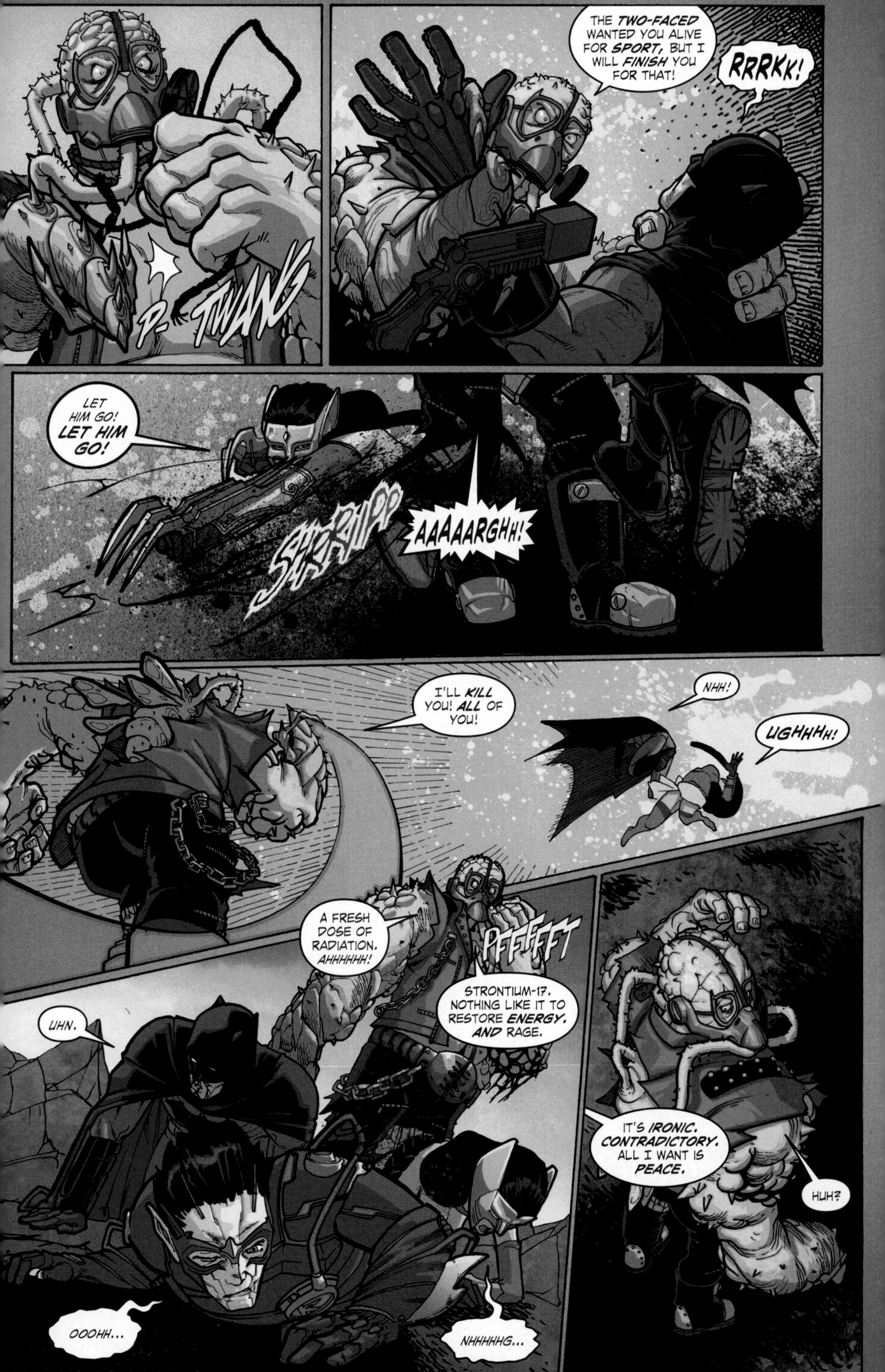
P-TWANG
THE TWO-FACED WANTED YOU ALIVE FOR SPORT, BUT I WILL FINISH YOU FOR THAT!
RRRKK!
LET HIM GO! LET HIM GO!
SSHRRIPP
AAAAARGHH!
I'LL KILL YOU! ALL OF YOU!
NHH!
UGHHHH!
A FRESH DOSE OF RADIATION. AHHHHHH!
PFFFFFT
STRONTIUM-17. NOTHING LIKE IT TO RESTORE ENERGY. AND RAGE.
UHN.
OOOHH...
NHHHHHG...
IT'S IRONIC. CONTRADICTORY. ALL I WANT IS PEACE.
HUH?

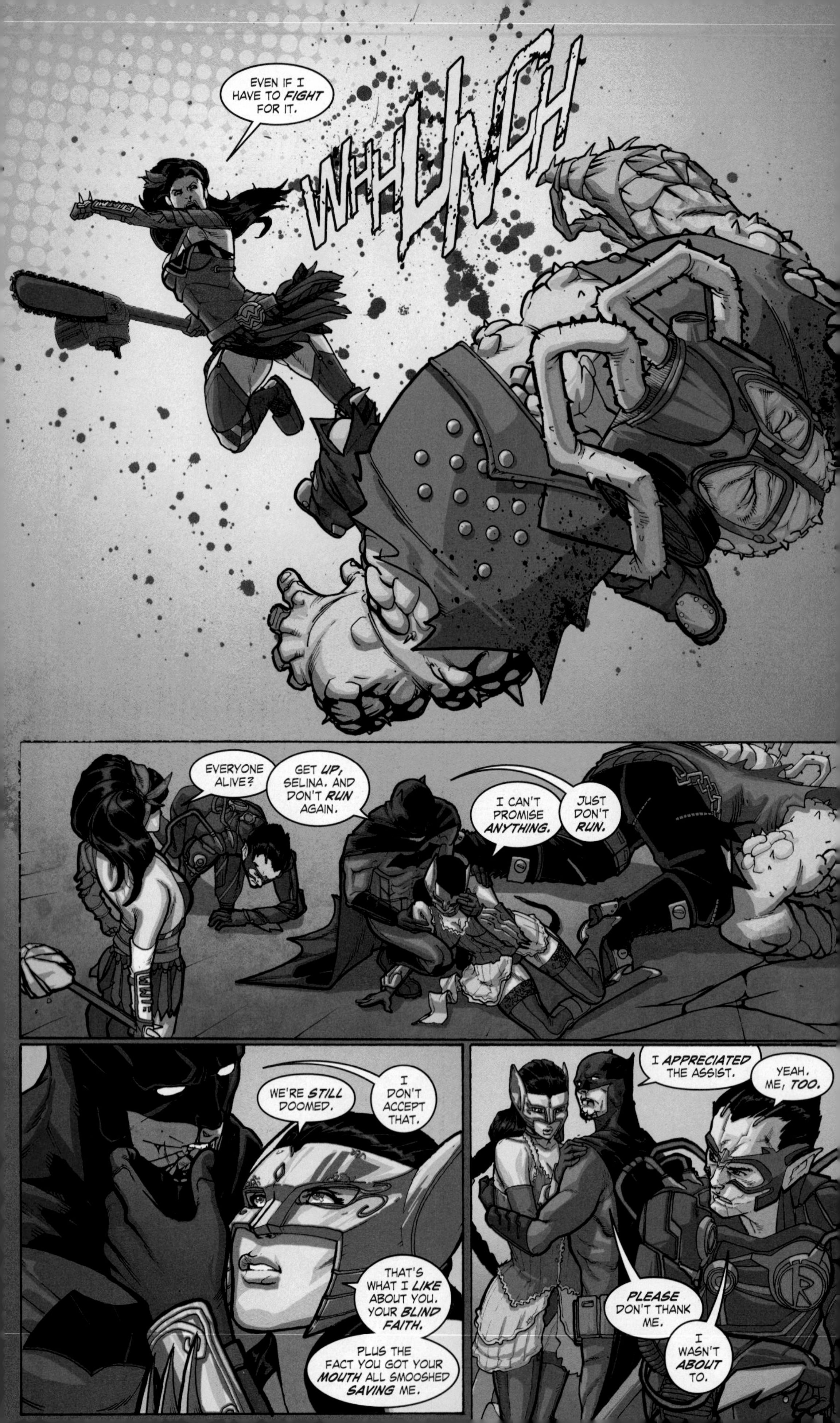
EVEN IF I HAVE TO FIGHT FOR IT.
WHUNCH
EVERYONE ALIVE?
GET UP, SELINA. AND DON'T RUN AGAIN.
I CAN'T PROMISE ANYTHING.
JUST DON'T RUN.
WE'RE STILL DOOMED.
I DON'T ACCEPT THAT.
THAT'S WHAT I LIKE ABOUT YOU. YOUR BLIND FAITH.
PLUS THE FACT YOU GOT YOUR MOUTH ALL SMOOSHED SAVING ME.
I APPRECIATED THE ASSIST.
YEAH. ME, TOO.
PLEASE DON'T THANK ME.
I WASN'T ABOUT TO.

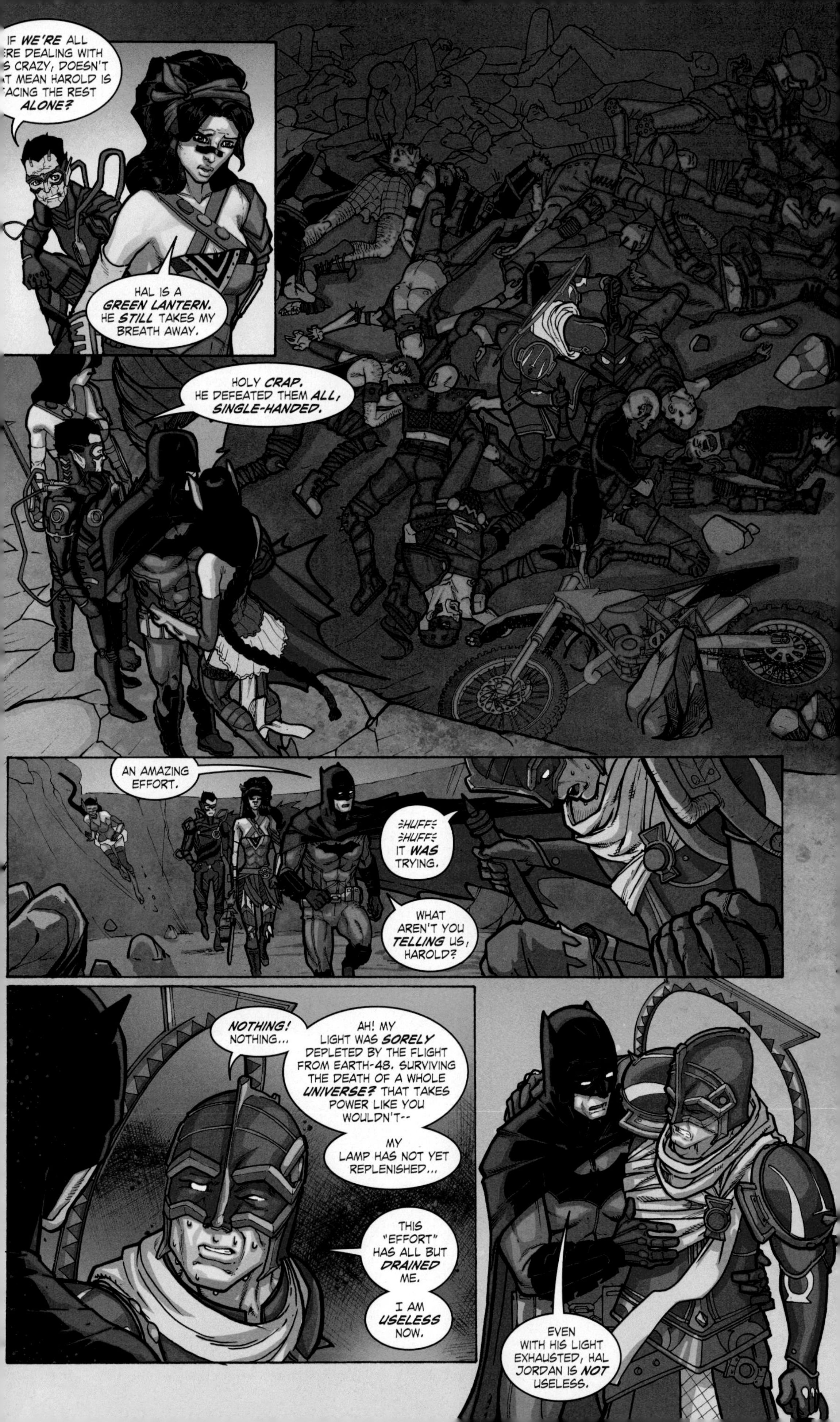

IF WE'RE ALL ERE DEALING WITH S CRAZY, DOESN'T T MEAN HAROLD IS ACING THE REST ALONE?
HAL IS A GREEN LANTERN. HE STILL TAKES MY BREATH AWAY.
HOLY CRAP. HE DEFEATED THEM ALL, SINGLE-HANDED.
AN AMAZING EFFORT.
HUFF HUFF IT WAS TRYING.
WHAT AREN'T YOU TELLING US, HAROLD?
NOTHING! NOTHING...
AH! MY LIGHT WAS SORELY DEPLETED BY THE FLIGHT FROM EARTH-48. SURVIVING THE DEATH OF A WHOLE UNIVERSE? THAT TAKES POWER LIKE YOU WOULDN'T--
MY LAMP HAS NOT YET REPLENISHED...
THIS "EFFORT" HAS ALL BUT DRAINED ME.
I AM USELESS NOW.
EVEN WITH HIS LIGHT EXHAUSTED, HAL JORDAN IS NOT USELESS.

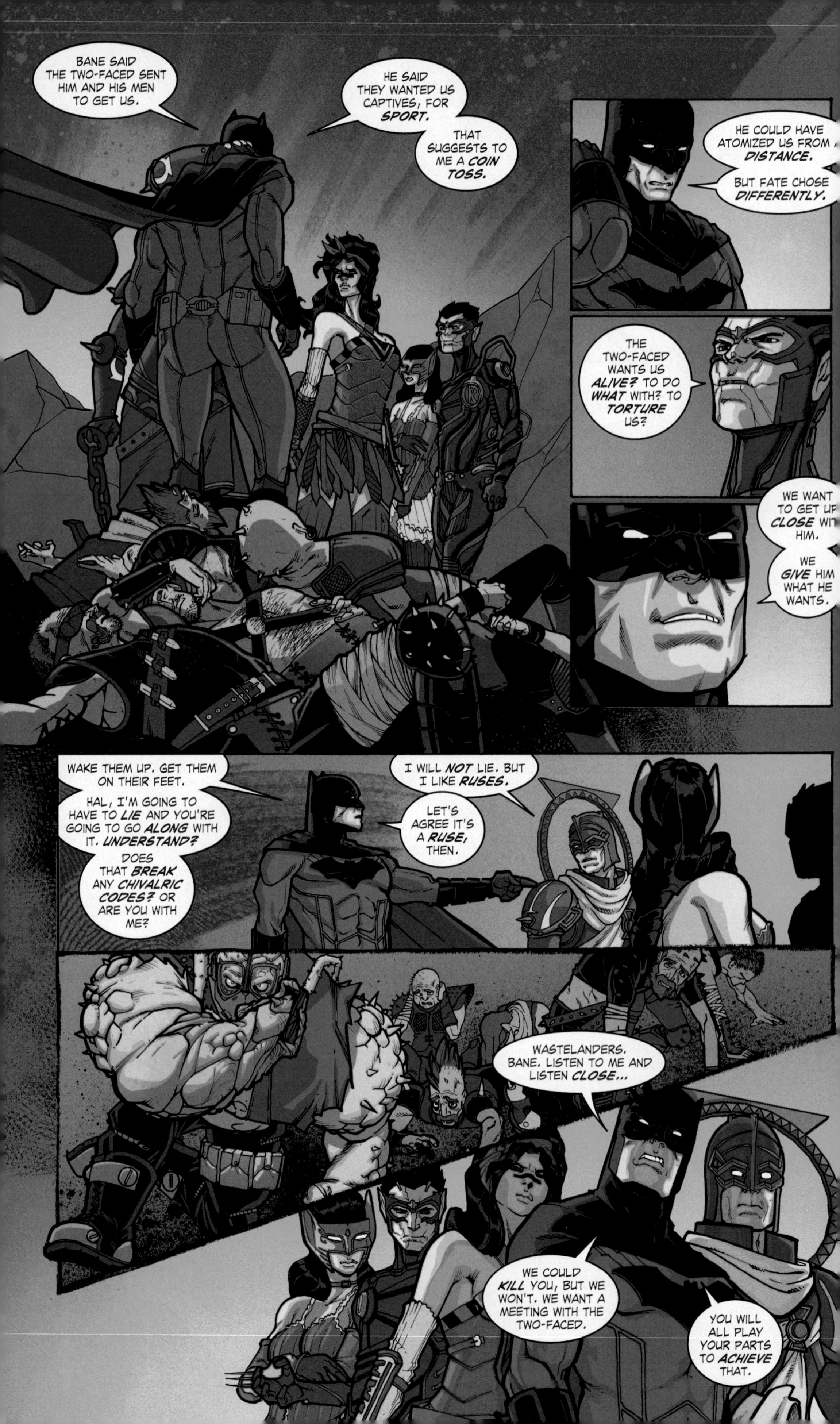
BANE SAID THE TWO-FACED SENT HIM AND HIS MEN TO GET US.
HE SAID THEY WANTED US CAPTIVES, FOR SPORT.
THAT SUGGESTS TO ME A COIN TOSS.
HE COULD HAVE ATOMIZED US FROM A DISTANCE.
BUT FATE CHOSE DIFFERENTLY.
THE TWO-FACED WANTS US ALIVE? TO DO WHAT WITH? TO TORTURE US?
WE WANT TO GET UP CLOSE WITH HIM.
WE GIVE HIM WHAT HE WANTS.
WAKE THEM UP. GET THEM ON THEIR FEET.
HAL, I'M GOING TO HAVE TO LIE AND YOU'RE GOING TO GO ALONG WITH IT. UNDERSTAND?
DOES THAT BREAK ANY CHIVALRIC CODES? OR ARE YOU WITH ME?
I WILL NOT LIE. BUT I LIKE RUSES.
LET'S AGREE IT'S A RUSE, THEN.
WASTELANDERS. BANE. LISTEN TO ME AND LISTEN CLOSE...
WE COULD KILL YOU, BUT WE WON'T. WE WANT A MEETING WITH THE TWO-FACED.
YOU WILL ALL PLAY YOUR PARTS TO ACHIEVE THAT.

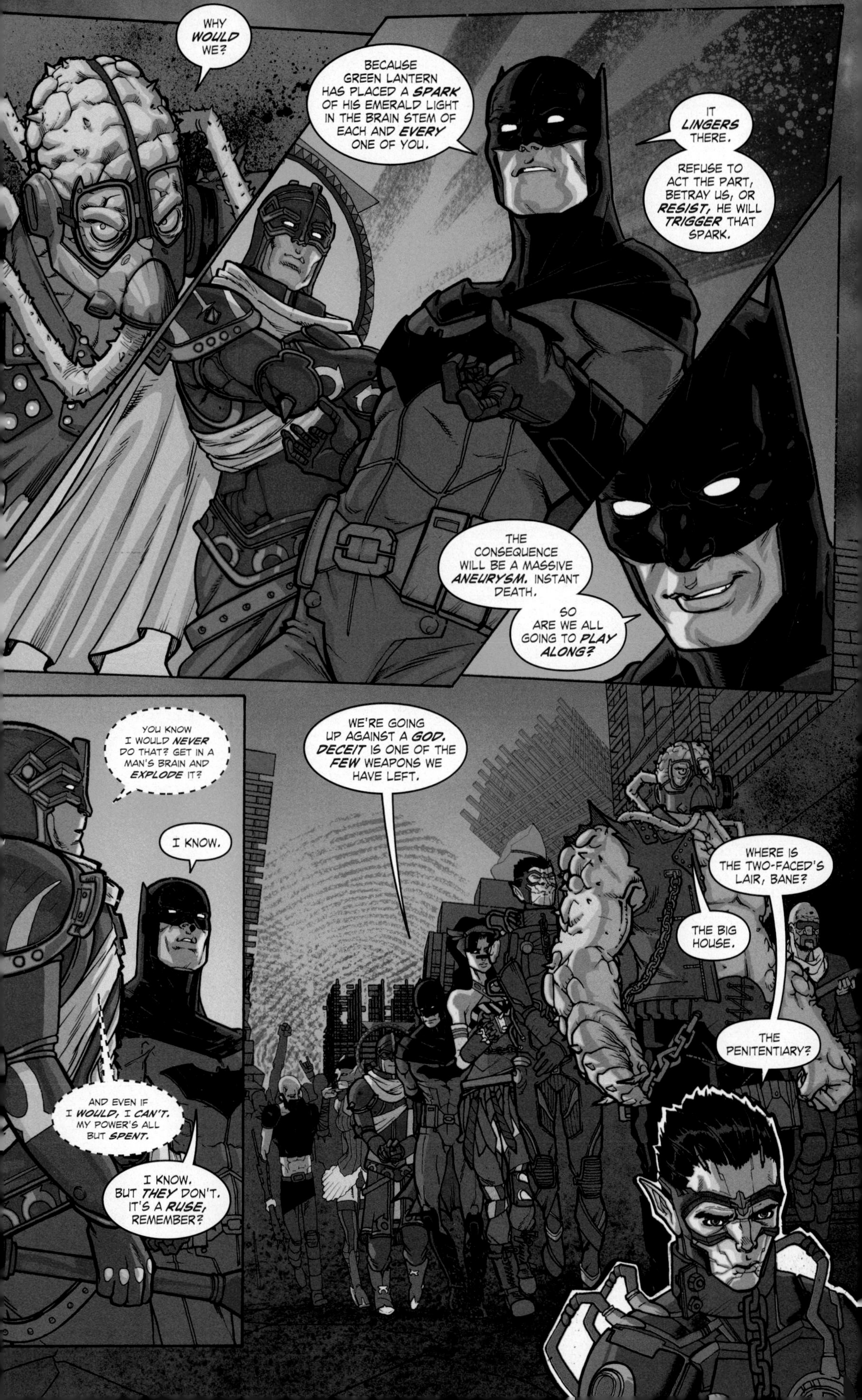

WHY WOULD WE?
BECAUSE GREEN LANTERN HAS PLACED A SPARK OF HIS EMERALD LIGHT IN THE BRAIN STEM OF EACH AND EVERY ONE OF YOU.
IT LINGERS THERE.
REFUSE TO ACT THE PART, BETRAY US, OR RESIST, HE WILL TRIGGER THAT SPARK.
THE CONSEQUENCE WILL BE A MASSIVE ANEURYSM. INSTANT DEATH.
SO ARE WE ALL GOING TO PLAY ALONG?
YOU KNOW I WOULD NEVER DO THAT? GET IN A MAN'S BRAIN AND EXPLODE IT?
I KNOW.
AND EVEN IF I WOULD, I CAN'T. MY POWER'S ALL BUT SPENT.
I KNOW. BUT THEY DON'T. IT'S A RUSE, REMEMBER?
WE'RE GOING UP AGAINST A GOD. DECEIT IS ONE OF THE FEW WEAPONS WE HAVE LEFT.
WHERE IS THE TWO-FACED'S LAIR, BANE?
THE BIG HOUSE.
THE PENITENTIARY?

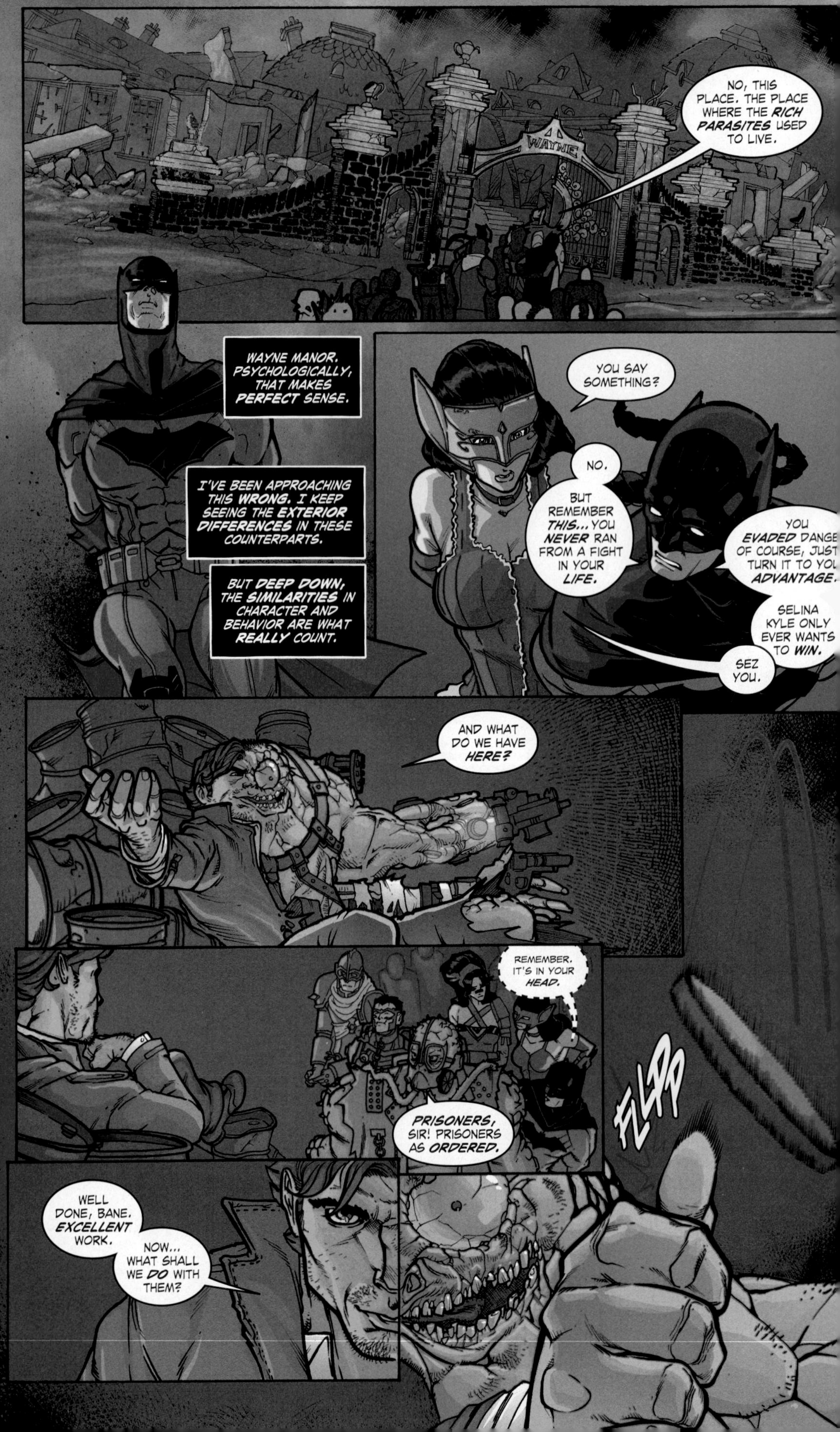
NO, THIS PLACE. THE PLACE WHERE THE RICH PARASITES USED TO LIVE.
WAYNE
WAYNE MANOR. PSYCHOLOGICALLY, THAT MAKES PERFECT SENSE.
I'VE BEEN APPROACHING THIS WRONG. I KEEP SEEING THE EXTERIOR DIFFERENCES IN THESE COUNTERPARTS.
BUT DEEP DOWN, THE SIMILARITIES IN CHARACTER AND BEHAVIOR ARE WHAT REALLY COUNT.
YOU SAY SOMETHING?
NO.
BUT REMEMBER THIS... YOU NEVER RAN FROM A FIGHT IN YOUR LIFE.
SELINA KYLE ONLY EVER WANTS TO WIN.
SEZ YOU.
AND WHAT DO WE HAVE HERE?
REMEMBER. IT'S IN YOUR HEAD.
PRISONERS, SIR! PRISONERS AS ORDERED.
FLPP
WELL DONE, BANE. EXCELLENT WORK.
NOW... WHAT SHALL WE DO WITH THEM?

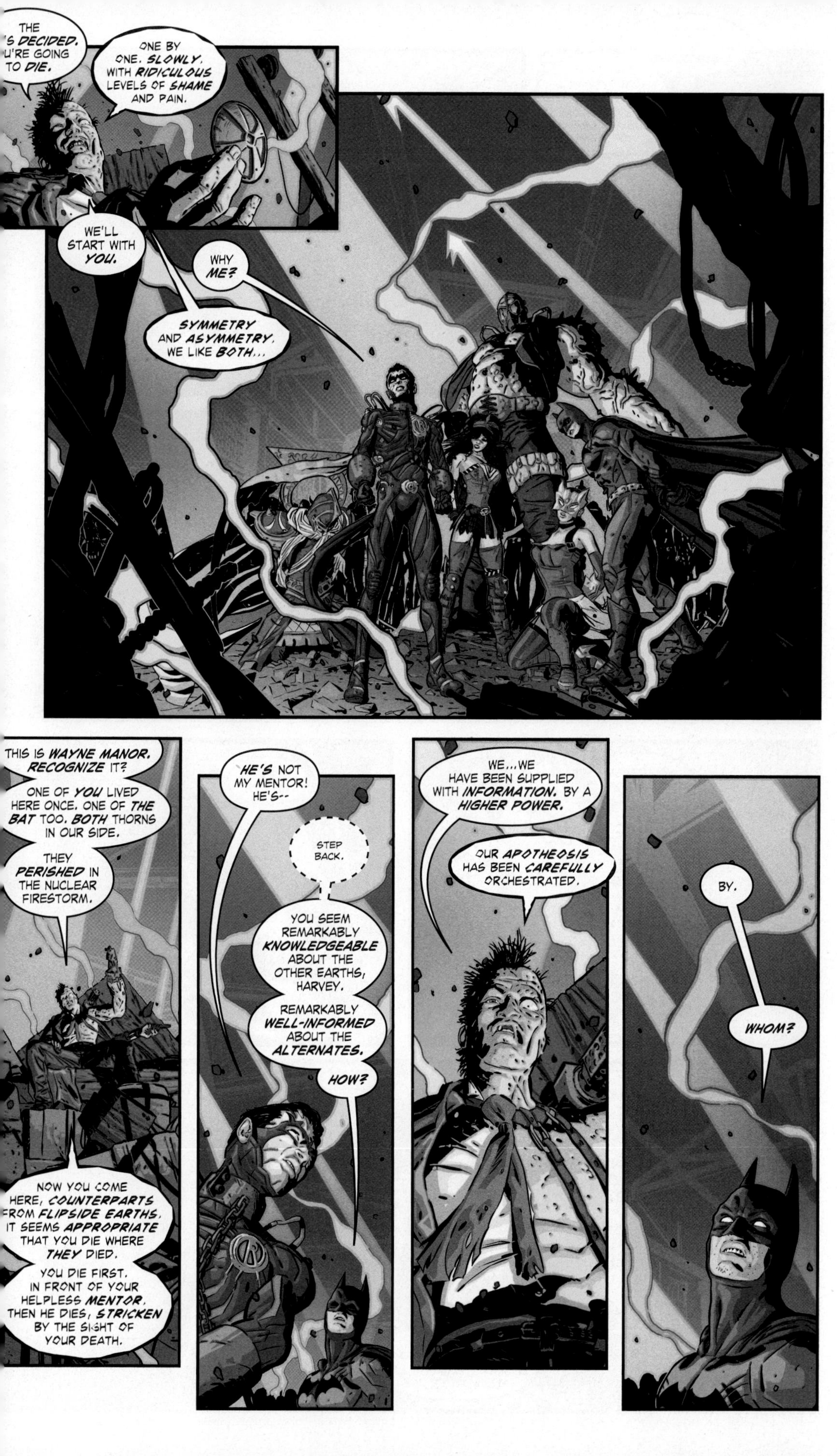
THE 'S DECIDED. U'RE GOING TO DIE.
ONE BY ONE. SLOWLY. WITH RIDICULOUS LEVELS OF SHAME AND PAIN.
WE'LL START WITH YOU.
WHY ME?
SYMMETRY AND ASYMMETRY. WE LIKE BOTH...
THIS IS WAYNE MANOR. RECOGNIZE IT?
ONE OF YOU LIVED HERE ONCE. ONE OF THE BAT TOO. BOTH THORNS IN OUR SIDE.
THEY PERISHED IN THE NUCLEAR FIRESTORM.
NOW YOU COME HERE, COUNTERPARTS FROM FLIPSIDE EARTHS. IT SEEMS APPROPRIATE THAT YOU DIE WHERE THEY DIED.
YOU DIE FIRST. IN FRONT OF YOUR HELPLESS MENTOR. THEN HE DIES, STRICKEN BY THE SIGHT OF YOUR DEATH.
HE'S NOT MY MENTOR! HE'S--
STEP BACK.
YOU SEEM REMARKABLY KNOWLEDGEABLE ABOUT THE OTHER EARTHS, HARVEY.
REMARKABLY WELL-INFORMED ABOUT THE ALTERNATES.
HOW?
WE...WE HAVE BEEN SUPPLIED WITH INFORMATION. BY A HIGHER POWER.
OUR APOTHEOSIS HAS BEEN CAREFULLY ORCHESTRATED.
BY.
WHOM?

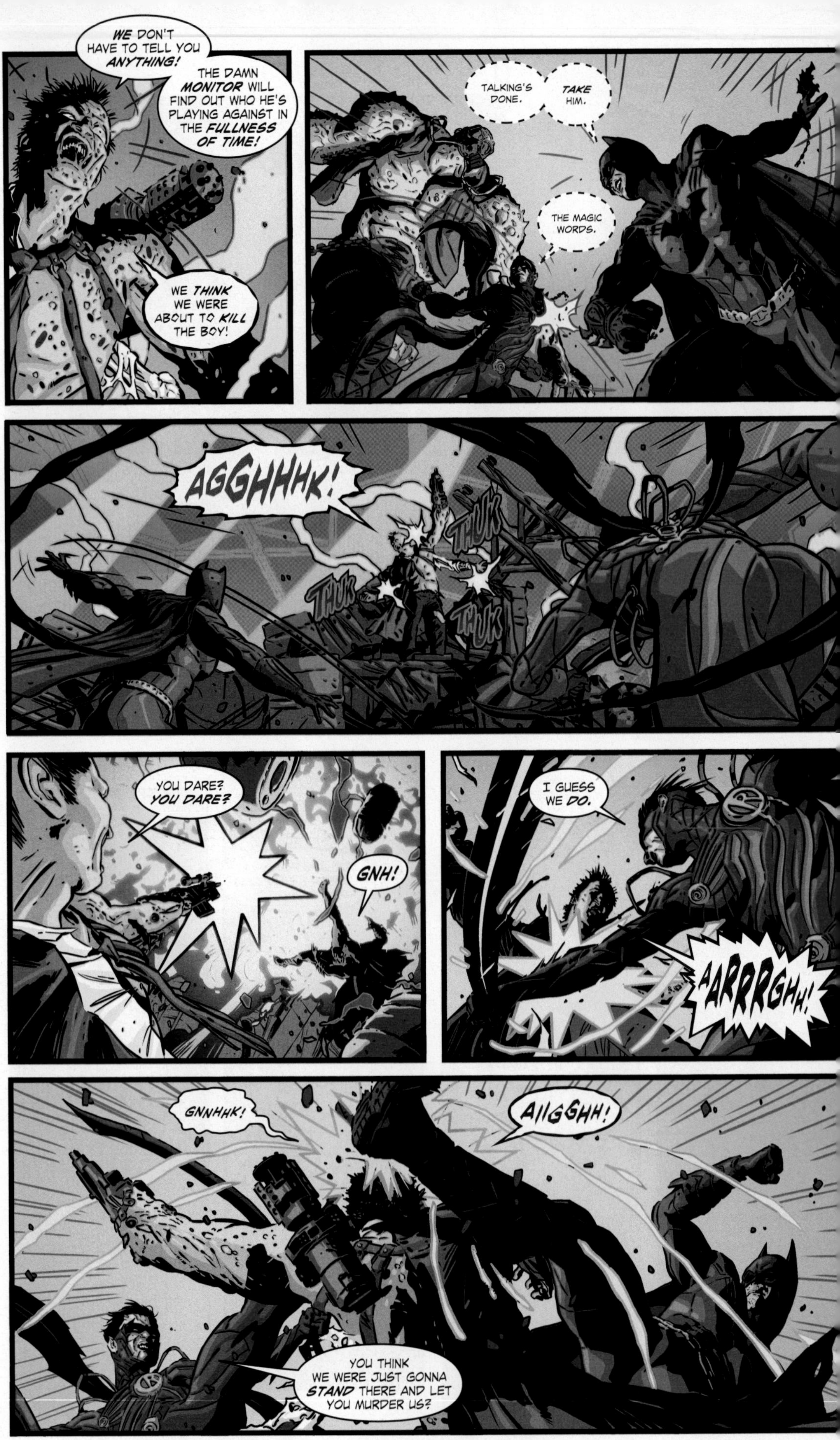
WE DON'T HAVE TO TELL YOU ANYTHING!
THE DAMN MONITOR WILL FIND OUT WHO HE'S PLAYING AGAINST IN THE FULLNESS OF TIME!
WE THINK WE WERE ABOUT TO KILL THE BOY!
TALKING'S DONE.
TAKE HIM.
THE MAGIC WORDS.
AGGHHHK!
THUK
THUK
THUK
YOU DARE? YOU DARE?
GNH!
I GUESS WE DO.
AARRRGHH!
GNNHHK!
AIIGGHH!
YOU THINK WE WERE JUST GONNA STAND THERE AND LET YOU MURDER US?

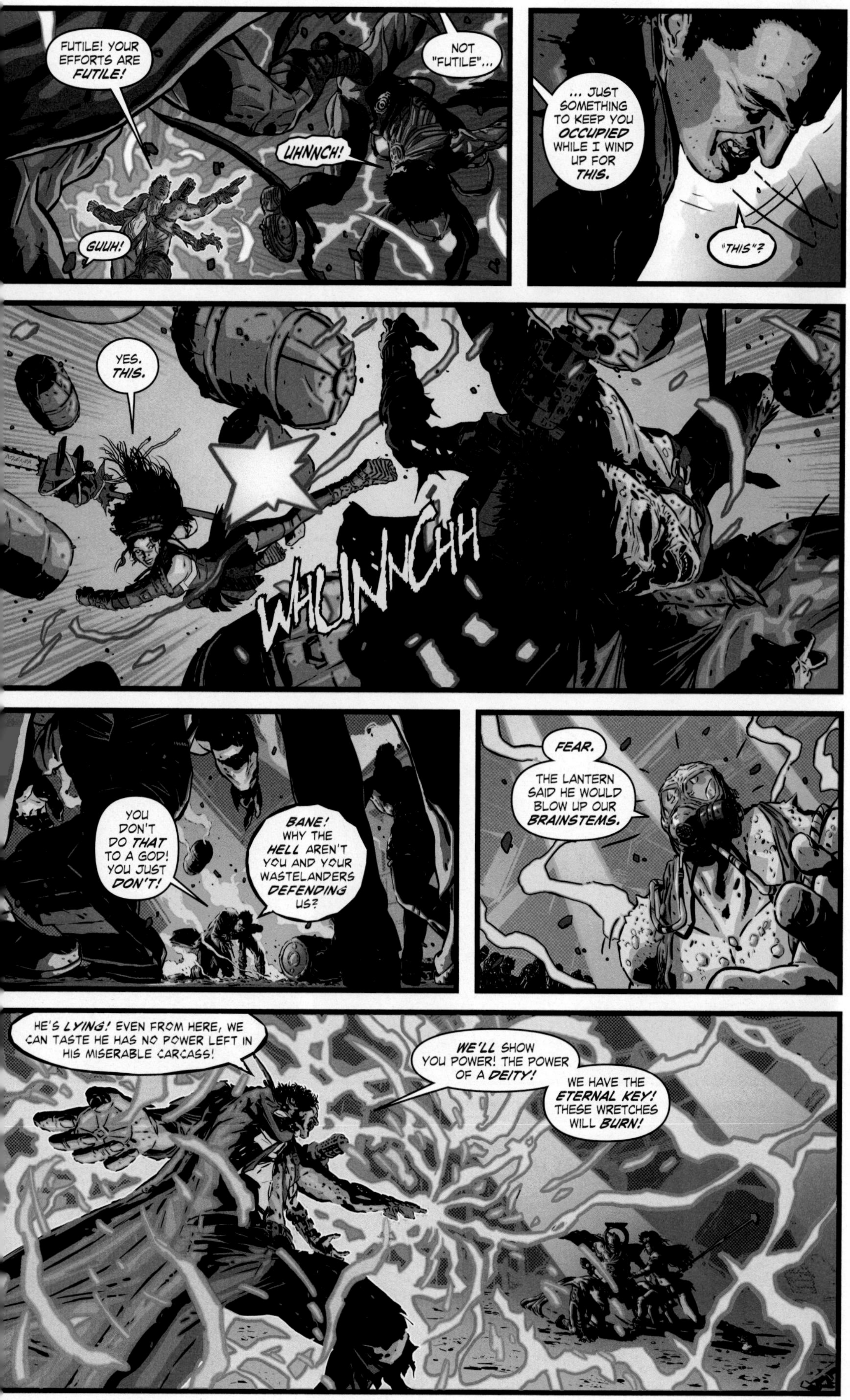
FUTILE! YOUR EFFORTS ARE FUTILE!
GUUH!
NOT "FUTILE"...
UHNNCH!
... JUST SOMETHING TO KEEP YOU OCCUPIED WHILE I WIND UP FOR THIS.
"THIS"?
YES. THIS.
WHUNNCHH
YOU DON'T DO THAT TO A GOD! YOU JUST DON'T!
BANE! WHY THE HELL AREN'T YOU AND YOUR WASTELANDERS DEFENDING US?
FEAR.
THE LANTERN SAID HE WOULD BLOW UP OUR BRAINSTEMS.
HE'S LYING! EVEN FROM HERE, WE CAN TASTE HE HAS NO POWER LEFT IN HIS MISERABLE CARCASS!
WE'LL SHOW YOU POWER! THE POWER OF A DEITY!
WE HAVE THE ETERNAL KEY! THESE WRETCHES WILL BURN!

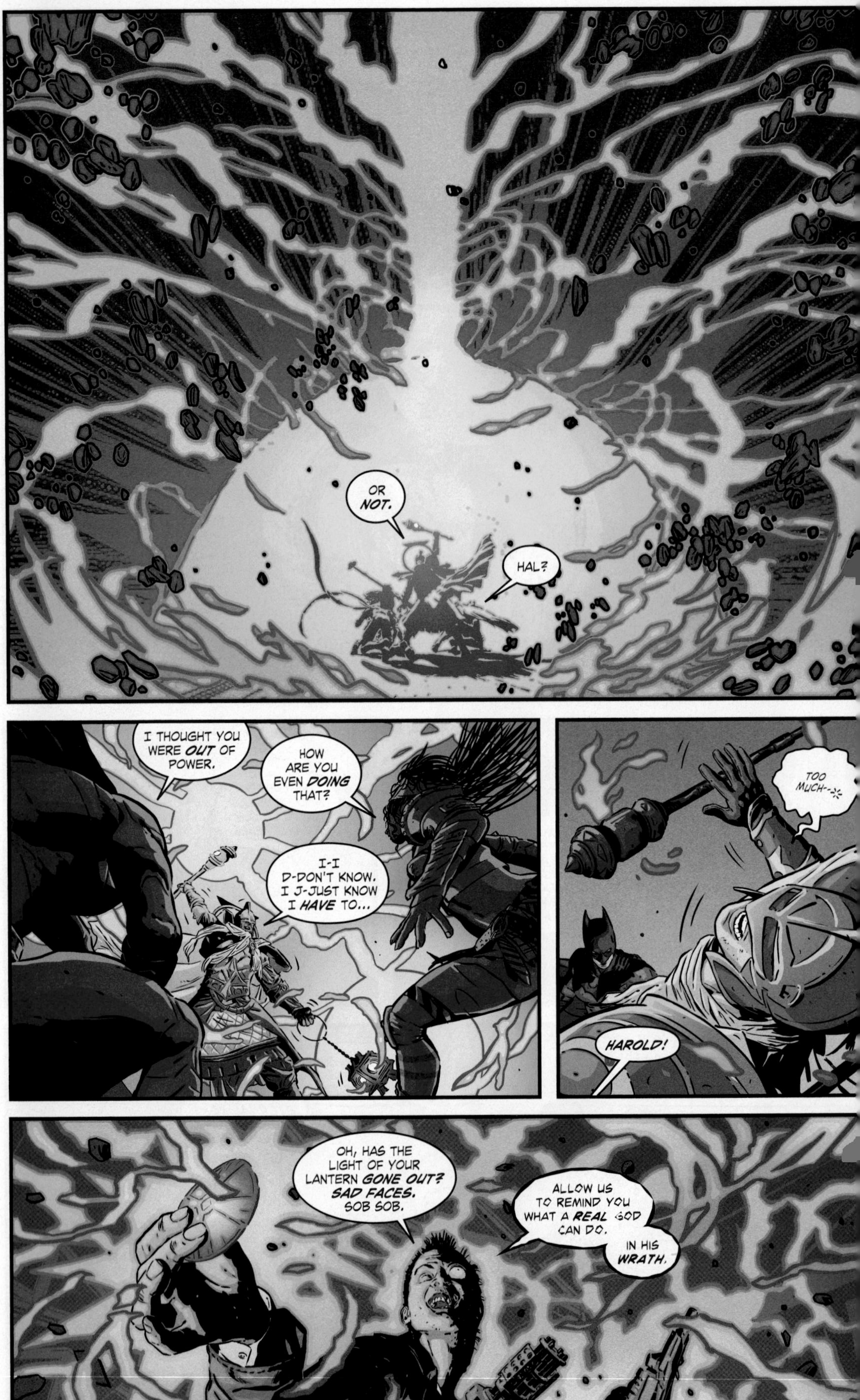
OR NOT.
HAL?
I THOUGHT YOU WERE OUT OF POWER.
HOW ARE YOU EVEN DOING THAT?
I-I D-DON'T KNOW. I J-JUST KNOW I HAVE TO...
TOO MUCH--
HAROLD!
OH, HAS THE LIGHT OF YOUR LANTERN GONE OUT? SAD FACES. SOB SOB.
ALLOW US TO REMIND YOU WHAT A REAL GOD CAN DO.
IN HIS WRATH.

WITH *WHAT?*

HUH?

FWIP

GIVE THAT *BACK* TO US!

SHAN'T. *WON'T.* *NOT* GONNA HAPPEN.

GOOD GIRL.

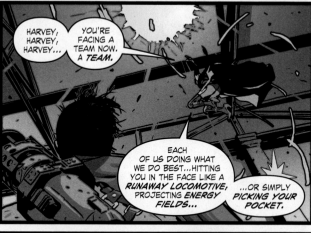

HARVEY, HARVEY, HARVEY...

YOU'RE FACING A TEAM NOW. A *TEAM.*

EACH OF US DOING WHAT WE DO BEST...HITTING YOU IN THE FACE LIKE A *RUNAWAY LOCOMOTIVE,* PROJECTING *ENERGY FIELDS...*

...OR SIMPLY *PICKING YOUR POCKET.*

WE DON'T *NEED* THAT! THE POWER IT BEQUEATHED IS *STILL INSIDE* US!

WE'RE *STILL* A *GOD!* WE CAN *STILL* BURN YOU!

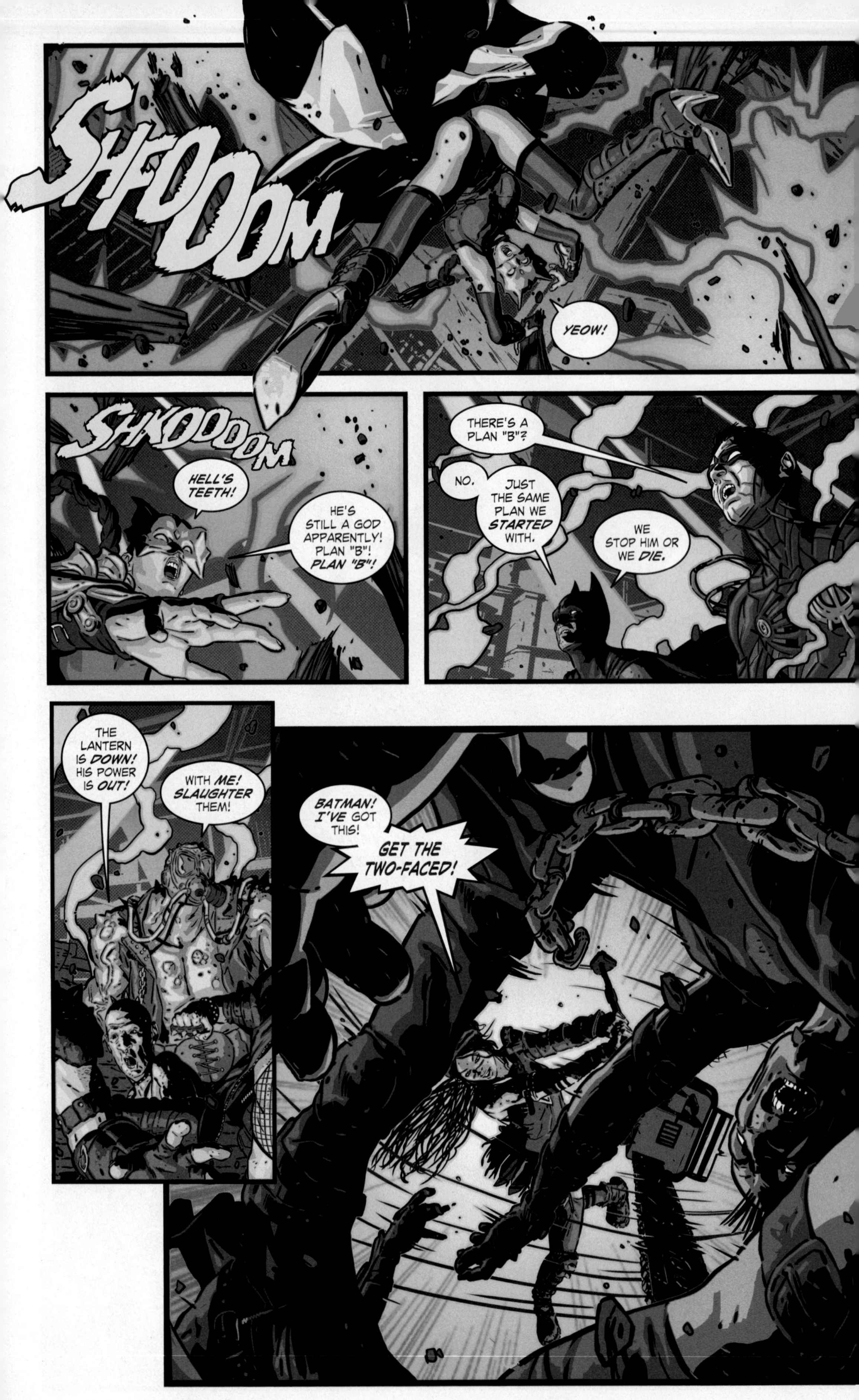
SHOOOM
YEOW!
SHKOOOOM
HELL'S TEETH!
HE'S STILL A GOD APPARENTLY! PLAN "B"! PLAN "B"!
THERE'S A PLAN "B"?
NO.
JUST THE SAME PLAN WE STARTED WITH.
WE STOP HIM OR WE DIE.
THE LANTERN IS DOWN! HIS POWER IS OUT!
WITH ME! SLAUGHTER THEM!
BATMAN! I'VE GOT THIS!
GET THE TWO-FACED!

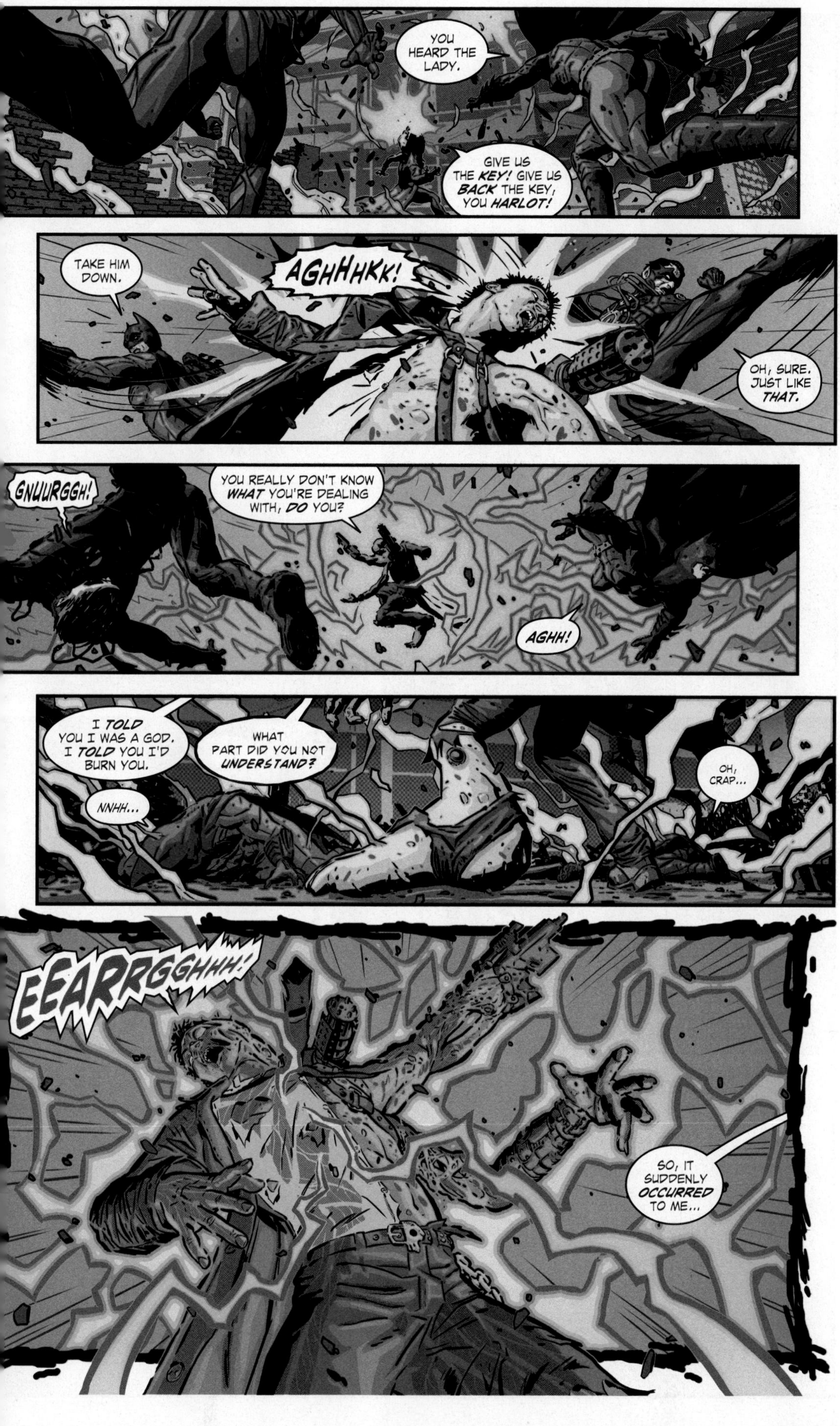

YOU HEARD THE LADY.
GIVE US THE KEY! GIVE US BACK THE KEY, YOU HARLOT!
TAKE HIM DOWN.
AGHHHKK!
OH, SURE. JUST LIKE THAT.
GNUURGGH!
YOU REALLY DON'T KNOW WHAT YOU'RE DEALING WITH, DO YOU?
AGHH!
I TOLD YOU I WAS A GOD. I TOLD YOU I'D BURN YOU.
WHAT PART DID YOU NOT UNDERSTAND?
NNHH...
OH, CRAP...
EEARRGGHHH!
SO, IT SUDDENLY OCCURRED TO ME...

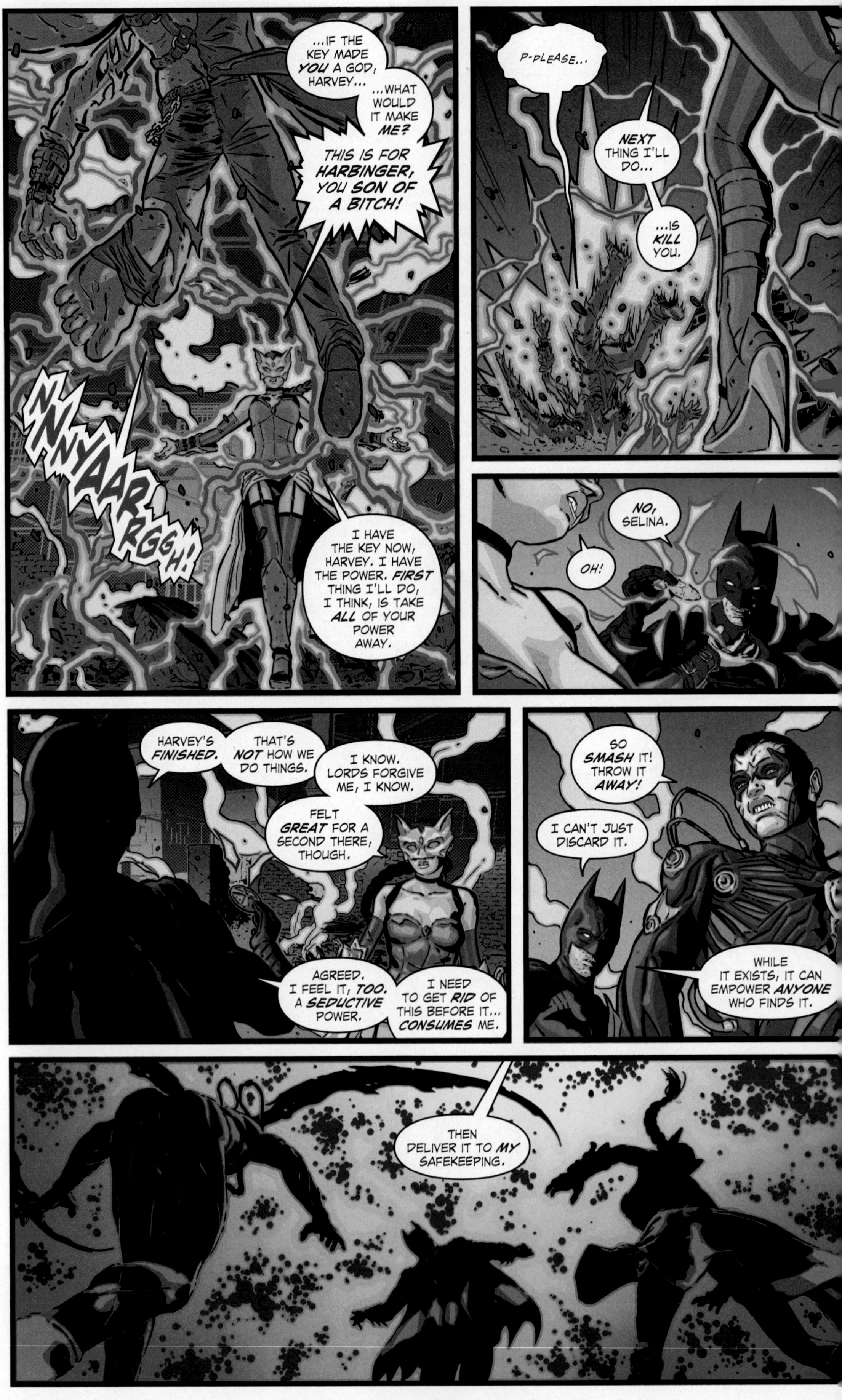
...IF THE KEY MADE YOU A GOD, HARVEY...
...WHAT WOULD IT MAKE ME?
THIS IS FOR HARBINGER, YOU SON OF A BITCH!
NNNYAARRGGH!
I HAVE THE KEY NOW, HARVEY. I HAVE THE POWER. FIRST THING I'LL DO, I THINK, IS TAKE ALL OF YOUR POWER AWAY.
P-PLEASE...
NEXT THING I'LL DO...
...IS KILL YOU.
NO, SELINA.
OH!
HARVEY'S FINISHED.
THAT'S NOT HOW WE DO THINGS.
I KNOW. LORDS FORGIVE ME, I KNOW.
FELT GREAT FOR A SECOND THERE, THOUGH.
AGREED. I FEEL IT, TOO. A SEDUCTIVE POWER.
I NEED TO GET RID OF THIS BEFORE IT... CONSUMES ME.
SO SMASH IT! THROW IT AWAY!
I CAN'T JUST DISCARD IT.
WHILE IT EXISTS, IT CAN EMPOWER ANYONE WHO FINDS IT.
THEN DELIVER IT TO MY SAFEKEEPING.

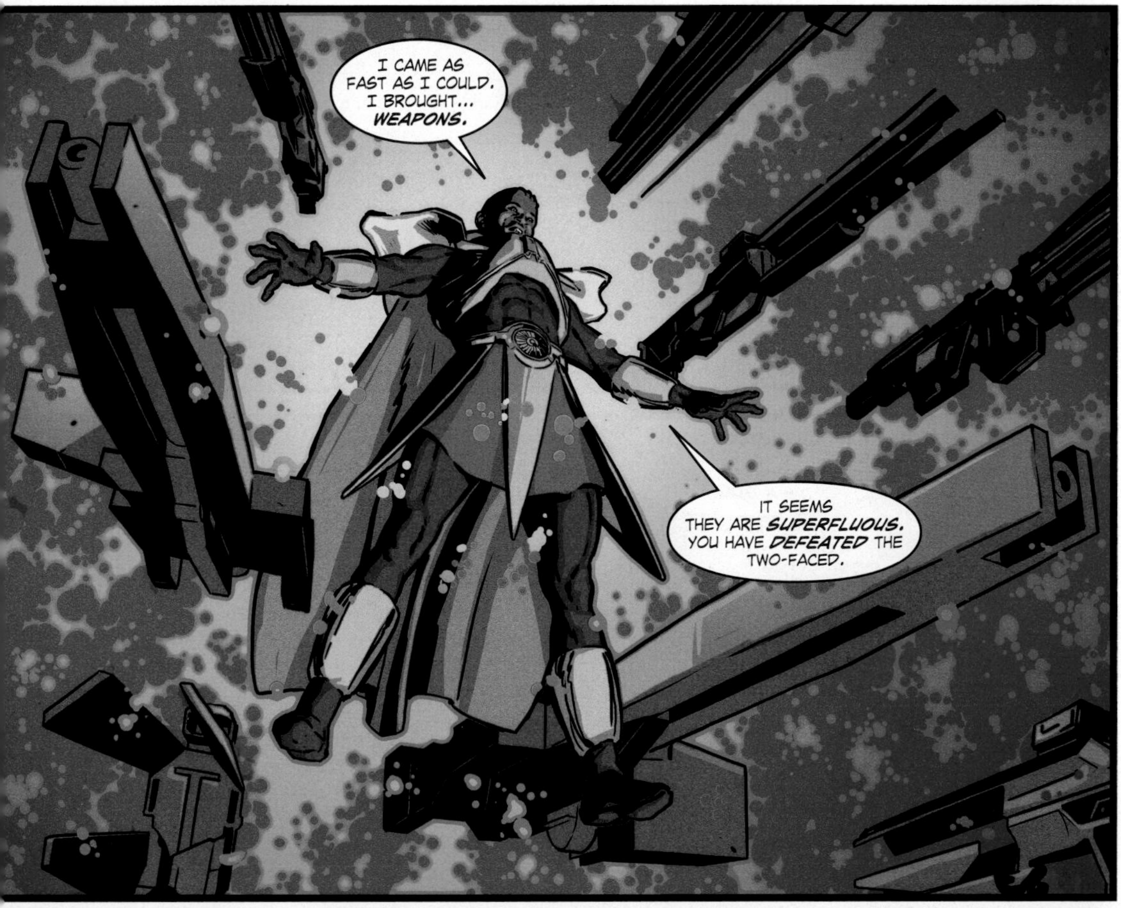
I CAME AS FAST AS I COULD. I BROUGHT... WEAPONS.
IT SEEMS THEY ARE SUPERFLUOUS. YOU HAVE DEFEATED THE TWO-FACED.

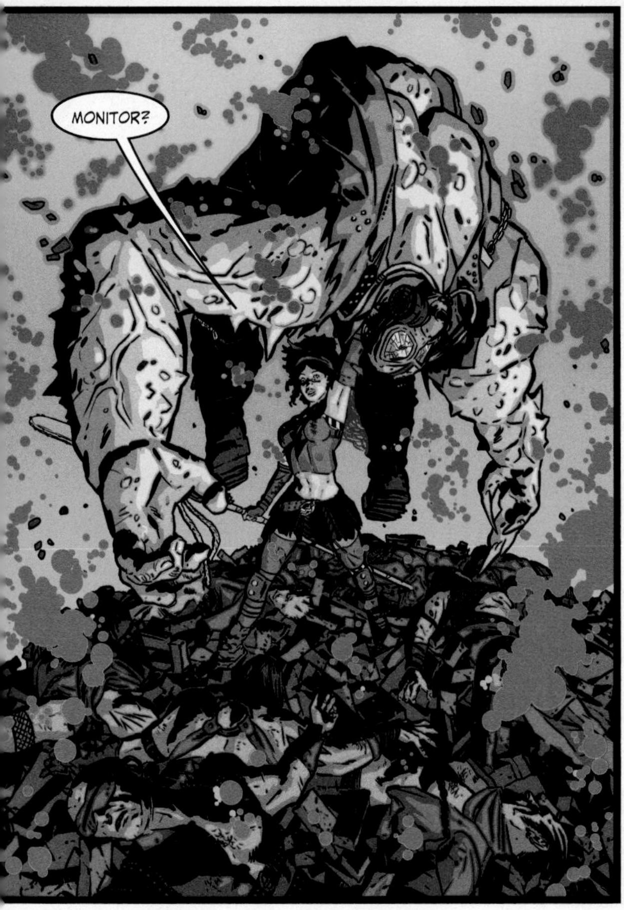
MONITOR?

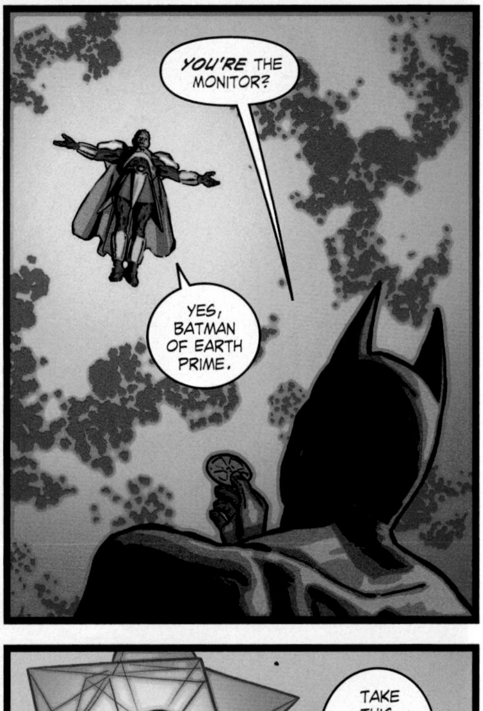
YOU'RE THE MONITOR?
YES, BATMAN OF EARTH PRIME.

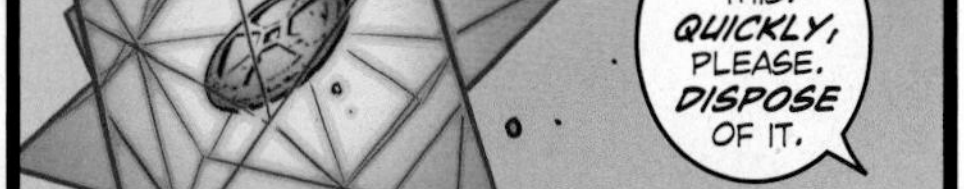
TAKE THIS. QUICKLY, PLEASE. DISPOSE OF IT.

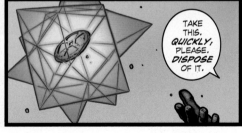

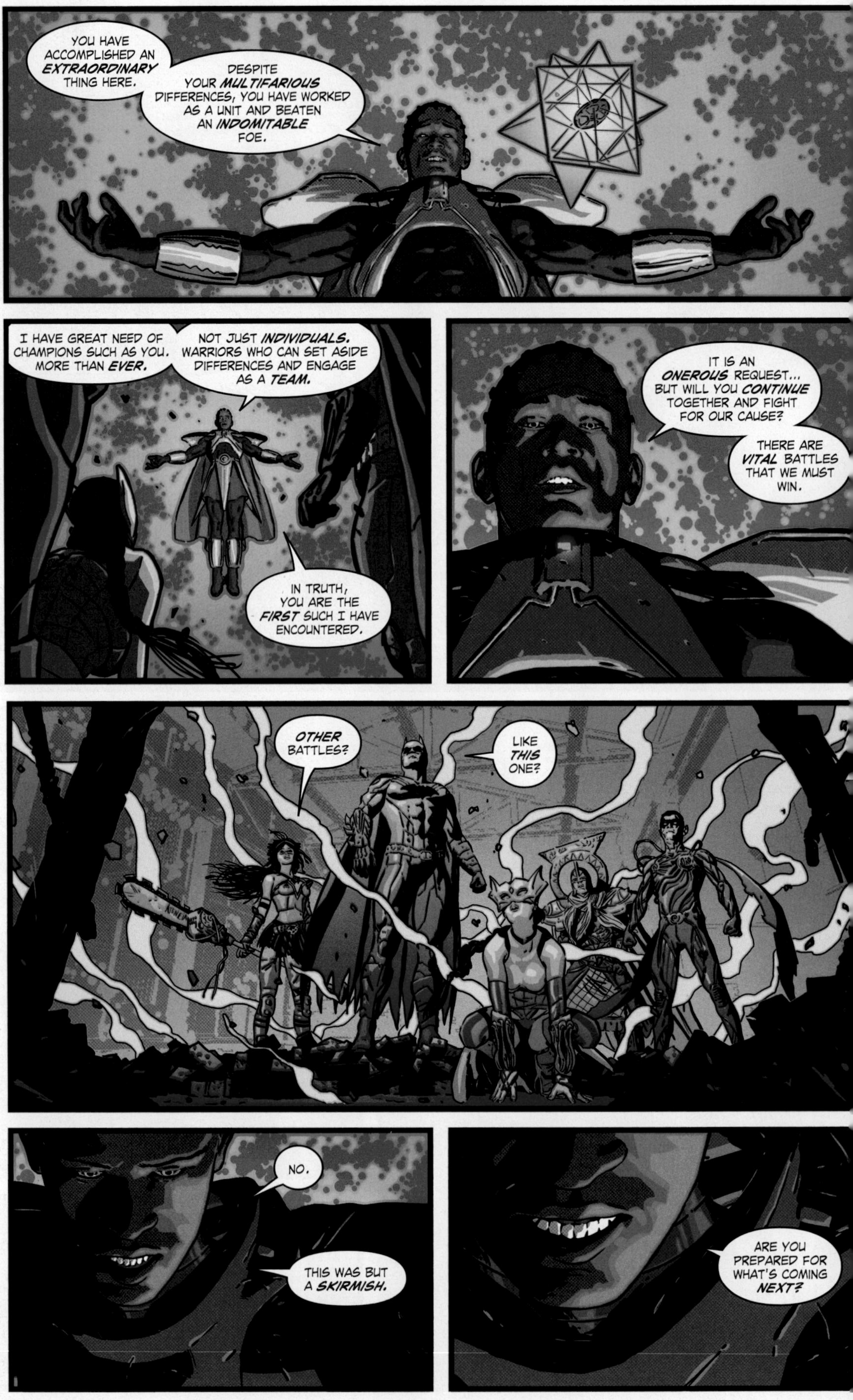
YOU HAVE ACCOMPLISHED AN EXTRAORDINARY THING HERE.
DESPITE YOUR MULTIFARIOUS DIFFERENCES, YOU HAVE WORKED AS A UNIT AND BEATEN AN INDOMITABLE FOE.
I HAVE GREAT NEED OF CHAMPIONS SUCH AS YOU. MORE THAN EVER.
NOT JUST INDIVIDUALS. WARRIORS WHO CAN SET ASIDE DIFFERENCES AND ENGAGE AS A TEAM.
IN TRUTH, YOU ARE THE FIRST SUCH I HAVE ENCOUNTERED.
IT IS AN ONEROUS REQUEST... BUT WILL YOU CONTINUE TOGETHER AND FIGHT FOR OUR CAUSE?
THERE ARE VITAL BATTLES THAT WE MUST WIN.
OTHER BATTLES?
LIKE THIS ONE?
NO.
THIS WAS BUT A SKIRMISH.
ARE YOU PREPARED FOR WHAT'S COMING NEXT?

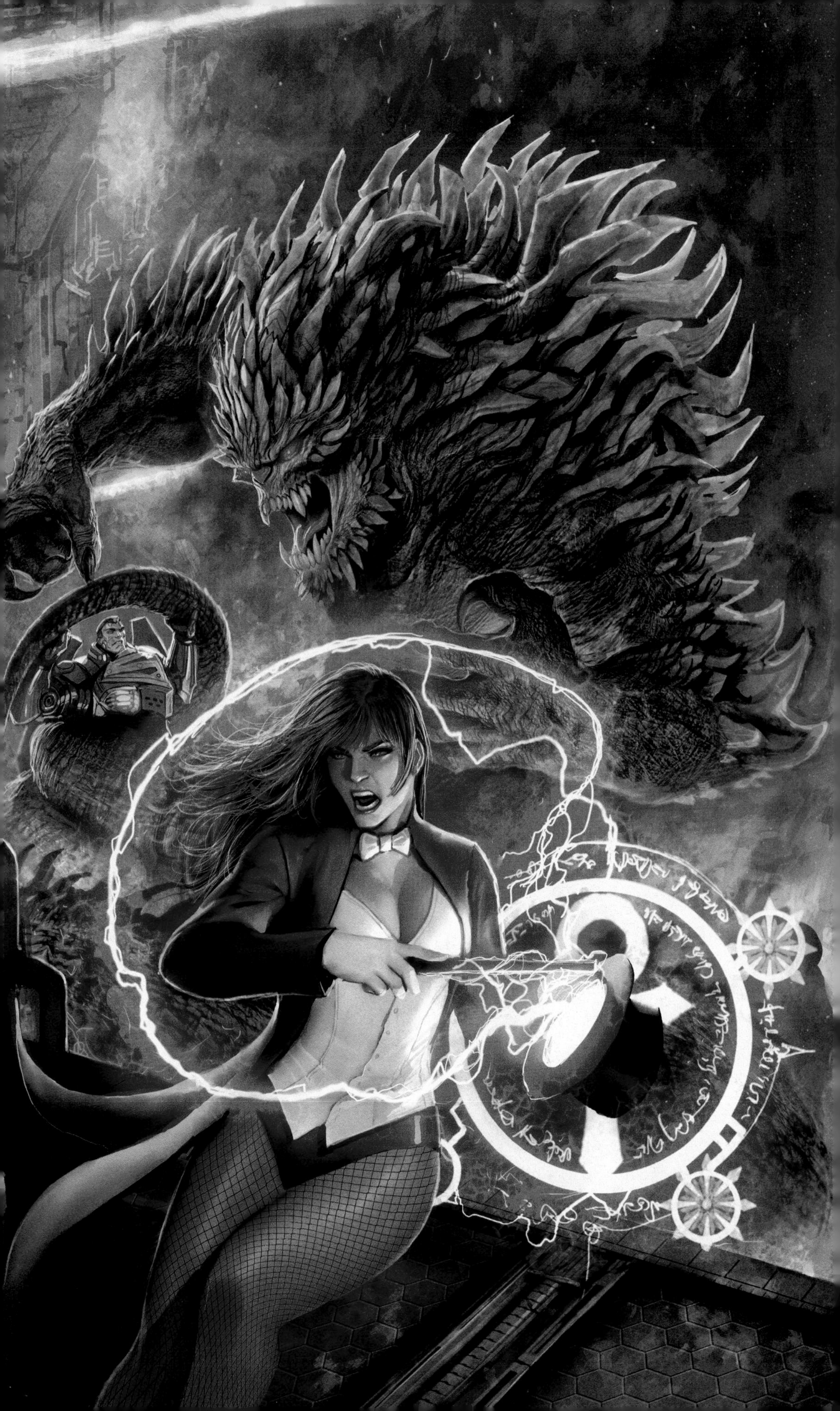

MECHA PART 1

Tom Derenick Artist **Alejandro Sanchez** Colorist
Cover Art by **Stjepan Sejic**

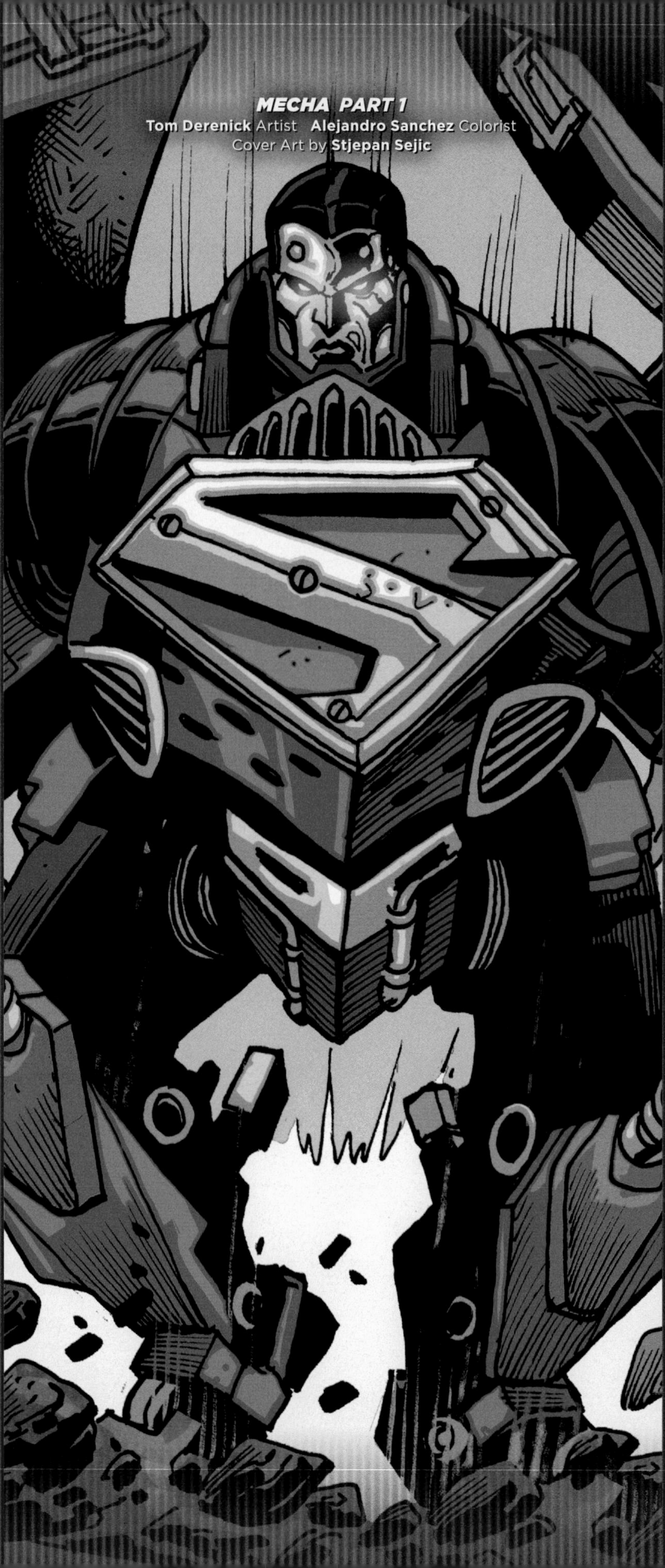

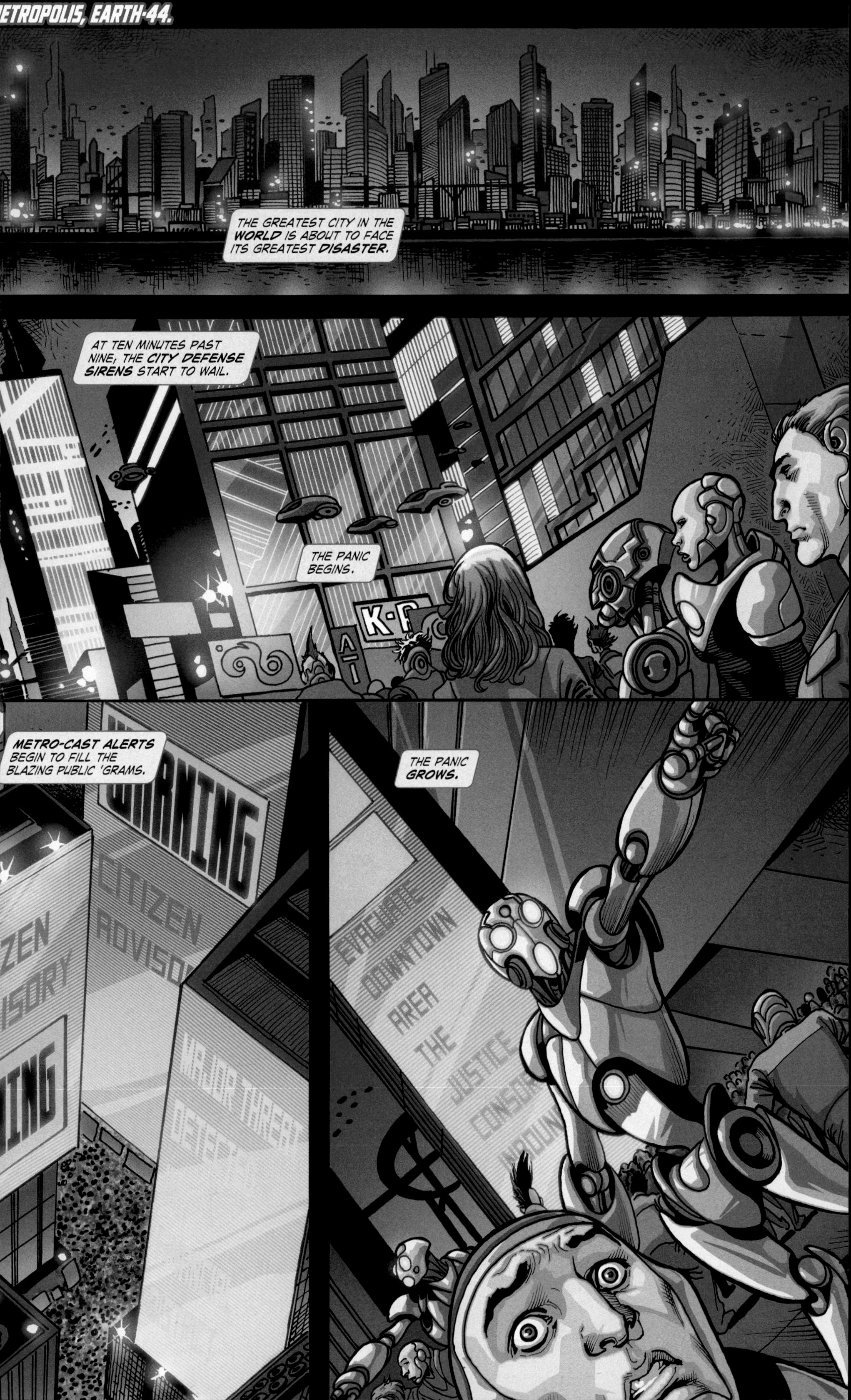
ETROPOLIS, EARTH-44.
THE GREATEST CITY IN THE WORLD IS ABOUT TO FACE ITS GREATEST DISASTER.
AT TEN MINUTES PAST NINE, THE CITY DEFENSE SIRENS START TO WAIL.
THE PANIC BEGINS.
METRO-CAST ALERTS BEGIN TO FILL THE BLAZING PUBLIC 'GRAMS.
CITIZEN
THE PANIC GROWS.
EVACUATE
DOWNTOWN
AREA
THE

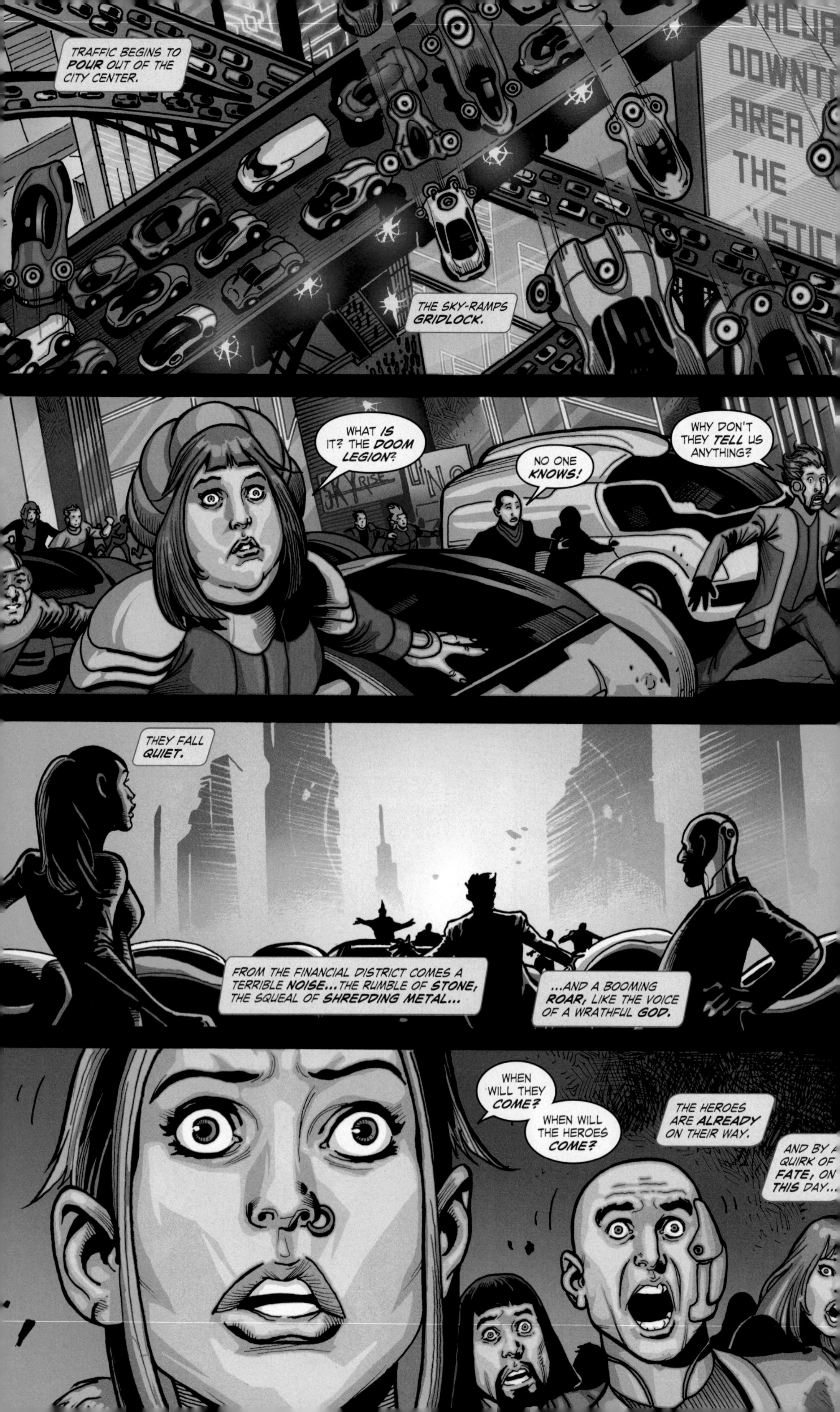
TRAFFIC BEGINS TO POUR OUT OF THE CITY CENTER.
THE SKY-RAMPS GRIDLOCK.
WHAT IS IT? THE DOOM LEGION?
NO ONE KNOWS!
WHY DON'T THEY TELL US ANYTHING?
THEY FALL QUIET.
FROM THE FINANCIAL DISTRICT COMES A TERRIBLE NOISE...THE RUMBLE OF STONE, THE SQUEAL OF SHREDDING METAL...
...AND A BOOMING ROAR, LIKE THE VOICE OF A WRATHFUL GOD.
WHEN WILL THEY COME?
WHEN WILL THE HEROES COME?
THE HEROES ARE ALREADY ON THEIR WAY.
AND BY A QUIRK OF FATE, ON THIS DAY...

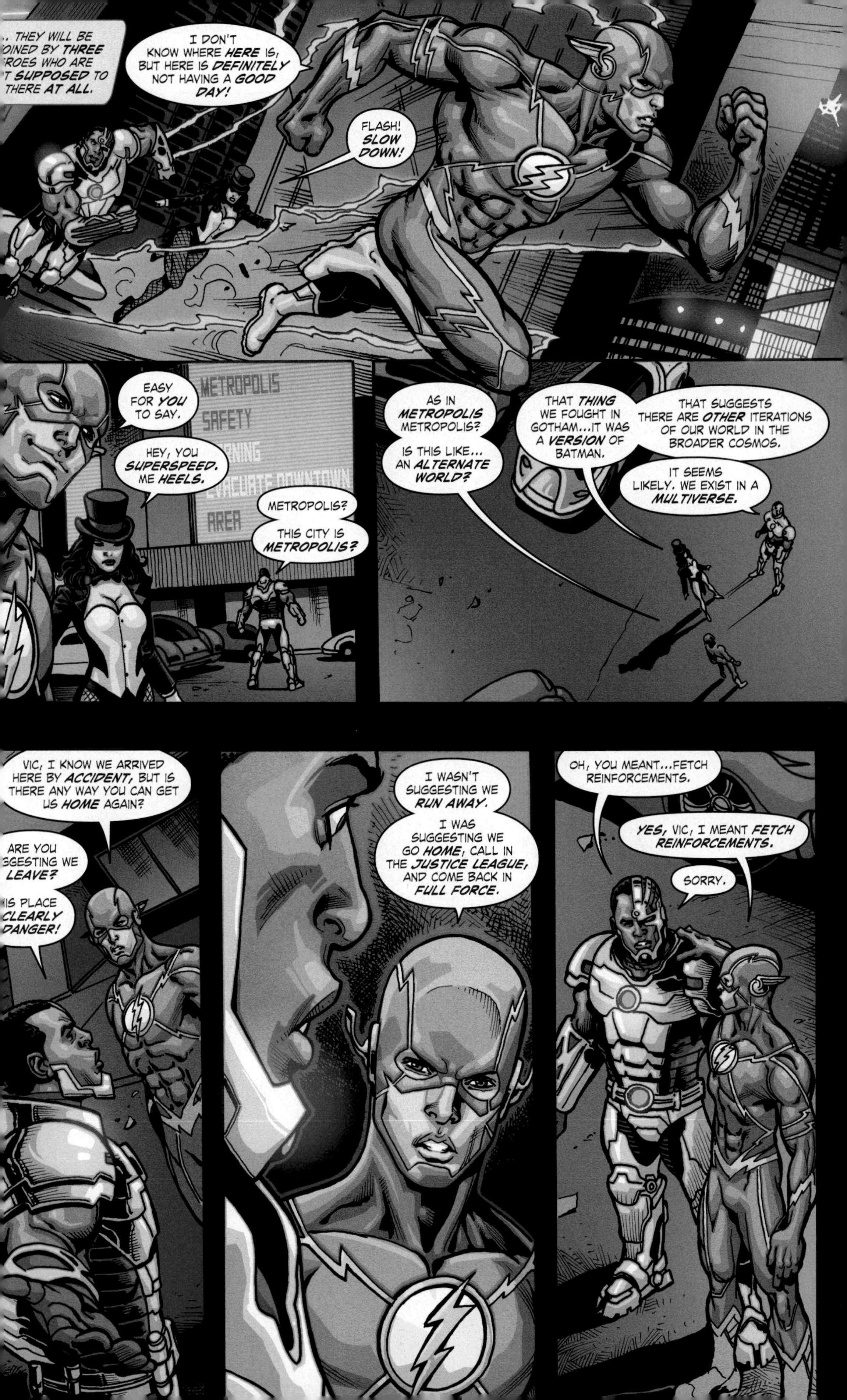
.. THEY WILL BE
JOINED BY THREE
ROES WHO ARE
'T SUPPOSED TO
THERE AT ALL.
I DON'T KNOW WHERE HERE IS, BUT HERE IS DEFINITELY NOT HAVING A GOOD DAY!
FLASH! SLOW DOWN!
EASY FOR YOU TO SAY.
HEY, YOU SUPERSPEED. ME HEELS.
METROPOLIS SAFETY
ARNING
EVACUATE DOWNTOWN
AREA
METROPOLIS?
THIS CITY IS METROPOLIS?
AS IN METROPOLIS METROPOLIS?
IS THIS LIKE... AN ALTERNATE WORLD?
THAT THING WE FOUGHT IN GOTHAM...IT WAS A VERSION OF BATMAN.
THAT SUGGESTS THERE ARE OTHER ITERATIONS OF OUR WORLD IN THE BROADER COSMOS.
IT SEEMS LIKELY. WE EXIST IN A MULTIVERSE.
VIC, I KNOW WE ARRIVED HERE BY ACCIDENT, BUT IS THERE ANY WAY YOU CAN GET US HOME AGAIN?
ARE YOU
GGESTING WE
LEAVE?
IS PLACE
CLEARLY
DANGER!
I WASN'T SUGGESTING WE RUN AWAY.
I WAS SUGGESTING WE GO HOME, CALL IN THE JUSTICE LEAGUE, AND COME BACK IN FULL FORCE.
OH, YOU MEANT...FETCH REINFORCEMENTS.
YES, VIC, I MEANT FETCH REINFORCEMENTS.
SORRY.

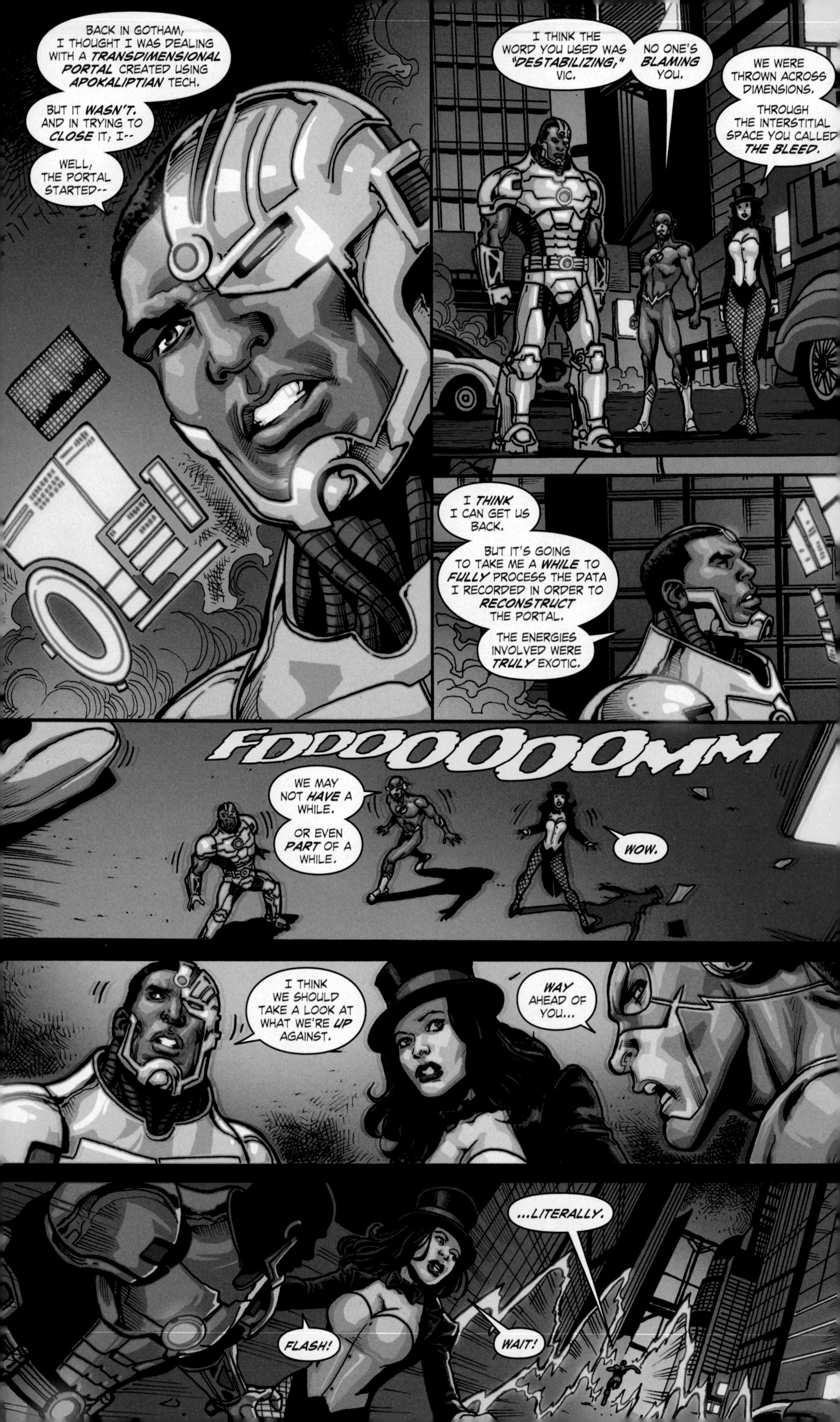
BACK IN GOTHAM, I THOUGHT I WAS DEALING WITH A TRANSDIMENSIONAL PORTAL CREATED USING APOKALIPTIAN TECH.
BUT IT WASN'T. AND IN TRYING TO CLOSE IT, I--
WELL, THE PORTAL STARTED--
I THINK THE WORD YOU USED WAS "DESTABILIZING," VIC.
NO ONE'S BLAMING YOU.
WE WERE THROWN ACROSS DIMENSIONS.
THROUGH THE INTERSTITIAL SPACE YOU CALLED THE BLEED.
I THINK I CAN GET US BACK.
BUT IT'S GOING TO TAKE ME A WHILE TO FULLY PROCESS THE DATA I RECORDED IN ORDER TO RECONSTRUCT THE PORTAL.
THE ENERGIES INVOLVED WERE TRULY EXOTIC.
FDDOOOOOOMM
WE MAY NOT HAVE A WHILE.
OR EVEN PART OF A WHILE.
WOW.
I THINK WE SHOULD TAKE A LOOK AT WHAT WE'RE UP AGAINST.
WAY AHEAD OF YOU...
...LITERALLY.
FLASH!
WAIT!

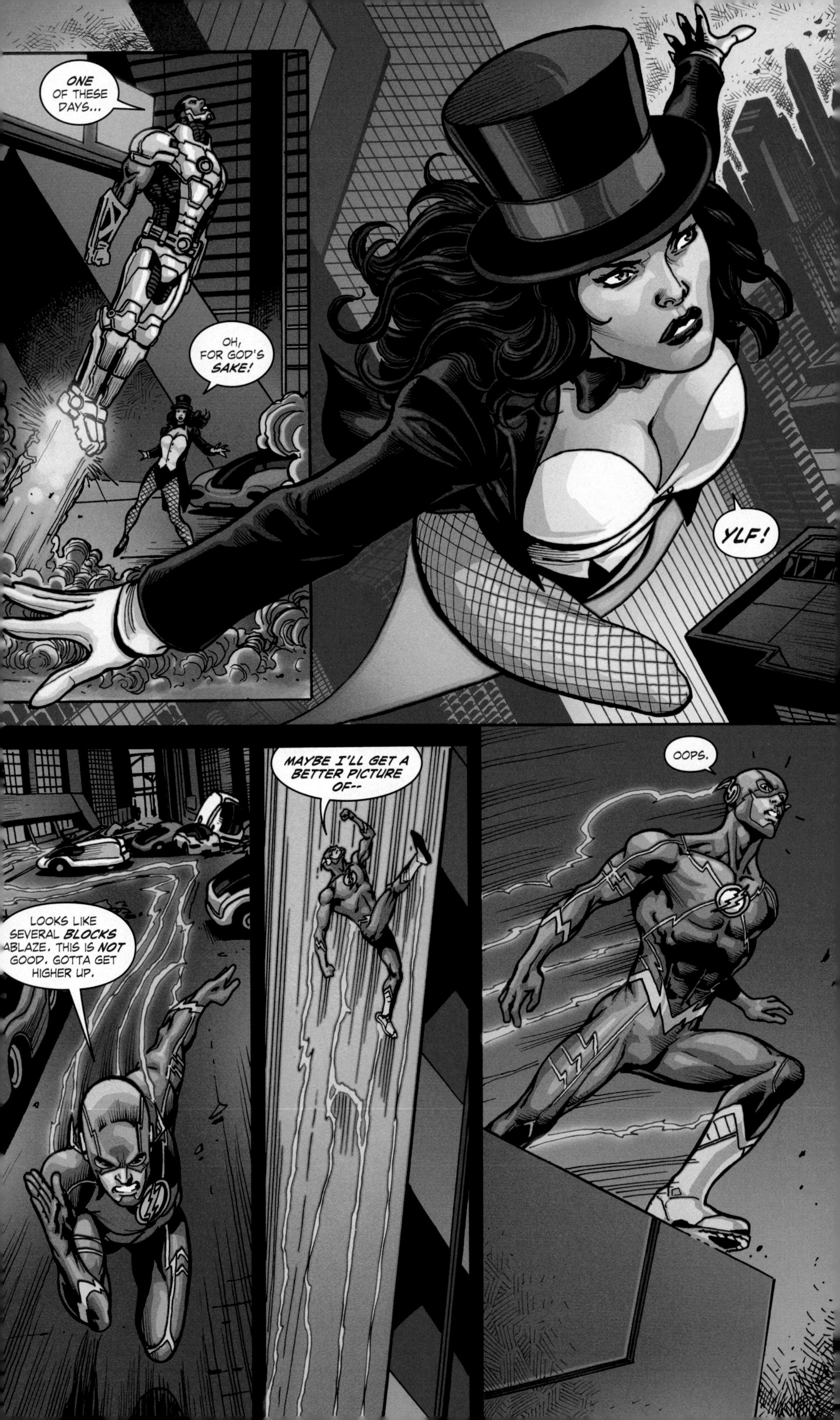
ONE OF THESE DAYS...
OH, FOR GOD'S SAKE!
YLF!
LOOKS LIKE SEVERAL BLOCKS ABLAZE. THIS IS NOT GOOD. GOTTA GET HIGHER UP.
MAYBE I'LL GET A BETTER PICTURE OF--
OOPS.

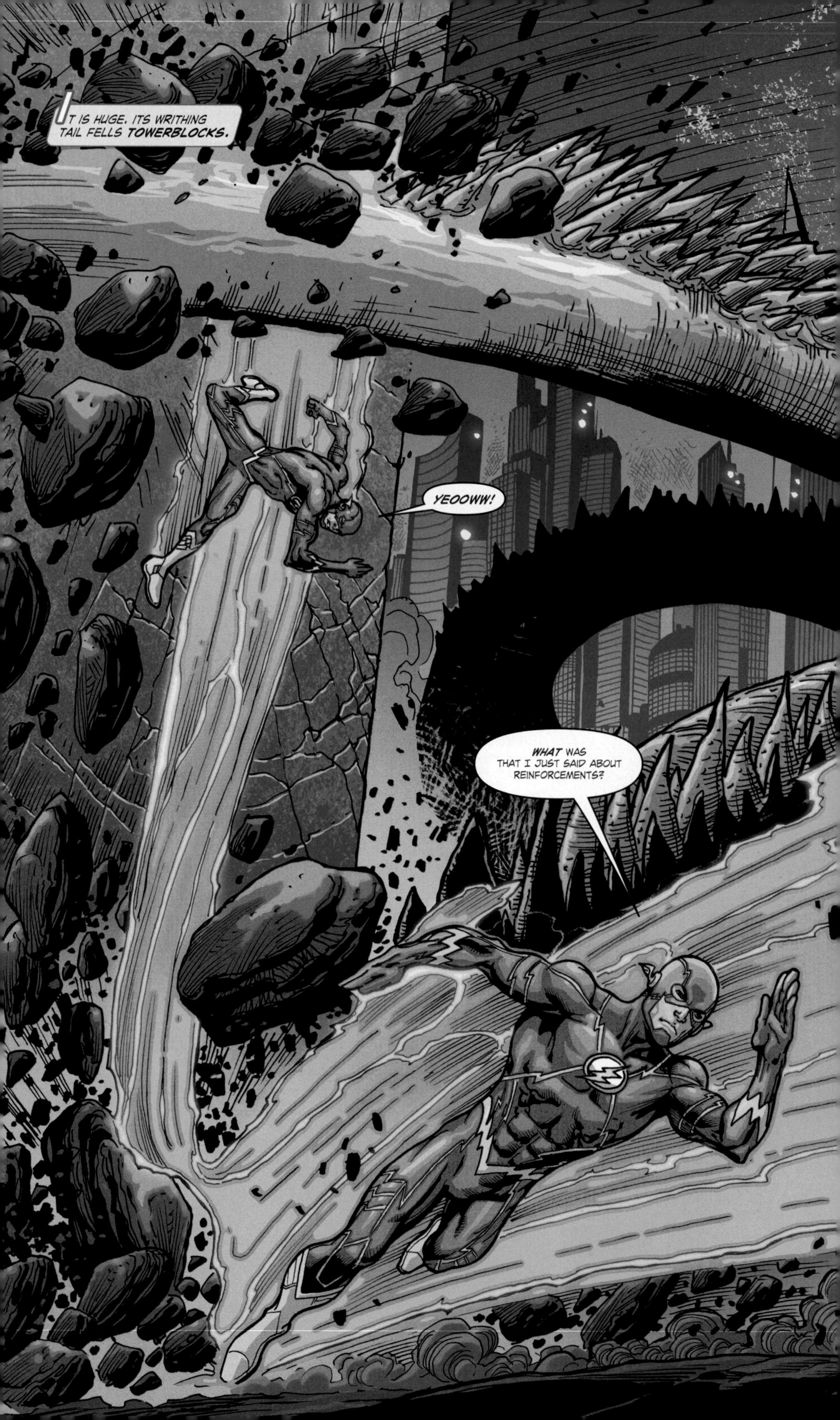
IT IS HUGE. ITS WRITHING TAIL FELLS TOWERBLOCKS.
YEOOWW!
WHAT WAS THAT I JUST SAID ABOUT REINFORCEMENTS?

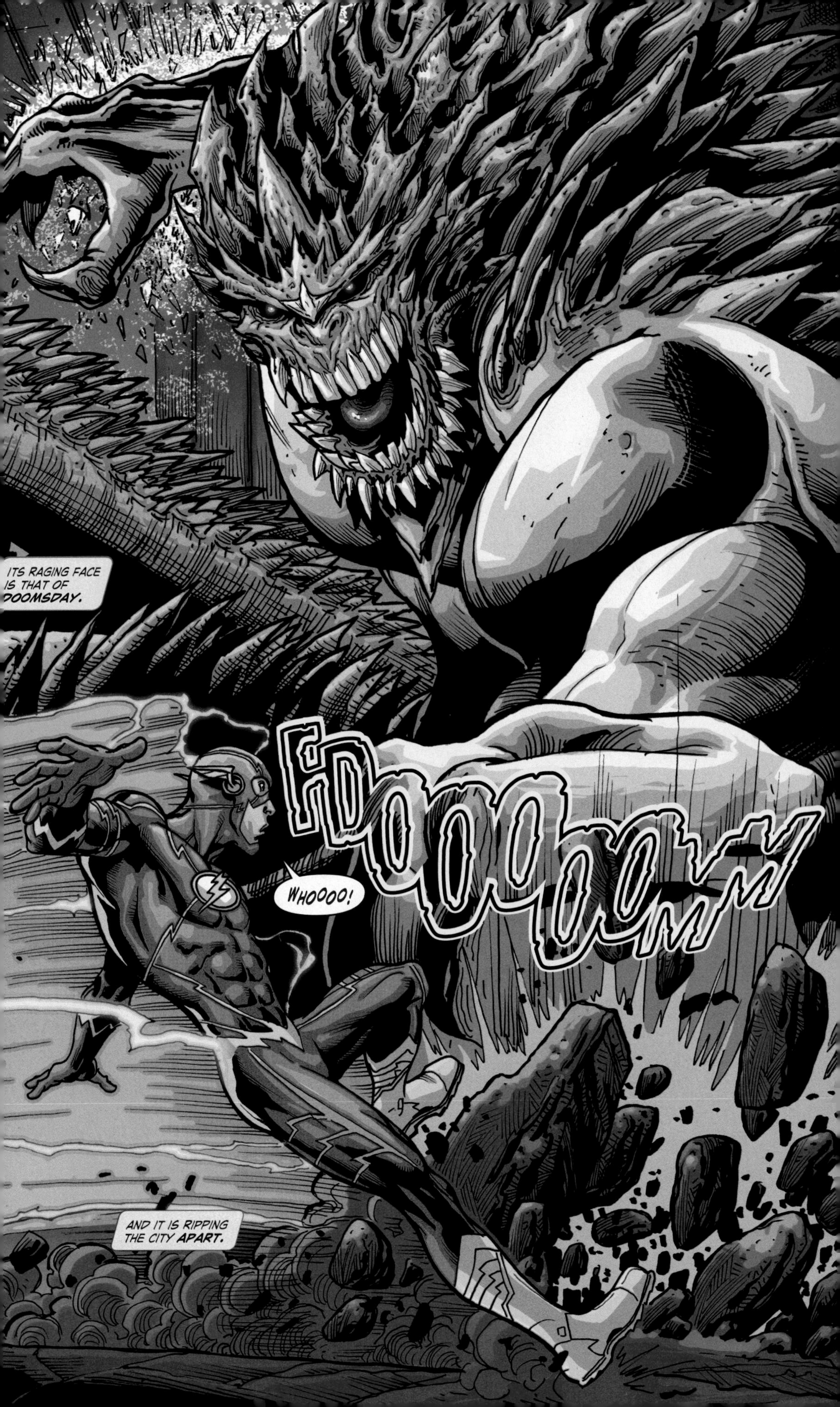
ITS RAGING FACE IS THAT OF DOOMSDAY.
WHOOOO!
FDOOOOOOMM
AND IT IS RIPPING THE CITY APART.

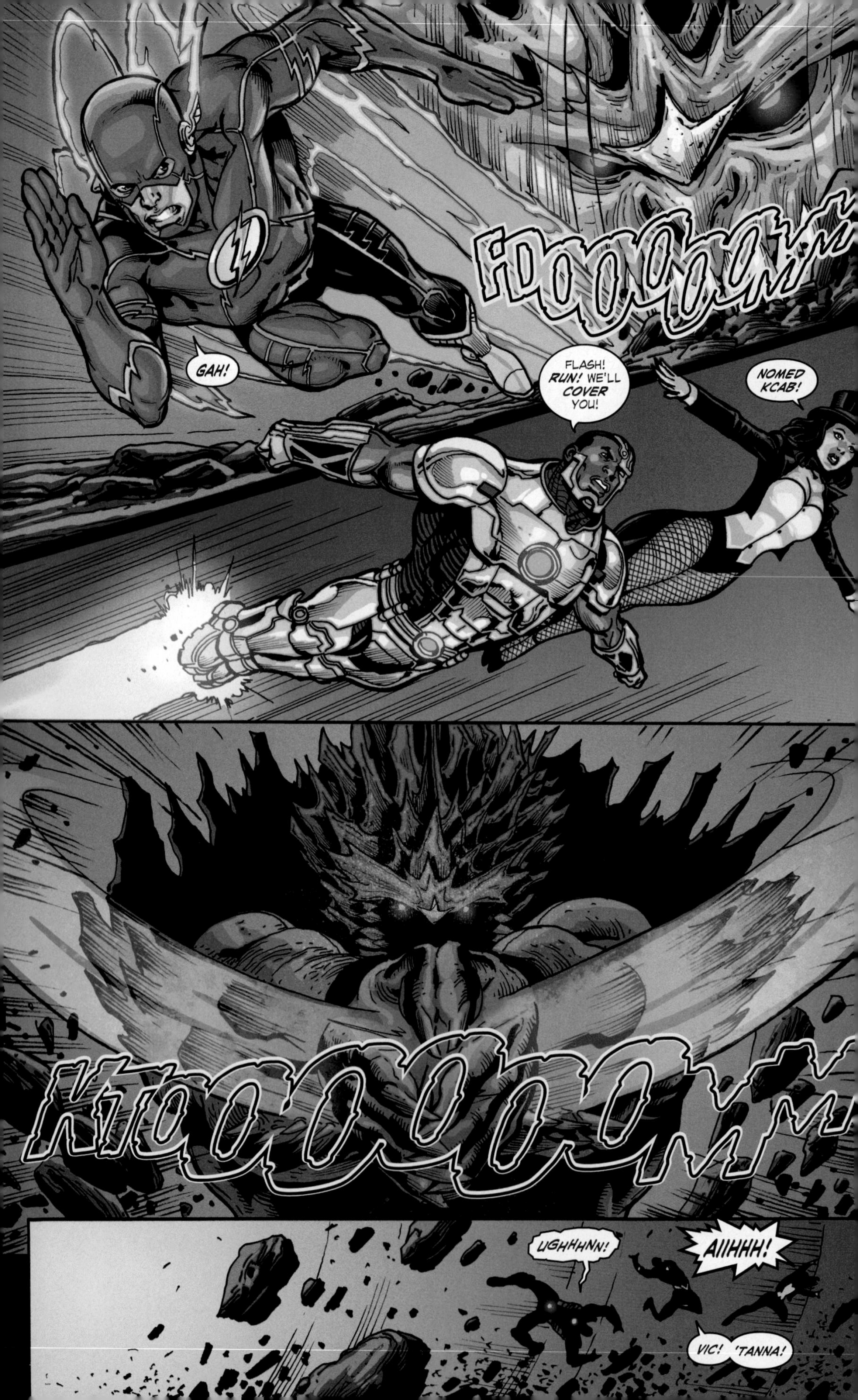
FDOOOOOOM!
GAH!
FLASH! RUN! WE'LL COVER YOU!
NOMED KCAB!
KROOOOOOM!
UGHHHNN!
AIIHHH!
VIC! 'TANNA!

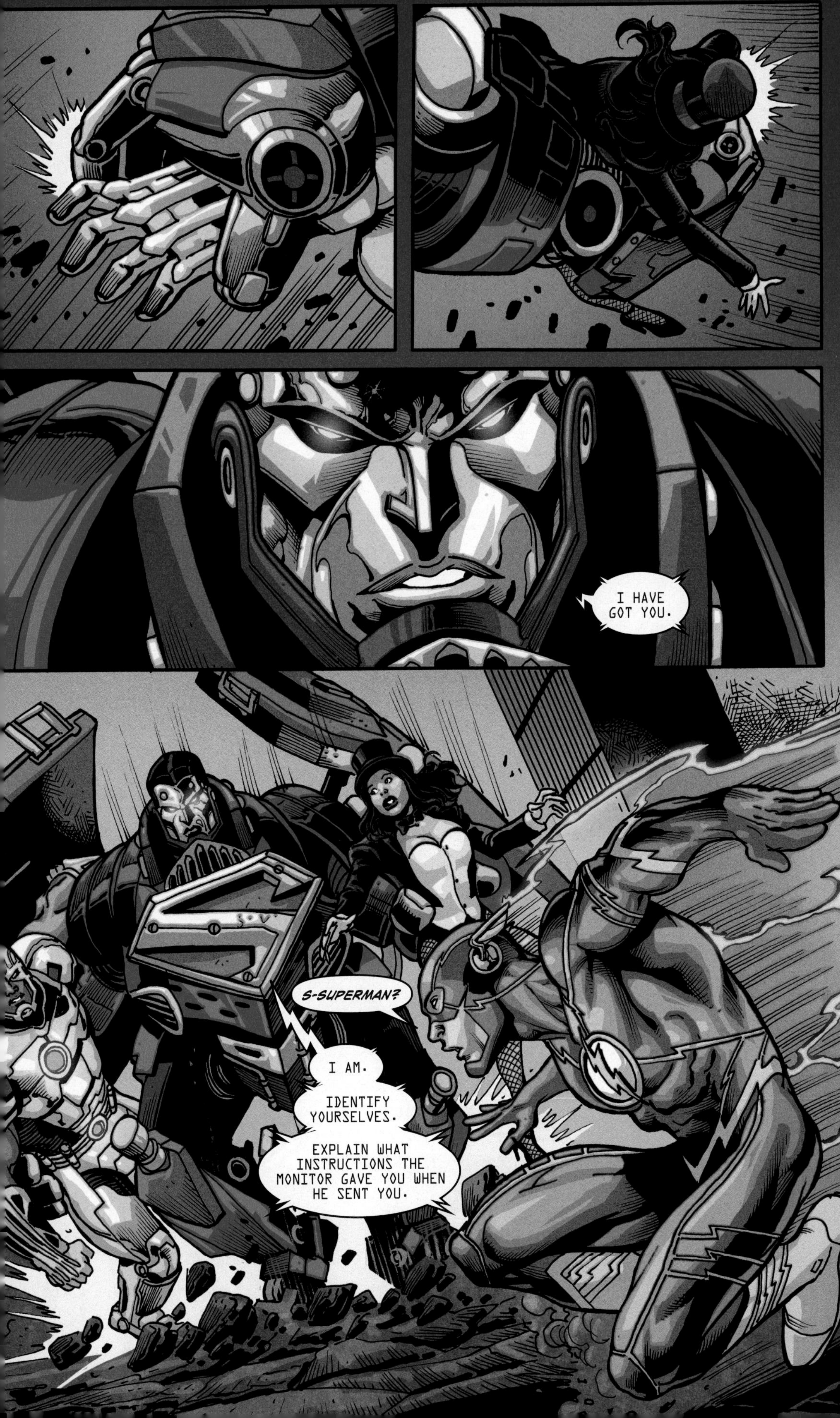
I HAVE GOT YOU.
S-SUPERMAN?
I AM.
IDENTIFY YOURSELVES.
EXPLAIN WHAT INSTRUCTIONS THE MONITOR GAVE YOU WHEN HE SENT YOU.

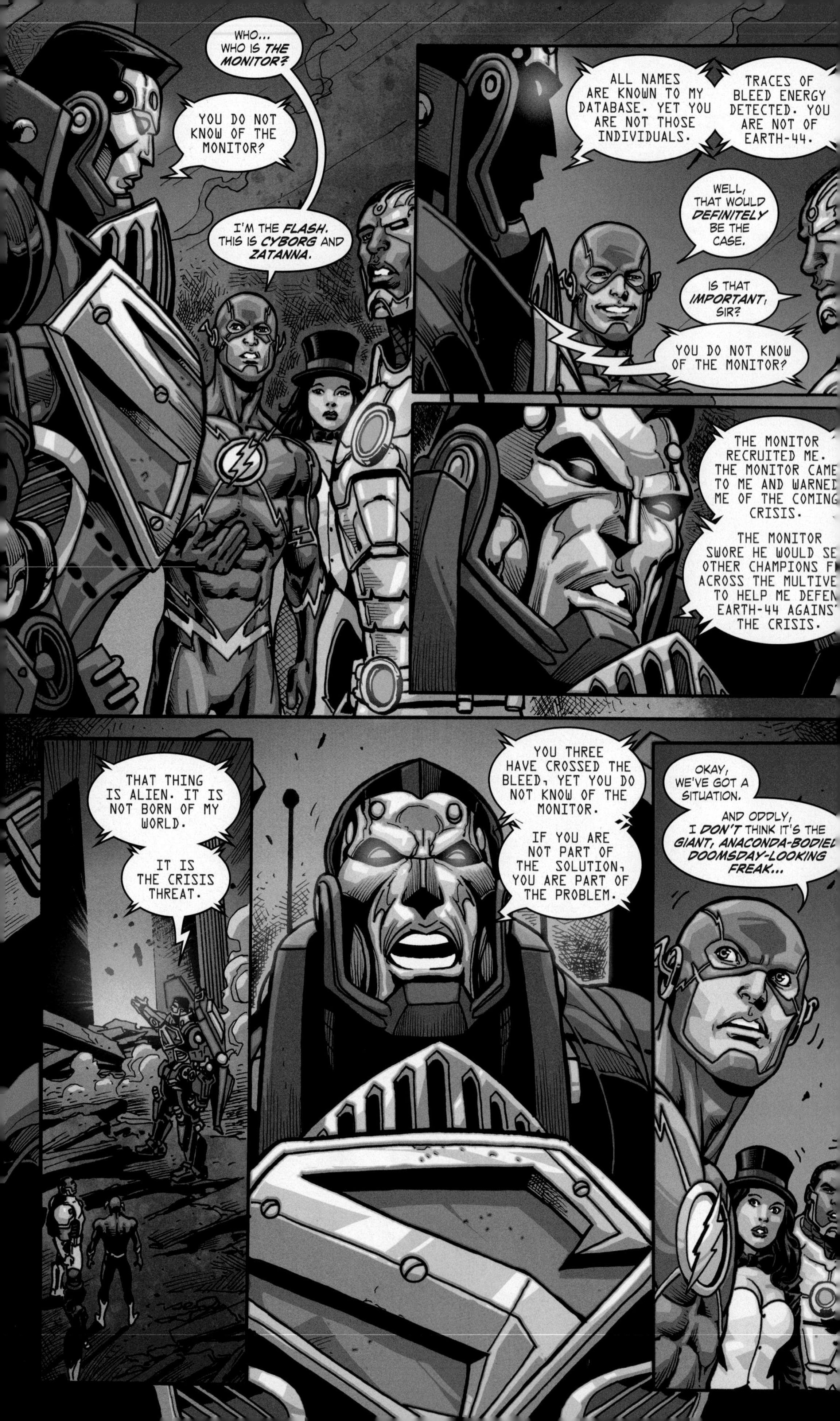
WHO... WHO IS THE MONITOR?
YOU DO NOT KNOW OF THE MONITOR?
I'M THE FLASH. THIS IS CYBORG AND ZATANNA.
ALL NAMES ARE KNOWN TO MY DATABASE. YET YOU ARE NOT THOSE INDIVIDUALS.
TRACES OF BLEED ENERGY DETECTED. YOU ARE NOT OF EARTH-44.
WELL, THAT WOULD DEFINITELY BE THE CASE.
IS THAT IMPORTANT, SIR?
YOU DO NOT KNOW OF THE MONITOR?
THE MONITOR RECRUITED ME. THE MONITOR CAME TO ME AND WARNED ME OF THE COMING CRISIS.
THE MONITOR SWORE HE WOULD SE OTHER CHAMPIONS F ACROSS THE MULTIVE TO HELP ME DEFEN EARTH-44 AGAINS THE CRISIS.
THAT THING IS ALIEN. IT IS NOT BORN OF MY WORLD.
IT IS THE CRISIS THREAT.
YOU THREE HAVE CROSSED THE BLEED, YET YOU DO NOT KNOW OF THE MONITOR.
IF YOU ARE NOT PART OF THE SOLUTION, YOU ARE PART OF THE PROBLEM.
OKAY, WE'VE GOT A SITUATION.
AND ODDLY, I DON'T THINK IT'S THE GIANT, ANACONDA-BODIE DOOMSDAY-LOOKING FREAK...

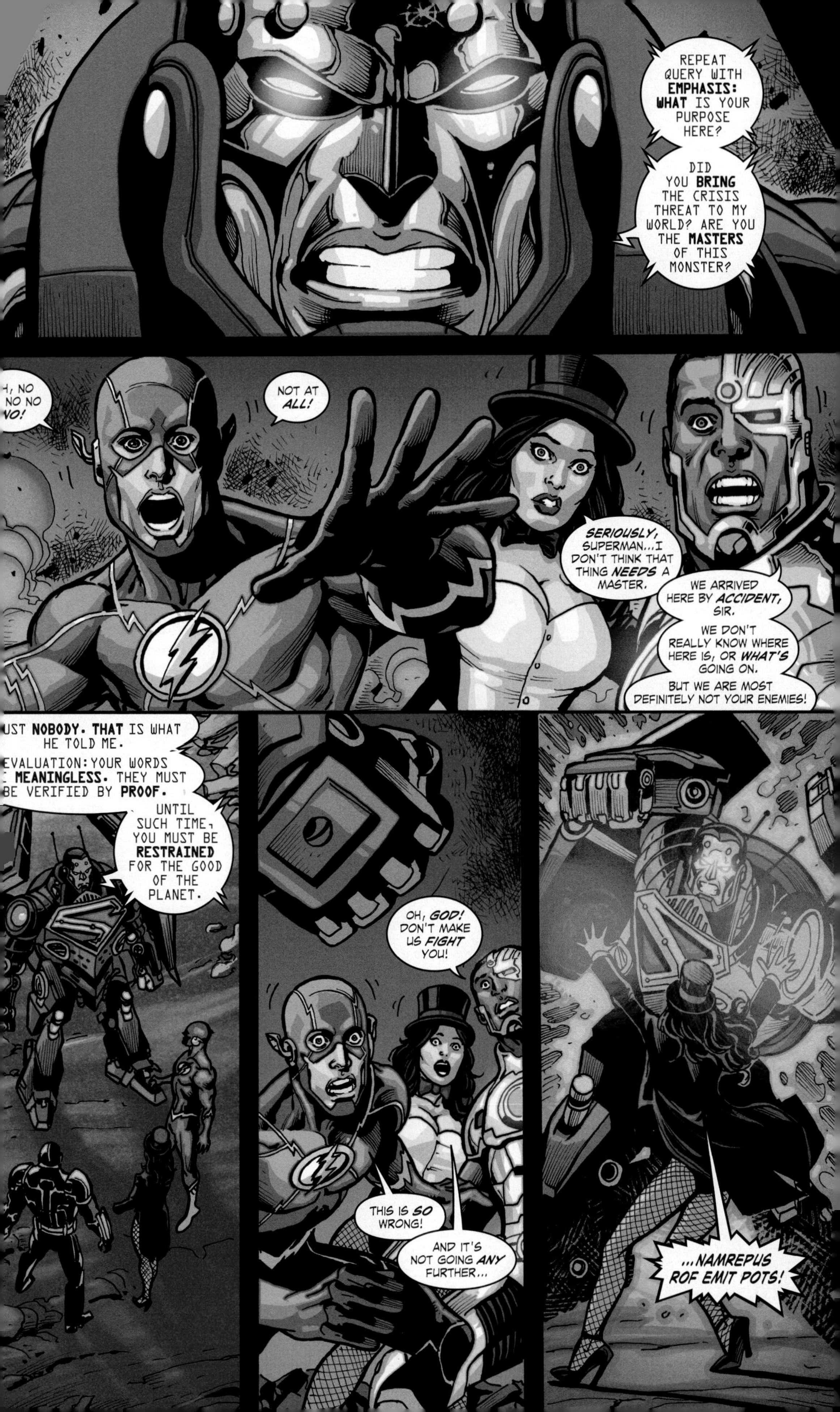
REPEAT QUERY WITH **EMPHASIS: WHAT** IS YOUR PURPOSE HERE?
DID YOU **BRING** THE CRISIS THREAT TO MY WORLD? ARE YOU THE **MASTERS** OF THIS MONSTER?
H, NO NO NO NO!
NOT AT *ALL!*
SERIOUSLY, SUPERMAN...I DON'T THINK THAT THING *NEEDS* A MASTER.
WE ARRIVED HERE BY *ACCIDENT,* SIR.
WE DON'T REALLY KNOW WHERE HERE IS, OR *WHAT'S* GOING ON.
BUT WE ARE MOST DEFINITELY NOT YOUR ENEMIES!
UST **NOBODY. THAT** IS WHAT HE TOLD ME.
EVALUATION: YOUR WORDS **MEANINGLESS.** THEY MUST BE VERIFIED BY **PROOF.**
UNTIL SUCH TIME, YOU MUST BE **RESTRAINED** FOR THE GOOD OF THE PLANET.
OH, *GOD!* DON'T MAKE US *FIGHT* YOU!
THIS IS *SO* WRONG!
AND IT'S NOT GOING *ANY* FURTHER...
...NAMREPUS ROF EMIT POTS!

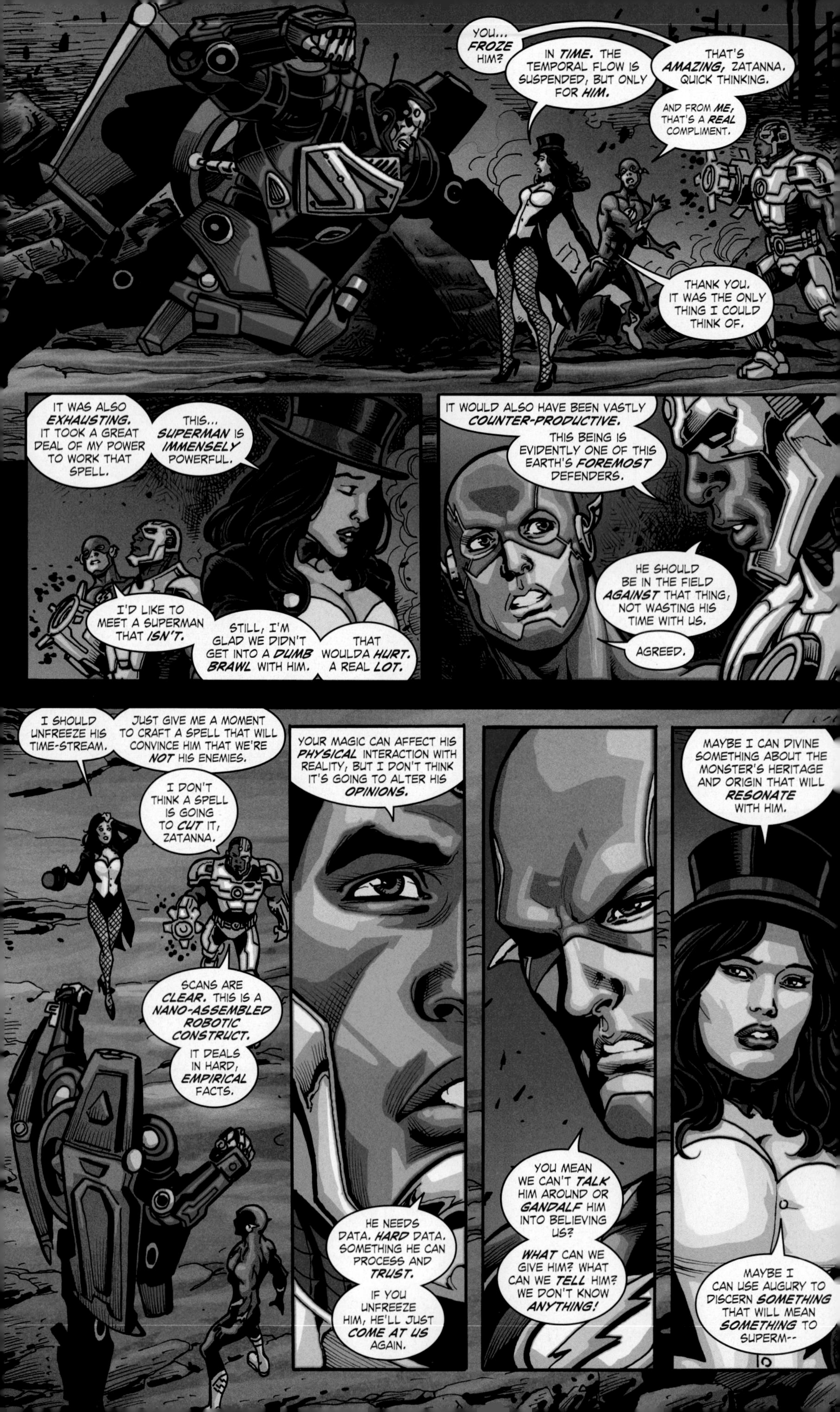

YOU... FROZE HIM?
IN TIME. THE TEMPORAL FLOW IS SUSPENDED, BUT ONLY FOR HIM.
THAT'S AMAZING, ZATANNA. QUICK THINKING.
AND FROM ME, THAT'S A REAL COMPLIMENT.
THANK YOU. IT WAS THE ONLY THING I COULD THINK OF.
IT WAS ALSO EXHAUSTING. IT TOOK A GREAT DEAL OF MY POWER TO WORK THAT SPELL.
THIS... SUPERMAN IS IMMENSELY POWERFUL.
I'D LIKE TO MEET A SUPERMAN THAT ISN'T.
STILL, I'M GLAD WE DIDN'T GET INTO A DUMB BRAWL WITH HIM.
THAT WOULDA HURT. A REAL LOT.
IT WOULD ALSO HAVE BEEN VASTLY COUNTER-PRODUCTIVE.
THIS BEING IS EVIDENTLY ONE OF THIS EARTH'S FOREMOST DEFENDERS.
HE SHOULD BE IN THE FIELD AGAINST THAT THING, NOT WASTING HIS TIME WITH US.
AGREED.
I SHOULD UNFREEZE HIS TIME-STREAM.
JUST GIVE ME A MOMENT TO CRAFT A SPELL THAT WILL CONVINCE HIM THAT WE'RE NOT HIS ENEMIES.
I DON'T THINK A SPELL IS GOING TO CUT IT, ZATANNA.
SCANS ARE CLEAR. THIS IS A NANO-ASSEMBLED ROBOTIC CONSTRUCT.
IT DEALS IN HARD, EMPIRICAL FACTS.
YOUR MAGIC CAN AFFECT HIS PHYSICAL INTERACTION WITH REALITY, BUT I DON'T THINK IT'S GOING TO ALTER HIS OPINIONS.
HE NEEDS DATA. HARD DATA. SOMETHING HE CAN PROCESS AND TRUST.
IF YOU UNFREEZE HIM, HE'LL JUST COME AT US AGAIN.
YOU MEAN WE CAN'T TALK HIM AROUND OR GANDALF HIM INTO BELIEVING US?
WHAT CAN WE GIVE HIM? WHAT CAN WE TELL HIM? WE DON'T KNOW ANYTHING!
MAYBE I CAN DIVINE SOMETHING ABOUT THE MONSTER'S HERITAGE AND ORIGIN THAT WILL RESONATE WITH HIM.
MAYBE I CAN USE AUGURY TO DISCERN SOMETHING THAT WILL MEAN SOMETHING TO SUPERM--

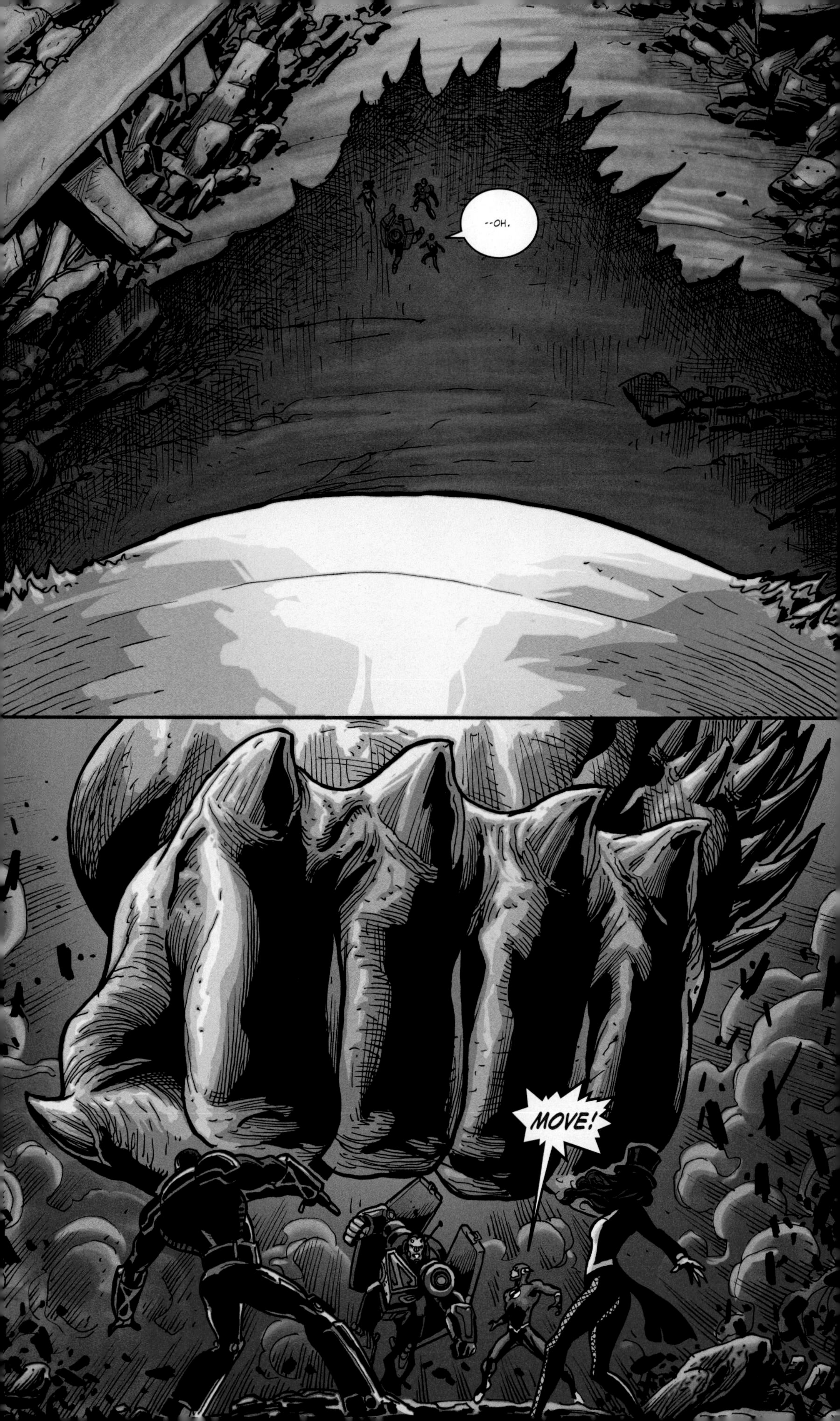
--OH.
MOVE!

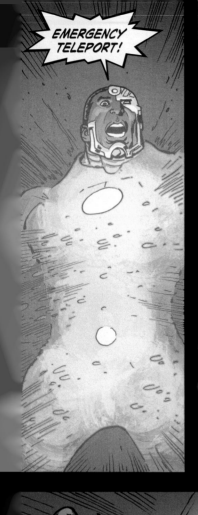

EMERGENCY TELEPORT!

WHHAA--?

PARDON MY *FAMILIARITY*, BUT WE HAVE TO BE GONE!

"BUT... SUPERMAN!"

KKTHOOOOOOMM

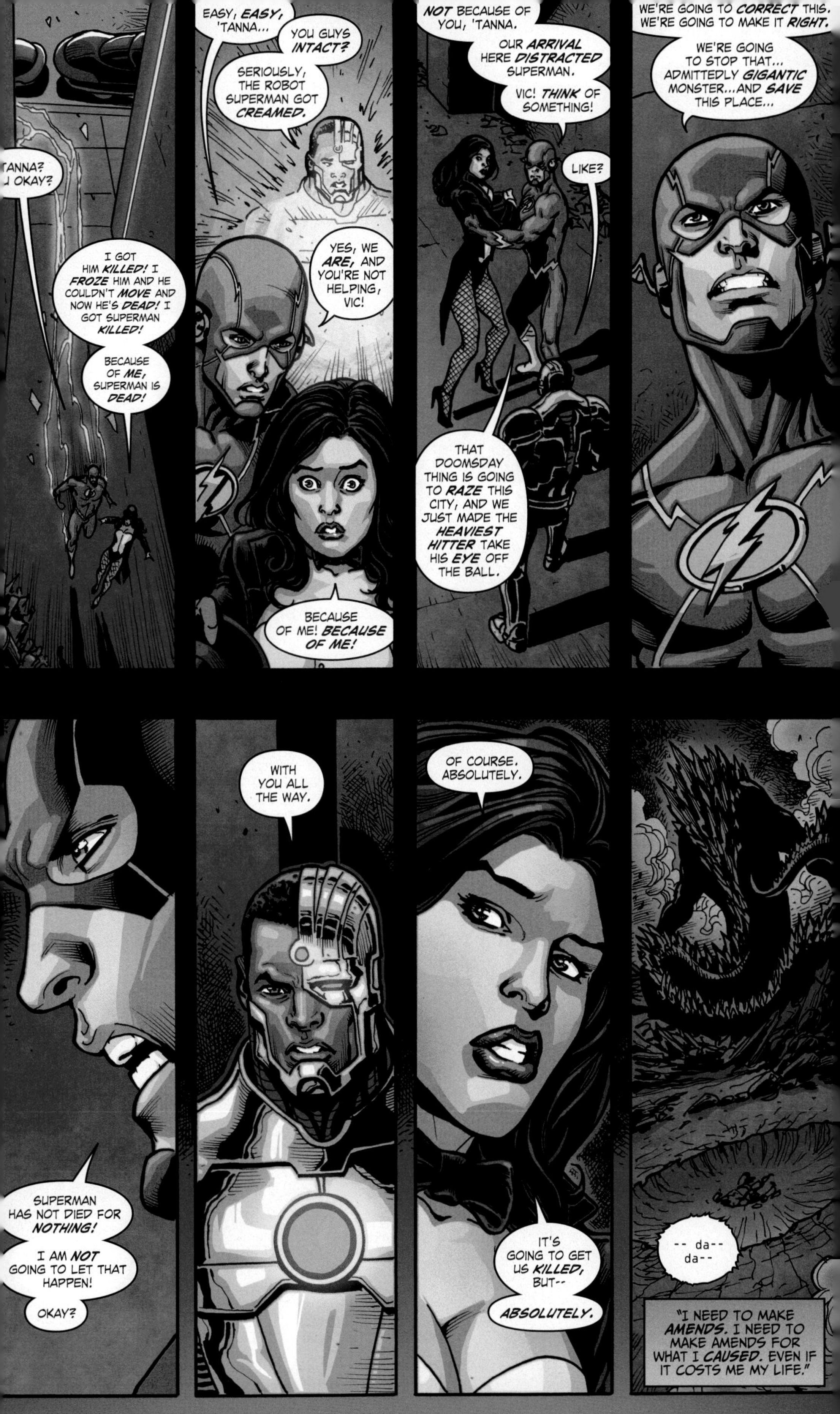

'TANNA?
U OKAY?
I GOT HIM KILLED! I FROZE HIM AND HE COULDN'T MOVE AND NOW HE'S DEAD! I GOT SUPERMAN KILLED!
BECAUSE OF ME, SUPERMAN IS DEAD!
EASY, EASY, 'TANNA...
YOU GUYS INTACT?
SERIOUSLY, THE ROBOT SUPERMAN GOT CREAMED.
YES, WE ARE, AND YOU'RE NOT HELPING, VIC!
BECAUSE OF ME! BECAUSE OF ME!
NOT BECAUSE OF YOU, 'TANNA.
OUR ARRIVAL HERE DISTRACTED SUPERMAN.
VIC! THINK OF SOMETHING!
LIKE?
THAT DOOMSDAY THING IS GOING TO RAZE THIS CITY, AND WE JUST MADE THE HEAVIEST HITTER TAKE HIS EYE OFF THE BALL.
WE'RE GOING TO CORRECT THIS. WE'RE GOING TO MAKE IT RIGHT.
WE'RE GOING TO STOP THAT... ADMITTEDLY GIGANTIC MONSTER...AND SAVE THIS PLACE...
SUPERMAN HAS NOT DIED FOR NOTHING!
I AM NOT GOING TO LET THAT HAPPEN!
OKAY?
WITH YOU ALL THE WAY.
OF COURSE. ABSOLUTELY.
IT'S GOING TO GET US KILLED, BUT--
ABSOLUTELY.
-- da-- da--
"I NEED TO MAKE AMENDS. I NEED TO MAKE AMENDS FOR WHAT I CAUSED. EVEN IF IT COSTS ME MY LIFE."

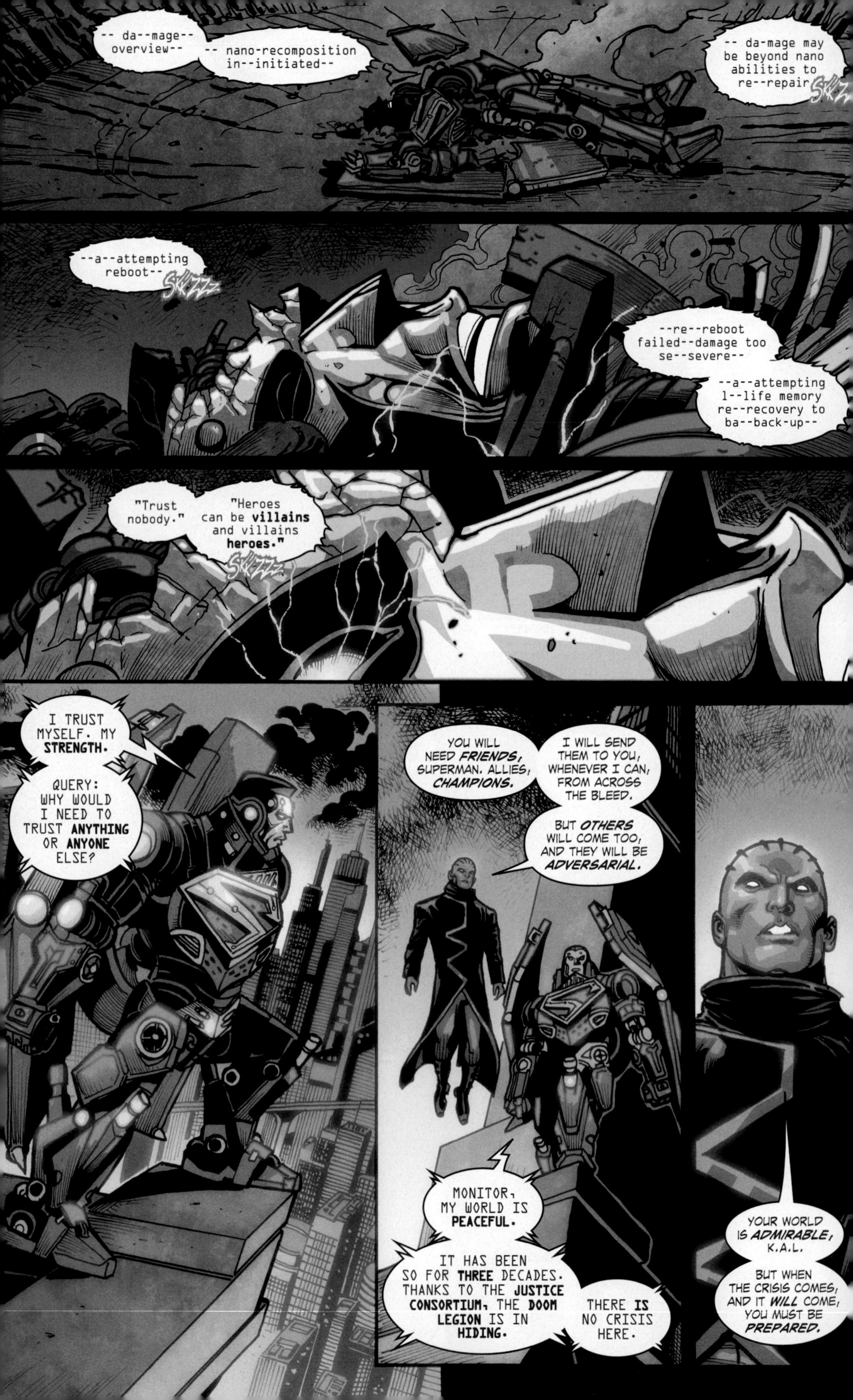
-- da--mage--
overview--
-- nano-recomposition
in--initiated--
-- da-mage may
be beyond nano
abilities to
re--repair
SKKZ
--a--attempting
reboot--
SKKZZZ
--re--reboot
failed--damage too
se--severe--
--a--attempting
l--life memory
re--recovery to
ba--back-up--
"Trust
nobody."
"Heroes
can be villains
and villains
heroes."
SKKZZZ
I TRUST
MYSELF. MY
STRENGTH.
QUERY:
WHY WOULD
I NEED TO
TRUST ANYTHING
OR ANYONE
ELSE?
YOU WILL
NEED FRIENDS,
SUPERMAN. ALLIES,
CHAMPIONS.
I WILL SEND
THEM TO YOU,
WHENEVER I CAN,
FROM ACROSS
THE BLEED.
BUT OTHERS
WILL COME TOO,
AND THEY WILL BE
ADVERSARIAL.
MONITOR,
MY WORLD IS
PEACEFUL.
IT HAS BEEN
SO FOR THREE DECADES.
THANKS TO THE JUSTICE
CONSORTIUM, THE DOOM
LEGION IS IN
HIDING.
THERE IS
NO CRISIS
HERE.
YOUR WORLD
IS ADMIRABLE,
K.A.L.
BUT WHEN
THE CRISIS COMES,
AND IT WILL COME,
YOU MUST BE
PREPARED.

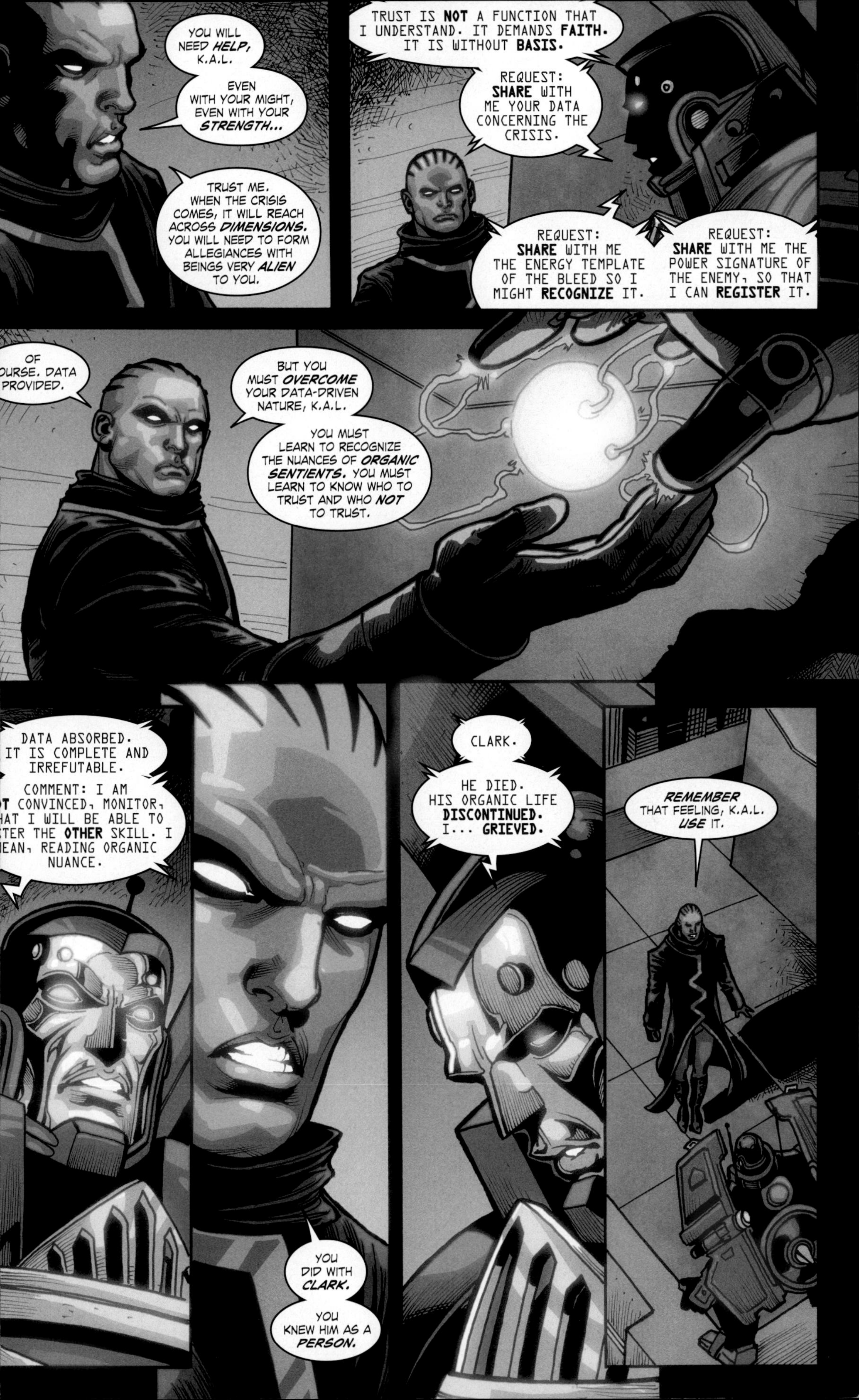
YOU WILL NEED HELP, K.A.L.
EVEN WITH YOUR MIGHT, EVEN WITH YOUR STRENGTH...
TRUST ME. WHEN THE CRISIS COMES, IT WILL REACH ACROSS DIMENSIONS. YOU WILL NEED TO FORM ALLEGIANCES WITH BEINGS VERY ALIEN TO YOU.
TRUST IS NOT A FUNCTION THAT I UNDERSTAND. IT DEMANDS FAITH. IT IS WITHOUT BASIS.
REQUEST: SHARE WITH ME YOUR DATA CONCERNING THE CRISIS.
REQUEST: SHARE WITH ME THE ENERGY TEMPLATE OF THE BLEED SO I MIGHT RECOGNIZE IT.
REQUEST: SHARE WITH ME THE POWER SIGNATURE OF THE ENEMY, SO THAT I CAN REGISTER IT.
OF OURSE. DATA PROVIDED.
BUT YOU MUST OVERCOME YOUR DATA-DRIVEN NATURE, K.A.L.
YOU MUST LEARN TO RECOGNIZE THE NUANCES OF ORGANIC SENTIENTS. YOU MUST LEARN TO KNOW WHO TO TRUST AND WHO NOT TO TRUST.
DATA ABSORBED. IT IS COMPLETE AND IRREFUTABLE.
COMMENT: I AM OT CONVINCED, MONITOR, HAT I WILL BE ABLE TO TER THE OTHER SKILL. I EAN, READING ORGANIC NUANCE.
YOU DID WITH CLARK.
YOU KNEW HIM AS A PERSON.
CLARK.
HE DIED. HIS ORGANIC LIFE DISCONTINUED. I... GRIEVED.
REMEMBER THAT FEELING, K.A.L. USE IT.

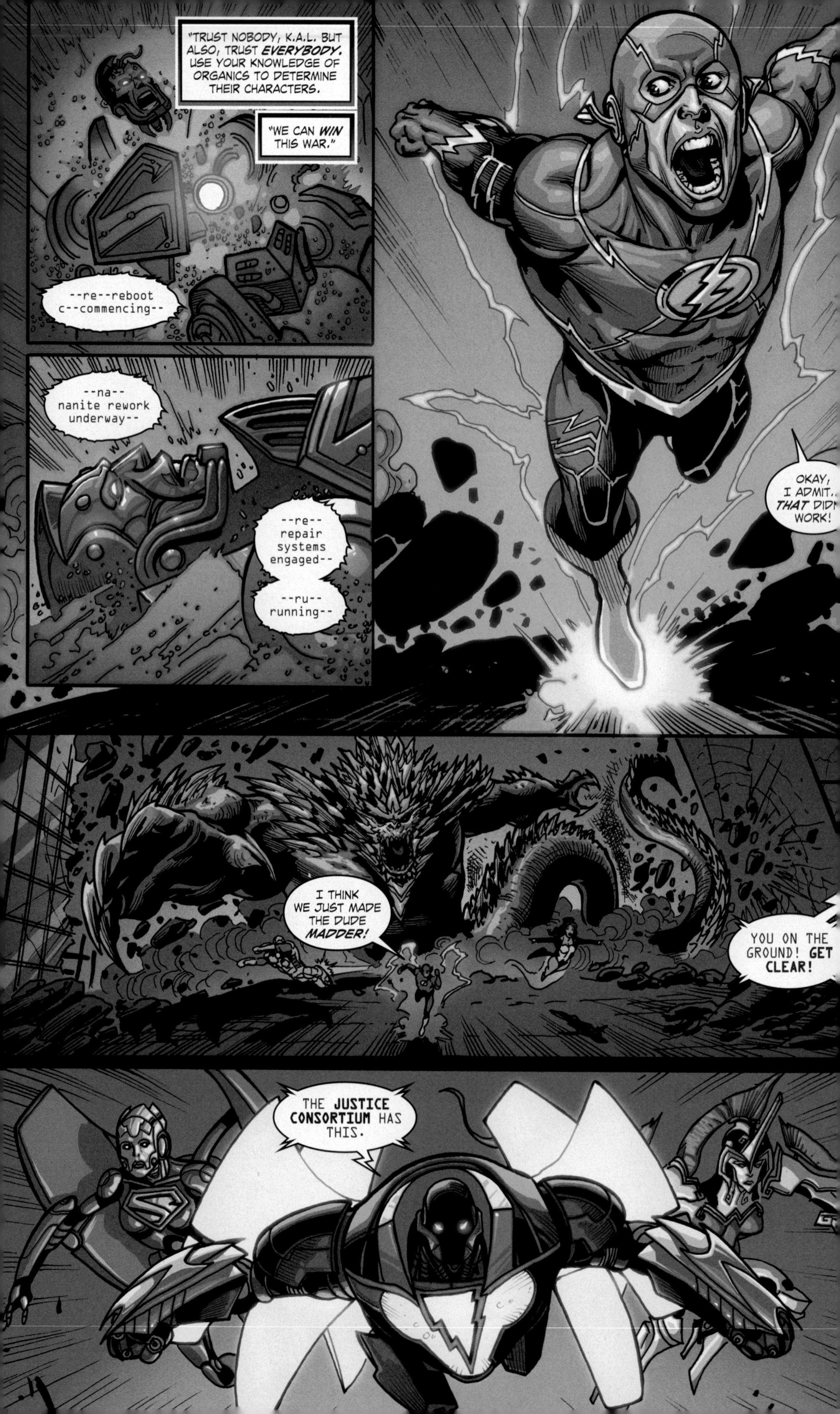
"TRUST NOBODY, K.A.L. BUT ALSO, TRUST *EVERYBODY.* USE YOUR KNOWLEDGE OF ORGANICS TO DETERMINE THEIR CHARACTERS.
"WE CAN *WIN* THIS WAR."
--re--reboot c--commencing--
--na-- nanite rework underway--
--re-- repair systems engaged--
--ru-- running--
OKAY, I ADMIT... *THAT* DIDN'T WORK!
I THINK WE JUST MADE THE DUDE *MADDER!*
YOU ON THE GROUND! **GET CLEAR!**
THE **JUSTICE CONSORTIUM** HAS THIS.

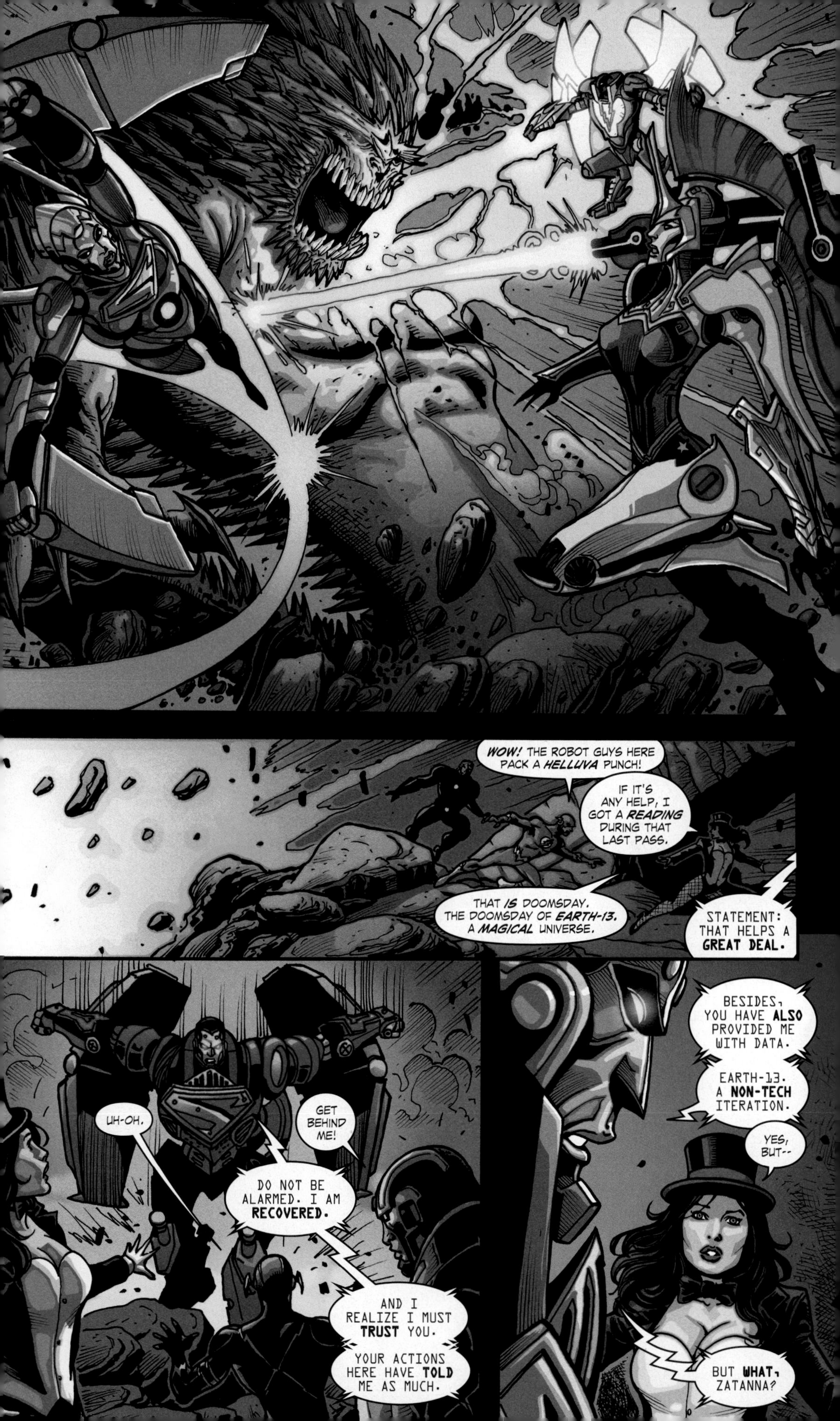
WOW! THE ROBOT GUYS HERE PACK A HELLUVA PUNCH!
IF IT'S ANY HELP, I GOT A READING DURING THAT LAST PASS.
THAT IS DOOMSDAY. THE DOOMSDAY OF EARTH-13. A MAGICAL UNIVERSE.
STATEMENT: THAT HELPS A GREAT DEAL.
UH-OH.
GET BEHIND ME!
DO NOT BE ALARMED. I AM RECOVERED.
AND I REALIZE I MUST TRUST YOU.
YOUR ACTIONS HERE HAVE TOLD ME AS MUCH.
BESIDES, YOU HAVE ALSO PROVIDED ME WITH DATA.
EARTH-13. A NON-TECH ITERATION.
YES, BUT--
BUT WHAT, ZATANNA?

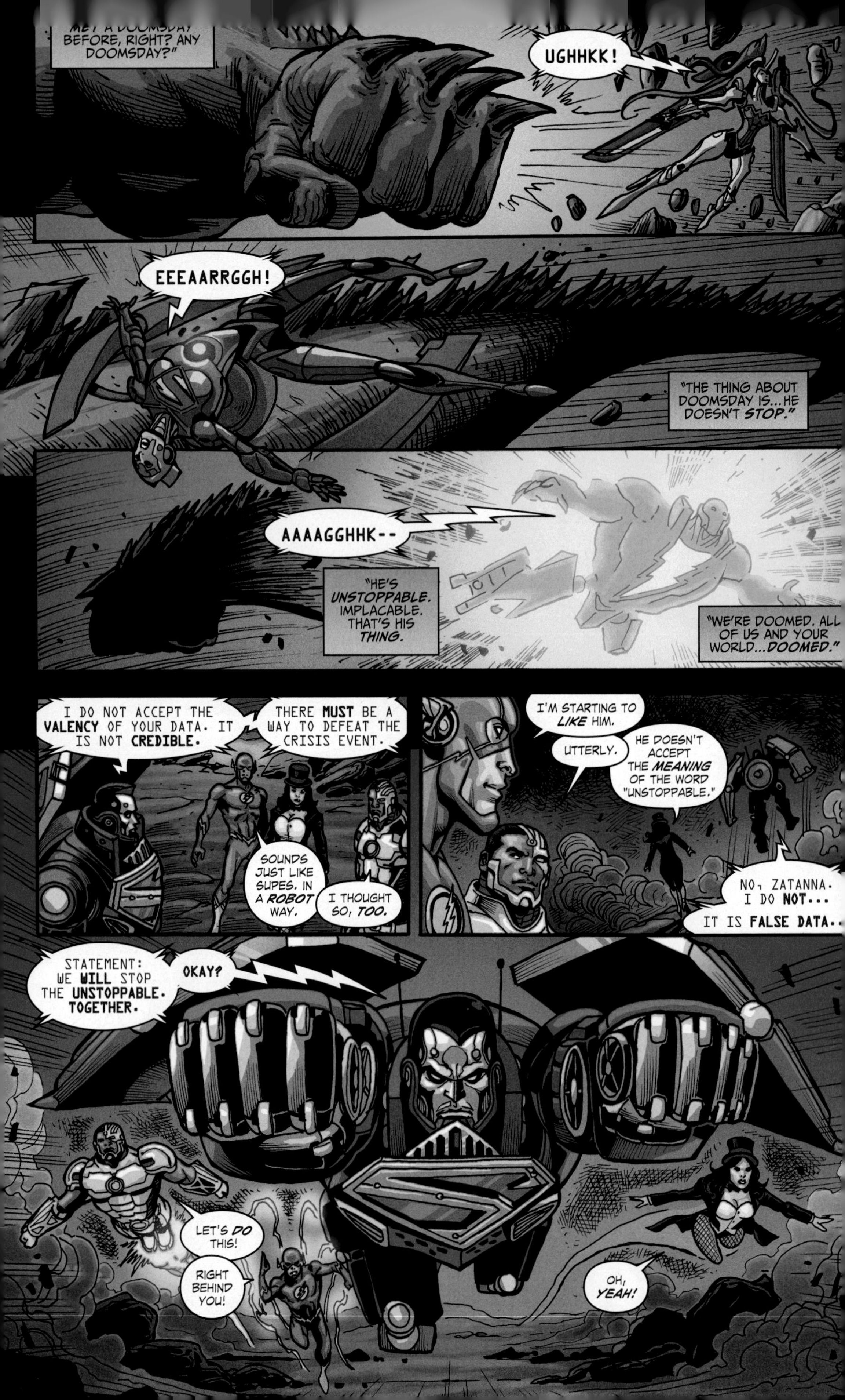

BEFORE, RIGHT? ANY DOOMSDAY?"
UGHHKK!
EEEAARRGGH!
"THE THING ABOUT DOOMSDAY IS...HE DOESN'T STOP."
AAAAGGHHK--
"HE'S UNSTOPPABLE. IMPLACABLE. THAT'S HIS THING.
"WE'RE DOOMED. ALL OF US AND YOUR WORLD...DOOMED."
I DO NOT ACCEPT THE VALENCY OF YOUR DATA. IT IS NOT CREDIBLE.
THERE MUST BE A WAY TO DEFEAT THE CRISIS EVENT.
SOUNDS JUST LIKE SUPES. IN A ROBOT WAY.
I THOUGHT SO, TOO.
I'M STARTING TO LIKE HIM.
UTTERLY.
HE DOESN'T ACCEPT THE MEANING OF THE WORD "UNSTOPPABLE."
NO, ZATANNA. I DO NOT...
IT IS FALSE DATA..
STATEMENT: WE WILL STOP THE UNSTOPPABLE. TOGETHER.
OKAY?
LET'S DO THIS!
RIGHT BEHIND YOU!
OH, YEAH!

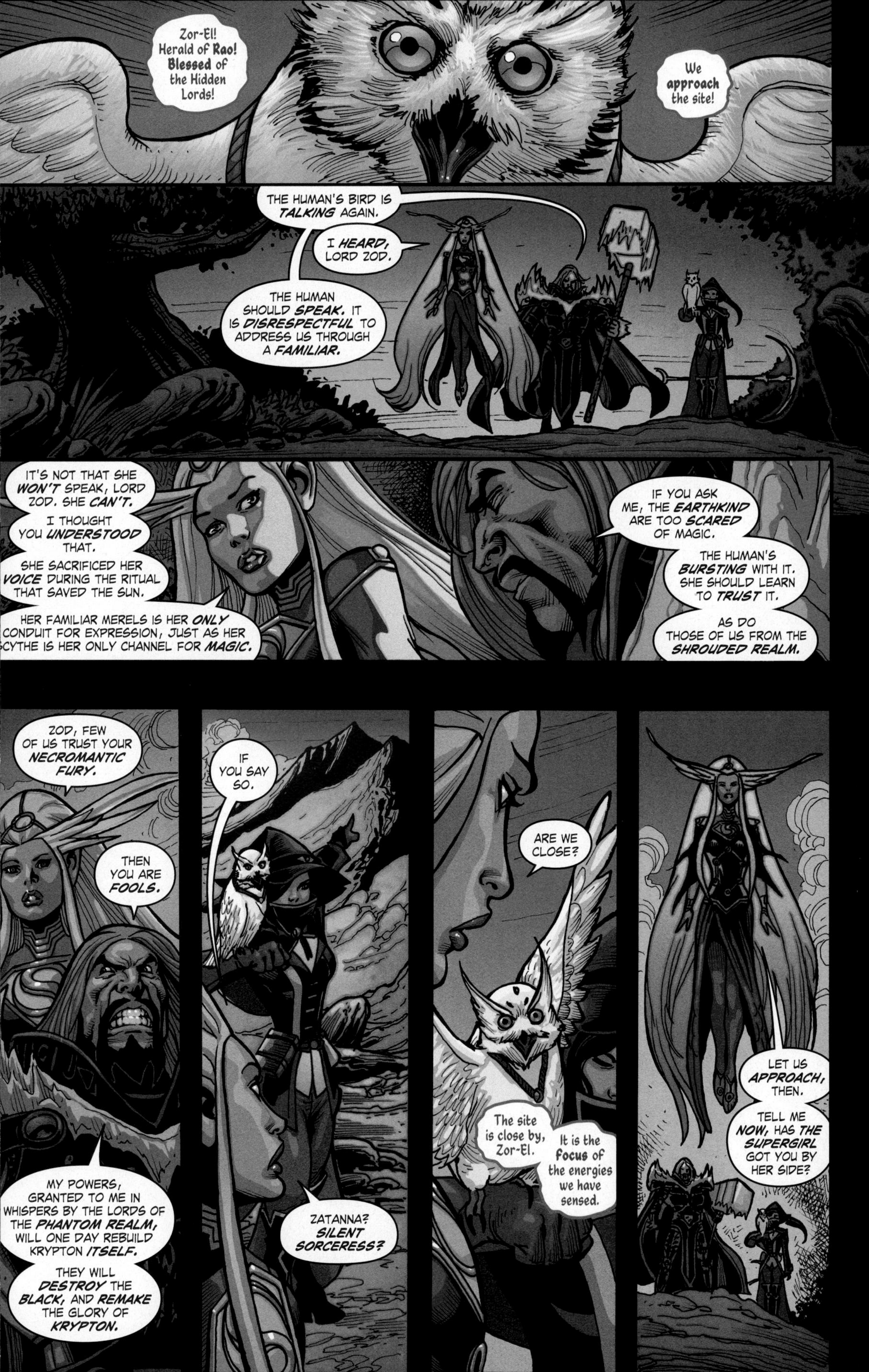
Zor-El! Herald of Rao! Blessed of the Hidden Lords!
We approach the site!
THE HUMAN'S BIRD IS TALKING AGAIN.
I HEARD, LORD ZOD.
THE HUMAN SHOULD SPEAK. IT IS DISRESPECTFUL TO ADDRESS US THROUGH A FAMILIAR.
IT'S NOT THAT SHE WON'T SPEAK, LORD ZOD. SHE CAN'T.
I THOUGHT YOU UNDERSTOOD THAT.
SHE SACRIFICED HER VOICE DURING THE RITUAL THAT SAVED THE SUN.
HER FAMILIAR MERELS IS HER ONLY CONDUIT FOR EXPRESSION, JUST AS HER SCYTHE IS HER ONLY CHANNEL FOR MAGIC.
IF YOU ASK ME, THE EARTHKIND ARE TOO SCARED OF MAGIC.
THE HUMAN'S BURSTING WITH IT. SHE SHOULD LEARN TO TRUST IT.
AS DO THOSE OF US FROM THE SHROUDED REALM.
ZOD, FEW OF US TRUST YOUR NECROMANTIC FURY.
THEN YOU ARE FOOLS.
MY POWERS, GRANTED TO ME IN WHISPERS BY THE LORDS OF THE PHANTOM REALM, WILL ONE DAY REBUILD KRYPTON ITSELF.
THEY WILL DESTROY THE BLACK, AND REMAKE THE GLORY OF KRYPTON.
IF YOU SAY SO.
ZATANNA? SILENT SORCERESS?
ARE WE CLOSE?
The site is close by, Zor-El.
It is the focus of the energies we have sensed.
LET US APPROACH, THEN.
TELL ME NOW, HAS THE SUPERGIRL GOT YOU BY HER SIDE?

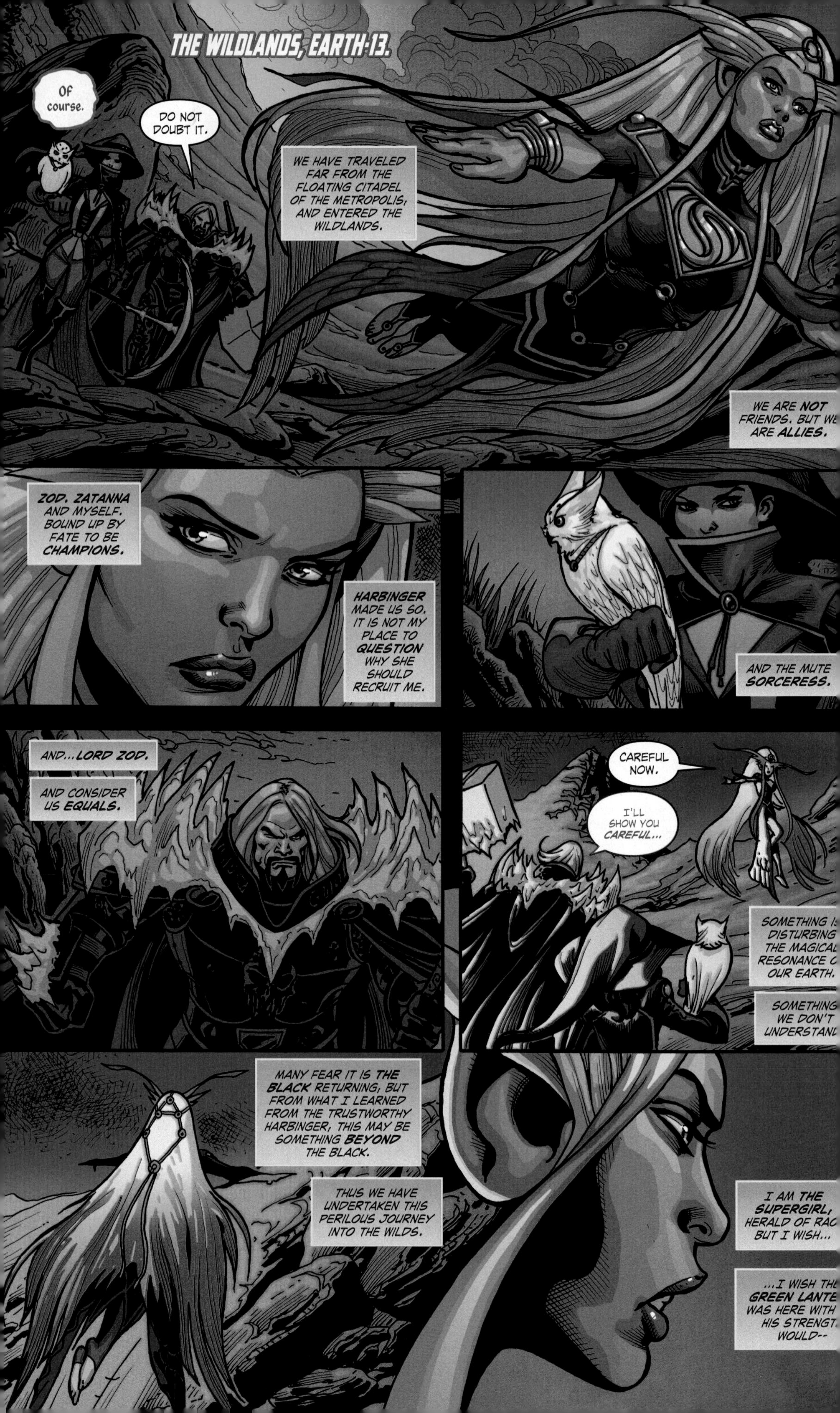
THE WILDLANDS, EARTH-13.
Of course.
DO NOT DOUBT IT.
WE HAVE TRAVELED FAR FROM THE FLOATING CITADEL OF THE METROPOLIS, AND ENTERED THE WILDLANDS.
WE ARE NOT FRIENDS. BUT WE ARE ALLIES.
ZOD. ZATANNA AND MYSELF. BOUND UP BY FATE TO BE CHAMPIONS.
HARBINGER MADE US SO. IT IS NOT MY PLACE TO QUESTION WHY SHE SHOULD RECRUIT ME.
AND THE MUTE SORCERESS.
AND...LORD ZOD.
AND CONSIDER US EQUALS.
CAREFUL NOW.
I'LL SHOW YOU CAREFUL...
SOMETHING IS DISTURBING THE MAGICAL RESONANCE OF OUR EARTH.
SOMETHING WE DON'T UNDERSTAND.
MANY FEAR IT IS THE BLACK RETURNING; BUT FROM WHAT I LEARNED FROM THE TRUSTWORTHY HARBINGER, THIS MAY BE SOMETHING BEYOND THE BLACK.
THUS WE HAVE UNDERTAKEN THIS PERILOUS JOURNEY INTO THE WILDS.
I AM THE SUPERGIRL, HERALD OF RAO
BUT I WISH...
...I WISH THE GREEN LANTERN WAS HERE WITH HIS STRENGTH WOULD--

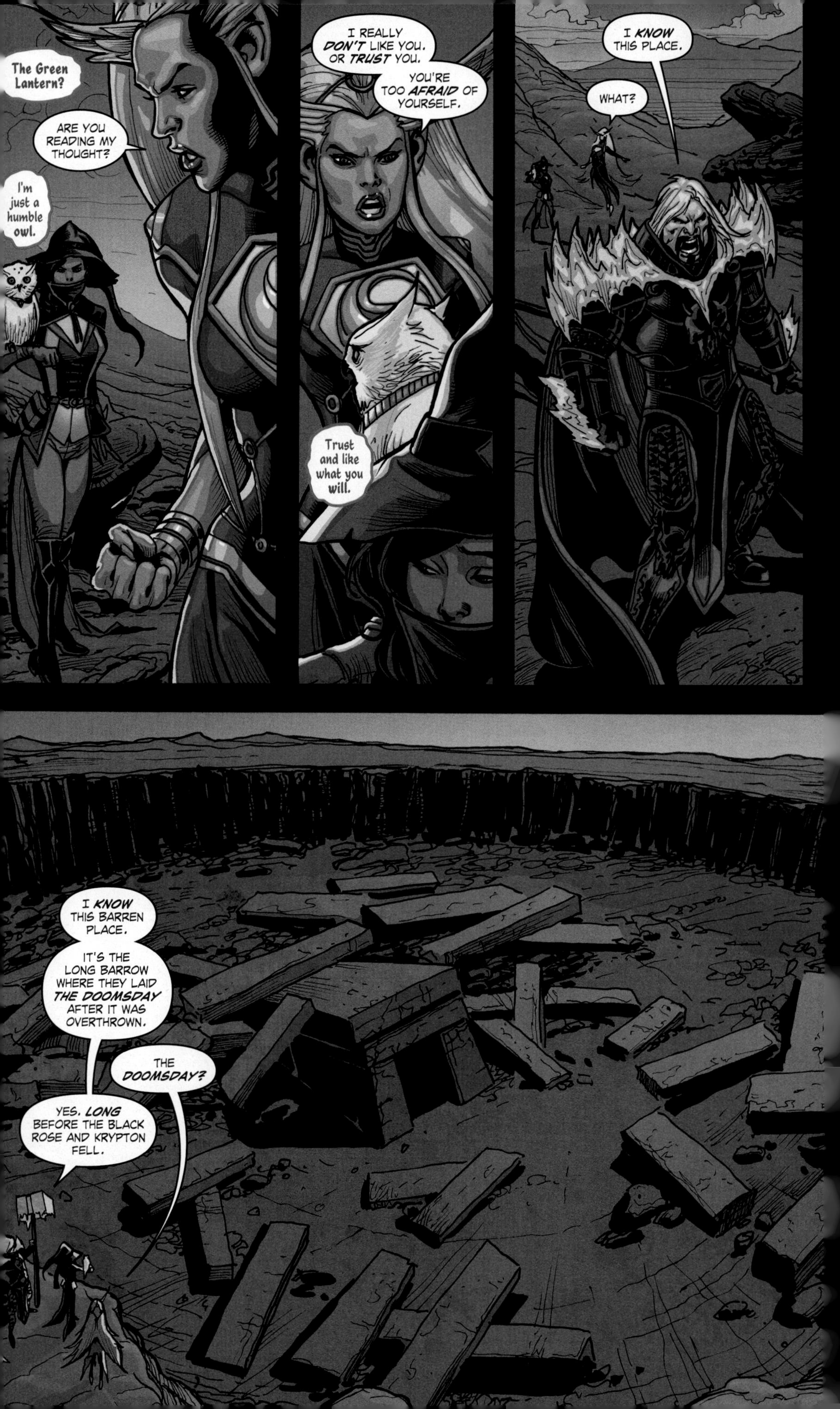

The Green Lantern?
ARE YOU READING MY THOUGHT?
I'm just a humble owl.
I REALLY DON'T LIKE YOU. OR TRUST YOU.
YOU'RE TOO AFRAID OF YOURSELF.
Trust and like what you will.
I KNOW THIS PLACE.
WHAT?
I KNOW THIS BARREN PLACE.
IT'S THE LONG BARROW WHERE THEY LAID THE DOOMSDAY AFTER IT WAS OVERTHROWN.
THE DOOMSDAY?
YES. LONG BEFORE THE BLACK ROSE AND KRYPTON FELL.

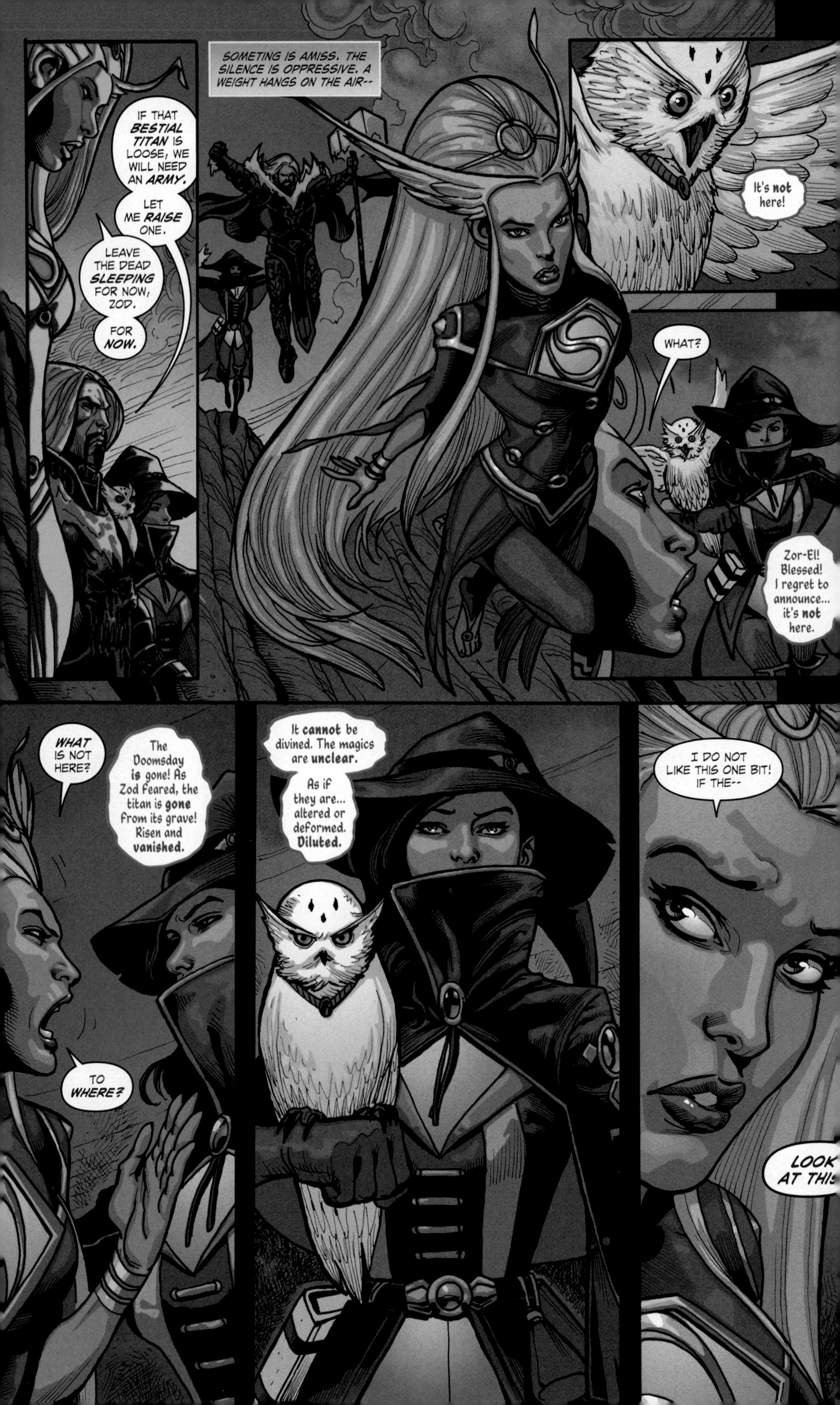

SOMETING IS AMISS. THE SILENCE IS OPPRESSIVE. A WEIGHT HANGS ON THE AIR--
IF THAT BESTIAL TITAN IS LOOSE, WE WILL NEED AN ARMY.
LET ME RAISE ONE.
LEAVE THE DEAD SLEEPING FOR NOW, ZOD.
FOR NOW.
It's not here!
WHAT?
Zor-El! Blessed! I regret to announce... it's not here.
WHAT IS NOT HERE?
The Doomsday is gone! As Zod feared, the titan is gone from its grave! Risen and vanished.
TO WHERE?
It cannot be divined. The magics are unclear.
As if they are... altered or deformed. Diluted.
I DO NOT LIKE THIS ONE BIT! IF THE--
LOOK AT THIS

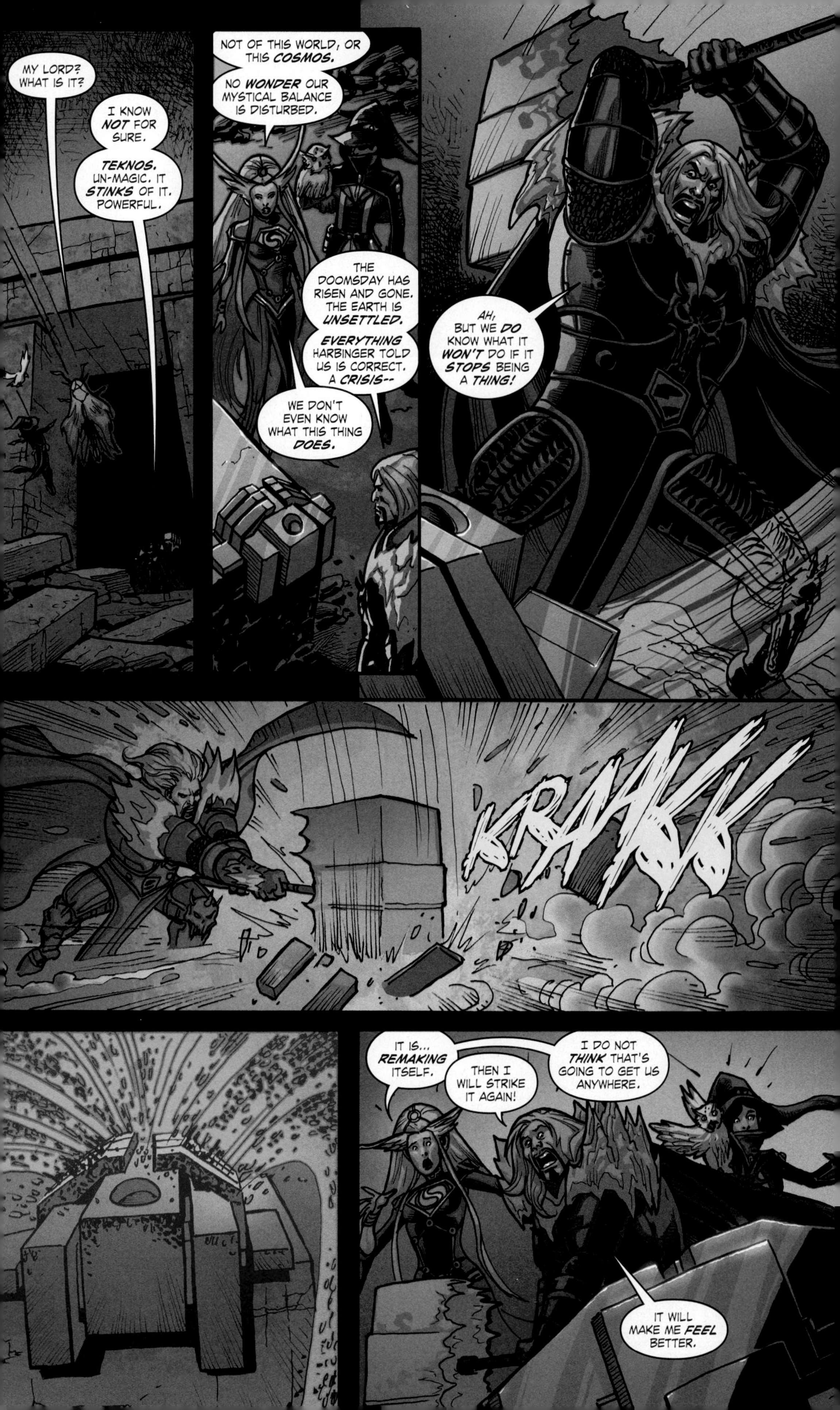

MY LORD? WHAT IS IT?
I KNOW NOT FOR SURE.
TEKNOS. UN-MAGIC. IT STINKS OF IT. POWERFUL.
NOT OF THIS WORLD, OR THIS COSMOS.
NO WONDER OUR MYSTICAL BALANCE IS DISTURBED.
THE DOOMSDAY HAS RISEN AND GONE. THE EARTH IS UNSETTLED.
EVERYTHING HARBINGER TOLD US IS CORRECT. A CRISIS--
WE DON'T EVEN KNOW WHAT THIS THING DOES.
AH, BUT WE DO KNOW WHAT IT WON'T DO IF IT STOPS BEING A THING!
KRAKKK
IT IS... REMAKING ITSELF.
THEN I WILL STRIKE IT AGAIN!
I DO NOT THINK THAT'S GOING TO GET US ANYWHERE.
IT WILL MAKE ME FEEL BETTER.

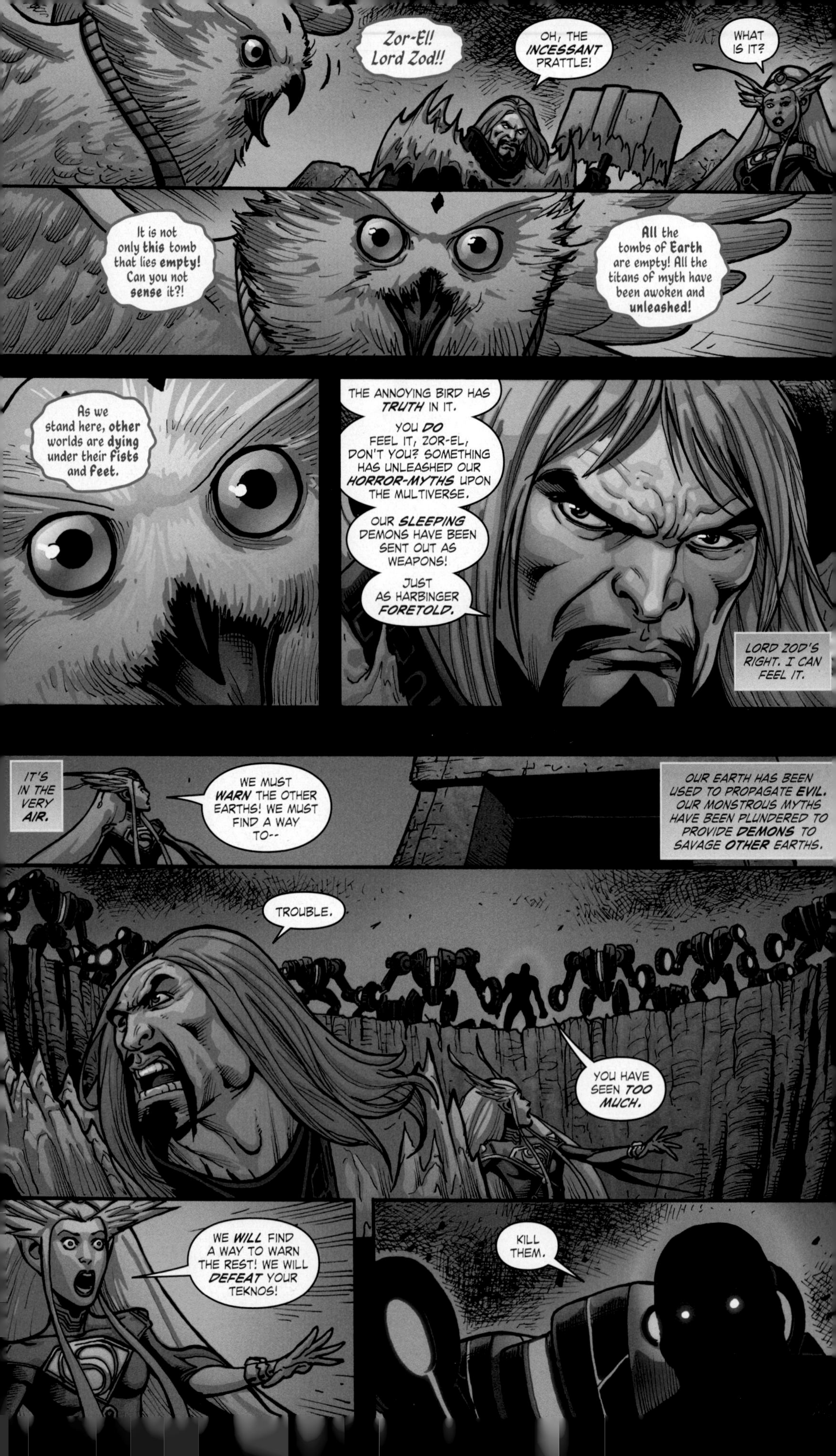
Zor-El! Lord Zod!!
OH, THE INCESSANT PRATTLE!
WHAT IS IT?
It is not only this tomb that lies empty! Can you not sense it?!
All the tombs of Earth are empty! All the titans of myth have been awoken and unleashed!
As we stand here, other worlds are dying under their fists and feet.
THE ANNOYING BIRD HAS TRUTH IN IT.
YOU DO FEEL IT, ZOR-EL, DON'T YOU? SOMETHING HAS UNLEASHED OUR HORROR-MYTHS UPON THE MULTIVERSE.
OUR SLEEPING DEMONS HAVE BEEN SENT OUT AS WEAPONS!
JUST AS HARBINGER FORETOLD.
LORD ZOD'S RIGHT. I CAN FEEL IT.
IT'S IN THE VERY AIR.
WE MUST WARN THE OTHER EARTHS! WE MUST FIND A WAY TO--
OUR EARTH HAS BEEN USED TO PROPAGATE EVIL. OUR MONSTROUS MYTHS HAVE BEEN PLUNDERED TO PROVIDE DEMONS TO SAVAGE OTHER EARTHS.
TROUBLE.
YOU HAVE SEEN TOO MUCH.
WE WILL FIND A WAY TO WARN THE REST! WE WILL DEFEAT YOUR TEKNOS!
KILL THEM.

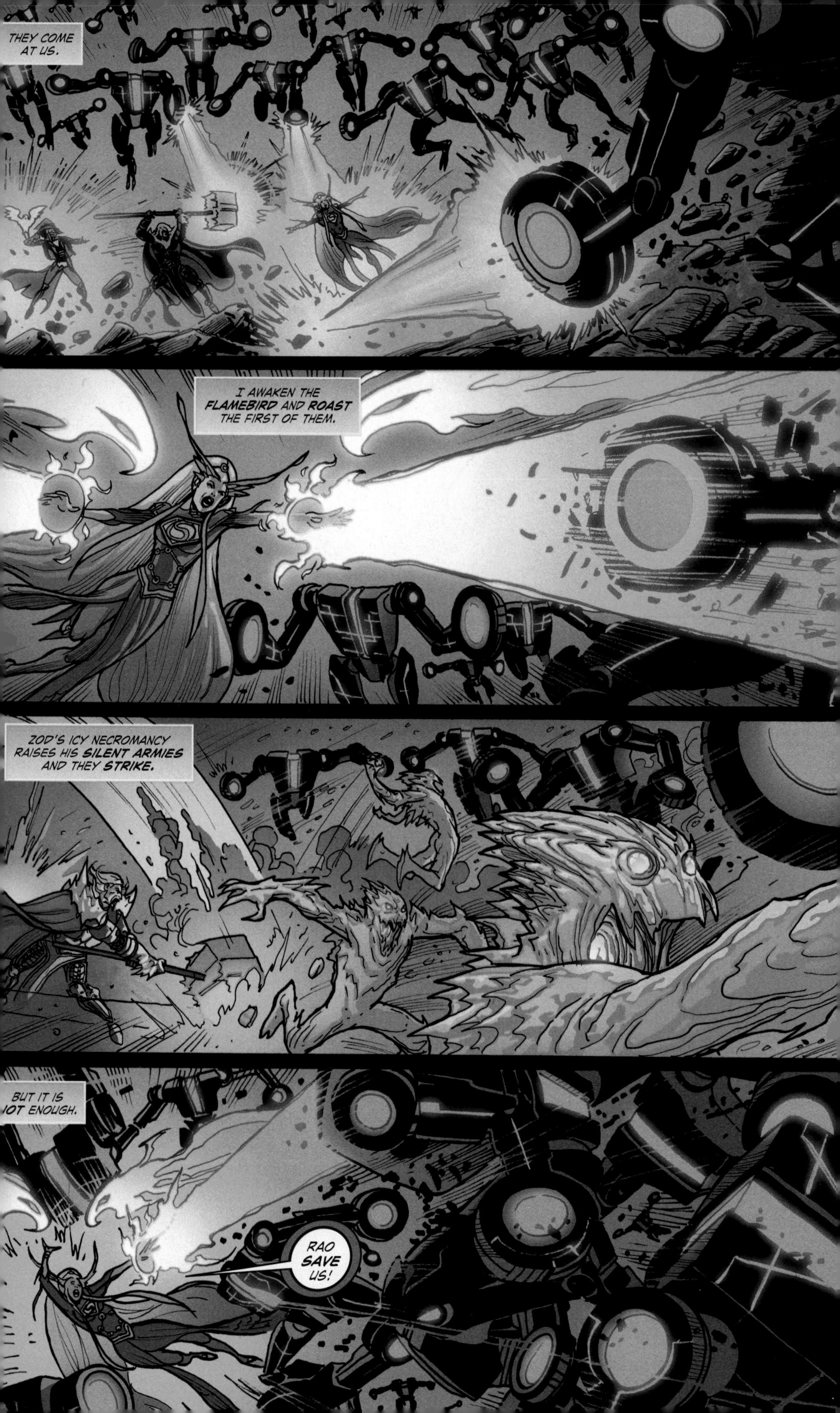
THEY COME AT US.
I AWAKEN THE FLAMEBIRD AND ROAST THE FIRST OF THEM.
ZOD'S ICY NECROMANCY RAISES HIS SILENT ARMIES AND THEY STRIKE.
BUT IT IS NOT ENOUGH.
RAO SAVE US!

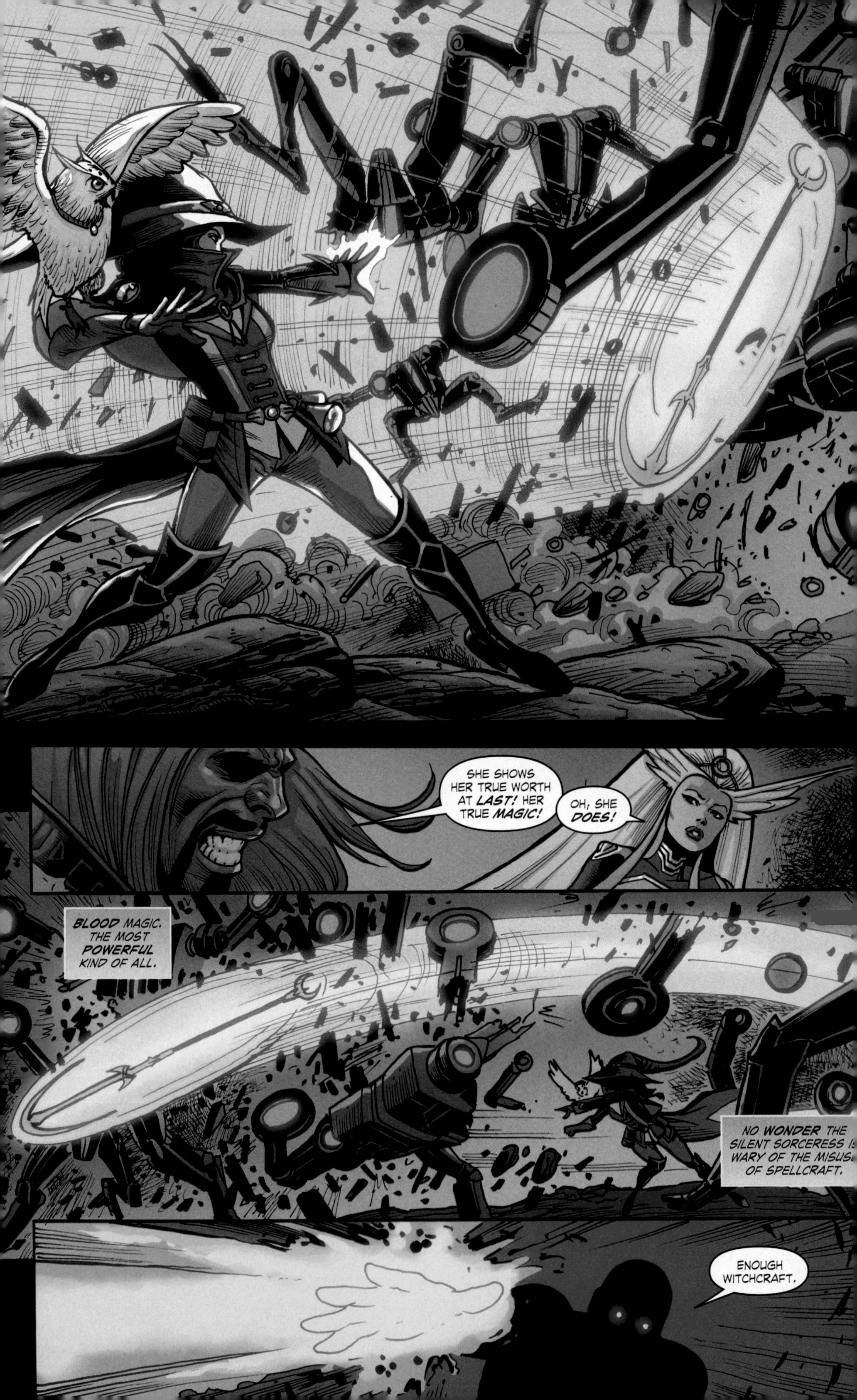
SHE SHOWS HER TRUE WORTH AT LAST! HER TRUE MAGIC!
OH, SHE DOES!
BLOOD MAGIC. THE MOST POWERFUL KIND OF ALL.
NO WONDER THE SILENT SORCERESS IS WARY OF THE MISUSE OF SPELLCRAFT.
ENOUGH WITCHCRAFT.

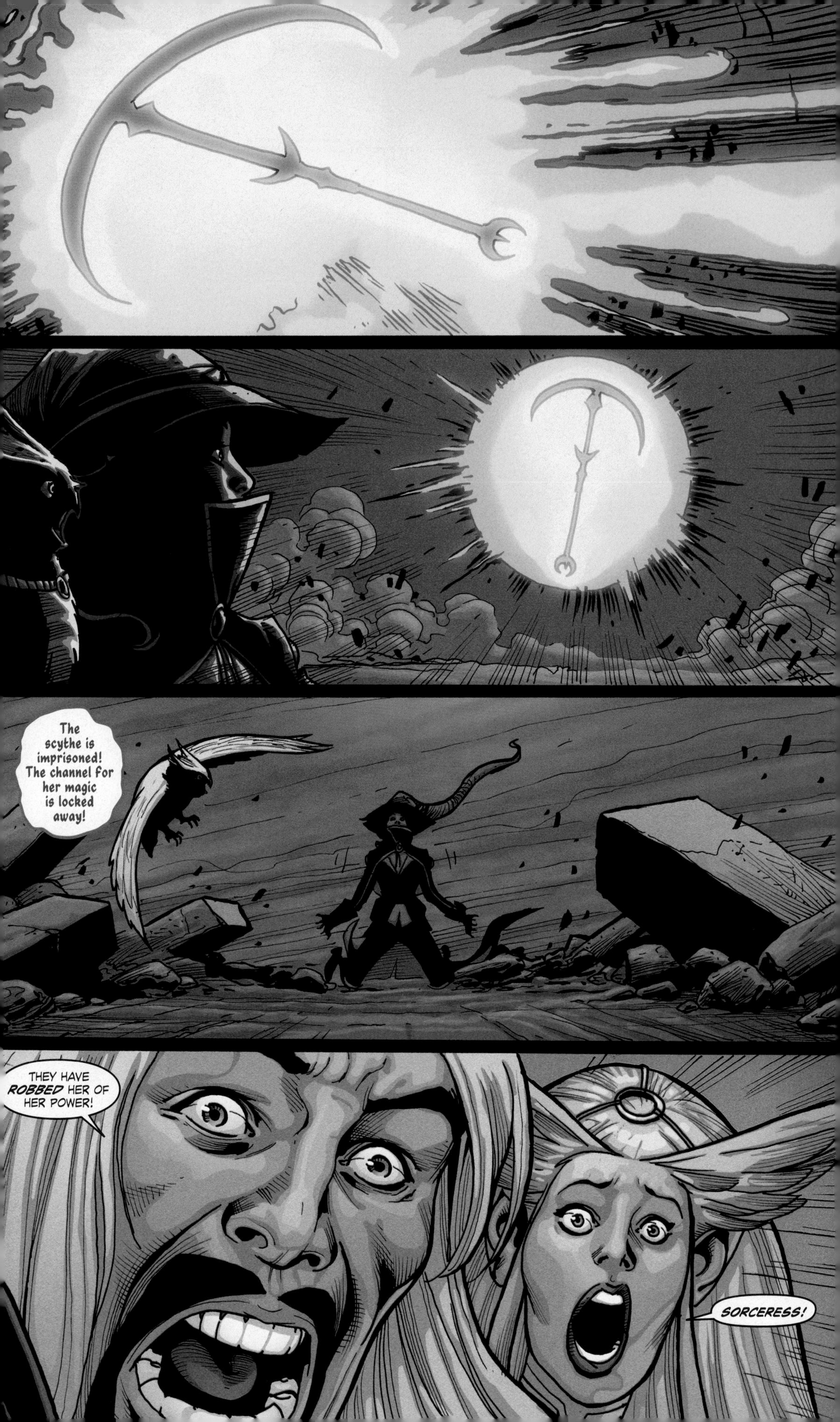
The scythe is imprisoned! The channel for her magic is locked away!
THEY HAVE **ROBBED** HER OF HER POWER!
SORCERESS!

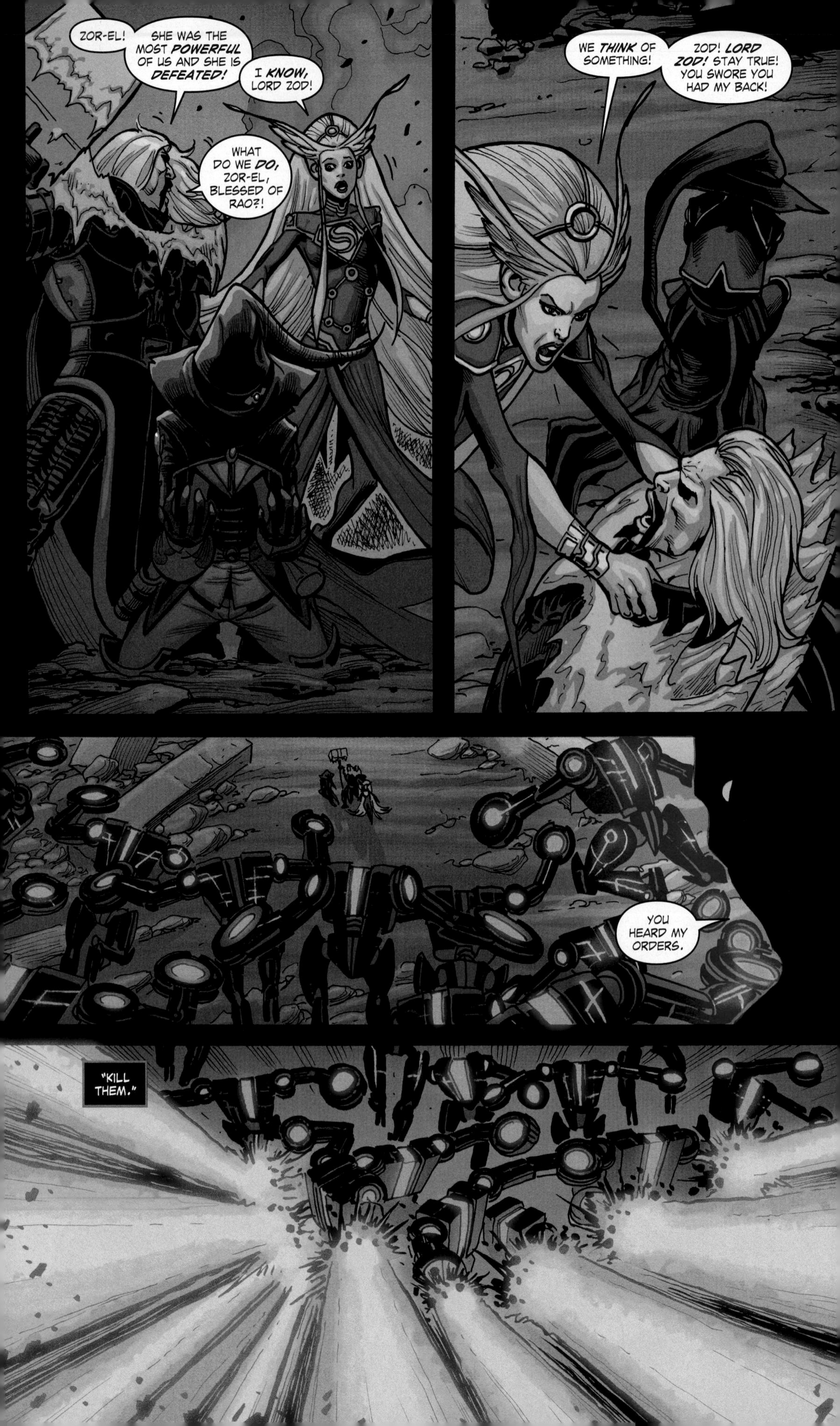
ZOR-EL!
SHE WAS THE MOST POWERFUL OF US AND SHE IS DEFEATED!
I KNOW, LORD ZOD!
WHAT DO WE DO, ZOR-EL, BLESSED OF RAO?!
WE THINK OF SOMETHING!
ZOD! LORD ZOD! STAY TRUE! YOU SWORE YOU HAD MY BACK!
YOU HEARD MY ORDERS.
"KILL THEM."

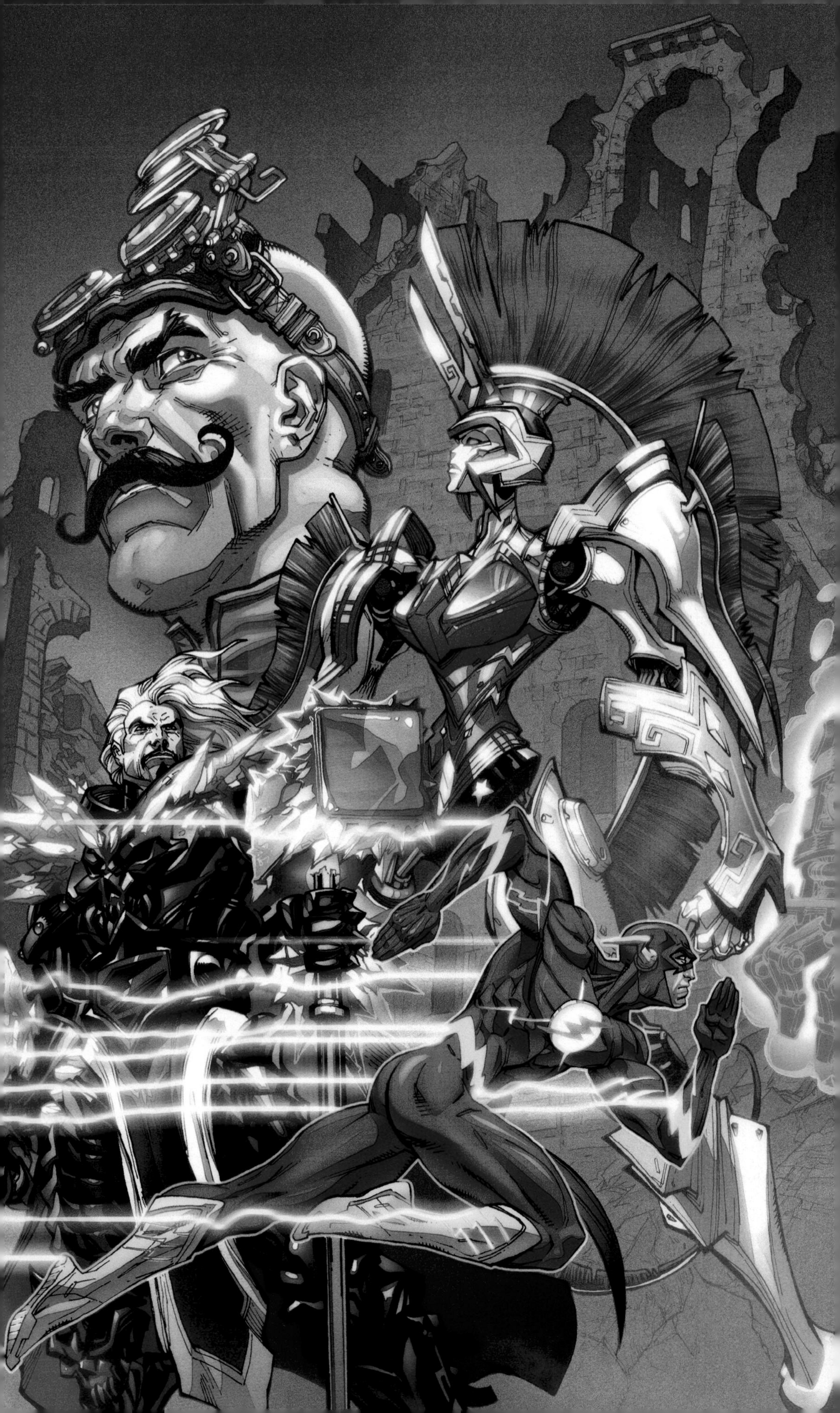

MECHA PART 2

Freddie Williams III **Tom Derenick** Artists **Alejandro Sanchez** Colorist
Cover Art by **Carlos D'Anda**

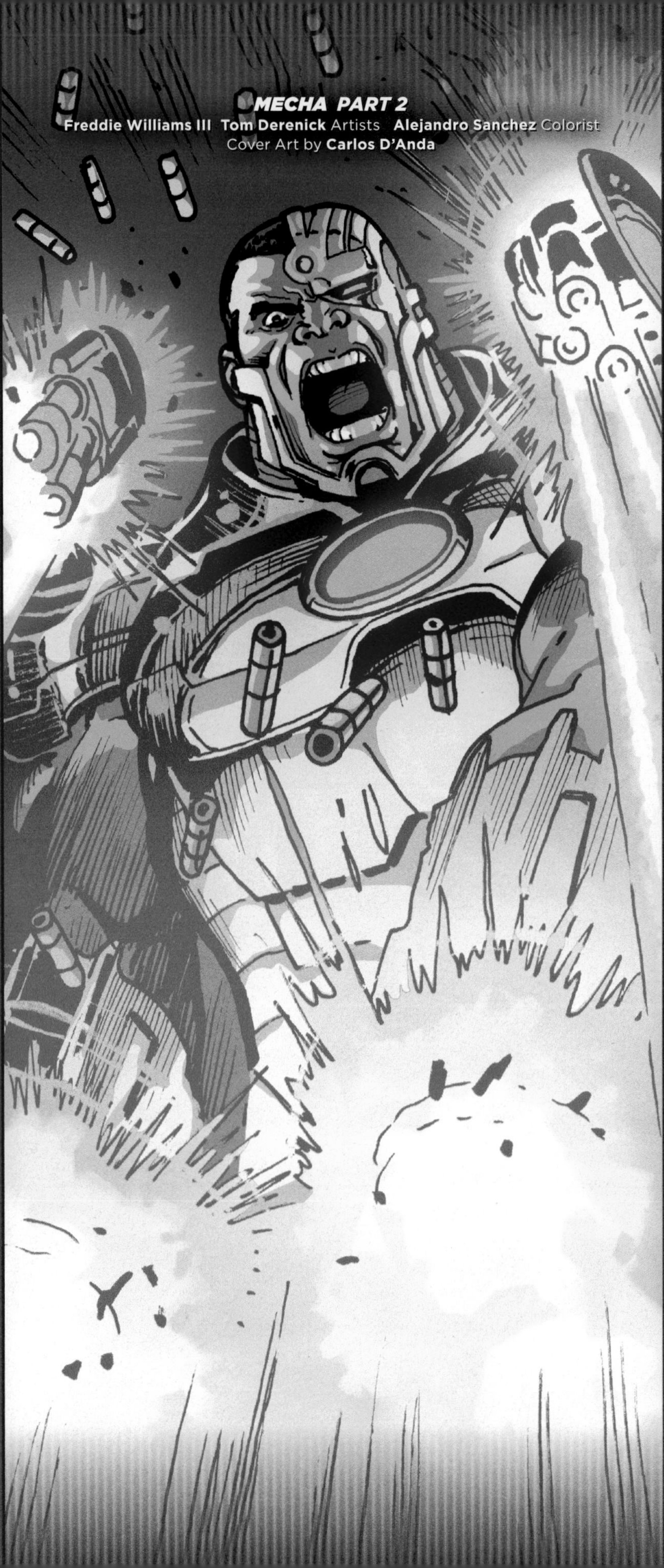

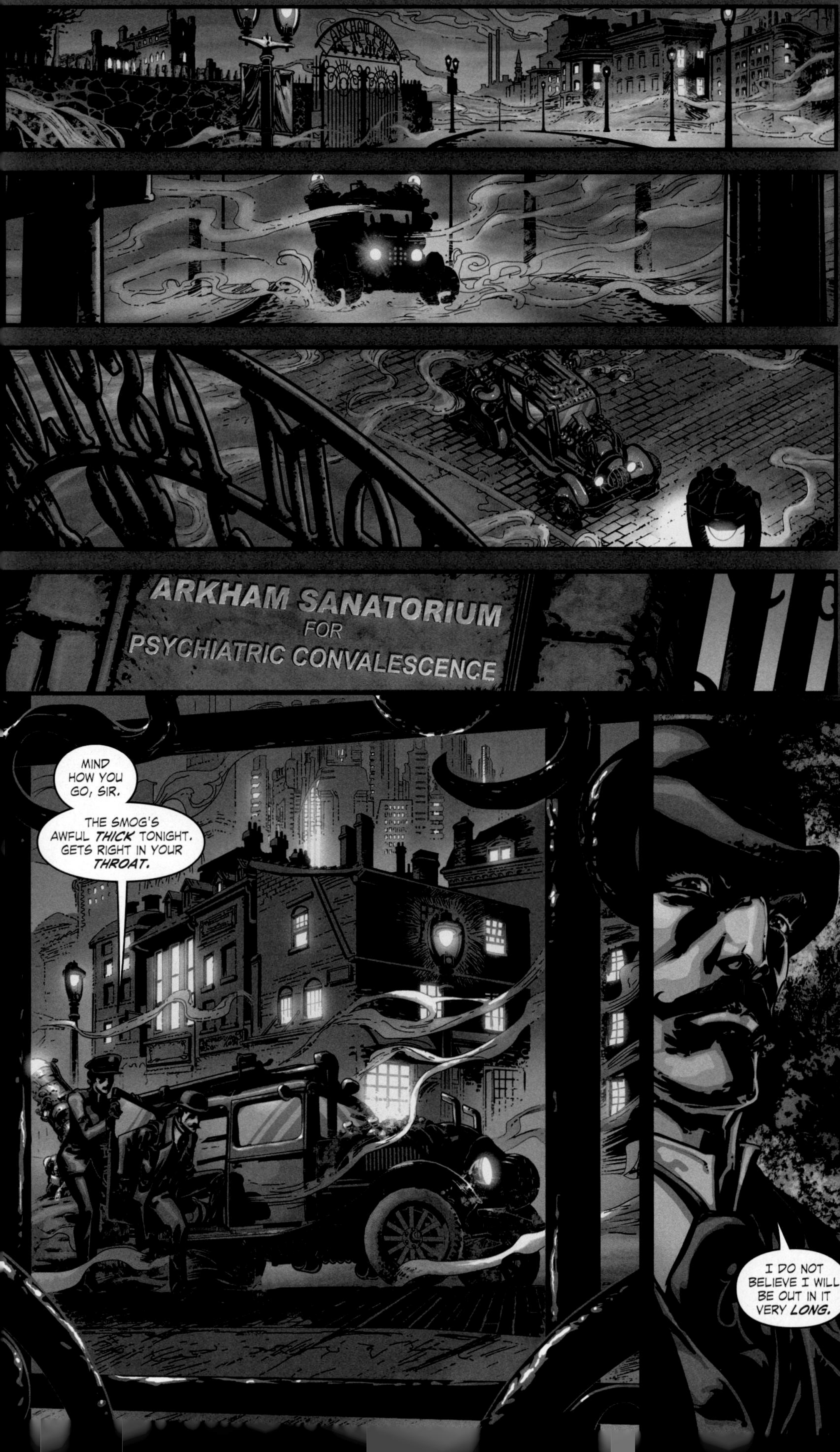
ARKHAM SANATORIUM
FOR
PSYCHIATRIC CONVALESCENCE
MIND HOW YOU GO, SIR.
THE SMOG'S AWFUL THICK TONIGHT. GETS RIGHT IN YOUR THROAT.
I DO NOT BELIEVE I WILL BE OUT IN IT VERY LONG.

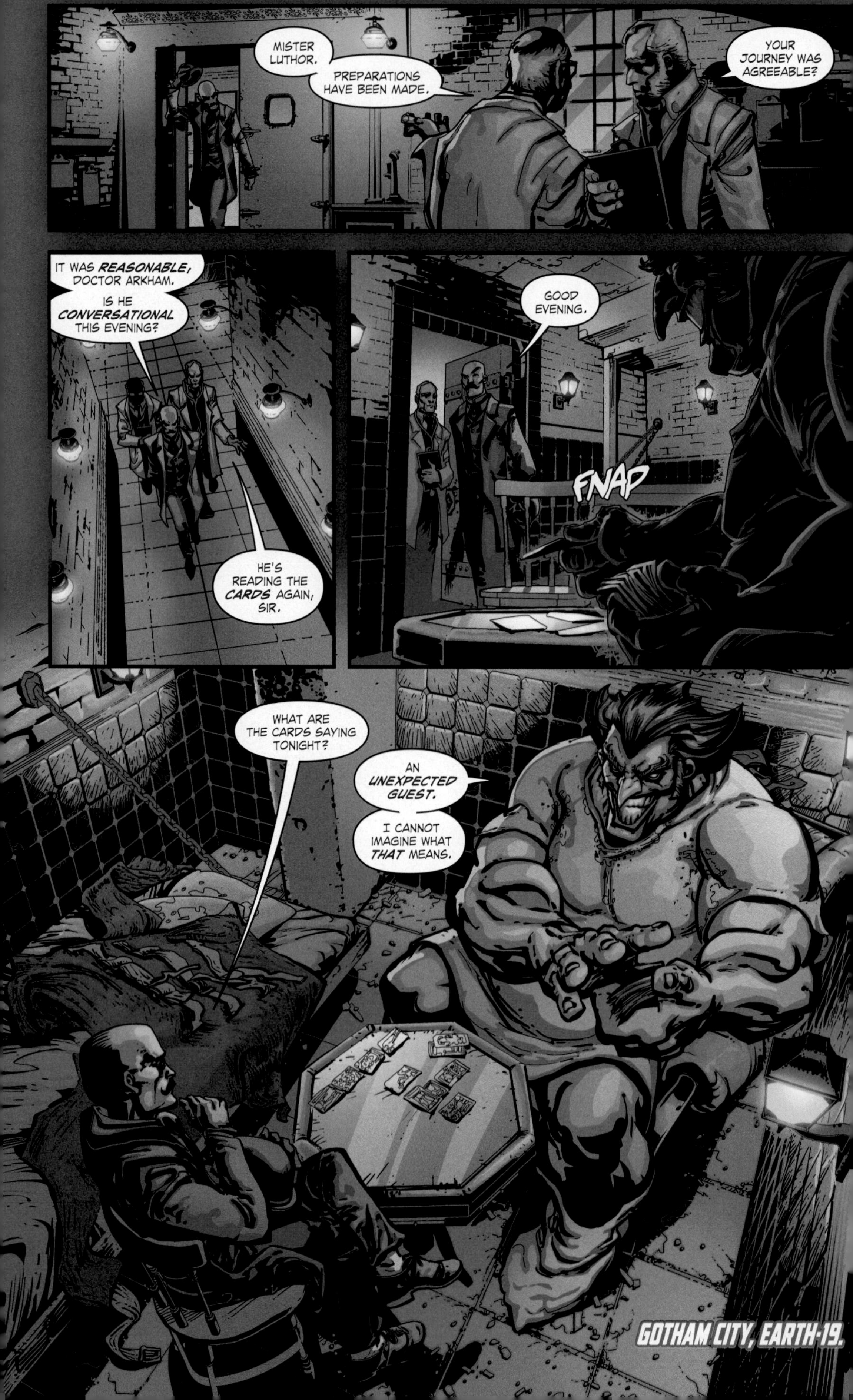
MISTER LUTHOR.
PREPARATIONS HAVE BEEN MADE.
YOUR JOURNEY WAS AGREEABLE?
IT WAS *REASONABLE,* DOCTOR ARKHAM.
IS HE *CONVERSATIONAL* THIS EVENING?
HE'S READING THE *CARDS* AGAIN, SIR.
GOOD EVENING.
FNAP
WHAT ARE THE CARDS SAYING TONIGHT?
AN *UNEXPECTED GUEST.*
I CANNOT IMAGINE WHAT *THAT* MEANS.
GOTHAM CITY, EARTH-19.

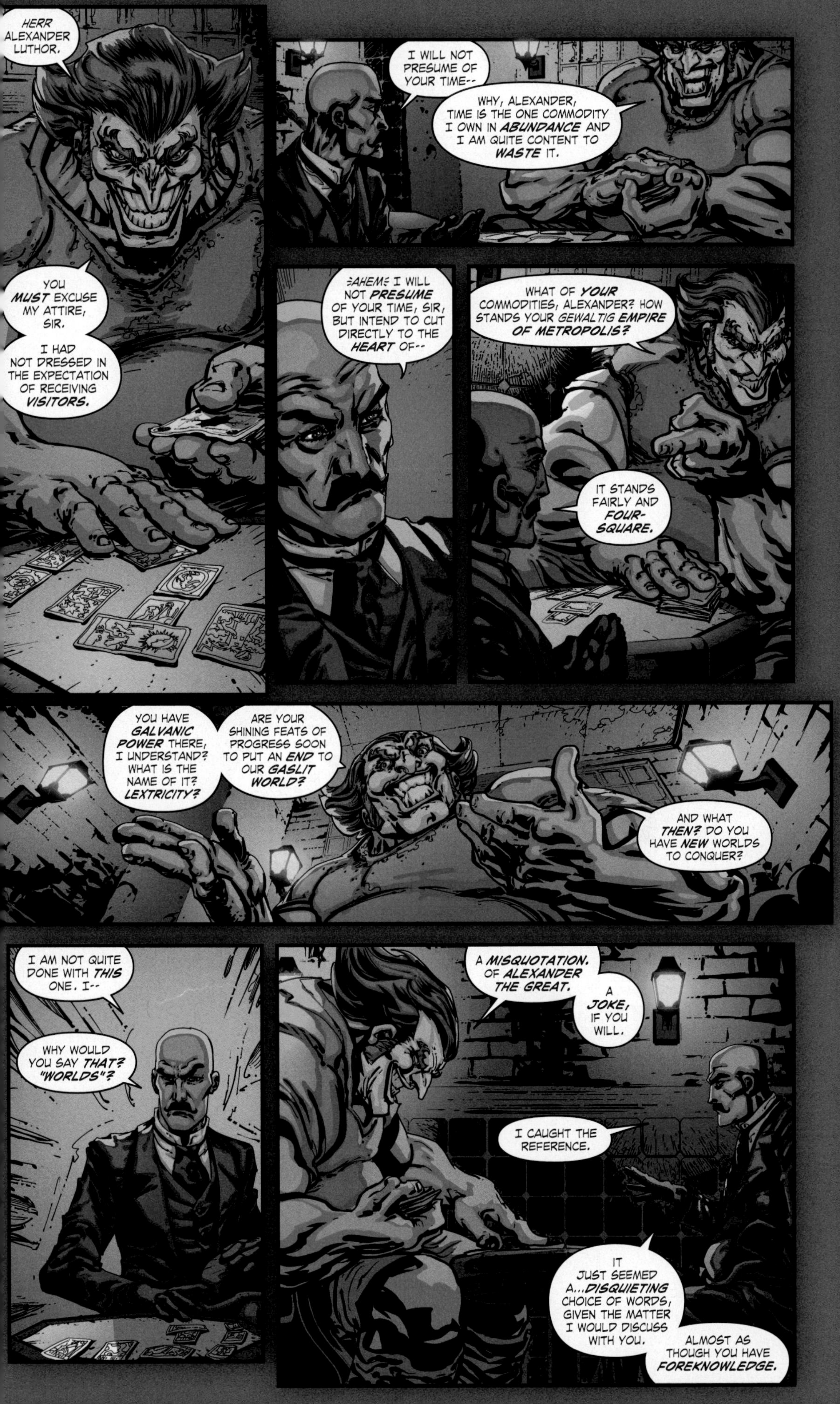
HERR ALEXANDER LUTHOR.
I WILL NOT PRESUME OF YOUR TIME--
WHY, ALEXANDER, TIME IS THE ONE COMMODITY I OWN IN ABUNDANCE AND I AM QUITE CONTENT TO WASTE IT.
YOU MUST EXCUSE MY ATTIRE, SIR.
I HAD NOT DRESSED IN THE EXPECTATION OF RECEIVING VISITORS.
AHEM I WILL NOT PRESUME OF YOUR TIME, SIR, BUT INTEND TO CUT DIRECTLY TO THE HEART OF--
WHAT OF YOUR COMMODITIES, ALEXANDER? HOW STANDS YOUR GEWALTIG EMPIRE OF METROPOLIS?
IT STANDS FAIRLY AND FOUR-SQUARE.
YOU HAVE GALVANIC POWER THERE, I UNDERSTAND? WHAT IS THE NAME OF IT? LEXTRICITY?
ARE YOUR SHINING FEATS OF PROGRESS SOON TO PUT AN END TO OUR GASLIT WORLD?
AND WHAT THEN? DO YOU HAVE NEW WORLDS TO CONQUER?
I AM NOT QUITE DONE WITH THIS ONE. I--
WHY WOULD YOU SAY THAT? "WORLDS"?
A MISQUOTATION. OF ALEXANDER THE GREAT.
A JOKE, IF YOU WILL.
I CAUGHT THE REFERENCE.
IT JUST SEEMED A...DISQUIETING CHOICE OF WORDS, GIVEN THE MATTER I WOULD DISCUSS WITH YOU.
ALMOST AS THOUGH YOU HAVE FOREKNOWLEDGE.

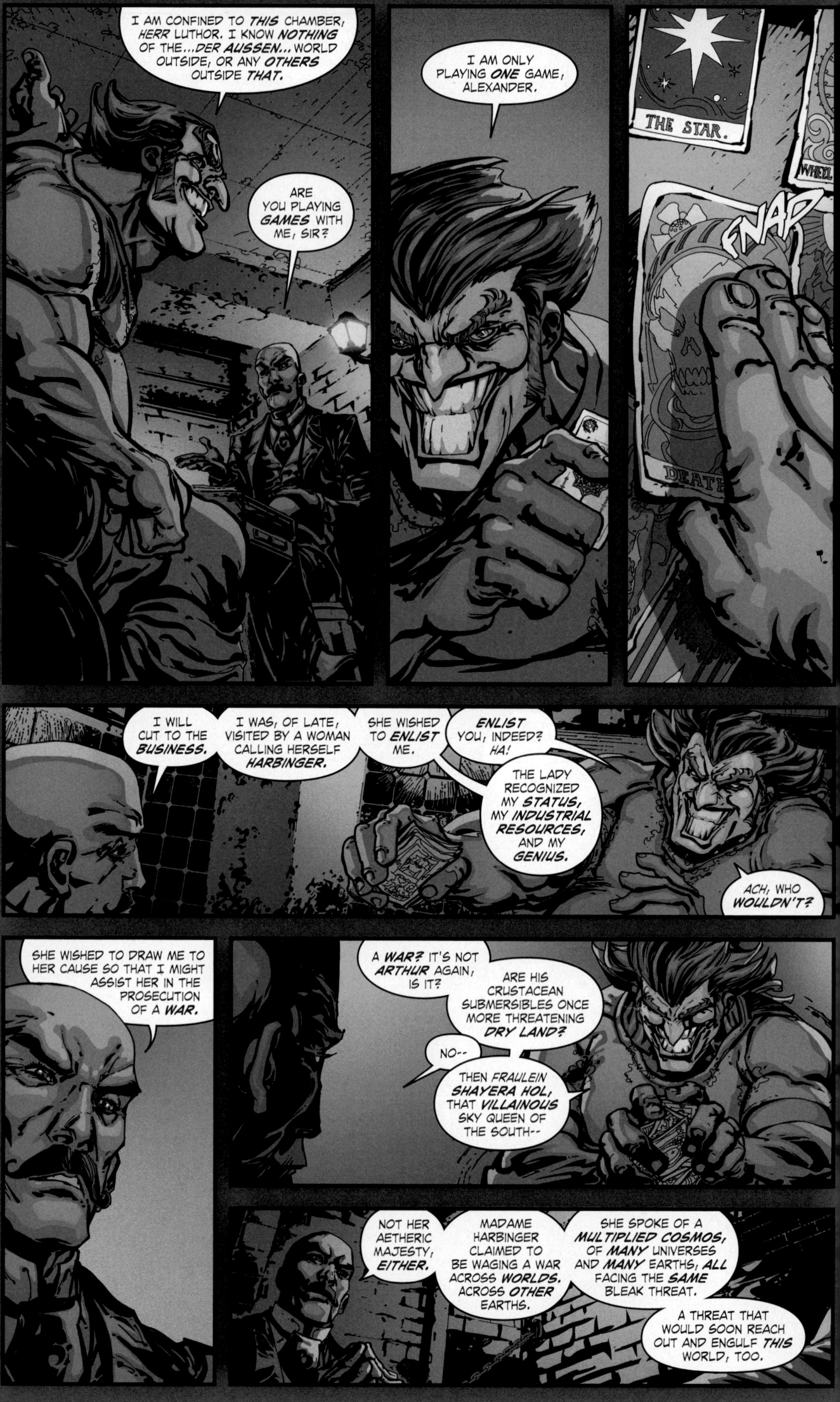
I AM CONFINED TO THIS CHAMBER, HERR LUTHOR. I KNOW NOTHING OF THE...DER AUSSEN...WORLD OUTSIDE, OR ANY OTHERS OUTSIDE THAT.
ARE YOU PLAYING GAMES WITH ME, SIR?
I AM ONLY PLAYING ONE GAME, ALEXANDER.
THE STAR.
WHEEL
FNAP
DEATH
I WILL CUT TO THE BUSINESS.
I WAS, OF LATE, VISITED BY A WOMAN CALLING HERSELF HARBINGER.
SHE WISHED TO ENLIST ME.
ENLIST YOU, INDEED? HA!
THE LADY RECOGNIZED MY STATUS, MY INDUSTRIAL RESOURCES, AND MY GENIUS.
ACH, WHO WOULDN'T?
SHE WISHED TO DRAW ME TO HER CAUSE SO THAT I MIGHT ASSIST HER IN THE PROSECUTION OF A WAR.
A WAR? IT'S NOT ARTHUR AGAIN, IS IT?
ARE HIS CRUSTACEAN SUBMERSIBLES ONCE MORE THREATENING DRY LAND?
NO--
THEN FRAULEIN SHAYERA HOL, THAT VILLAINOUS SKY QUEEN OF THE SOUTH--
NOT HER AETHERIC MAJESTY, EITHER.
MADAME HARBINGER CLAIMED TO BE WAGING A WAR ACROSS WORLDS. ACROSS OTHER EARTHS.
SHE SPOKE OF A MULTIPLIED COSMOS, OF MANY UNIVERSES AND MANY EARTHS, ALL FACING THE SAME BLEAK THREAT.
A THREAT THAT WOULD SOON REACH OUT AND ENGULF THIS WORLD, TOO.

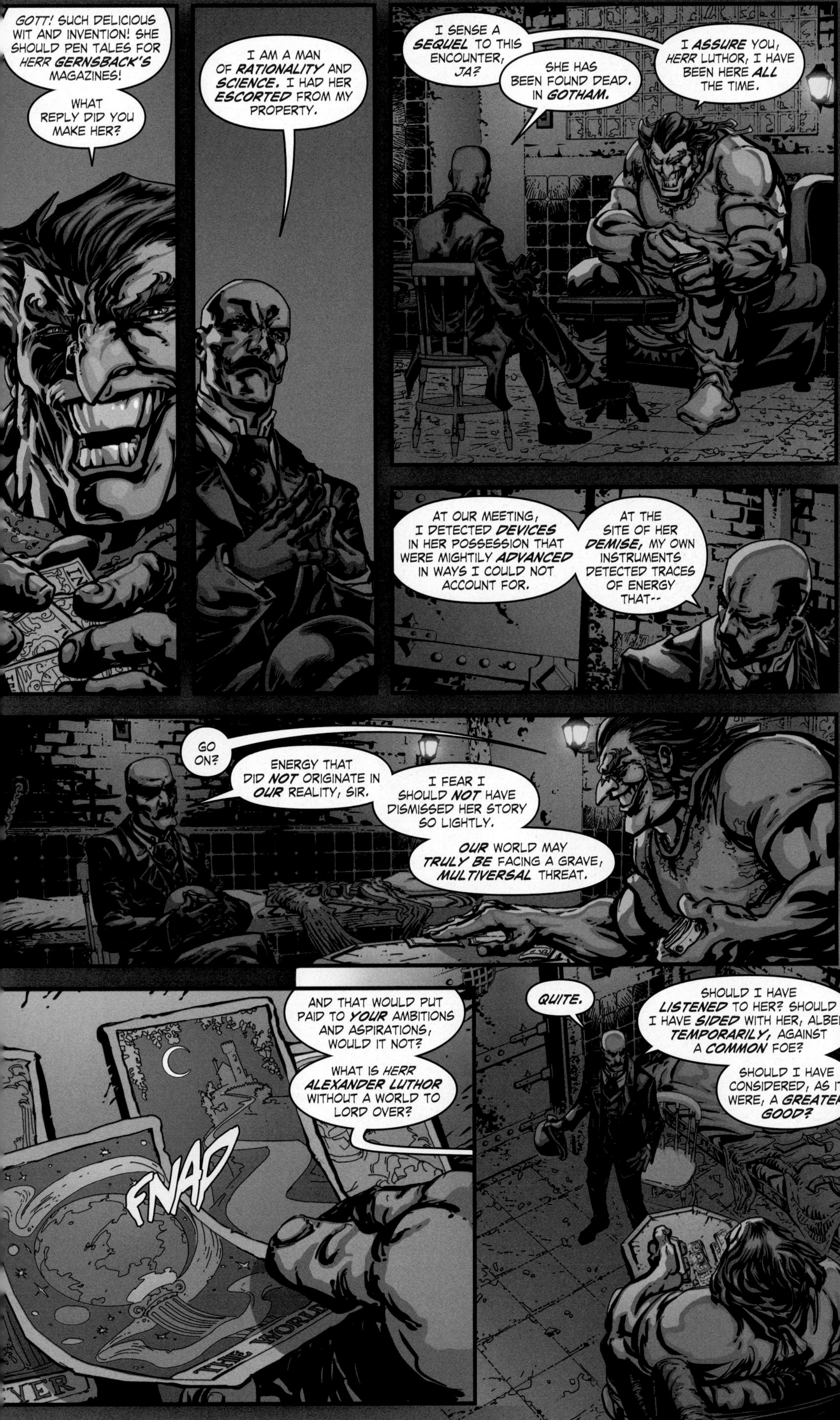
GOTT! SUCH DELICIOUS WIT AND INVENTION! SHE SHOULD PEN TALES FOR HERR GERNSBACK'S MAGAZINES!
WHAT REPLY DID YOU MAKE HER?
I AM A MAN OF RATIONALITY AND SCIENCE. I HAD HER ESCORTED FROM MY PROPERTY.
I SENSE A SEQUEL TO THIS ENCOUNTER, JA?
SHE HAS BEEN FOUND DEAD. IN GOTHAM.
I ASSURE YOU, HERR LUTHOR, I HAVE BEEN HERE ALL THE TIME.
AT OUR MEETING, I DETECTED DEVICES IN HER POSSESSION THAT WERE MIGHTILY ADVANCED IN WAYS I COULD NOT ACCOUNT FOR.
AT THE SITE OF HER DEMISE, MY OWN INSTRUMENTS DETECTED TRACES OF ENERGY THAT--
GO ON?
ENERGY THAT DID NOT ORIGINATE IN OUR REALITY, SIR.
I FEAR I SHOULD NOT HAVE DISMISSED HER STORY SO LIGHTLY.
OUR WORLD MAY TRULY BE FACING A GRAVE, MULTIVERSAL THREAT.
AND THAT WOULD PUT PAID TO YOUR AMBITIONS AND ASPIRATIONS, WOULD IT NOT?
WHAT IS HERR ALEXANDER LUTHOR WITHOUT A WORLD TO LORD OVER?
FNAP
THE WORLD
QUITE.
SHOULD I HAVE LISTENED TO HER? SHOULD I HAVE SIDED WITH HER, ALBEIT TEMPORARILY, AGAINST A COMMON FOE?
SHOULD I HAVE CONSIDERED, AS IT WERE, A GREATER GOOD?

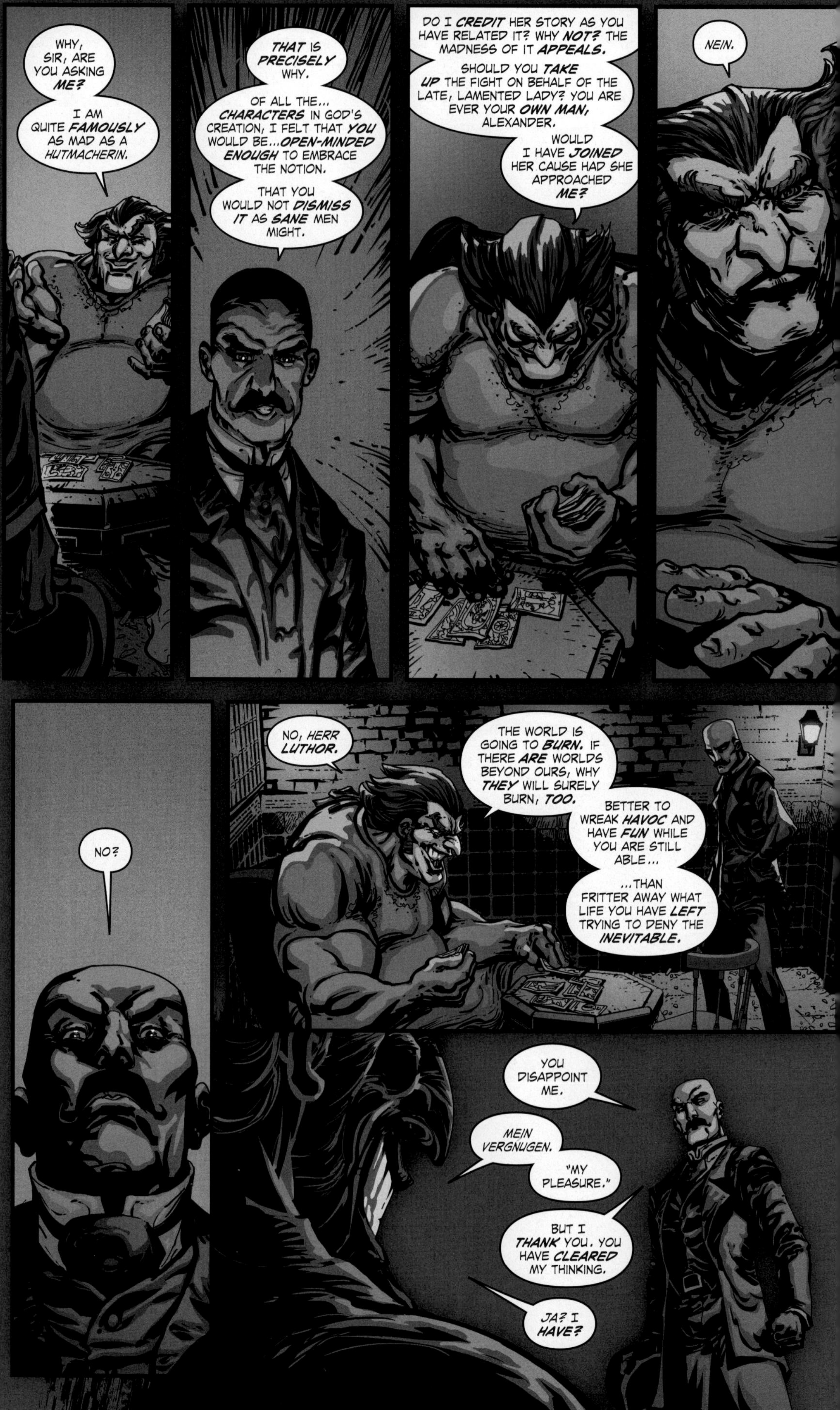

WHY, SIR, ARE YOU ASKING ME?
I AM QUITE FAMOUSLY AS MAD AS A HUTMACHERIN.
THAT IS PRECISELY WHY.
OF ALL THE... CHARACTERS IN GOD'S CREATION, I FELT THAT YOU WOULD BE...OPEN-MINDED ENOUGH TO EMBRACE THE NOTION.
THAT YOU WOULD NOT DISMISS IT AS SANE MEN MIGHT.
DO I CREDIT HER STORY AS YOU HAVE RELATED IT? WHY NOT? THE MADNESS OF IT APPEALS.
SHOULD YOU TAKE UP THE FIGHT ON BEHALF OF THE LATE, LAMENTED LADY? YOU ARE EVER YOUR OWN MAN, ALEXANDER.
WOULD I HAVE JOINED HER CAUSE HAD SHE APPROACHED ME?
NEIN.
NO?
NO, HERR LUTHOR.
THE WORLD IS GOING TO BURN. IF THERE ARE WORLDS BEYOND OURS, WHY THEY WILL SURELY BURN, TOO.
BETTER TO WREAK HAVOC AND HAVE FUN WHILE YOU ARE STILL ABLE...
...THAN FRITTER AWAY WHAT LIFE YOU HAVE LEFT TRYING TO DENY THE INEVITABLE.
YOU DISAPPOINT ME.
MEIN VERGNUGEN.
"MY PLEASURE."
BUT I THANK YOU. YOU HAVE CLEARED MY THINKING.
JA? I HAVE?

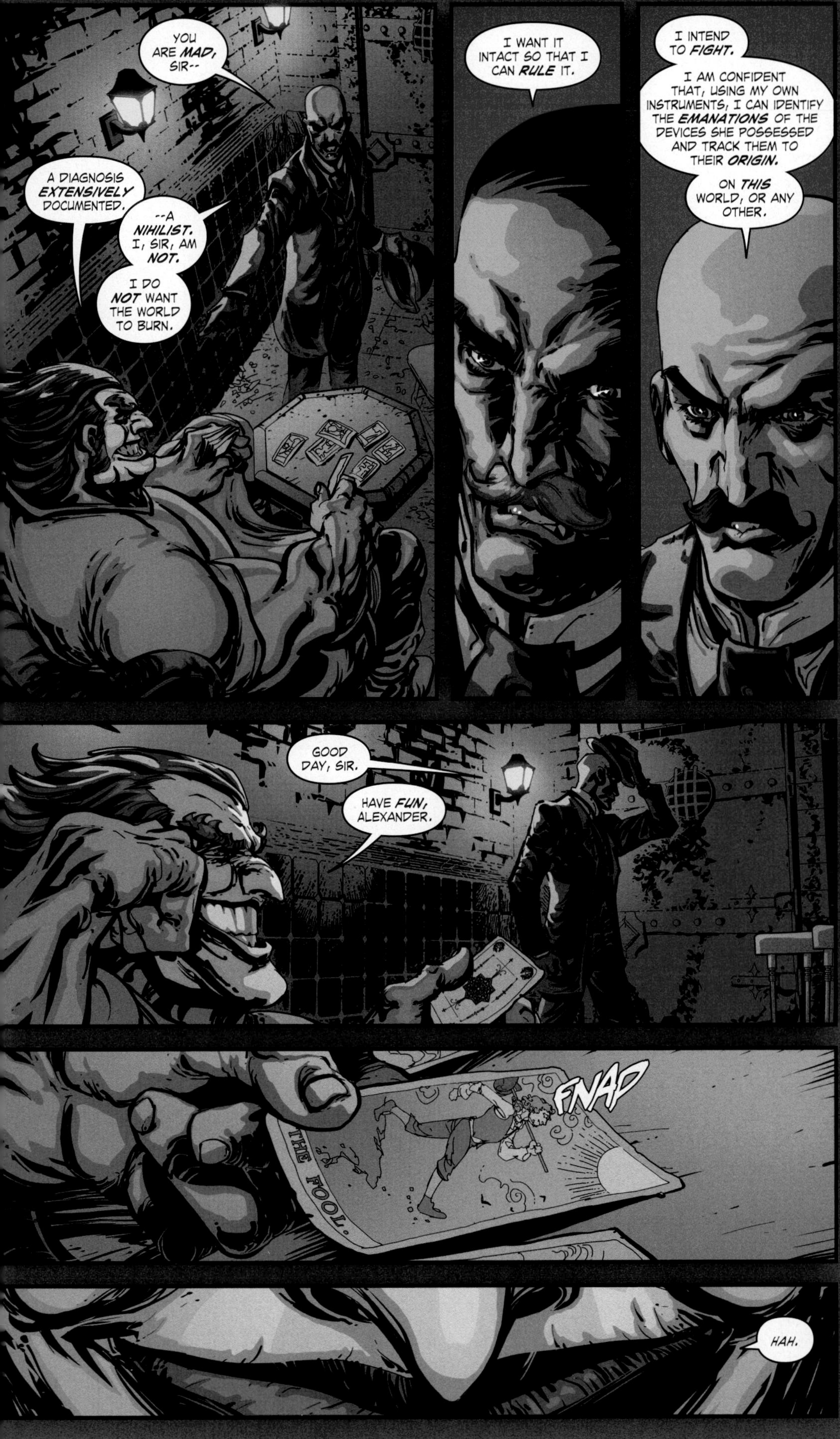
YOU ARE MAD, SIR--
A DIAGNOSIS EXTENSIVELY DOCUMENTED.
--A NIHILIST. I, SIR, AM NOT.
I DO NOT WANT THE WORLD TO BURN.
I WANT IT INTACT SO THAT I CAN RULE IT.
I INTEND TO FIGHT.
I AM CONFIDENT THAT, USING MY OWN INSTRUMENTS, I CAN IDENTIFY THE EMANATIONS OF THE DEVICES SHE POSSESSED AND TRACK THEM TO THEIR ORIGIN.
ON THIS WORLD, OR ANY OTHER.
GOOD DAY, SIR.
HAVE FUN, ALEXANDER.
FNAP
THE FOOL.
HAH.

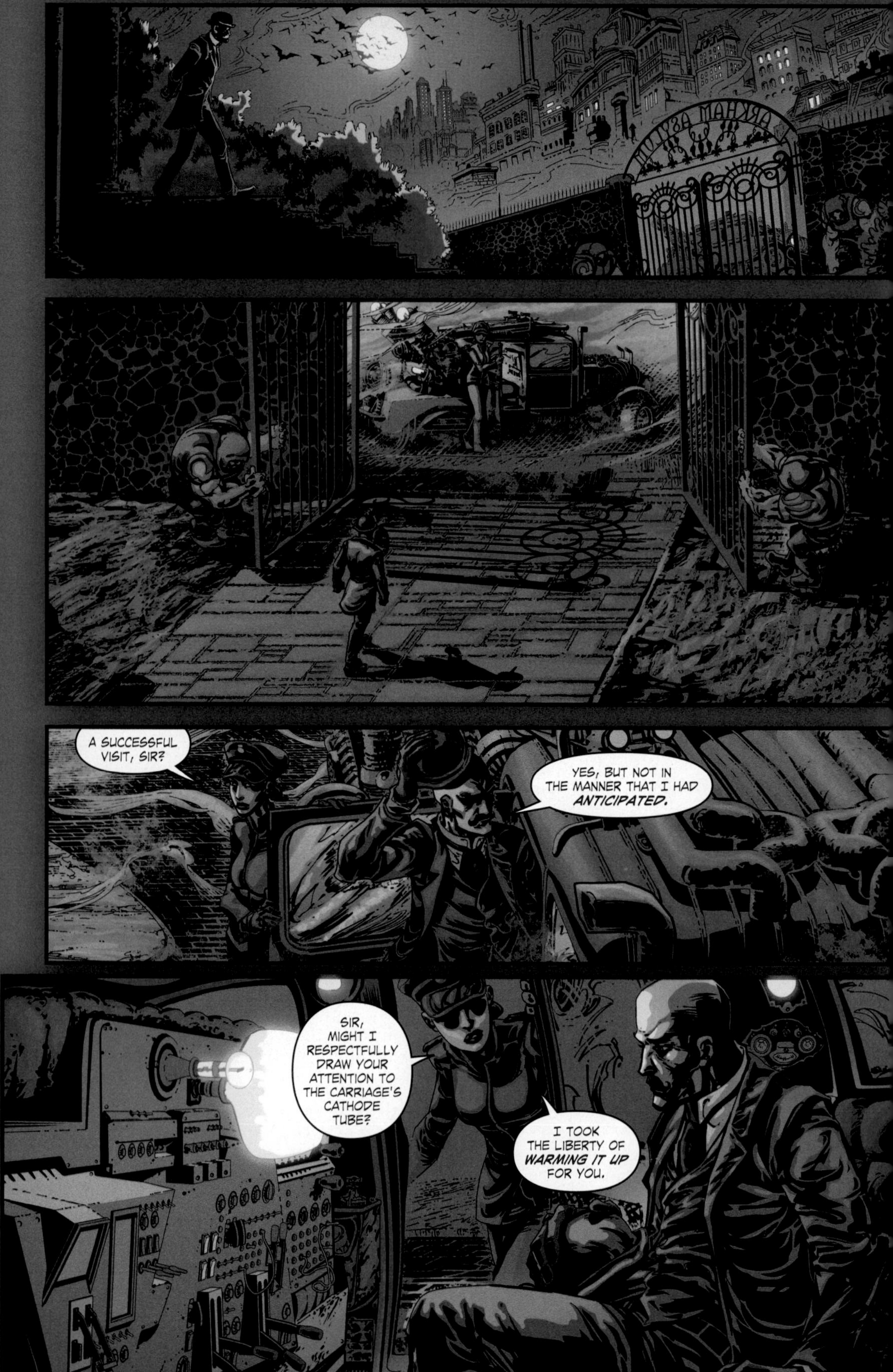
ARKHAM ASYLUM
A SUCCESSFUL VISIT, SIR?
YES, BUT NOT IN THE MANNER THAT I HAD ANTICIPATED.
SIR, MIGHT I RESPECTFULLY DRAW YOUR ATTENTION TO THE CARRIAGE'S CATHODE TUBE?
I TOOK THE LIBERTY OF WARMING IT UP FOR YOU.

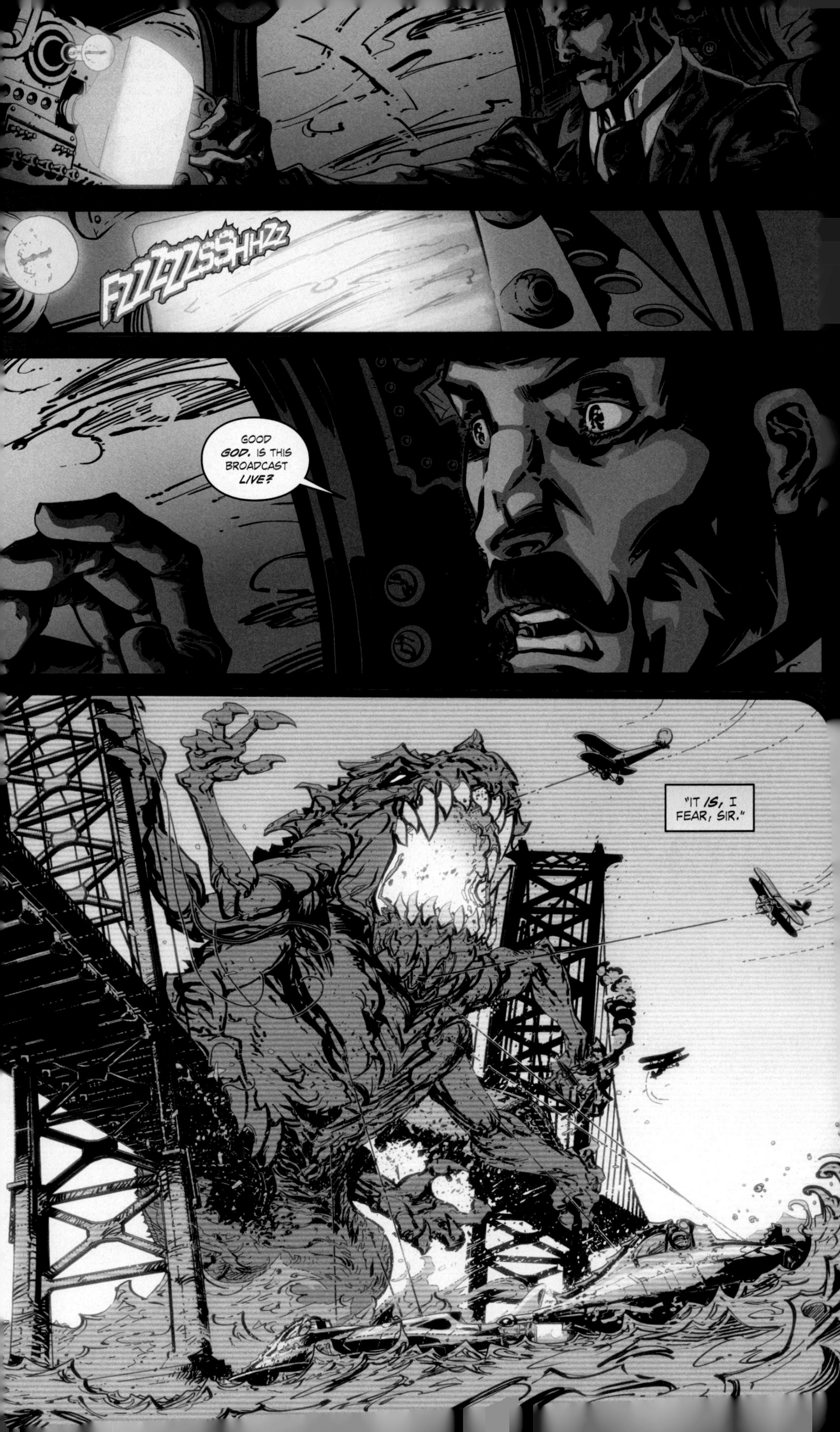
FZZZZZZSSHHZZ
GOOD GOD. IS THIS BROADCAST LIVE?
"IT IS, I FEAR, SIR."

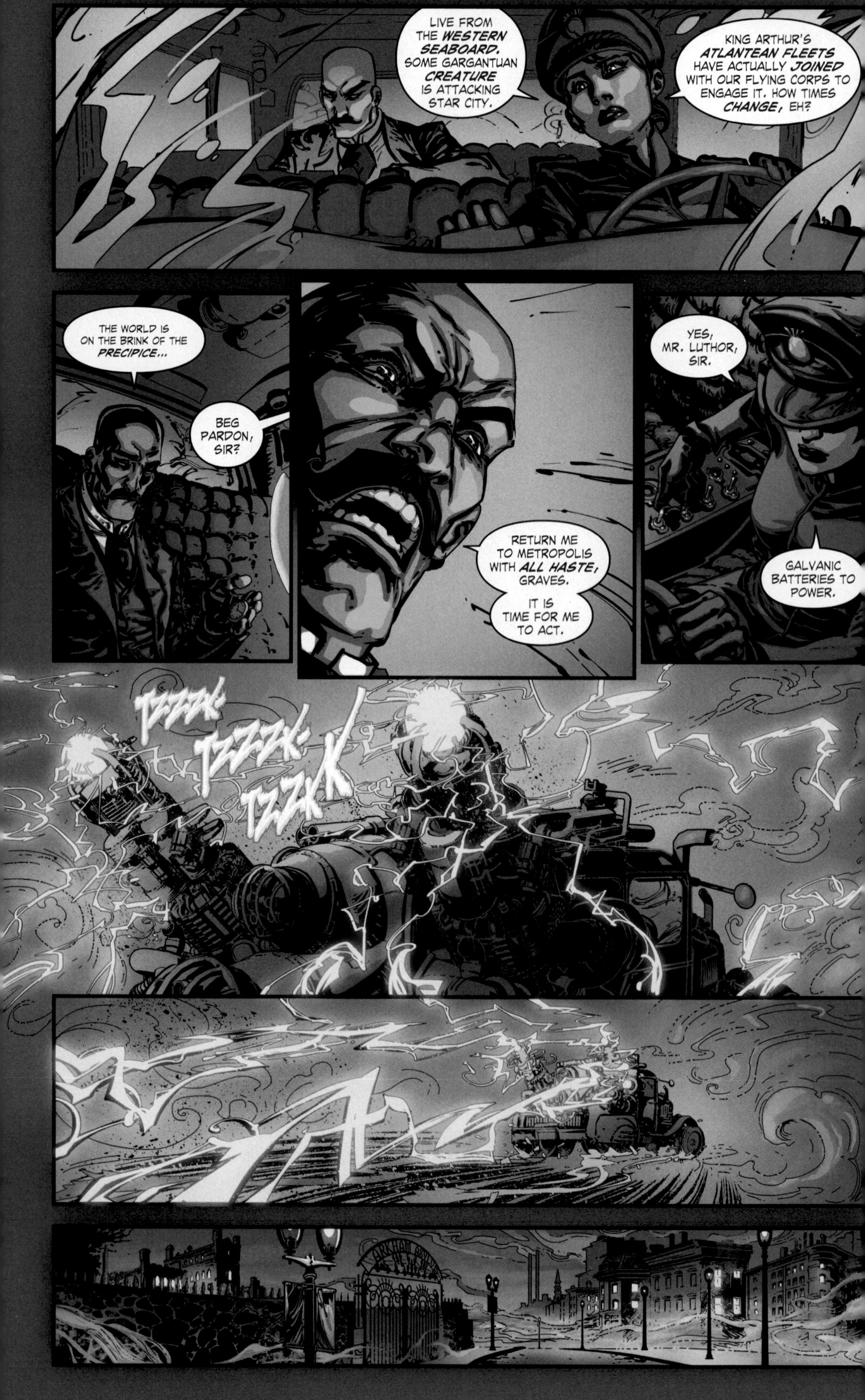
LIVE FROM THE WESTERN SEABOARD. SOME GARGANTUAN CREATURE IS ATTACKING STAR CITY.
KING ARTHUR'S ATLANTEAN FLEETS HAVE ACTUALLY JOINED WITH OUR FLYING CORPS TO ENGAGE IT. HOW TIMES CHANGE, EH?
THE WORLD IS ON THE BRINK OF THE PRECIPICE...
BEG PARDON, SIR?
RETURN ME TO METROPOLIS WITH ALL HASTE, GRAVES.
IT IS TIME FOR ME TO ACT.
YES, MR. LUTHOR, SIR.
GALVANIC BATTERIES TO POWER.
TZZZK!
TZZZK!
TZZKK

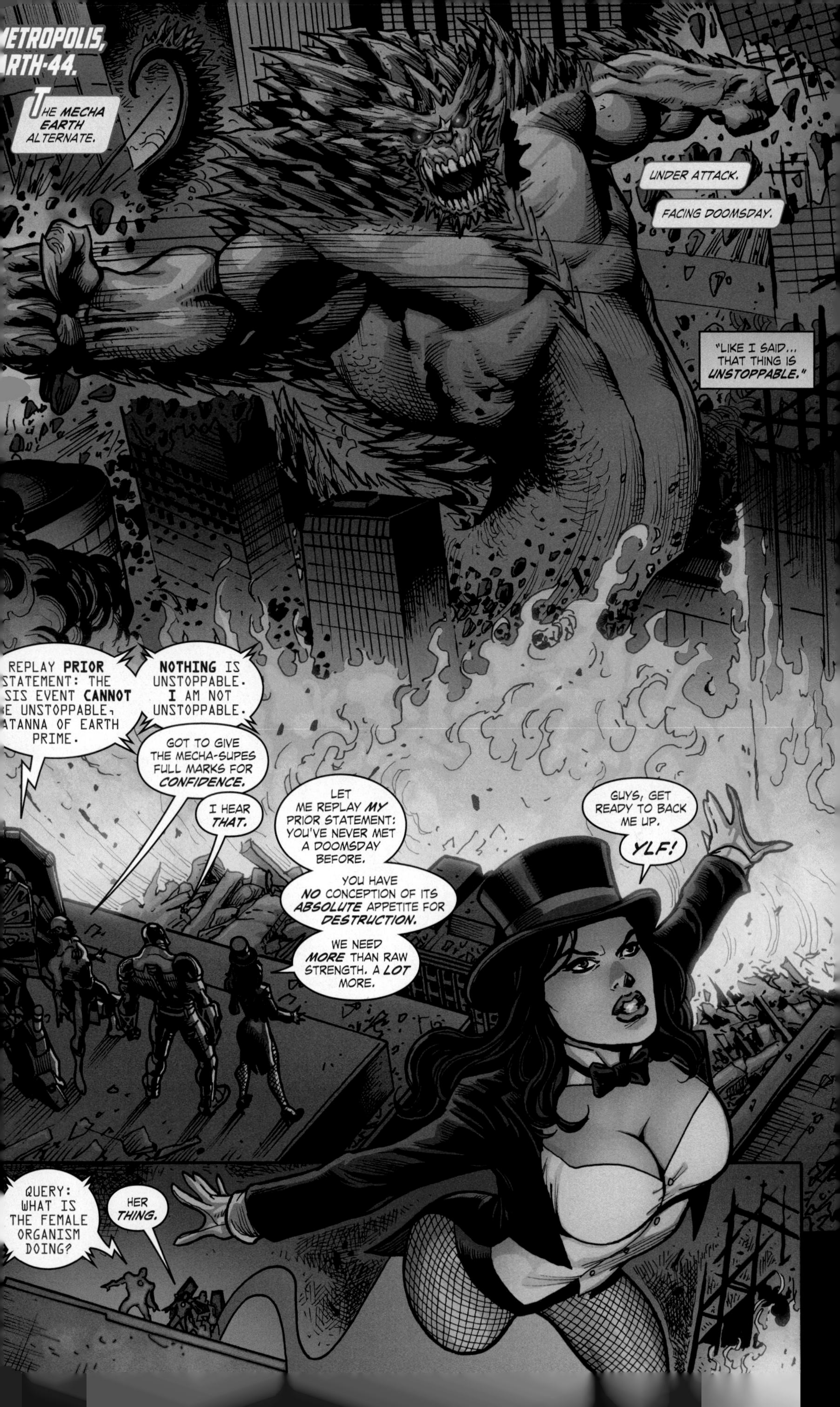

ETROPOLIS,
RTH-44.
THE MECHA EARTH ALTERNATE.
UNDER ATTACK.
FACING DOOMSDAY.
"LIKE I SAID... THAT THING IS UNSTOPPABLE."
REPLAY PRIOR STATEMENT: THE SIS EVENT CANNOT E UNSTOPPABLE, ATANNA OF EARTH PRIME.
NOTHING IS UNSTOPPABLE. I AM NOT UNSTOPPABLE.
GOT TO GIVE THE MECHA-SUPES FULL MARKS FOR CONFIDENCE.
I HEAR THAT.
LET ME REPLAY MY PRIOR STATEMENT: YOU'VE NEVER MET A DOOMSDAY BEFORE.
YOU HAVE NO CONCEPTION OF ITS ABSOLUTE APPETITE FOR DESTRUCTION.
WE NEED MORE THAN RAW STRENGTH. A LOT MORE.
GUYS, GET READY TO BACK ME UP.
YLF!
QUERY: WHAT IS THE FEMALE ORGANISM DOING?
HER THING.

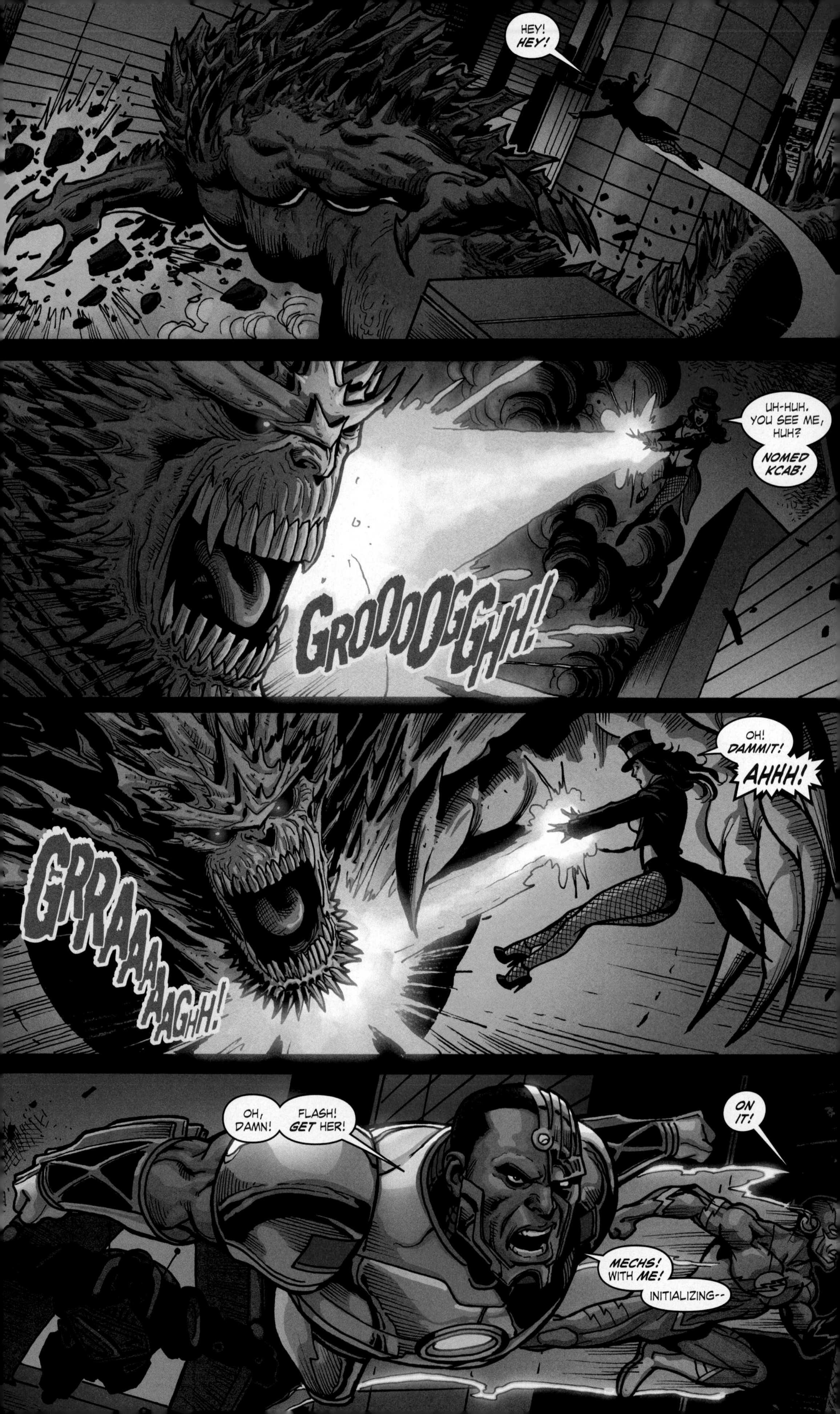
HEY! HEY!
UH-HUH. YOU SEE ME, HUH? NOMED KCAB!
GROOOOGGHH!
OH! DAMMIT! AHHH!
GRRAAAAAAGHH!
OH, DAMN!
FLASH! GET HER!
ON IT!
MECHS! WITH ME!
INITIALIZING--

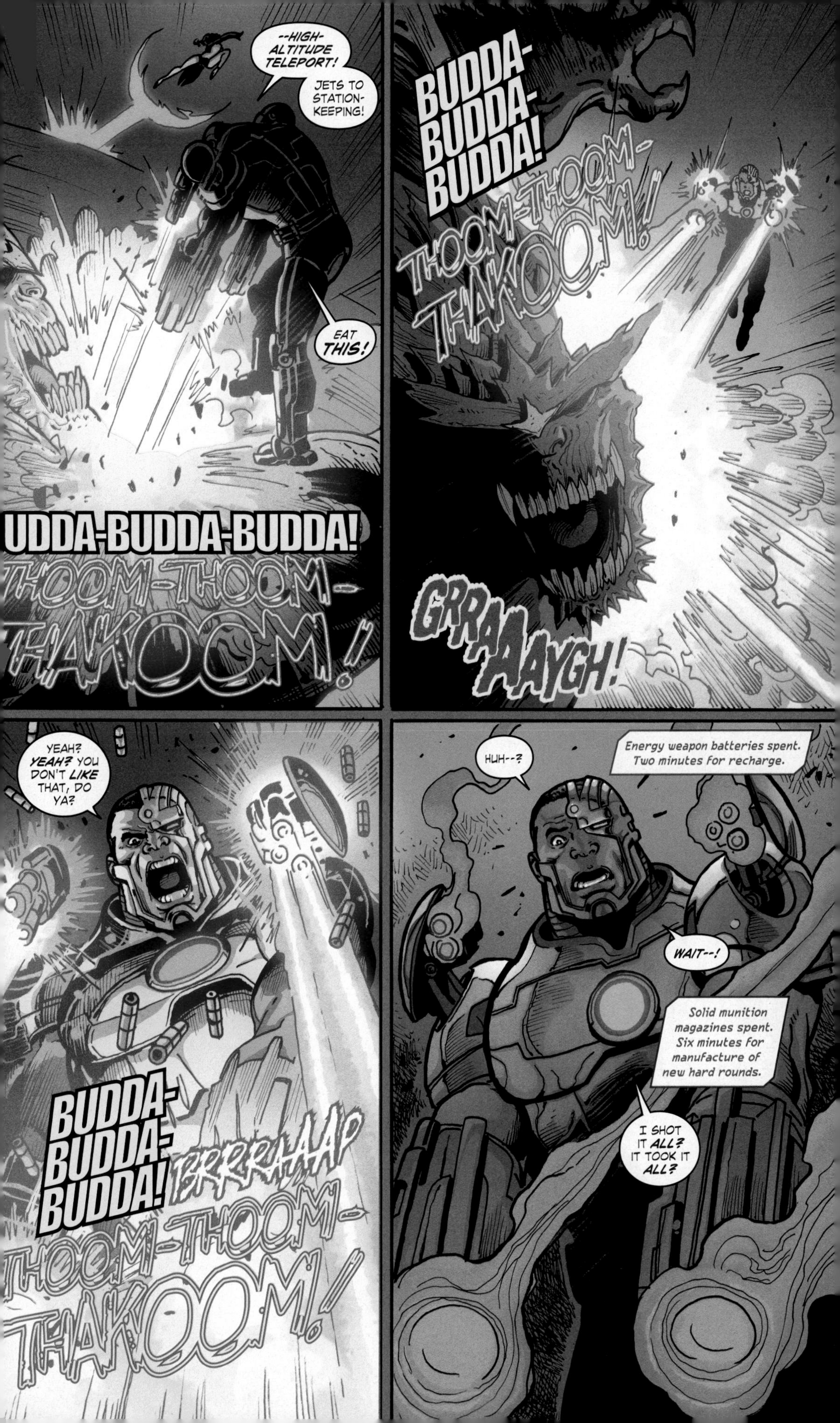
--HIGH-ALTITUDE TELEPORT!
JETS TO STATION-KEEPING!
EAT THIS!
UDDA-BUDDA-BUDDA!
THOOM-THOOM-THAKOOM!
BUDDA-BUDDA-BUDDA!
THOOM-THOOM-THAKOOM!
GRRAAAYGH!
YEAH? YEAH? YOU DON'T LIKE THAT, DO YA?
BUDDA-BUDDA-BUDDA!
BRRRAAAP
THOOM-THOOM-THAKOOM!
HUH--?
Energy weapon batteries spent. Two minutes for recharge.
WAIT--!
Solid munition magazines spent. Six minutes for manufacture of new hard rounds.
I SHOT IT ALL? IT TOOK IT ALL?

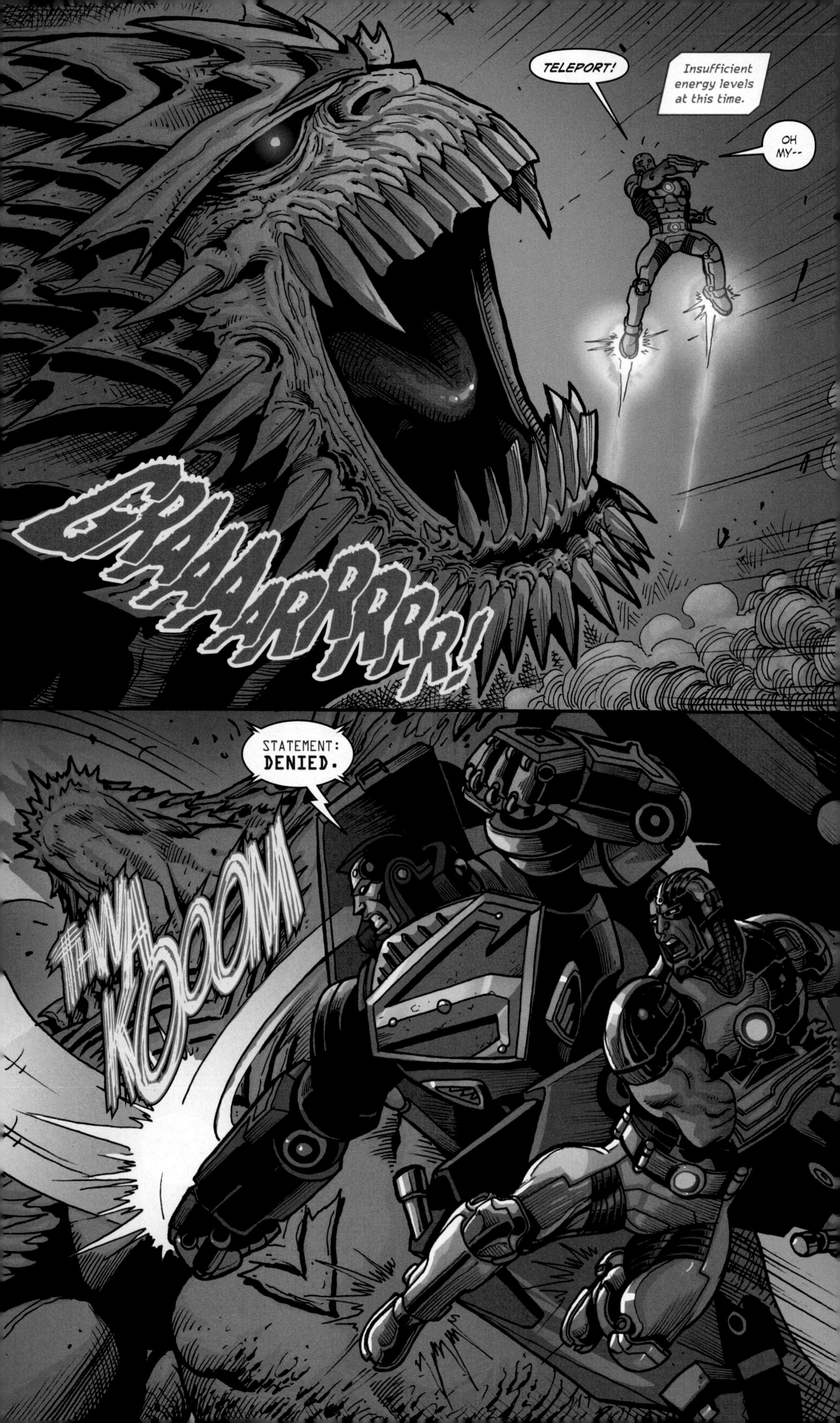
TELEPORT!
Insufficient energy levels at this time.
OH MY--
GRAAAARRRRRR!
STATEMENT: DENIED.
THWAKOOOM

UGHHHHNNKKK!

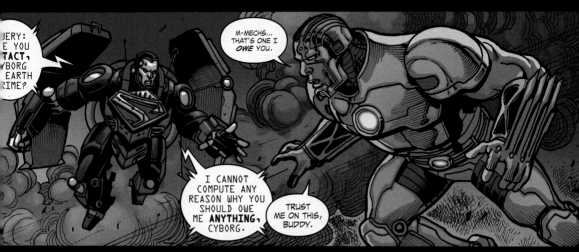

QUERY: ARE YOU INTACT, CYBORG OF EARTH PRIME?

M-MECHS... THAT'S ONE I OWE YOU.

I CANNOT COMPUTE ANY REASON WHY YOU SHOULD OWE ME ANYTHING, CYBORG.

TRUST ME ON THIS, BUDDY.

GEEZ-- GOTTA--

LYF!

FYL!

CAN'T PHRASE A--

OHMIGOD--

'TANNA! I GOT YA!

'TANNA!

YFL--

DAMMIT--

YOU ARE NOT GONNA BE PAVEMENT PIZZA, HONEY--

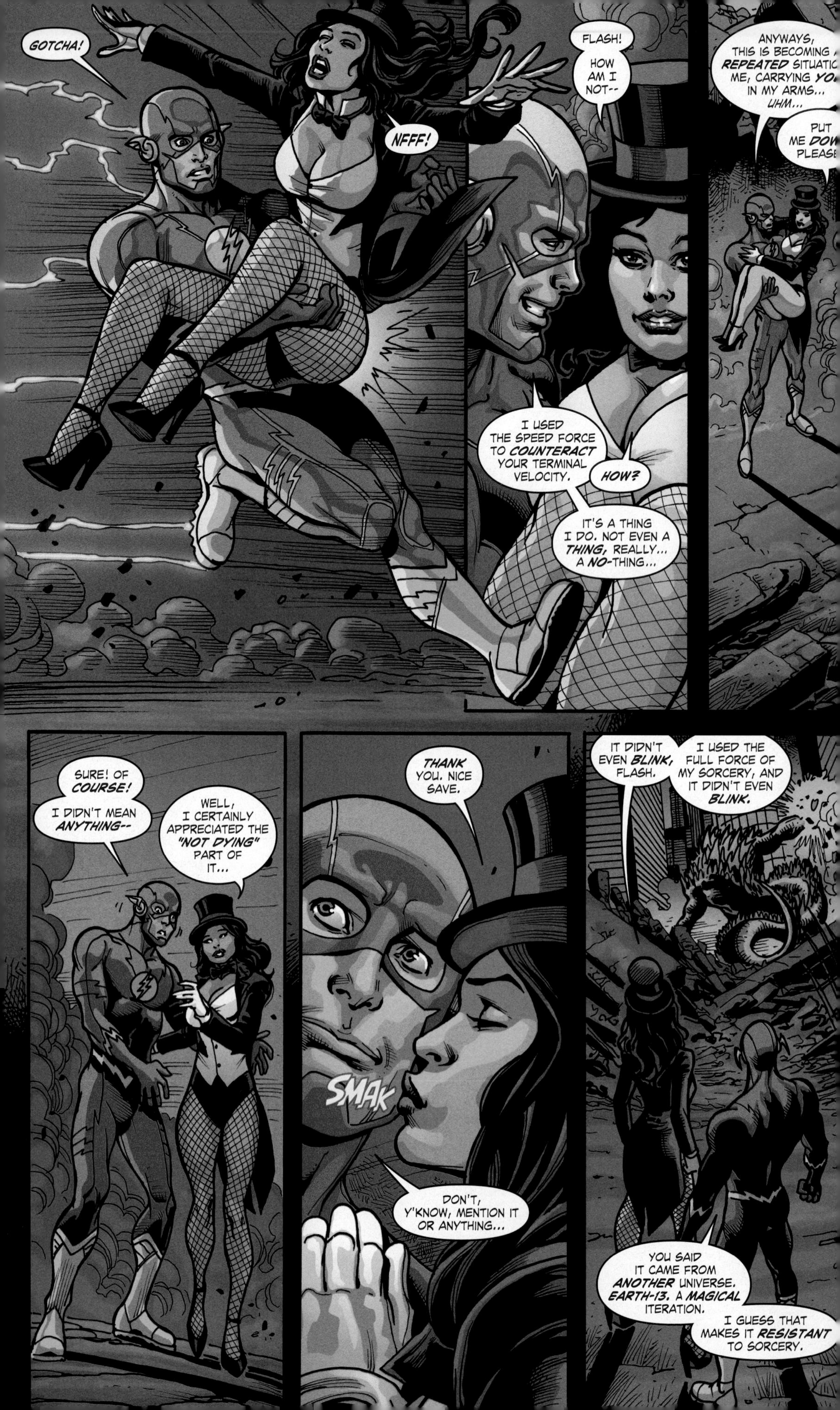

GOTCHA!
NFFF!
FLASH!
HOW AM I NOT--
I USED THE SPEED FORCE TO *COUNTERACT* YOUR TERMINAL VELOCITY.
HOW?
IT'S A THING I DO. NOT EVEN A *THING,* REALLY... A *NO-*THING...
ANYWAYS, THIS IS BECOMING A *REPEATED* SITUATIC ME, CARRYING *YO* IN MY ARMS... *UHM...*
PUT ME *DOW* PLEASE
SURE! OF *COURSE!*
I DIDN'T MEAN *ANYTHING--*
WELL, I CERTAINLY APPRECIATED THE *"NOT DYING"* PART OF IT...
THANK YOU. NICE SAVE.
SMAK
DON'T, Y'KNOW, MENTION IT OR ANYTHING...
IT DIDN'T EVEN *BLINK,* FLASH.
I USED THE FULL FORCE OF MY SORCERY, AND IT DIDN'T EVEN *BLINK.*
YOU SAID IT CAME FROM *ANOTHER* UNIVERSE. *EARTH-13.* A *MAGICAL* ITERATION.
I GUESS THAT MAKES IT *RESISTANT* TO SORCERY.

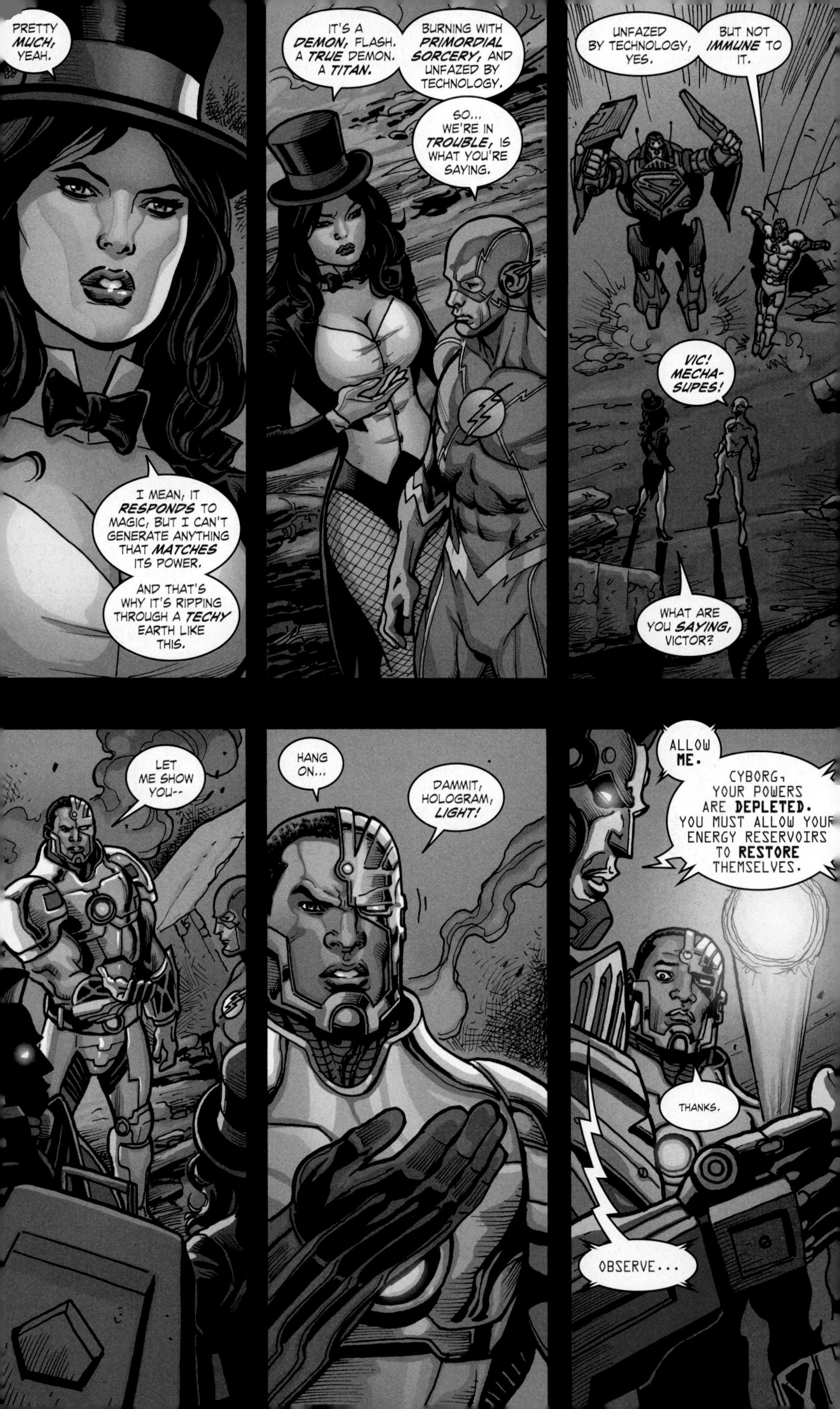
PRETTY MUCH, YEAH.
I MEAN, IT RESPONDS TO MAGIC, BUT I CAN'T GENERATE ANYTHING THAT MATCHES ITS POWER.
AND THAT'S WHY IT'S RIPPING THROUGH A TECHY EARTH LIKE THIS.
IT'S A DEMON, FLASH. A TRUE DEMON. A TITAN.
BURNING WITH PRIMORDIAL SORCERY, AND UNFAZED BY TECHNOLOGY.
SO... WE'RE IN TROUBLE, IS WHAT YOU'RE SAYING.
UNFAZED BY TECHNOLOGY, YES.
BUT NOT IMMUNE TO IT.
VIC! MECHA-SUPES!
WHAT ARE YOU SAYING, VICTOR?
LET ME SHOW YOU--
HANG ON...
DAMMIT, HOLOGRAM, LIGHT!
ALLOW ME.
CYBORG, YOUR POWERS ARE DEPLETED. YOU MUST ALLOW YOUR ENERGY RESERVOIRS TO RESTORE THEMSELVES.
THANKS.
OBSERVE...

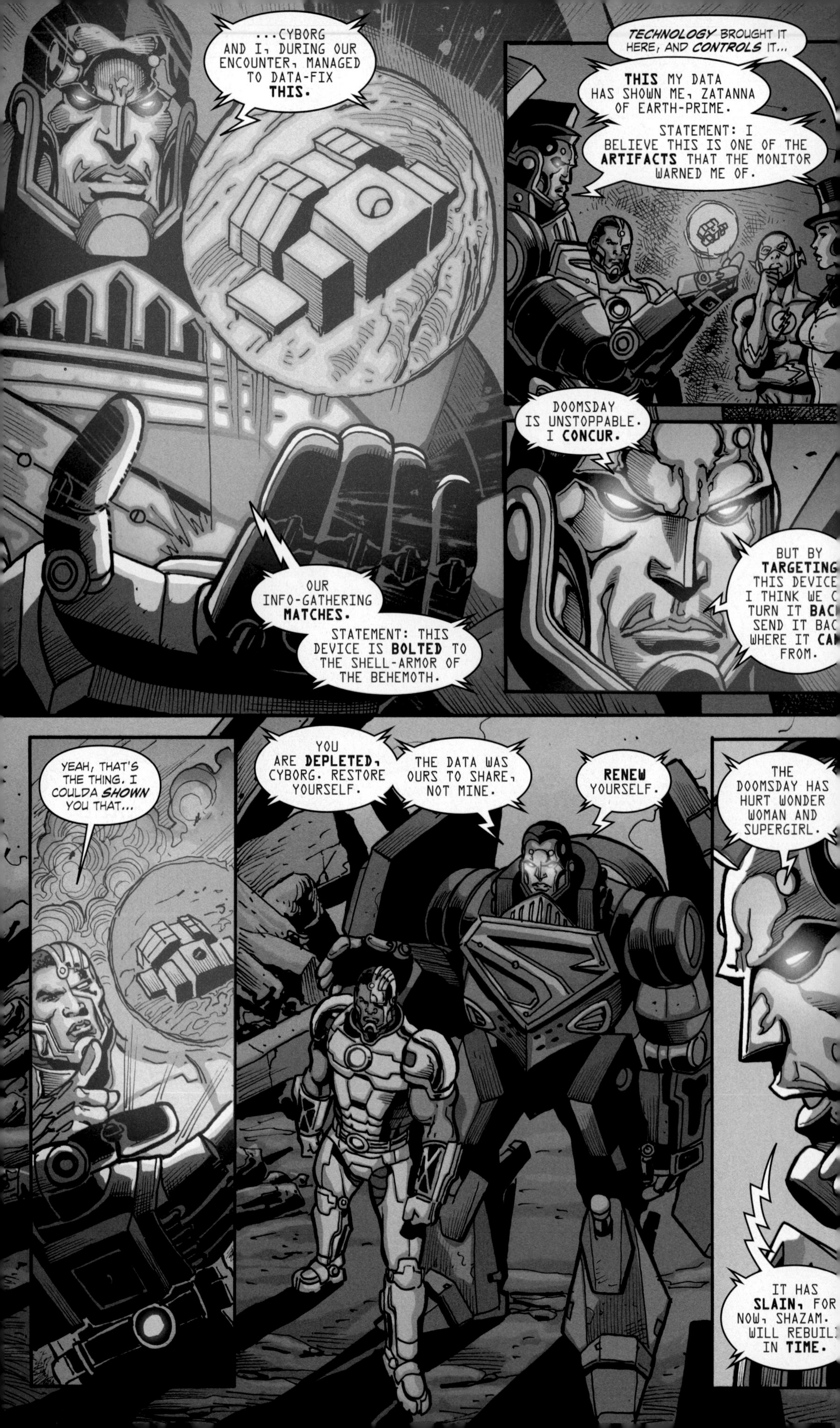
...CYBORG AND I, DURING OUR ENCOUNTER, MANAGED TO DATA-FIX **THIS.**
TECHNOLOGY BROUGHT IT HERE, AND *CONTROLS* IT...
THIS MY DATA HAS SHOWN ME, ZATANNA OF EARTH-PRIME.
STATEMENT: I BELIEVE THIS IS ONE OF THE **ARTIFACTS** THAT THE MONITOR WARNED ME OF.
OUR INFO-GATHERING **MATCHES.**
STATEMENT: THIS DEVICE IS **BOLTED** TO THE SHELL-ARMOR OF THE BEHEMOTH.
DOOMSDAY IS UNSTOPPABLE. I **CONCUR.**
BUT BY **TARGETING** THIS DEVICE I THINK WE C TURN IT **BAC** SEND IT BAC WHERE IT **CA** FROM.
YEAH, THAT'S THE THING. I COULDA *SHOWN* YOU THAT...
YOU ARE **DEPLETED,** CYBORG. RESTORE YOURSELF.
THE DATA WAS OURS TO SHARE, NOT MINE.
RENEW YOURSELF.
THE DOOMSDAY HAS HURT WONDER WOMAN AND SUPERGIRL.
IT HAS **SLAIN,** FOR NOW, SHAZAM. WILL REBUIL IN **TIME.**

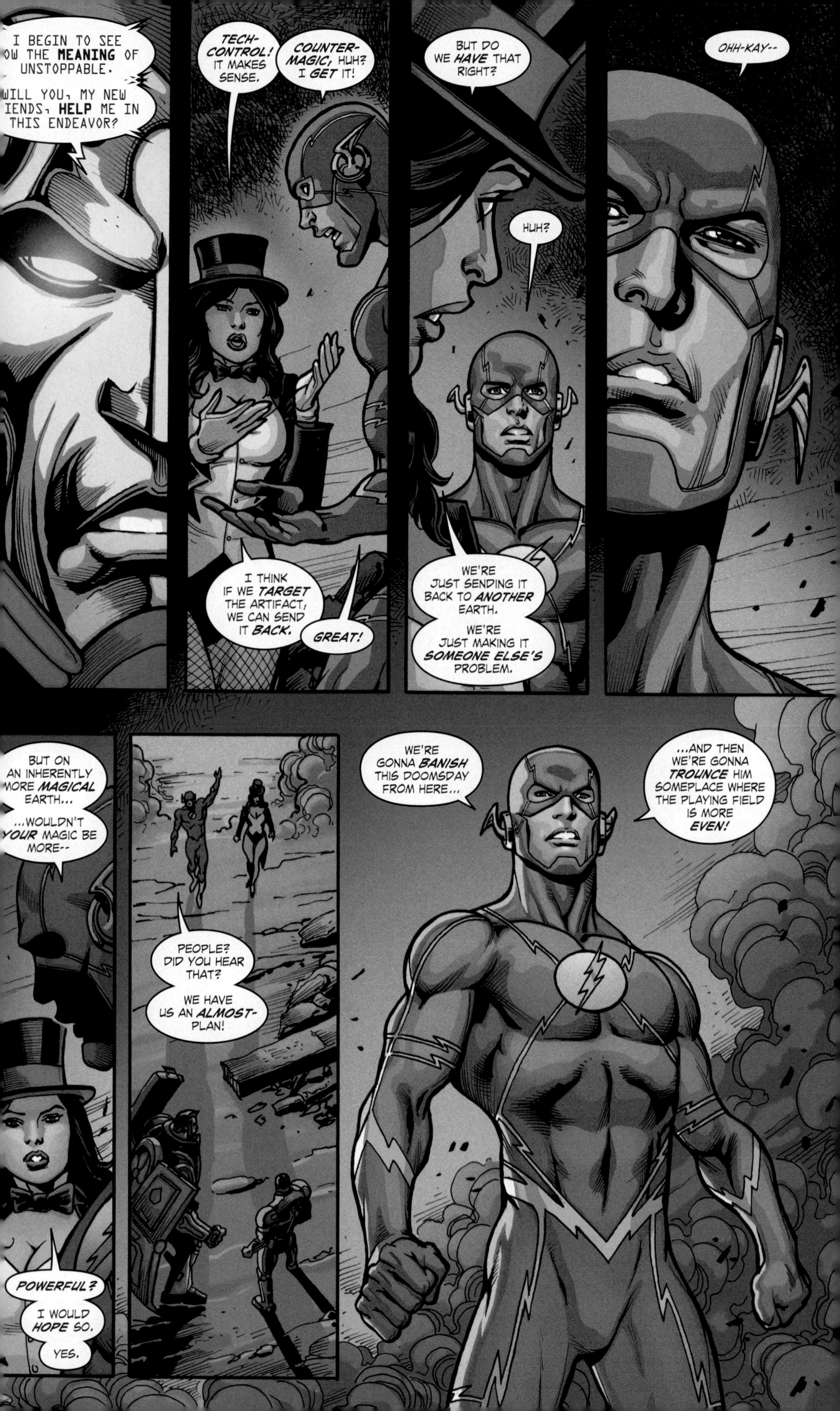
I BEGIN TO SEE
OW THE MEANING OF UNSTOPPABLE.
WILL YOU, MY NEW IENDS, HELP ME IN THIS ENDEAVOR?
TECH-CONTROL! IT MAKES SENSE.
COUNTER-MAGIC, HUH? I GET IT!
I THINK IF WE TARGET THE ARTIFACT, WE CAN SEND IT BACK.
GREAT!
BUT DO WE HAVE THAT RIGHT?
HUH?
WE'RE JUST SENDING IT BACK TO ANOTHER EARTH.
WE'RE JUST MAKING IT SOMEONE ELSE'S PROBLEM.
OHH-KAY--
BUT ON AN INHERENTLY MORE MAGICAL EARTH...
...WOULDN'T YOUR MAGIC BE MORE--
POWERFUL?
I WOULD HOPE SO.
YES.
PEOPLE? DID YOU HEAR THAT?
WE HAVE US AN ALMOST-PLAN!
WE'RE GONNA BANISH THIS DOOMSDAY FROM HERE...
...AND THEN WE'RE GONNA TROUNCE HIM SOMEPLACE WHERE THE PLAYING FIELD IS MORE EVEN!

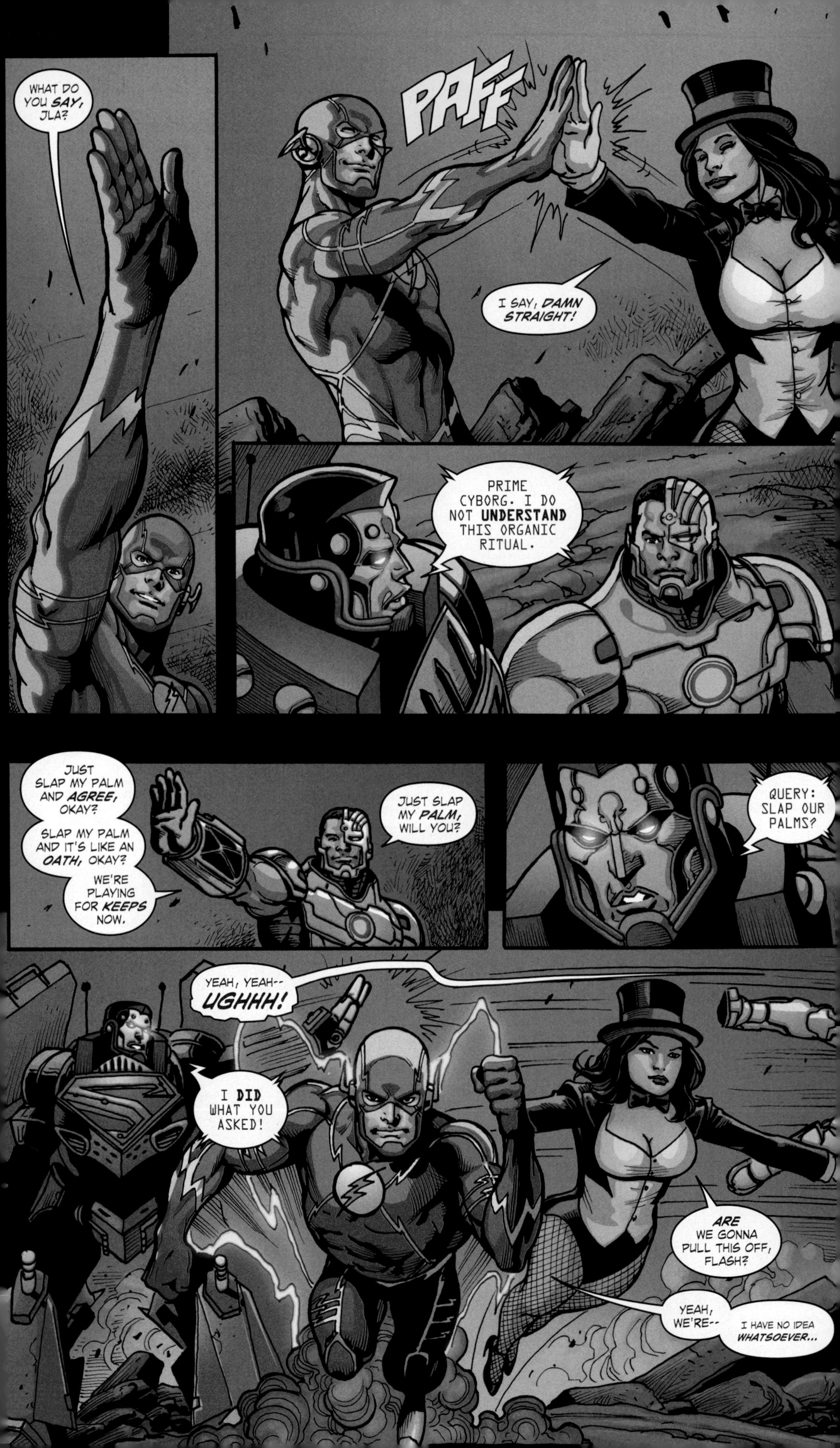
WHAT DO YOU SAY, JLA?
PAFF
I SAY, DAMN STRAIGHT!
PRIME CYBORG. I DO NOT UNDERSTAND THIS ORGANIC RITUAL.
JUST SLAP MY PALM AND AGREE, OKAY?
SLAP MY PALM AND IT'S LIKE AN OATH, OKAY?
WE'RE PLAYING FOR KEEPS NOW.
JUST SLAP MY PALM, WILL YOU?
QUERY: SLAP OUR PALMS?
YEAH, YEAH-- UGHHH!
I DID WHAT YOU ASKED!
ARE WE GONNA PULL THIS OFF, FLASH?
YEAH, WE'RE--
I HAVE NO IDEA WHATSOEVER...

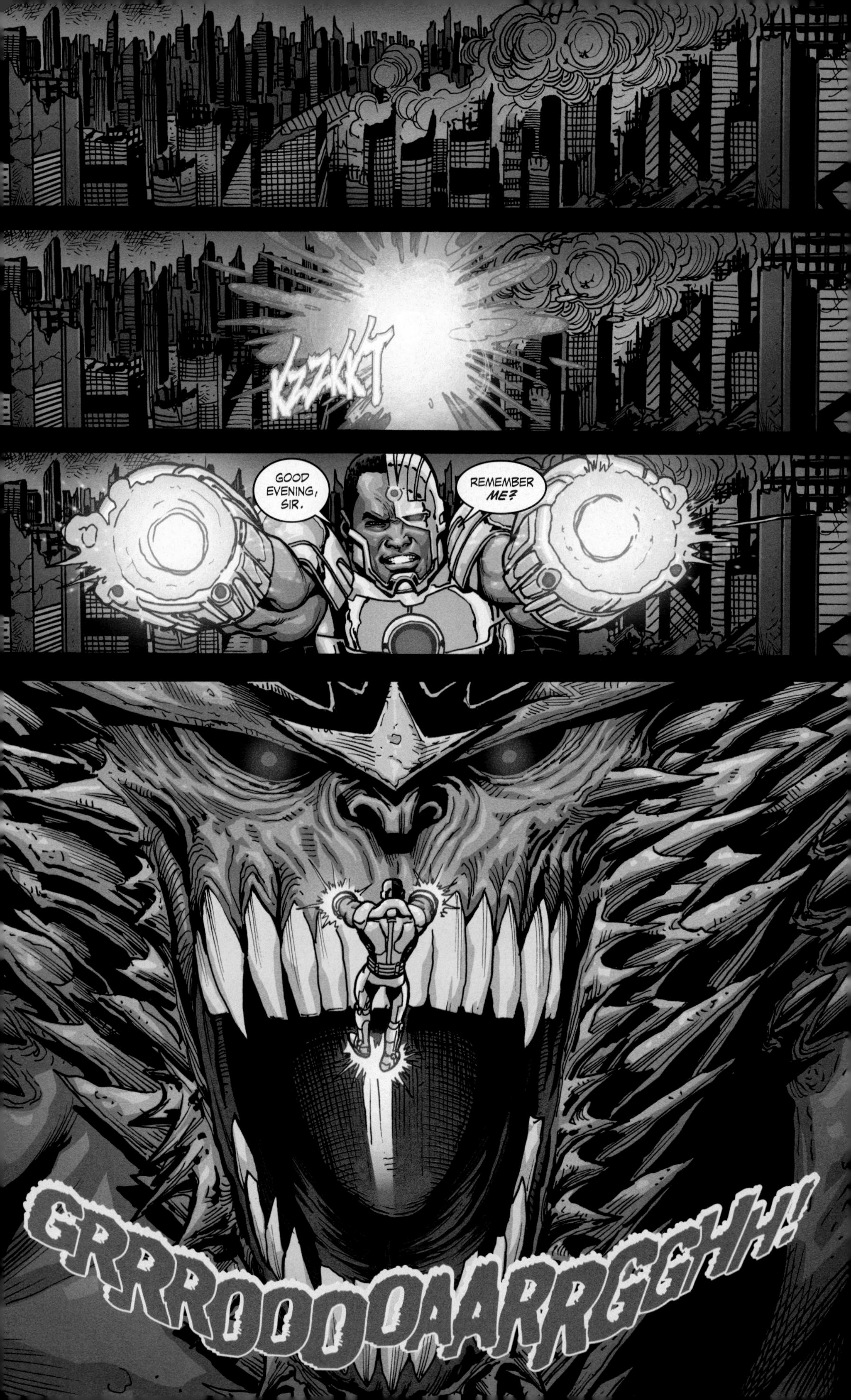
KZZKKT
GOOD EVENING, SIR.
REMEMBER ME?
GRRROOOOAARRGGHH!

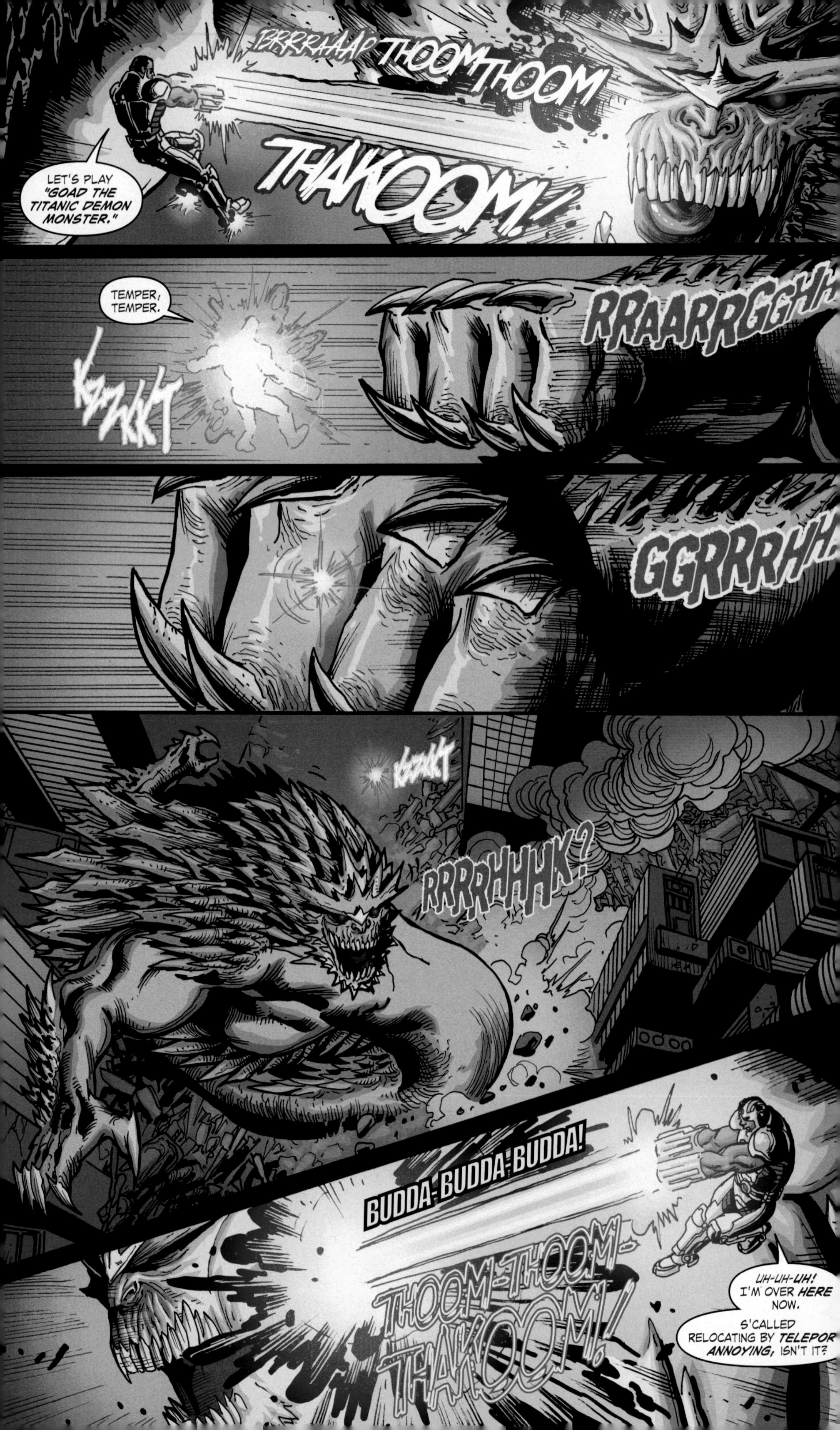
BRRRAAAP THOOM THOOM
THAKOOM!
LET'S PLAY "GOAD THE TITANIC DEMON MONSTER."
TEMPER, TEMPER.
KZZZKKT
RRAARRGGHH
GGRRRRH
KZZKKT
RRRRHHHK?
BUDDA-BUDDA-BUDDA!
THOOM-THOOM-THOOM-
THAKOOM!
UH-UH-UH! I'M OVER HERE NOW.
S'CALLED RELOCATING BY TELEPOR ANNOYING, ISN'T IT?

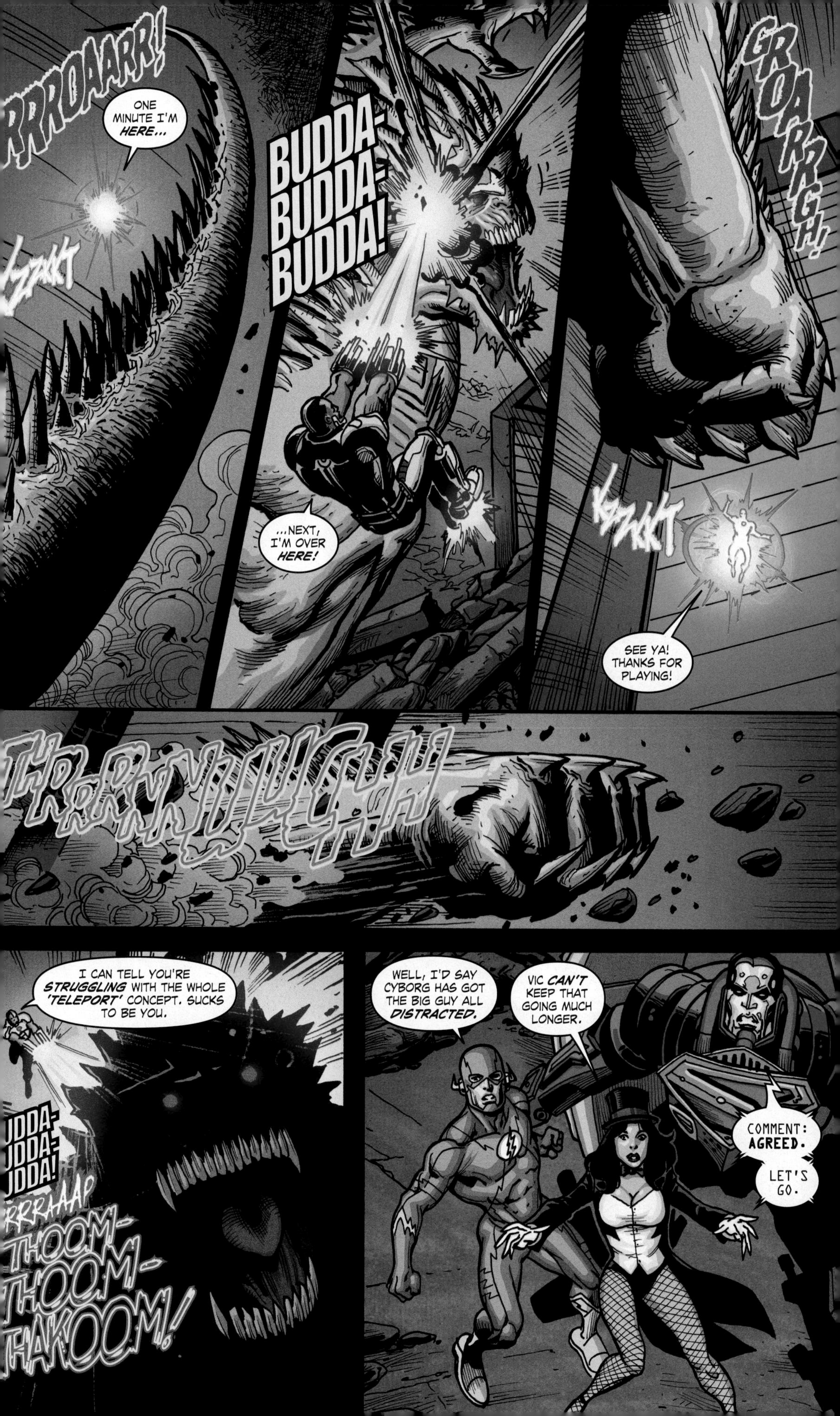
RRROAARR!
ONE MINUTE I'M *HERE...*
SZZKKT
BUDDA-BUDDA-BUDDA!
...NEXT, I'M OVER *HERE!*
GROARRGH!
KSSZKKT
SEE YA! THANKS FOR PLAYING!
THOOOMMMUUGHH
I CAN TELL YOU'RE *STRUGGLING* WITH THE WHOLE *'TELEPORT'* CONCEPT. SUCKS TO BE YOU.
UDDA-UDDA-UDDA!
RRRAAAP
THOOM-THOOM-THAKOOM!
WELL, I'D SAY CYBORG HAS GOT THE BIG GUY ALL *DISTRACTED.*
VIC *CAN'T* KEEP THAT GOING MUCH LONGER.
COMMENT: **AGREED.**
LET'S GO.

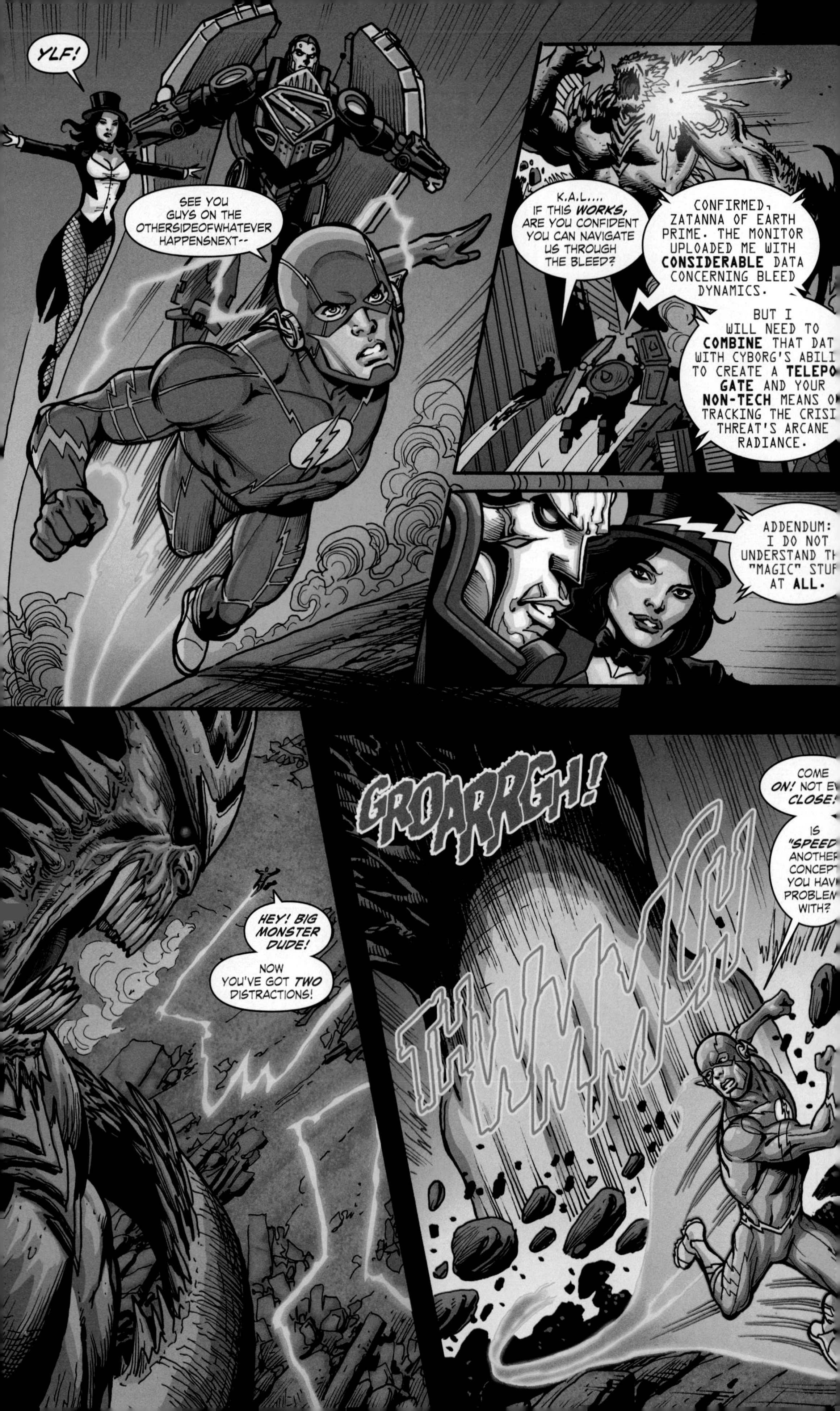
YLF!
SEE YOU GUYS ON THE OTHERSIDEOFWHATEVER HAPPENSNEXT--
K.A.L.... IF THIS WORKS, ARE YOU CONFIDENT YOU CAN NAVIGATE US THROUGH THE BLEED?
CONFIRMED, ZATANNA OF EARTH PRIME. THE MONITOR UPLOADED ME WITH CONSIDERABLE DATA CONCERNING BLEED DYNAMICS.
BUT I WILL NEED TO COMBINE THAT DAT WITH CYBORG'S ABILI TO CREATE A TELEPO GATE AND YOUR NON-TECH MEANS O TRACKING THE CRISI THREAT'S ARCANE RADIANCE.
ADDENDUM: I DO NOT UNDERSTAND TH "MAGIC" STUF AT ALL.
HEY! BIG MONSTER DUDE!
NOW YOU'VE GOT TWO DISTRACTIONS!
GROARRGH!
THWMMM
COME ON! NOT E CLOSE!
IS "SPEED ANOTHER CONCEPT YOU HAV PROBLEM WITH?

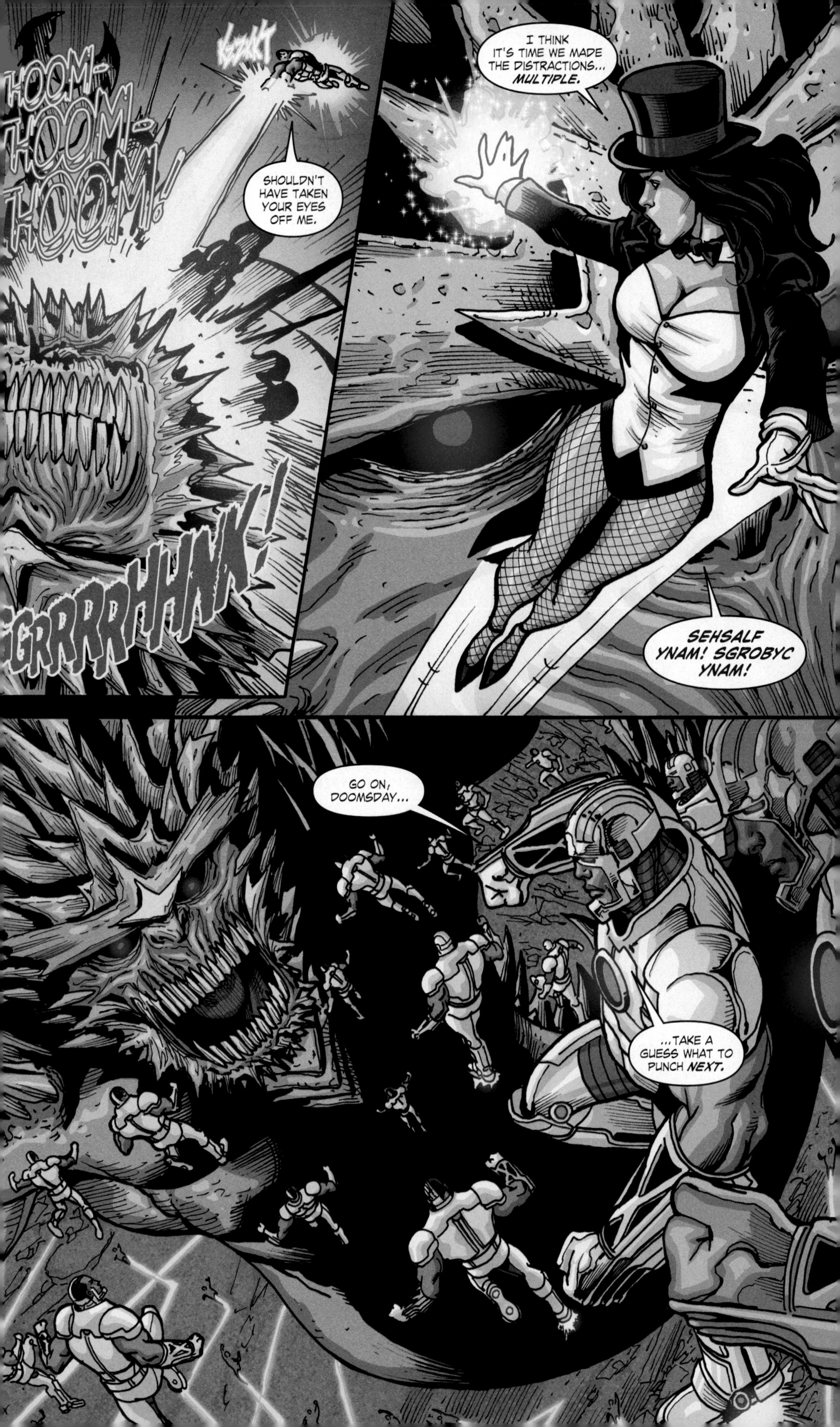
KZZKKT
THOOM-THOOM-THOOM-THOOM!
SHOULDN'T HAVE TAKEN YOUR EYES OFF ME.
GRRRRHHNK!
I THINK IT'S TIME WE MADE THE DISTRACTIONS... *MULTIPLE.*
SEHSALF YNAM! SGROBYC YNAM!
GO ON, DOOMSDAY...
...TAKE A GUESS WHAT TO PUNCH *NEXT.*

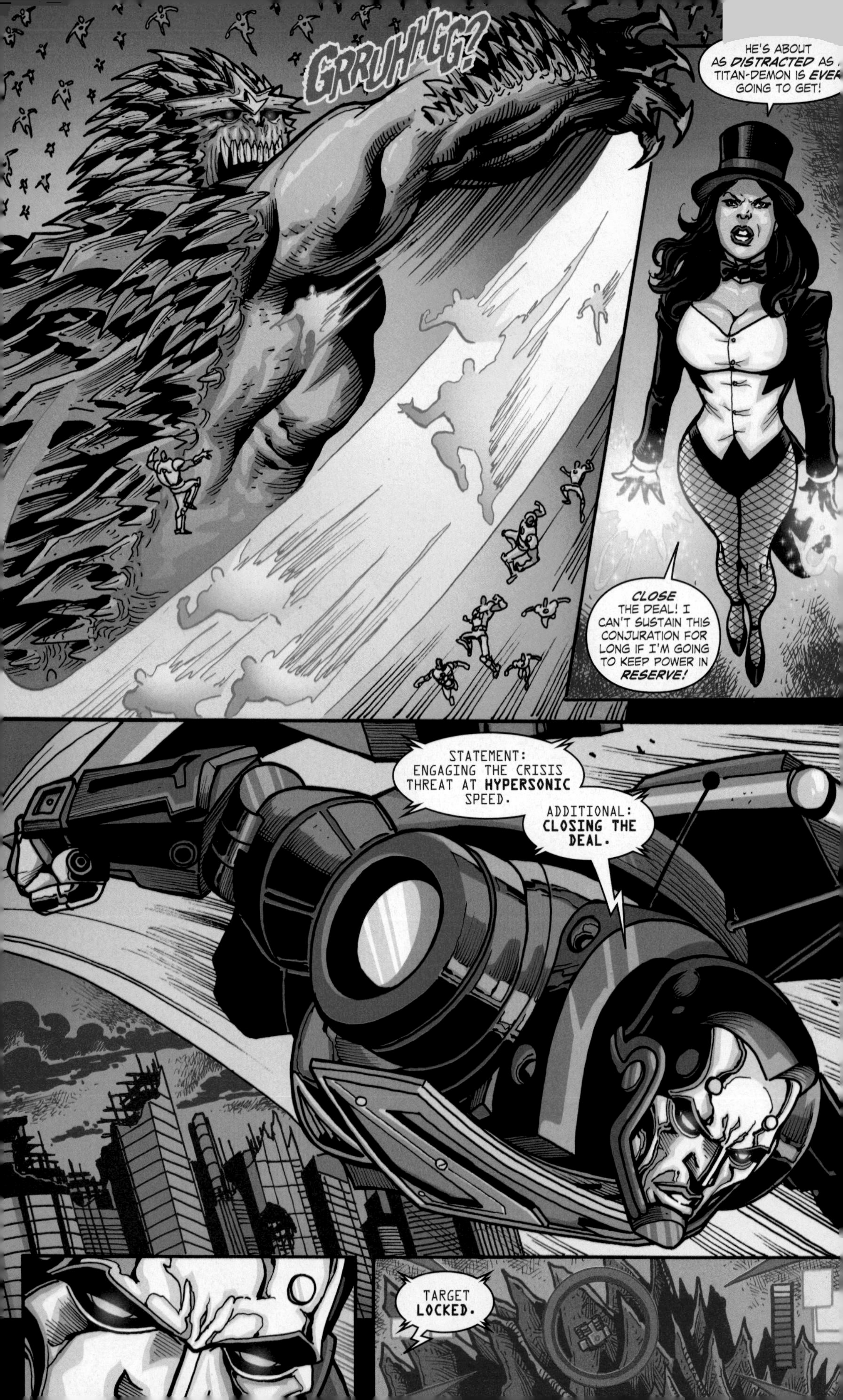
GRRUHHGG?
HE'S ABOUT AS DISTRACTED AS A TITAN-DEMON IS EVER GOING TO GET!
CLOSE THE DEAL! I CAN'T SUSTAIN THIS CONJURATION FOR LONG IF I'M GOING TO KEEP POWER IN RESERVE!
STATEMENT: ENGAGING THE CRISIS THREAT AT HYPERSONIC SPEED.
ADDITIONAL: CLOSING THE DEAL.
TARGET LOCKED.

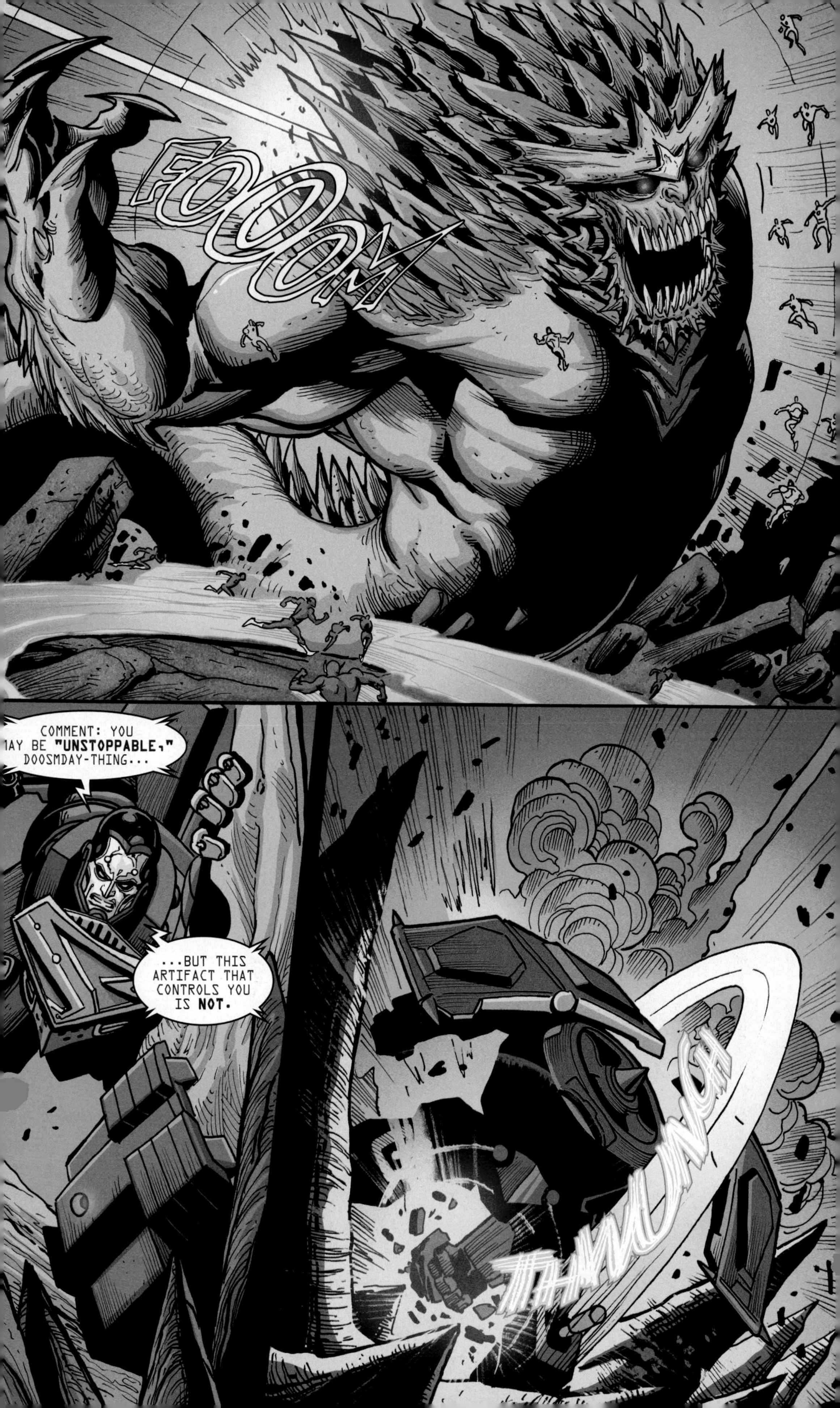
FOOOOM
COMMENT: YOU MAY BE "UNSTOPPABLE," DOOSMDAY-THING...
...BUT THIS ARTIFACT THAT CONTROLS YOU IS NOT.
THHWUNCH

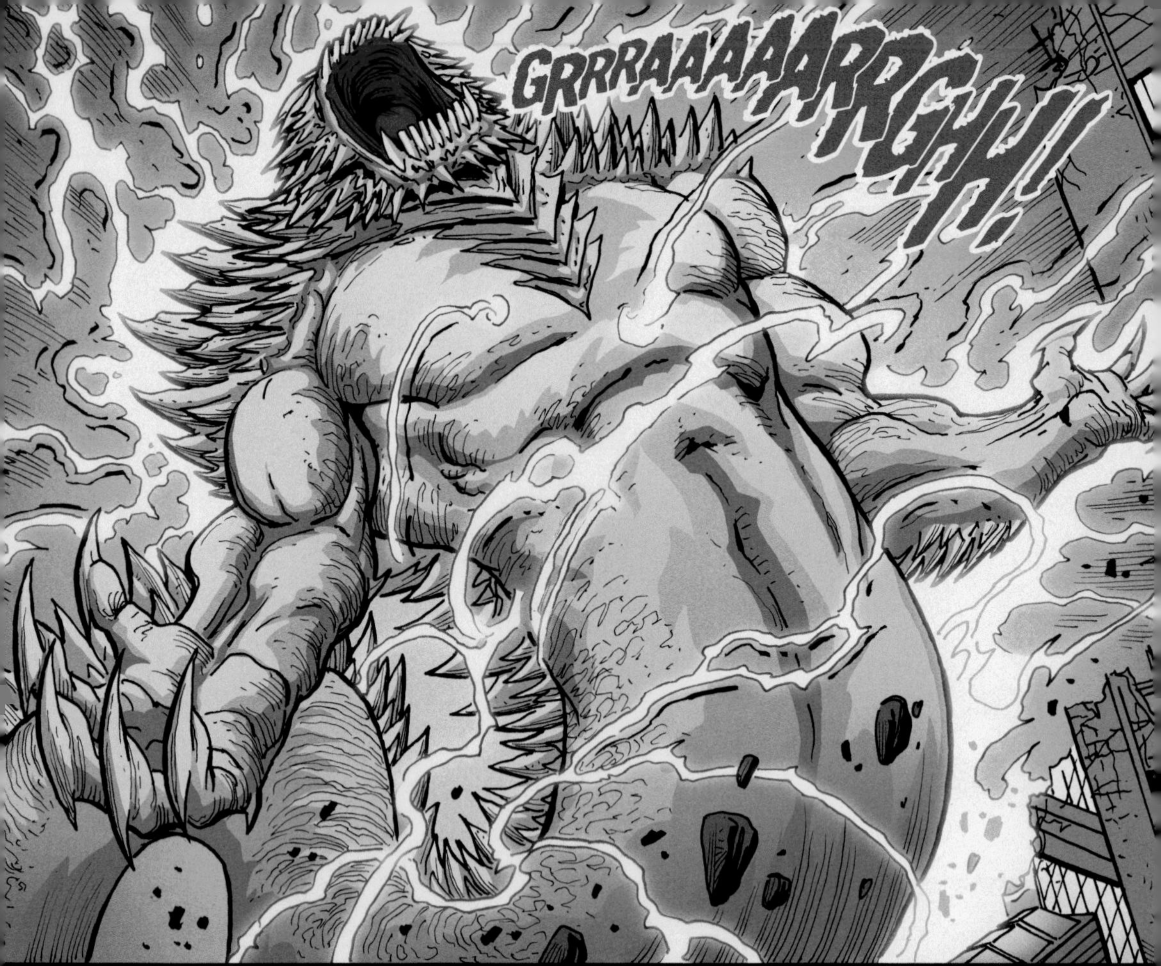
GRRRAAAAAARRGH!!

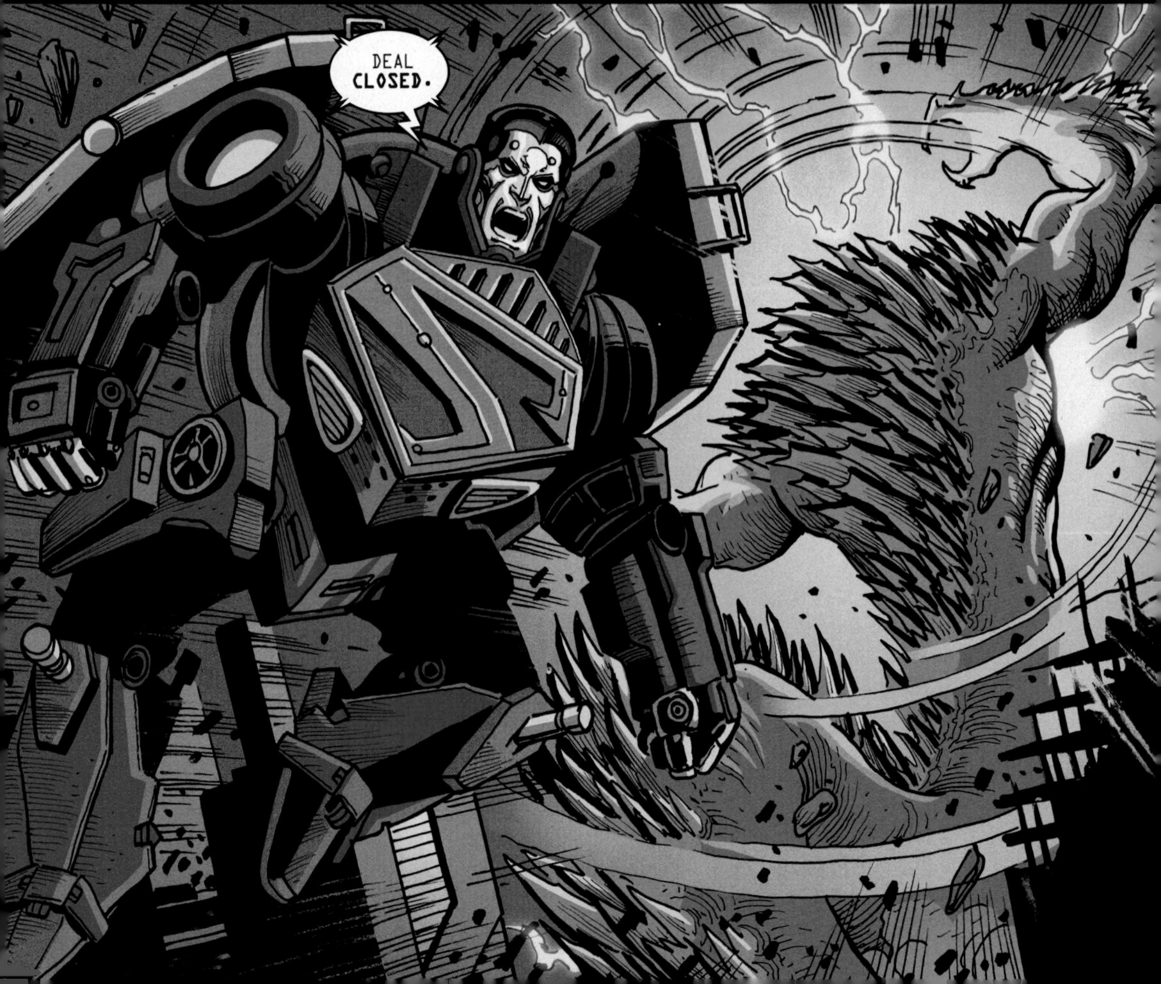
DEAL CLOSED.

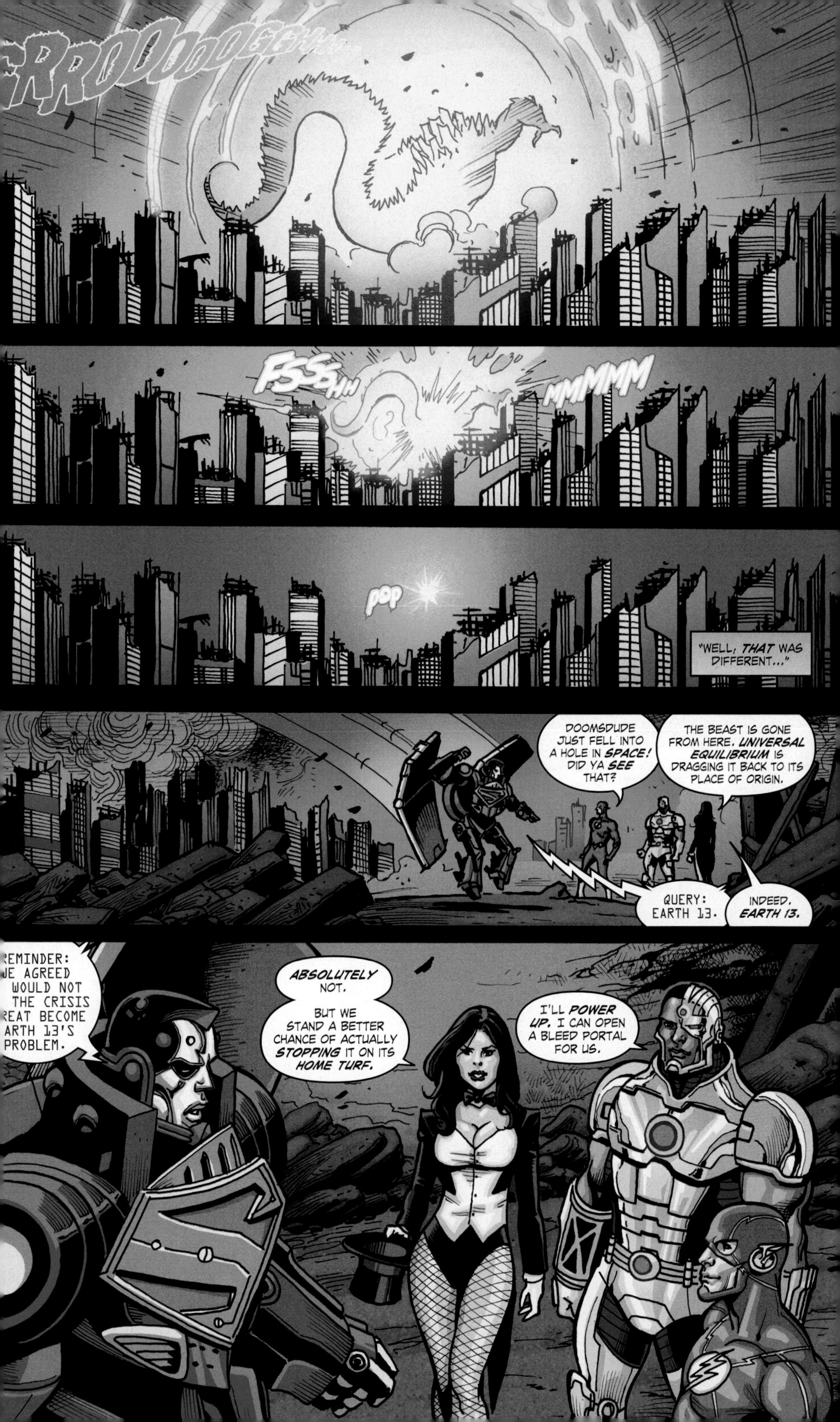
RRROOOOOGGHH
FSSSHH
MMMMMM
POP
"WELL, THAT WAS DIFFERENT..."
DOOMSDUDE JUST FELL INTO A HOLE IN SPACE! DID YA SEE THAT?
THE BEAST IS GONE FROM HERE. UNIVERSAL EQUILIBRIUM IS DRAGGING IT BACK TO ITS PLACE OF ORIGIN.
QUERY: EARTH 13.
INDEED. EARTH 13.
REMINDER: WE AGREED WOULD NOT THE CRISIS REAT BECOME ARTH 13'S PROBLEM.
ABSOLUTELY NOT.
BUT WE STAND A BETTER CHANCE OF ACTUALLY STOPPING IT ON ITS HOME TURF.
I'LL POWER UP. I CAN OPEN A BLEED PORTAL FOR US.

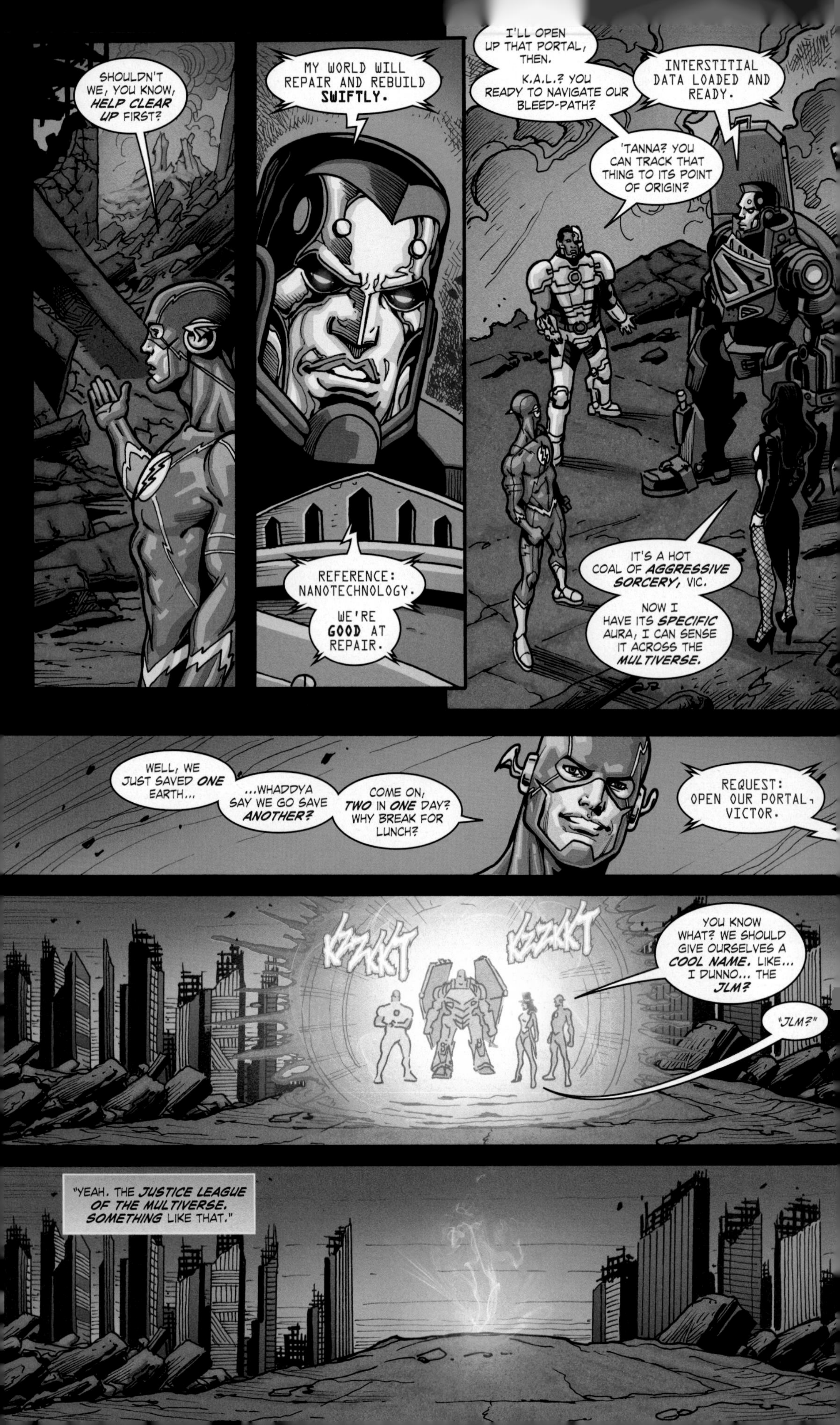
SHOULDN'T WE, YOU KNOW, *HELP CLEAR UP* FIRST?
MY WORLD WILL REPAIR AND REBUILD **SWIFTLY.**
REFERENCE: NANOTECHNOLOGY.
WE'RE **GOOD** AT REPAIR.
I'LL OPEN UP THAT PORTAL, THEN.
K.A.L.? YOU READY TO NAVIGATE OUR BLEED-PATH?
INTERSTITIAL DATA LOADED AND READY.
'TANNA? YOU CAN TRACK THAT THING TO ITS POINT OF ORIGIN?
IT'S A HOT COAL OF *AGGRESSIVE SORCERY,* VIC.
NOW I HAVE ITS *SPECIFIC* AURA, I CAN SENSE IT ACROSS THE *MULTIVERSE.*
WELL, WE JUST SAVED *ONE* EARTH...
...WHADDYA SAY WE GO SAVE *ANOTHER?*
COME ON, *TWO* IN *ONE* DAY? WHY BREAK FOR LUNCH?
REQUEST: OPEN OUR PORTAL, VICTOR.
KZZKKT
KZZKKT
YOU KNOW WHAT? WE SHOULD GIVE OURSELVES A *COOL NAME.* LIKE... I DUNNO... THE *JLM?*
"*JLM?*"
"YEAH. THE *JUSTICE LEAGUE OF THE MULTIVERSE. SOMETHING* LIKE THAT."

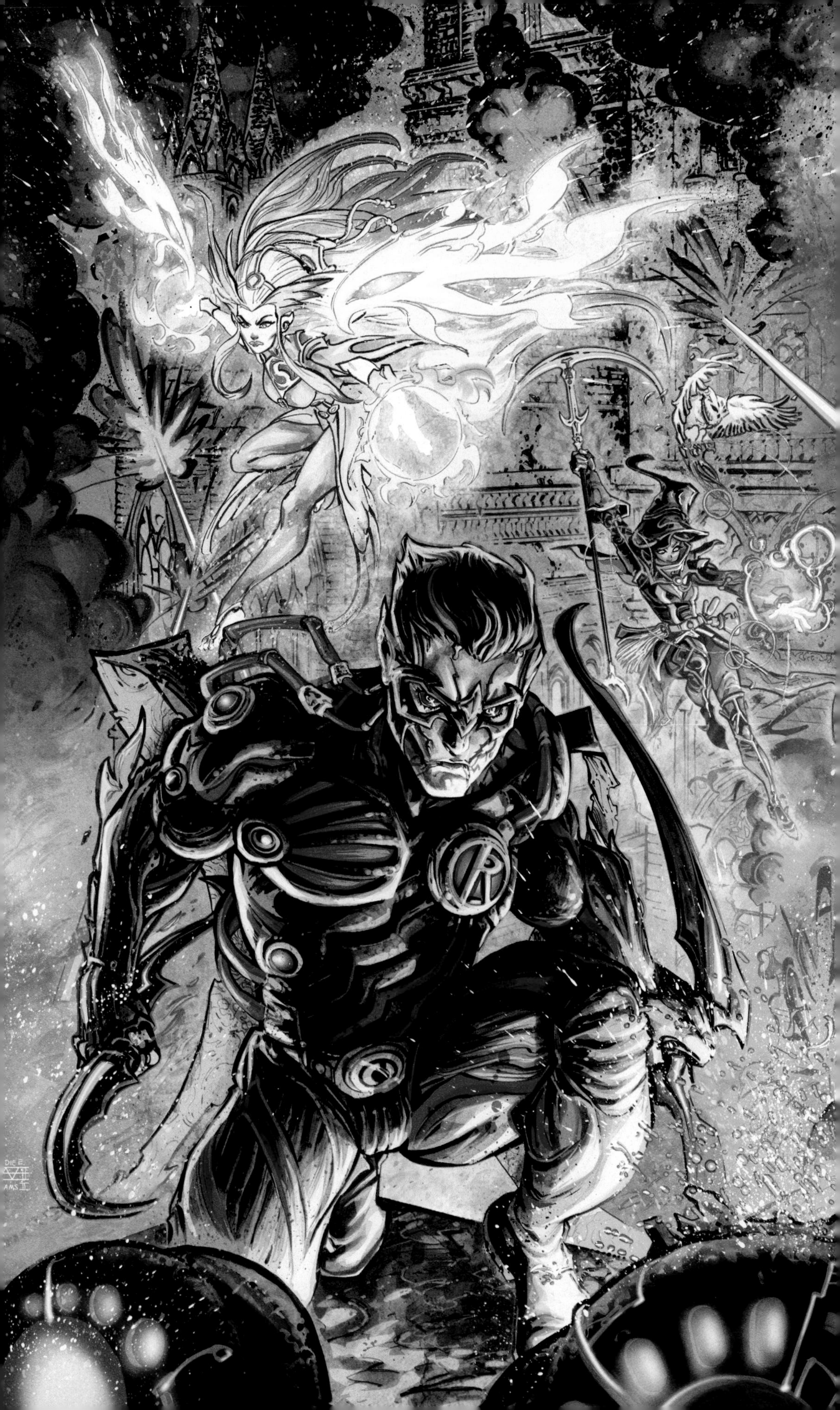

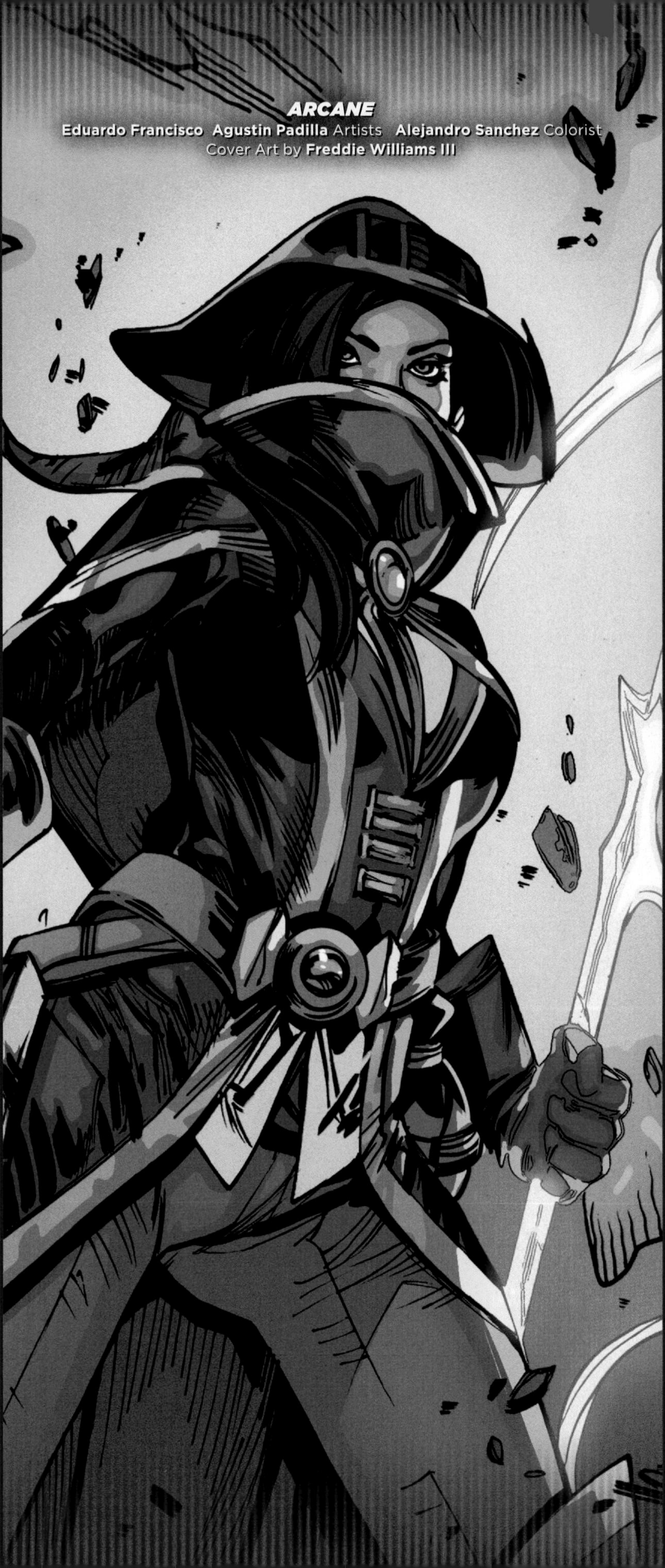
ARCANE
Eduardo Francisco Agustin Padilla Artists Alejandro Sanchez Colorist
Cover Art by Freddie Williams III

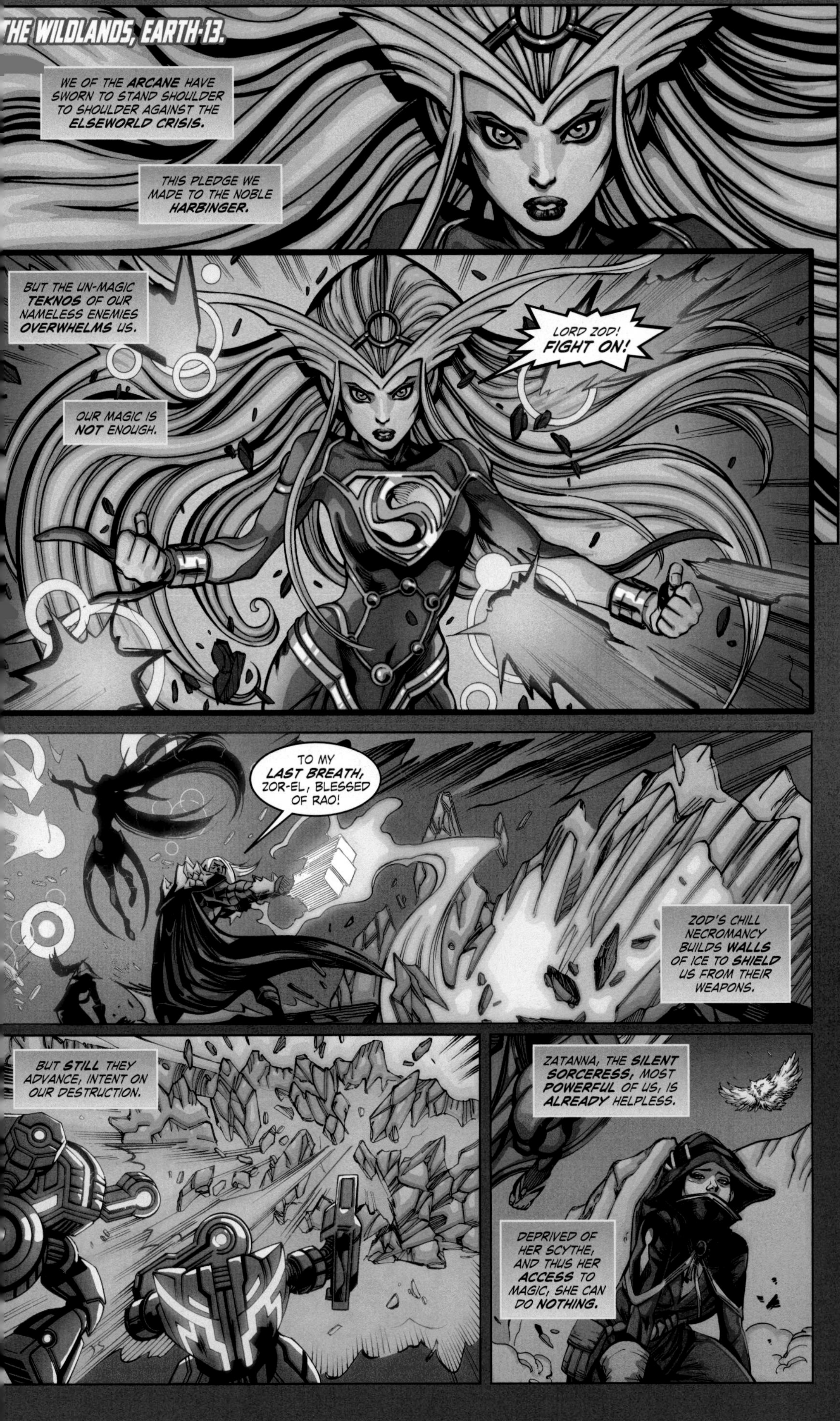
THE WILDLANDS, EARTH-13.
WE OF THE ARCANE HAVE SWORN TO STAND SHOULDER TO SHOULDER AGAINST THE ELSEWORLD CRISIS.
THIS PLEDGE WE MADE TO THE NOBLE HARBINGER.
BUT THE UN-MAGIC TEKNOS OF OUR NAMELESS ENEMIES OVERWHELMS US.
LORD ZOD! FIGHT ON!
OUR MAGIC IS NOT ENOUGH.
TO MY LAST BREATH, ZOR-EL, BLESSED OF RAO!
ZOD'S CHILL NECROMANCY BUILDS WALLS OF ICE TO SHIELD US FROM THEIR WEAPONS.
BUT STILL THEY ADVANCE, INTENT ON OUR DESTRUCTION.
ZATANNA, THE SILENT SORCERESS, MOST POWERFUL OF US, IS ALREADY HELPLESS.
DEPRIVED OF HER SCYTHE, AND THUS HER ACCESS TO MAGIC, SHE CAN DO NOTHING.

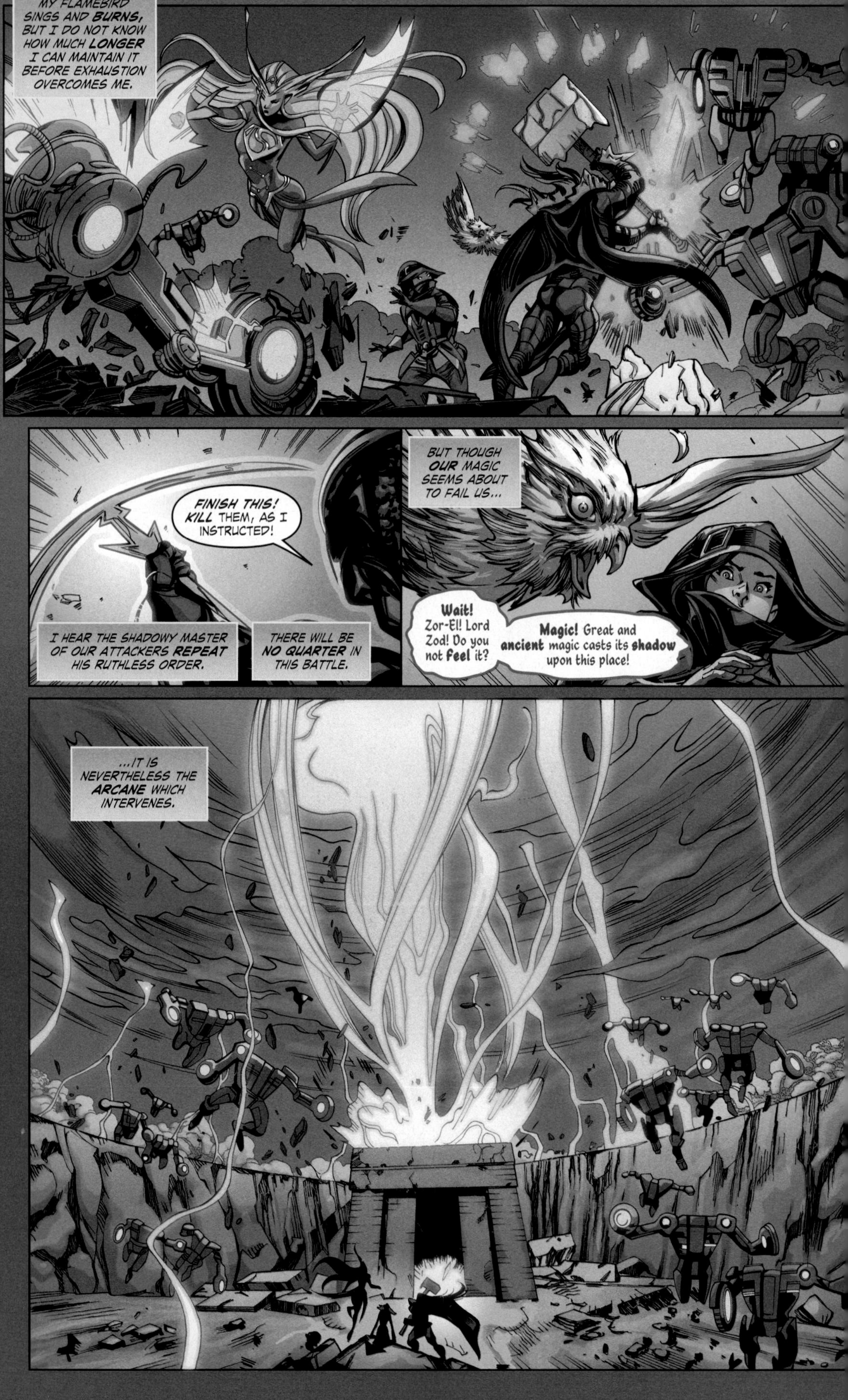
MY FLAMEBIRD SINGS AND BURNS, BUT I DO NOT KNOW HOW MUCH LONGER I CAN MAINTAIN IT BEFORE EXHAUSTION OVERCOMES ME.
FINISH THIS! KILL THEM, AS I INSTRUCTED!
I HEAR THE SHADOWY MASTER OF OUR ATTACKERS REPEAT HIS RUTHLESS ORDER.
THERE WILL BE NO QUARTER IN THIS BATTLE.
BUT THOUGH OUR MAGIC SEEMS ABOUT TO FAIL US...
Wait! Zor-El! Lord Zod! Do you not feel it?
Magic! Great and ancient magic casts its shadow upon this place!
...IT IS NEVERTHELESS THE ARCANE WHICH INTERVENES.

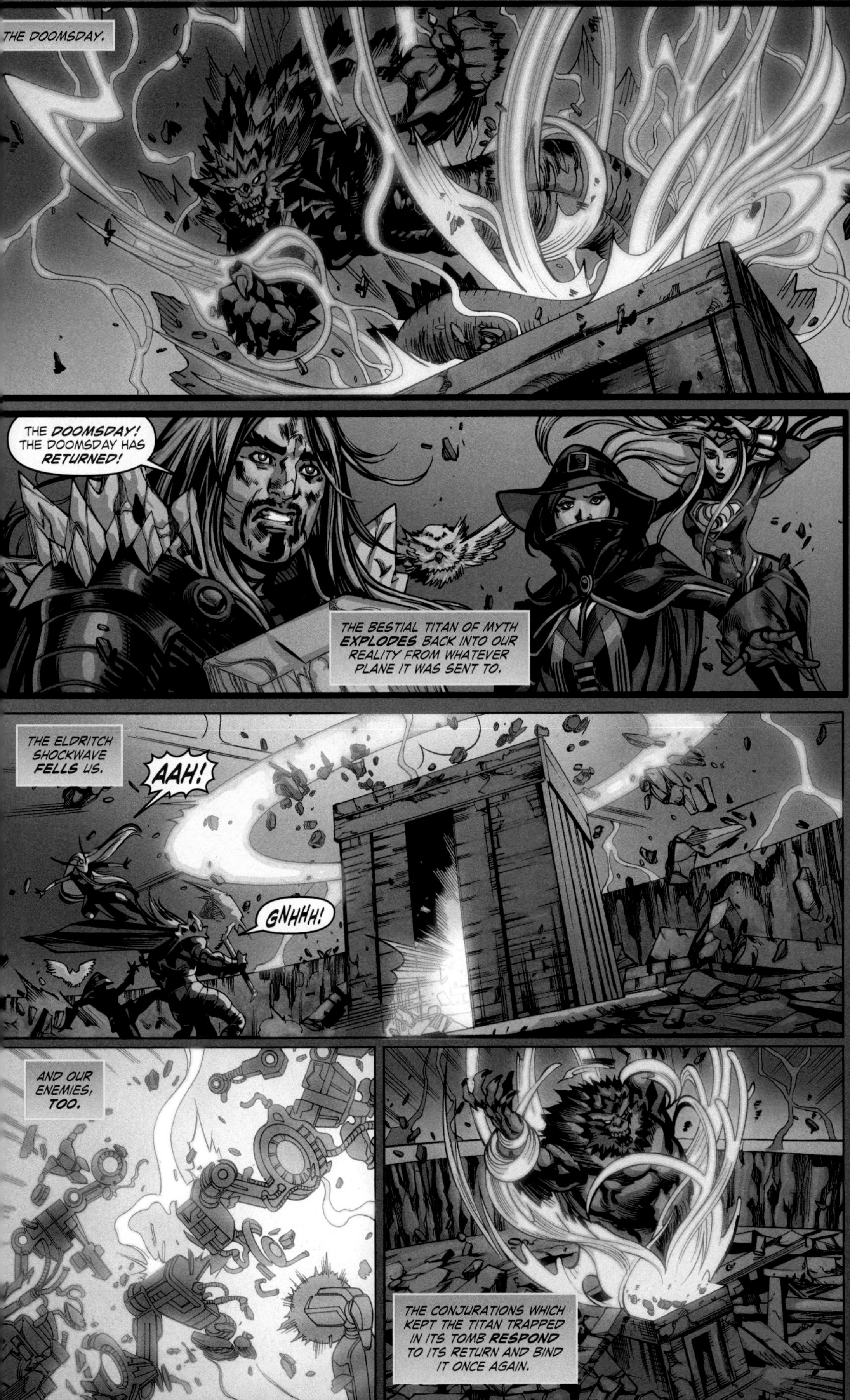
THE DOOMSDAY.
THE DOOMSDAY! THE DOOMSDAY HAS RETURNED!
THE BESTIAL TITAN OF MYTH EXPLODES BACK INTO OUR REALITY FROM WHATEVER PLANE IT WAS SENT TO.
THE ELDRITCH SHOCKWAVE FELLS US.
AAH!
GNHHH!
AND OUR ENEMIES, TOO.
THE CONJURATIONS WHICH KEPT THE TITAN TRAPPED IN ITS TOMB RESPOND TO ITS RETURN AND BIND IT ONCE AGAIN.

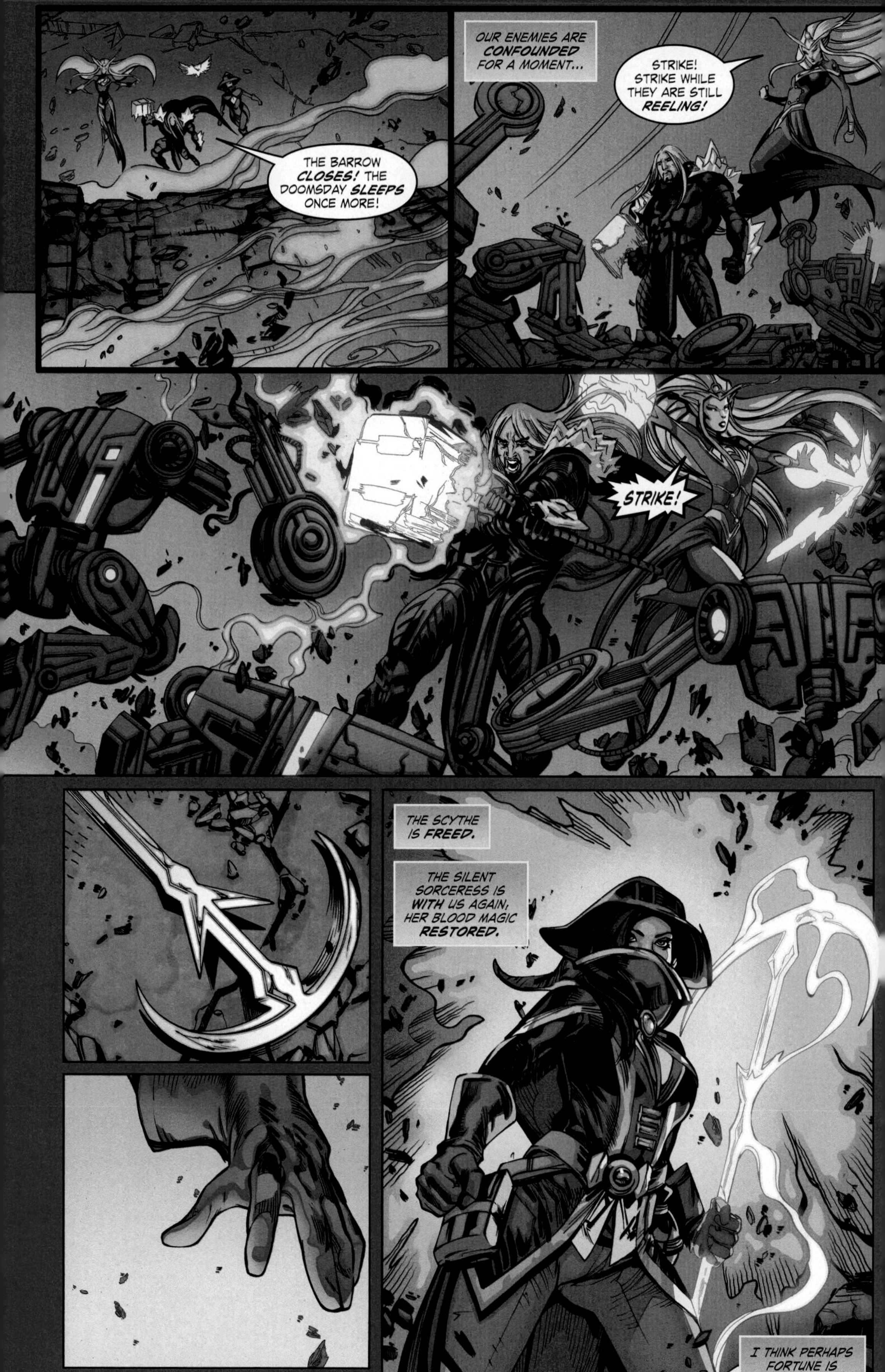
THE BARROW CLOSES! THE DOOMSDAY SLEEPS ONCE MORE!
OUR ENEMIES ARE CONFOUNDED FOR A MOMENT...
STRIKE! STRIKE WHILE THEY ARE STILL REELING!
STRIKE!
THE SCYTHE IS FREED.
THE SILENT SORCERESS IS WITH US AGAIN, HER BLOOD MAGIC RESTORED.
I THINK PERHAPS FORTUNE IS SMILING ON US ONCE MORE.

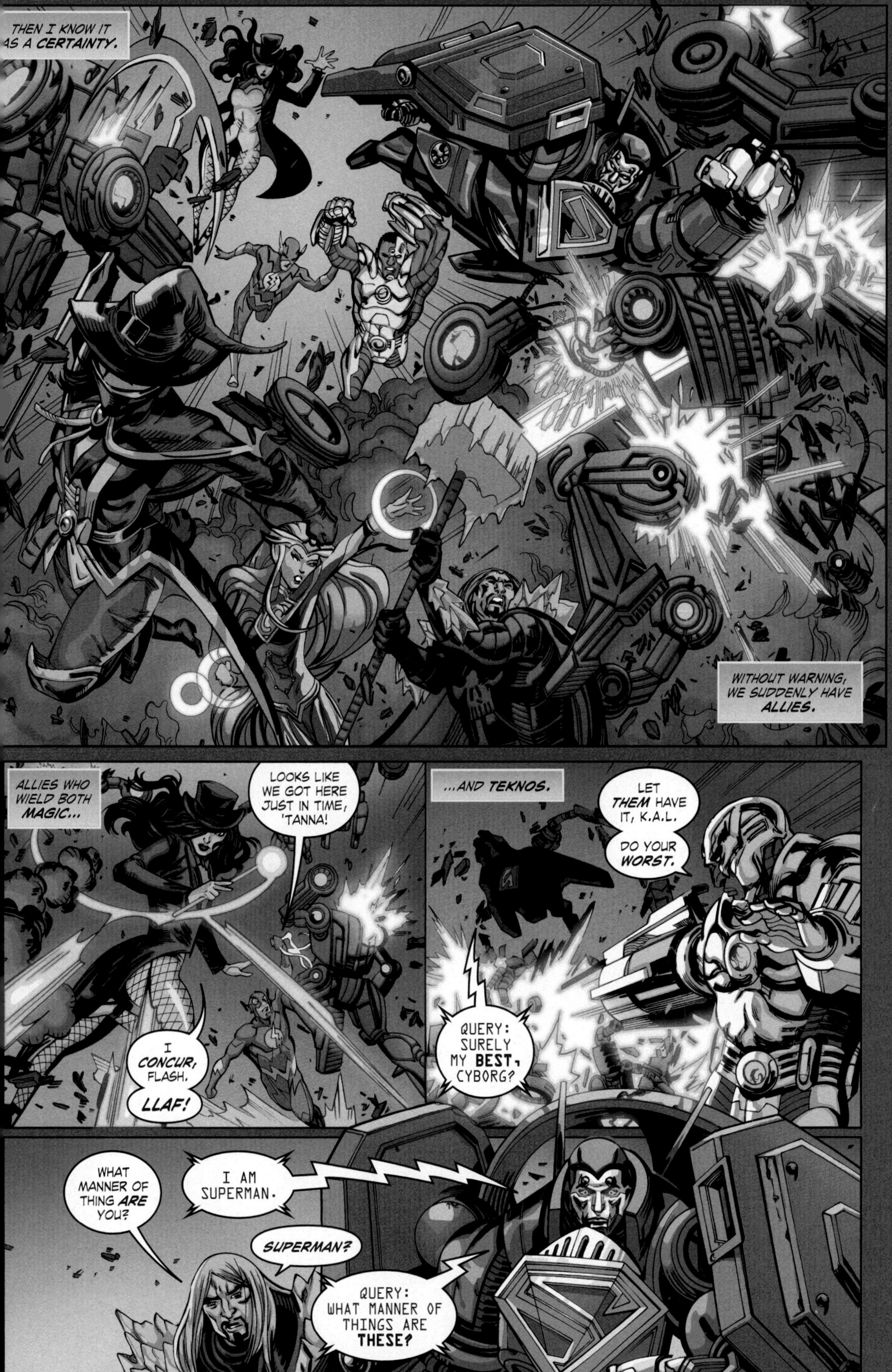
THEN I KNOW IT AS A CERTAINTY.
WITHOUT WARNING, WE SUDDENLY HAVE ALLIES.
ALLIES WHO WIELD BOTH MAGIC...
LOOKS LIKE WE GOT HERE JUST IN TIME, 'TANNA!
I CONCUR, FLASH. LLAF!
...AND TEKNOS.
LET THEM HAVE IT, K.A.L.
DO YOUR WORST.
QUERY: SURELY MY BEST, CYBORG?
WHAT MANNER OF THING ARE YOU?
I AM SUPERMAN.
SUPERMAN?
QUERY: WHAT MANNER OF THINGS ARE THESE?

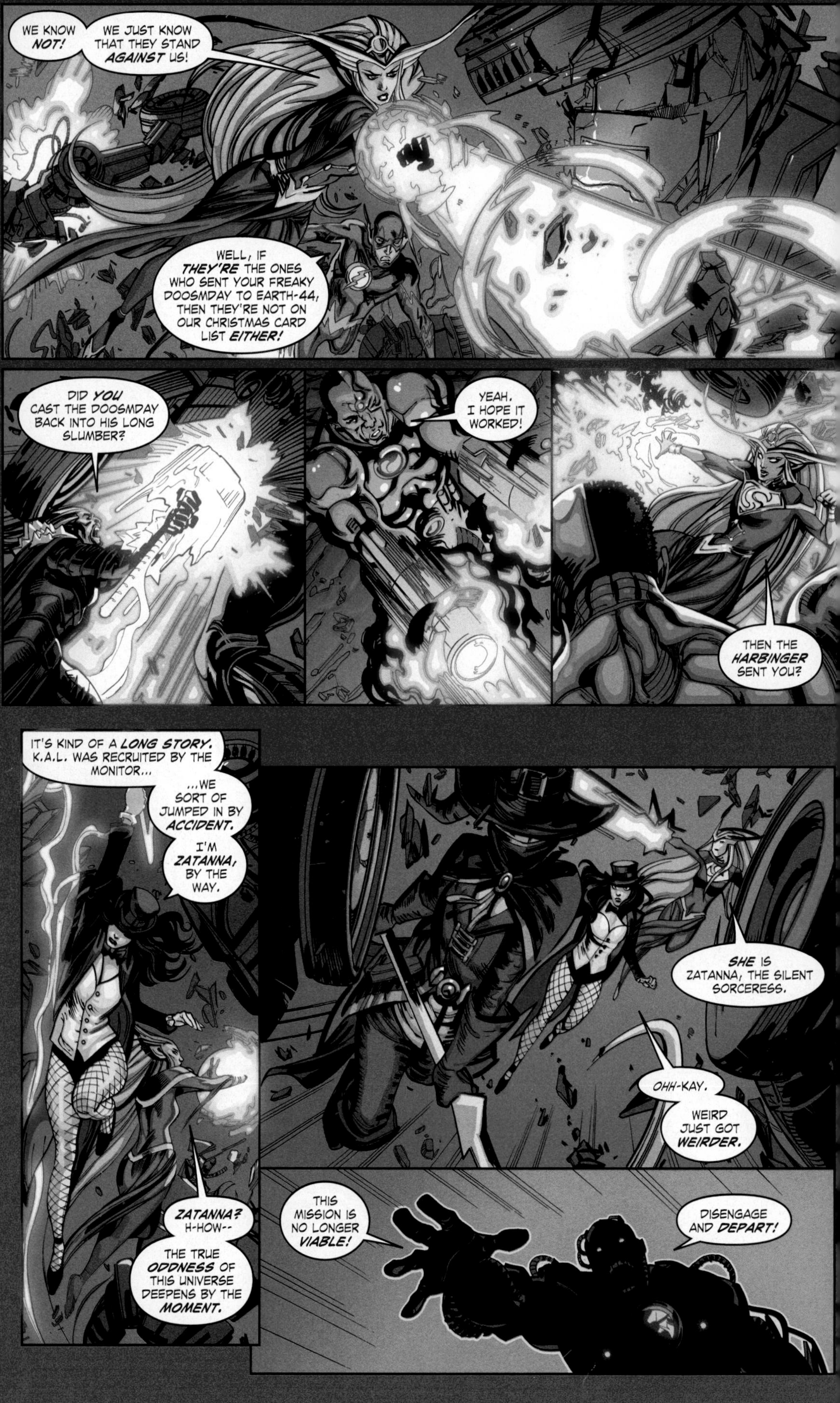
WE KNOW NOT!
WE JUST KNOW THAT THEY STAND AGAINST US!
WELL, IF THEY'RE THE ONES WHO SENT YOUR FREAKY DOOSMDAY TO EARTH-44, THEN THEY'RE NOT ON OUR CHRISTMAS CARD LIST EITHER!
DID YOU CAST THE DOOSMDAY BACK INTO HIS LONG SLUMBER?
YEAH. I HOPE IT WORKED!
THEN THE HARBINGER SENT YOU?
IT'S KIND OF A LONG STORY. K.A.L. WAS RECRUITED BY THE MONITOR...
...WE SORT OF JUMPED IN BY ACCIDENT.
I'M ZATANNA, BY THE WAY.
ZATANNA? H-HOW--
THE TRUE ODDNESS OF THIS UNIVERSE DEEPENS BY THE MOMENT.
SHE IS ZATANNA, THE SILENT SORCERESS.
OHH-KAY.
WEIRD JUST GOT WEIRDER.
THIS MISSION IS NO LONGER VIABLE!
DISENGAGE AND DEPART!

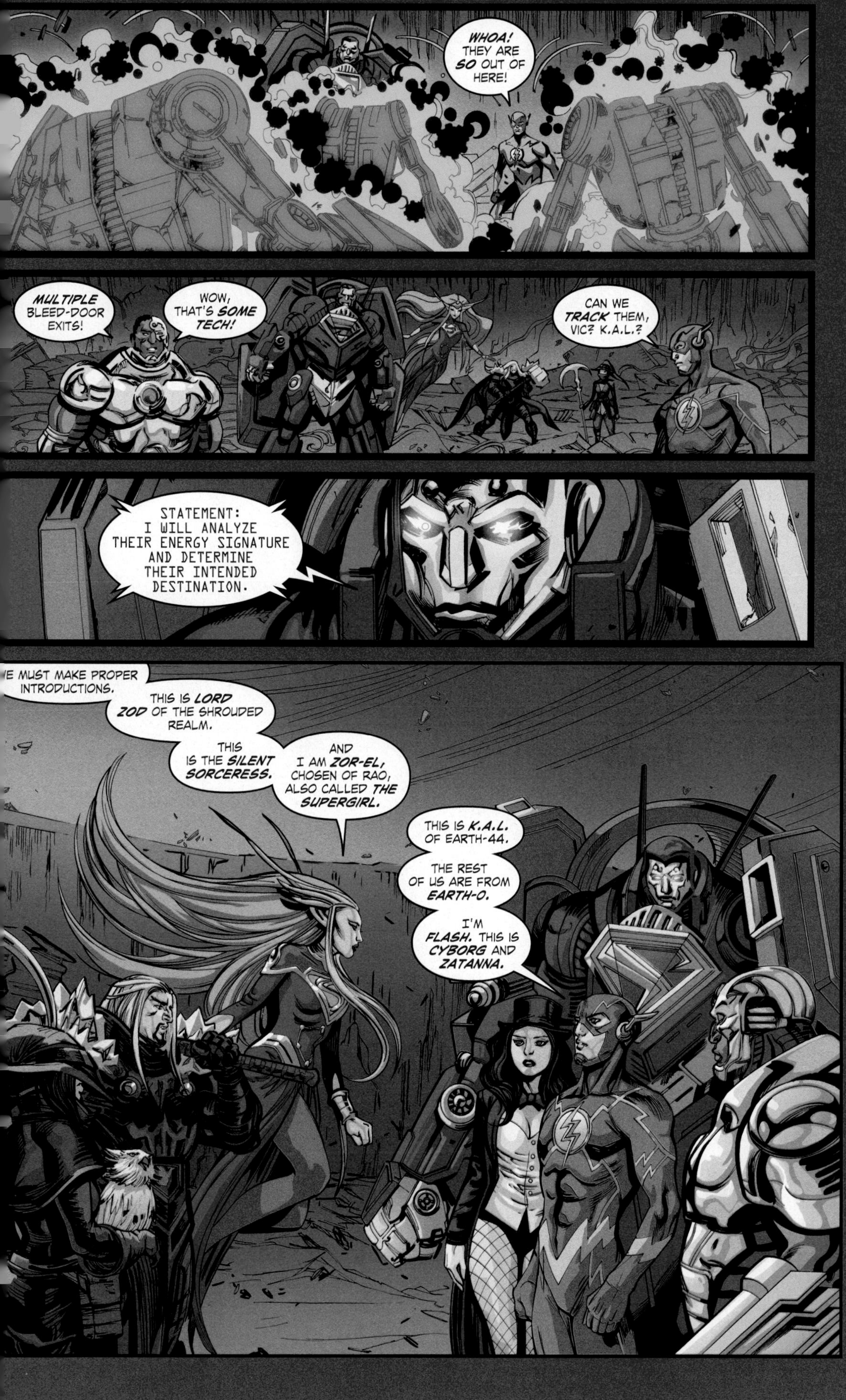
WHOA! THEY ARE SO OUT OF HERE!
MULTIPLE BLEED-DOOR EXITS!
WOW, THAT'S SOME TECH!
CAN WE TRACK THEM, VIC? K.A.L.?
STATEMENT: I WILL ANALYZE THEIR ENERGY SIGNATURE AND DETERMINE THEIR INTENDED DESTINATION.
E MUST MAKE PROPER INTRODUCTIONS.
THIS IS LORD ZOD OF THE SHROUDED REALM.
THIS IS THE SILENT SORCERESS.
AND I AM ZOR-EL, CHOSEN OF RAO, ALSO CALLED THE SUPERGIRL.
THIS IS K.A.L. OF EARTH-44.
THE REST OF US ARE FROM EARTH-0.
I'M FLASH. THIS IS CYBORG AND ZATANNA.

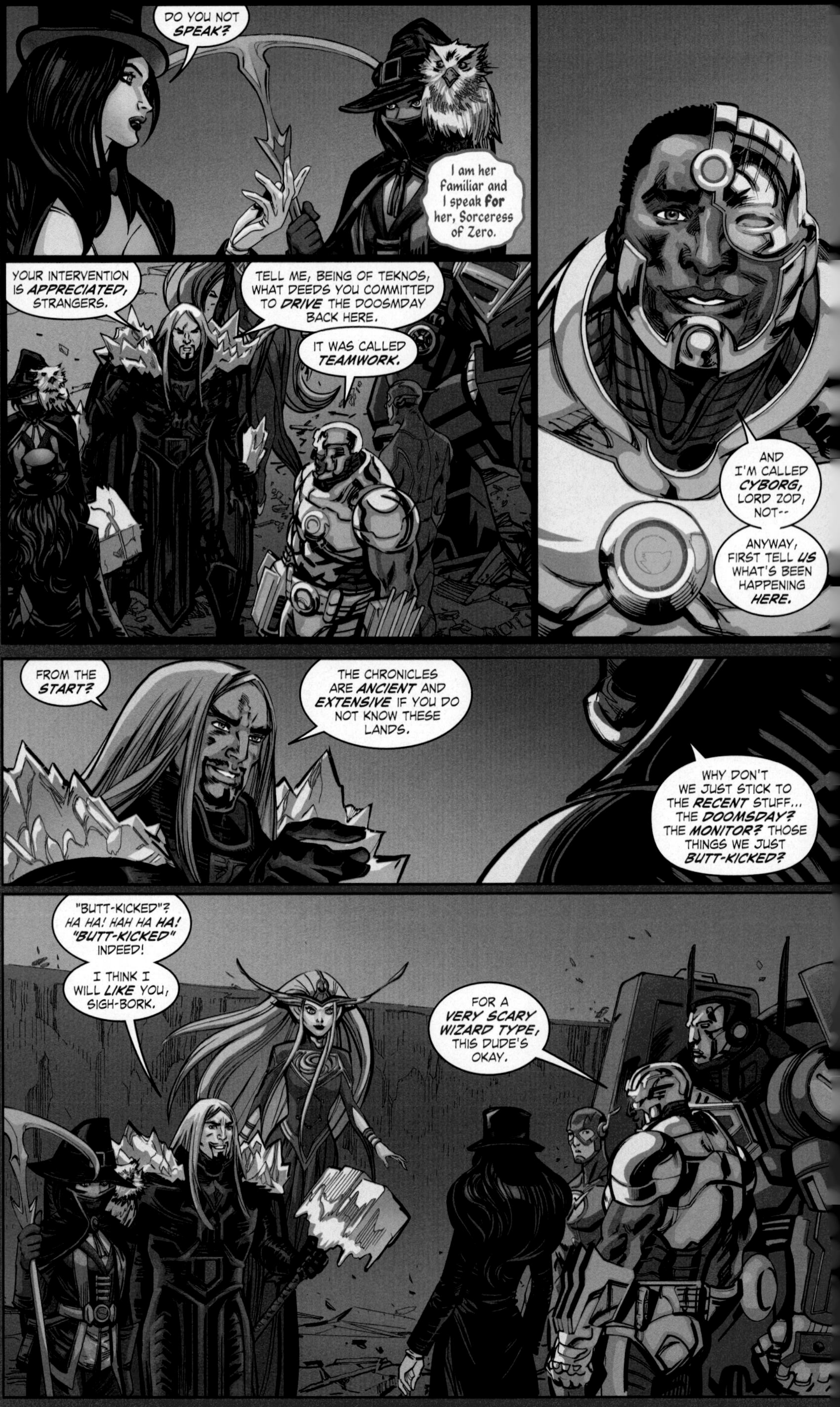
DO YOU NOT SPEAK?
I am her familiar and I speak for her, Sorceress of Zero.
YOUR INTERVENTION IS APPRECIATED, STRANGERS.
TELL ME, BEING OF TEKNOS, WHAT DEEDS YOU COMMITTED TO DRIVE THE DOOMSDAY BACK HERE.
IT WAS CALLED TEAMWORK.
AND I'M CALLED CYBORG, LORD ZOD, NOT--
ANYWAY, FIRST TELL US WHAT'S BEEN HAPPENING HERE.
FROM THE START?
THE CHRONICLES ARE ANCIENT AND EXTENSIVE IF YOU DO NOT KNOW THESE LANDS.
WHY DON'T WE JUST STICK TO THE RECENT STUFF... THE DOOMSDAY? THE MONITOR? THOSE THINGS WE JUST BUTT-KICKED?
"BUTT-KICKED"? HA HA! HAH HA HA! "BUTT-KICKED" INDEED!
I THINK I WILL LIKE YOU, SIGH-BORK.
FOR A VERY SCARY WIZARD TYPE, THIS DUDE'S OKAY.

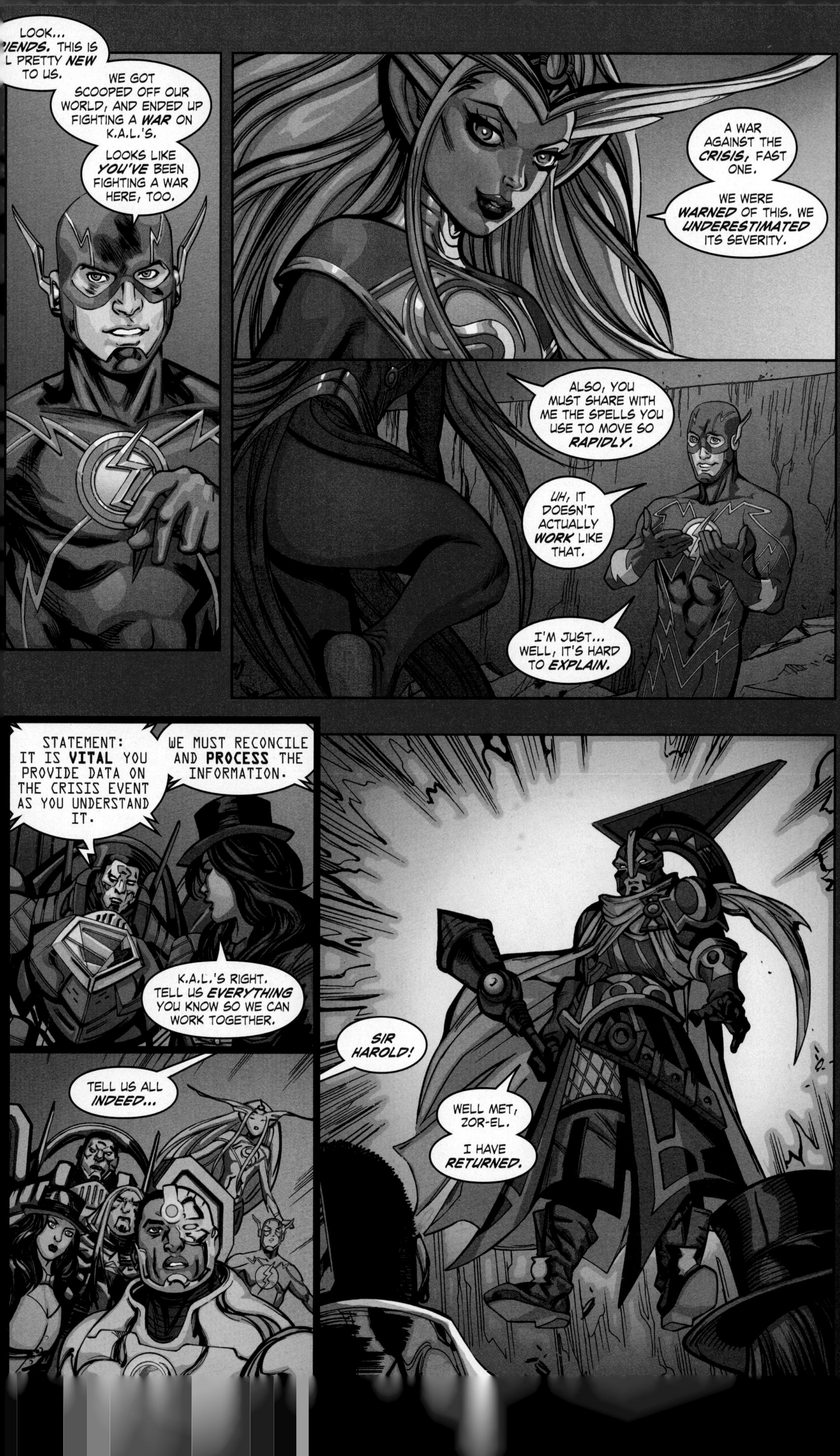
LOOK... FRIENDS. THIS IS ALL PRETTY NEW TO US.
WE GOT SCOOPED OFF OUR WORLD, AND ENDED UP FIGHTING A WAR ON K.A.L.'S.
LOOKS LIKE YOU'VE BEEN FIGHTING A WAR HERE, TOO.
A WAR AGAINST THE CRISIS, FAST ONE.
WE WERE WARNED OF THIS. WE UNDERESTIMATED ITS SEVERITY.
ALSO, YOU MUST SHARE WITH ME THE SPELLS YOU USE TO MOVE SO RAPIDLY.
UH, IT DOESN'T ACTUALLY WORK LIKE THAT.
I'M JUST... WELL, IT'S HARD TO EXPLAIN.
STATEMENT: IT IS VITAL YOU PROVIDE DATA ON THE CRISIS EVENT AS YOU UNDERSTAND IT.
WE MUST RECONCILE AND PROCESS THE INFORMATION.
K.A.L.'S RIGHT. TELL US EVERYTHING YOU KNOW SO WE CAN WORK TOGETHER.
TELL US ALL INDEED...
SIR HAROLD!
WELL MET, ZOR-EL.
I HAVE RETURNED.

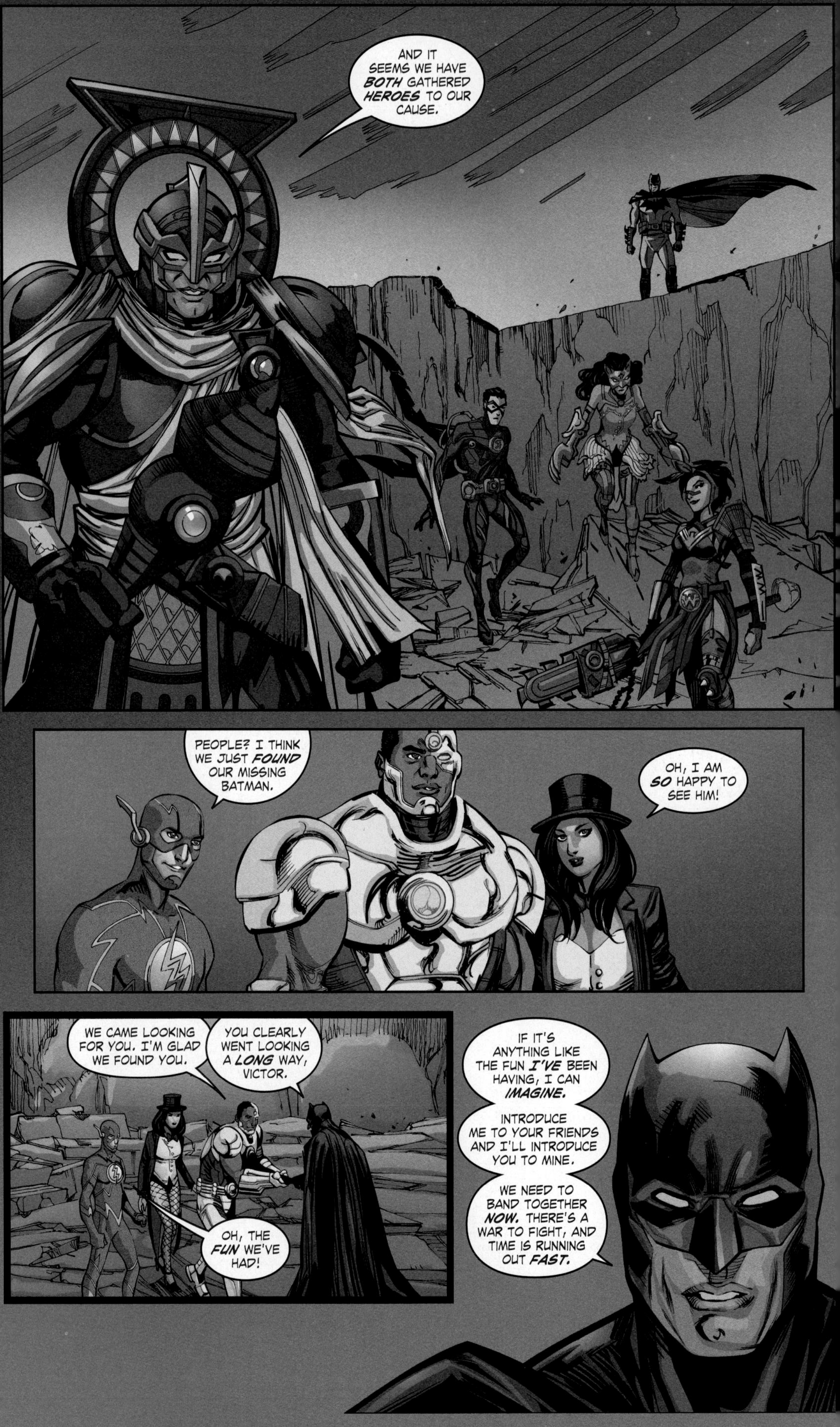

AND IT SEEMS WE HAVE BOTH GATHERED HEROES TO OUR CAUSE.
PEOPLE? I THINK WE JUST FOUND OUR MISSING BATMAN.
OH, I AM SO HAPPY TO SEE HIM!
WE CAME LOOKING FOR YOU. I'M GLAD WE FOUND YOU.
YOU CLEARLY WENT LOOKING A LONG WAY, VICTOR.
OH, THE FUN WE'VE HAD!
IF IT'S ANYTHING LIKE THE FUN I'VE BEEN HAVING, I CAN IMAGINE.
INTRODUCE ME TO YOUR FRIENDS AND I'LL INTRODUCE YOU TO MINE.
WE NEED TO BAND TOGETHER NOW. THERE'S A WAR TO FIGHT, AND TIME IS RUNNING OUT FAST.

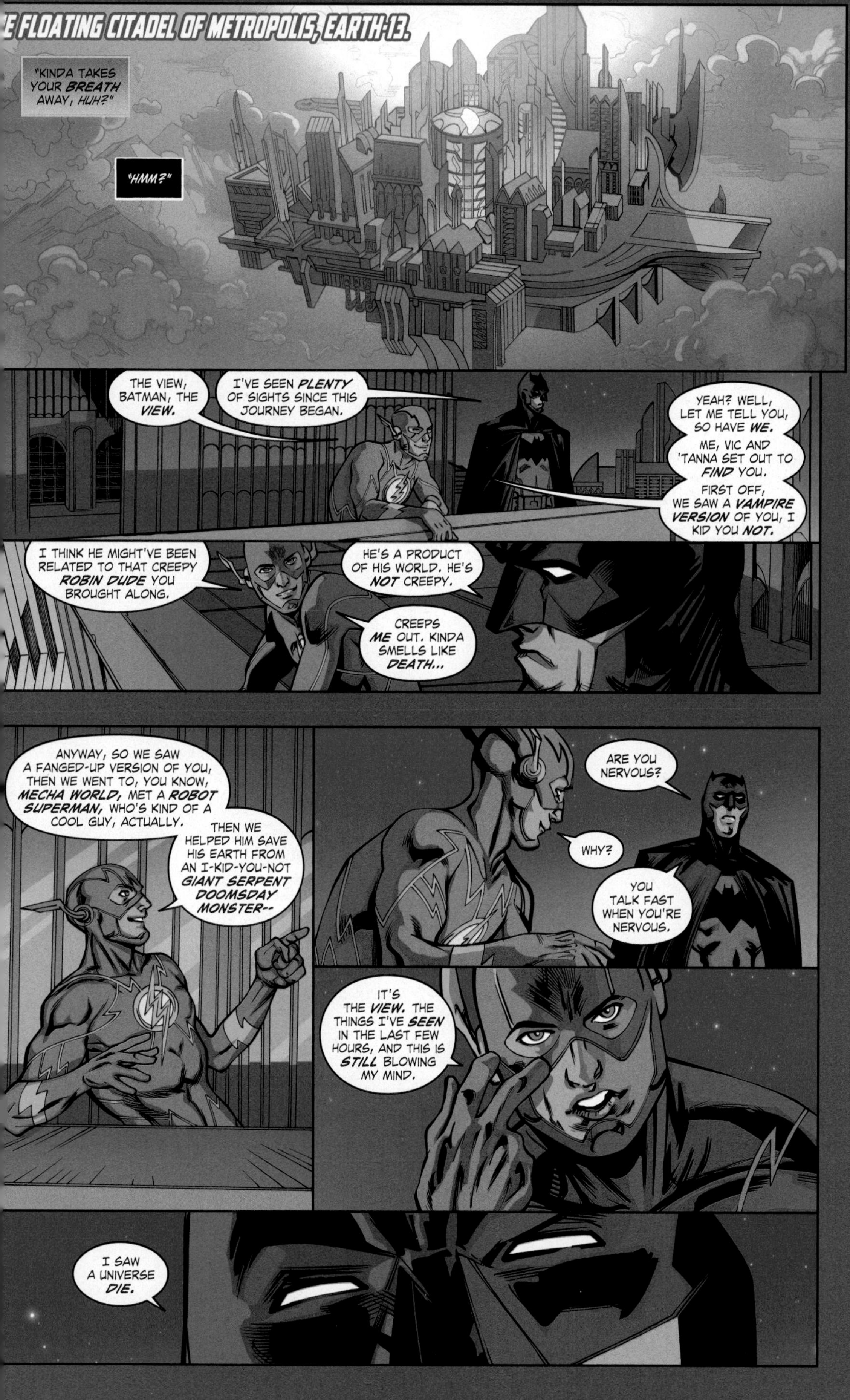
E FLOATING CITADEL OF METROPOLIS, EARTH-13.
"KINDA TAKES YOUR BREATH AWAY, HUH?"
"HMM?"
THE VIEW, BATMAN, THE VIEW.
I'VE SEEN PLENTY OF SIGHTS SINCE THIS JOURNEY BEGAN.
YEAH? WELL, LET ME TELL YOU, SO HAVE WE.
ME, VIC AND 'TANNA SET OUT TO FIND YOU.
FIRST OFF, WE SAW A VAMPIRE VERSION OF YOU, I KID YOU NOT.
I THINK HE MIGHT'VE BEEN RELATED TO THAT CREEPY ROBIN DUDE YOU BROUGHT ALONG.
HE'S A PRODUCT OF HIS WORLD. HE'S NOT CREEPY.
CREEPS ME OUT. KINDA SMELLS LIKE DEATH...
ANYWAY, SO WE SAW A FANGED-UP VERSION OF YOU, THEN WE WENT TO, YOU KNOW, MECHA WORLD, MET A ROBOT SUPERMAN, WHO'S KIND OF A COOL GUY, ACTUALLY.
THEN WE HELPED HIM SAVE HIS EARTH FROM AN I-KID-YOU-NOT GIANT SERPENT DOOMSDAY MONSTER--
ARE YOU NERVOUS?
WHY?
YOU TALK FAST WHEN YOU'RE NERVOUS.
IT'S THE VIEW. THE THINGS I'VE SEEN IN THE LAST FEW HOURS, AND THIS IS STILL BLOWING MY MIND.
I SAW A UNIVERSE DIE.

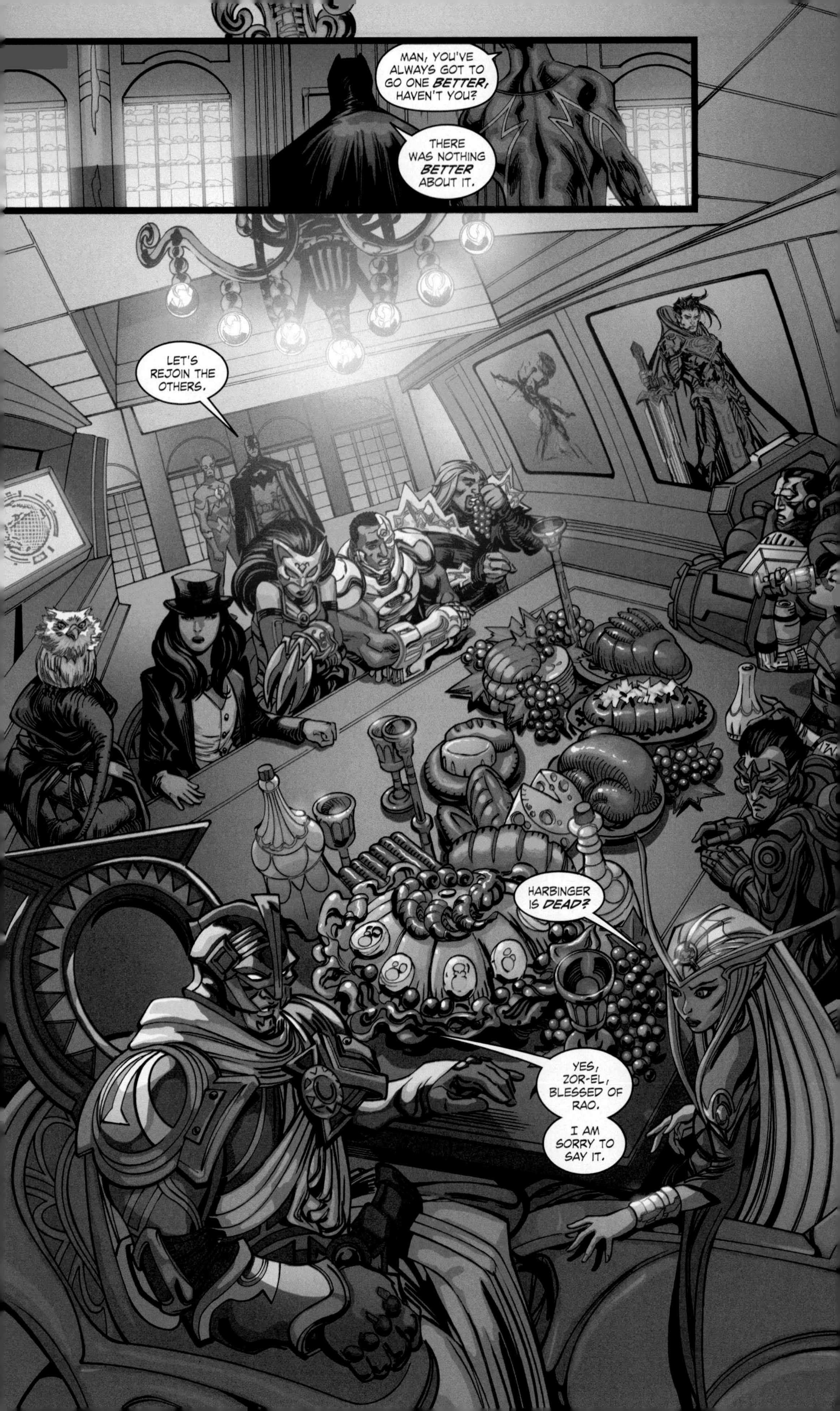
MAN, YOU'VE ALWAYS GOT TO GO ONE *BETTER,* HAVEN'T YOU?
THERE WAS NOTHING *BETTER* ABOUT IT.
LET'S REJOIN THE OTHERS.
HARBINGER IS *DEAD?*
YES, ZOR-EL, BLESSED OF RAO.
I AM SORRY TO SAY IT.

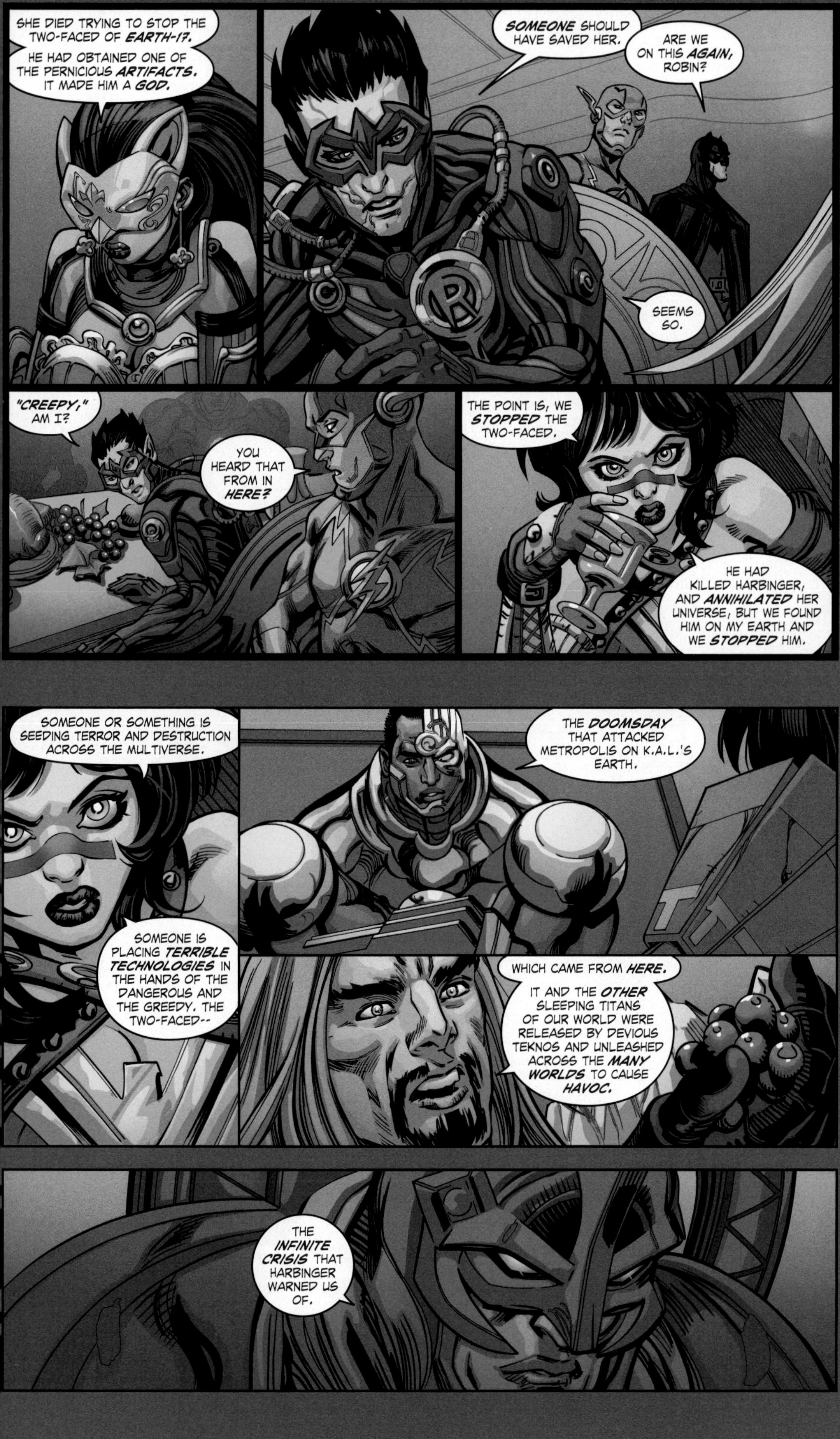
SHE DIED TRYING TO STOP THE TWO-FACED OF EARTH-17.
HE HAD OBTAINED ONE OF THE PERNICIOUS ARTIFACTS. IT MADE HIM A GOD.
SOMEONE SHOULD HAVE SAVED HER.
ARE WE ON THIS AGAIN, ROBIN?
SEEMS SO.
"CREEPY," AM I?
YOU HEARD THAT FROM IN HERE?
THE POINT IS, WE STOPPED THE TWO-FACED.
HE HAD KILLED HARBINGER, AND ANNIHILATED HER UNIVERSE, BUT WE FOUND HIM ON MY EARTH AND WE STOPPED HIM.
SOMEONE OR SOMETHING IS SEEDING TERROR AND DESTRUCTION ACROSS THE MULTIVERSE.
SOMEONE IS PLACING TERRIBLE TECHNOLOGIES IN THE HANDS OF THE DANGEROUS AND THE GREEDY. THE TWO-FACED--
THE DOOMSDAY THAT ATTACKED METROPOLIS ON K.A.L.'S EARTH.
WHICH CAME FROM HERE.
IT AND THE OTHER SLEEPING TITANS OF OUR WORLD WERE RELEASED BY DEVIOUS TEKNOS AND UNLEASHED ACROSS THE MANY WORLDS TO CAUSE HAVOC.
THE INFINITE CRISIS THAT HARBINGER WARNED US OF.

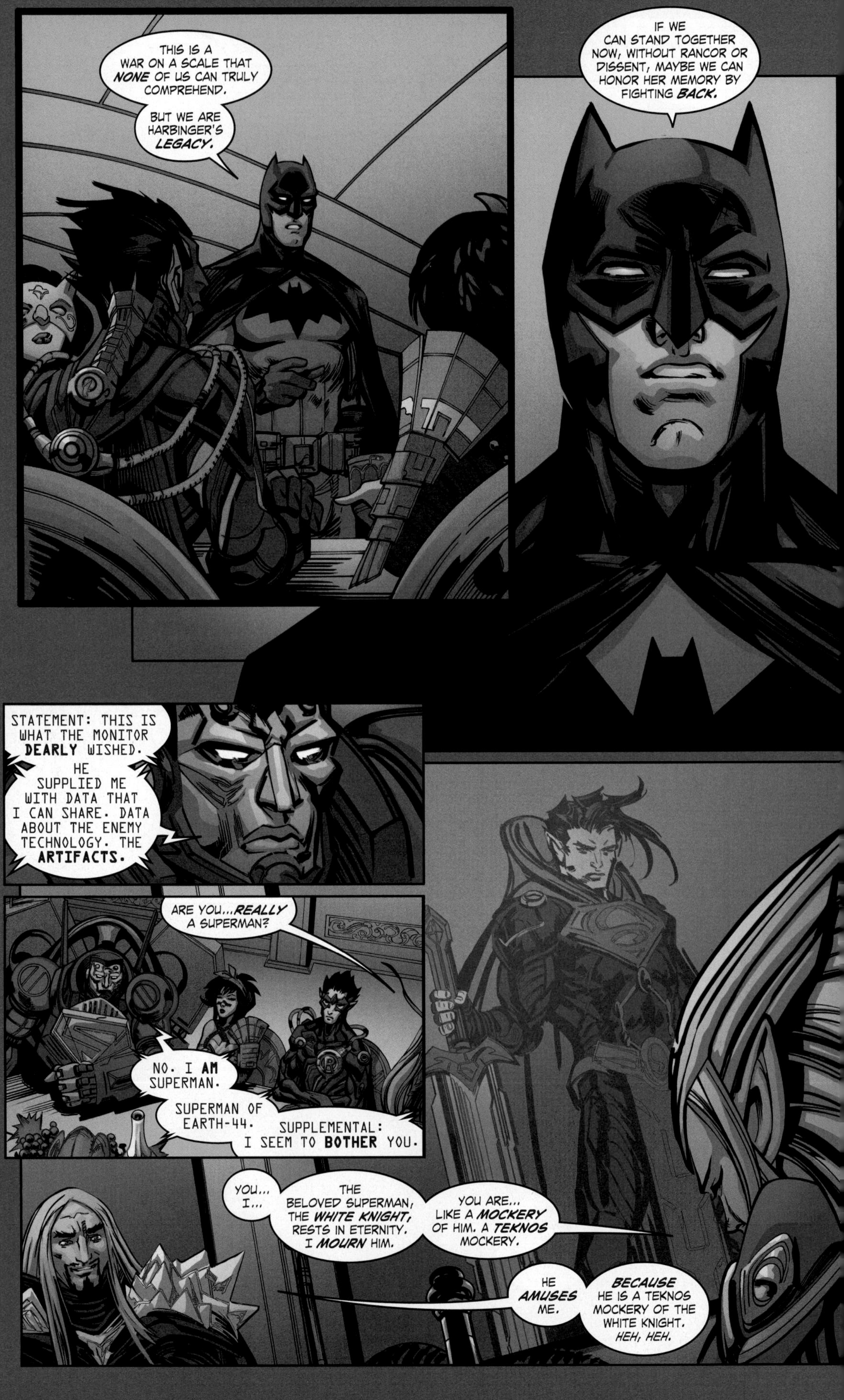
THIS IS A WAR ON A SCALE THAT NONE OF US CAN TRULY COMPREHEND.
BUT WE ARE HARBINGER'S LEGACY.
IF WE CAN STAND TOGETHER NOW, WITHOUT RANCOR OR DISSENT, MAYBE WE CAN HONOR HER MEMORY BY FIGHTING BACK.
STATEMENT: THIS IS WHAT THE MONITOR DEARLY WISHED.
HE SUPPLIED ME WITH DATA THAT I CAN SHARE. DATA ABOUT THE ENEMY TECHNOLOGY. THE ARTIFACTS.
ARE YOU...REALLY A SUPERMAN?
NO. I AM SUPERMAN.
SUPERMAN OF EARTH-44.
SUPPLEMENTAL: I SEEM TO BOTHER YOU.
YOU... I...
THE BELOVED SUPERMAN, THE WHITE KNIGHT, RESTS IN ETERNITY. I MOURN HIM.
YOU ARE... LIKE A MOCKERY OF HIM. A TEKNOS MOCKERY.
HE AMUSES ME.
BECAUSE HE IS A TEKNOS MOCKERY OF THE WHITE KNIGHT. HEH, HEH.

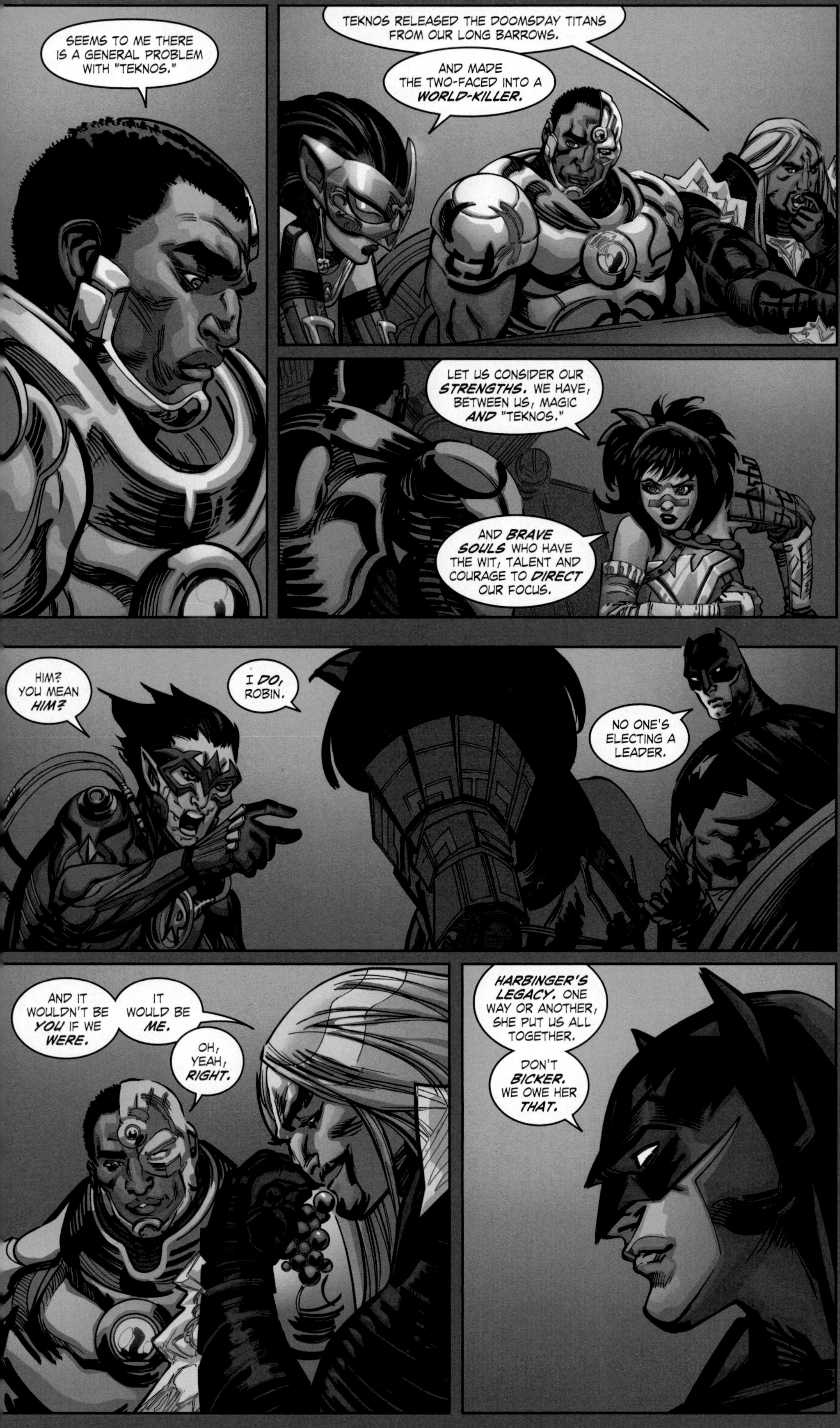

SEEMS TO ME THERE IS A GENERAL PROBLEM WITH "TEKNOS."
TEKNOS RELEASED THE DOOMSDAY TITANS FROM OUR LONG BARROWS.
AND MADE THE TWO-FACED INTO A WORLD-KILLER.
LET US CONSIDER OUR STRENGTHS. WE HAVE, BETWEEN US, MAGIC AND "TEKNOS."
AND BRAVE SOULS WHO HAVE THE WIT, TALENT AND COURAGE TO DIRECT OUR FOCUS.
HIM? YOU MEAN HIM?
I DO, ROBIN.
NO ONE'S ELECTING A LEADER.
AND IT WOULDN'T BE YOU IF WE WERE.
IT WOULD BE ME.
OH, YEAH, RIGHT.
HARBINGER'S LEGACY. ONE WAY OR ANOTHER, SHE PUT US ALL TOGETHER.
DON'T BICKER. WE OWE HER THAT.

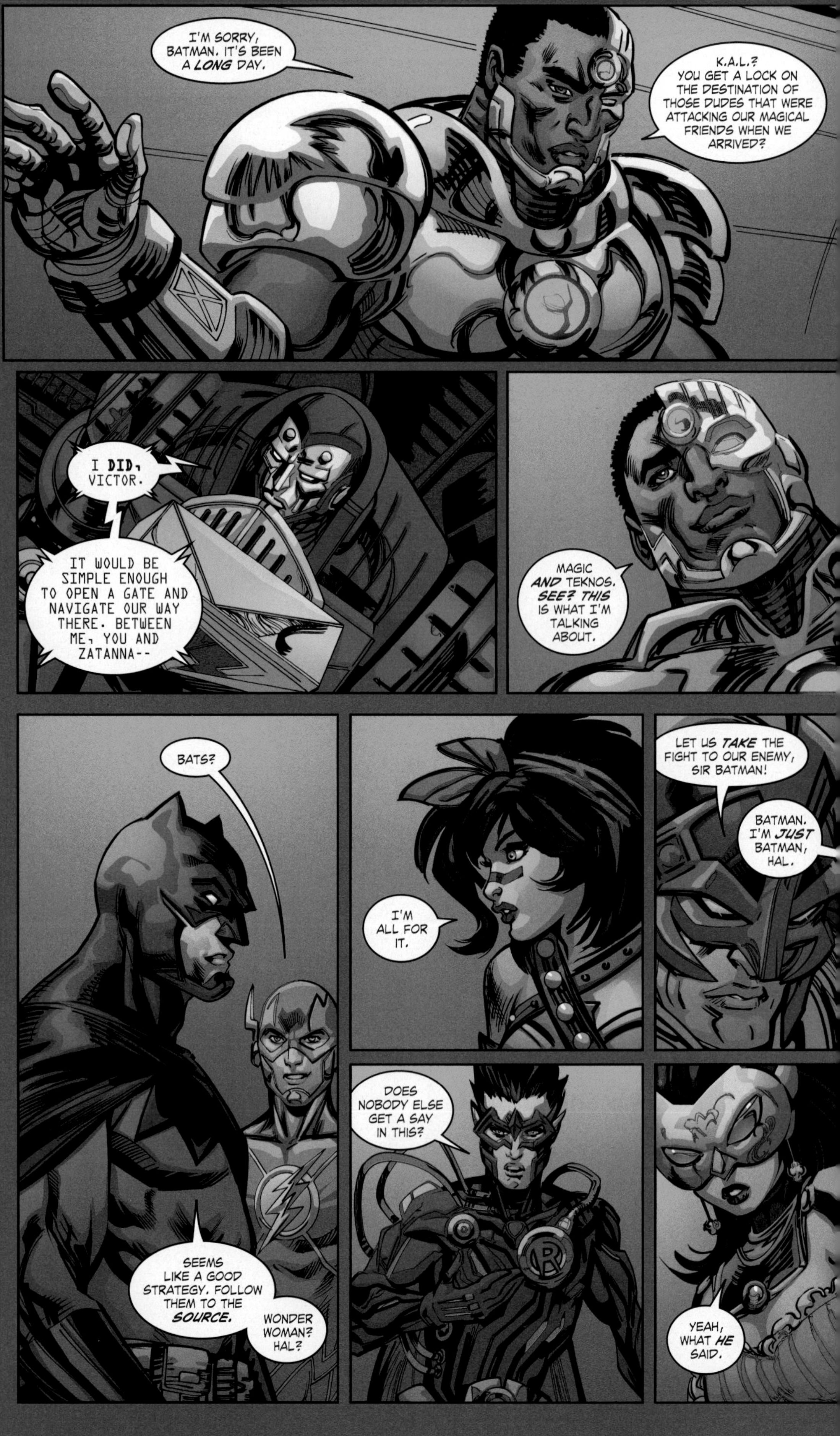
I'M SORRY, BATMAN. IT'S BEEN A *LONG* DAY.
K.A.L.? YOU GET A LOCK ON THE DESTINATION OF THOSE DUDES THAT WERE ATTACKING OUR MAGICAL FRIENDS WHEN WE ARRIVED?
I **DID**, VICTOR.
IT WOULD BE SIMPLE ENOUGH TO OPEN A GATE AND NAVIGATE OUR WAY THERE. BETWEEN ME, YOU AND ZATANNA--
MAGIC *AND* TEKNOS. *SEE? THIS* IS WHAT I'M TALKING ABOUT.
BATS?
SEEMS LIKE A GOOD STRATEGY. FOLLOW THEM TO THE *SOURCE.*
WONDER WOMAN? HAL?
I'M ALL FOR IT.
LET US *TAKE* THE FIGHT TO OUR ENEMY, SIR BATMAN!
BATMAN. I'M *JUST* BATMAN, HAL.
DOES NOBODY ELSE GET A SAY IN THIS?
YEAH, WHAT *HE* SAID.

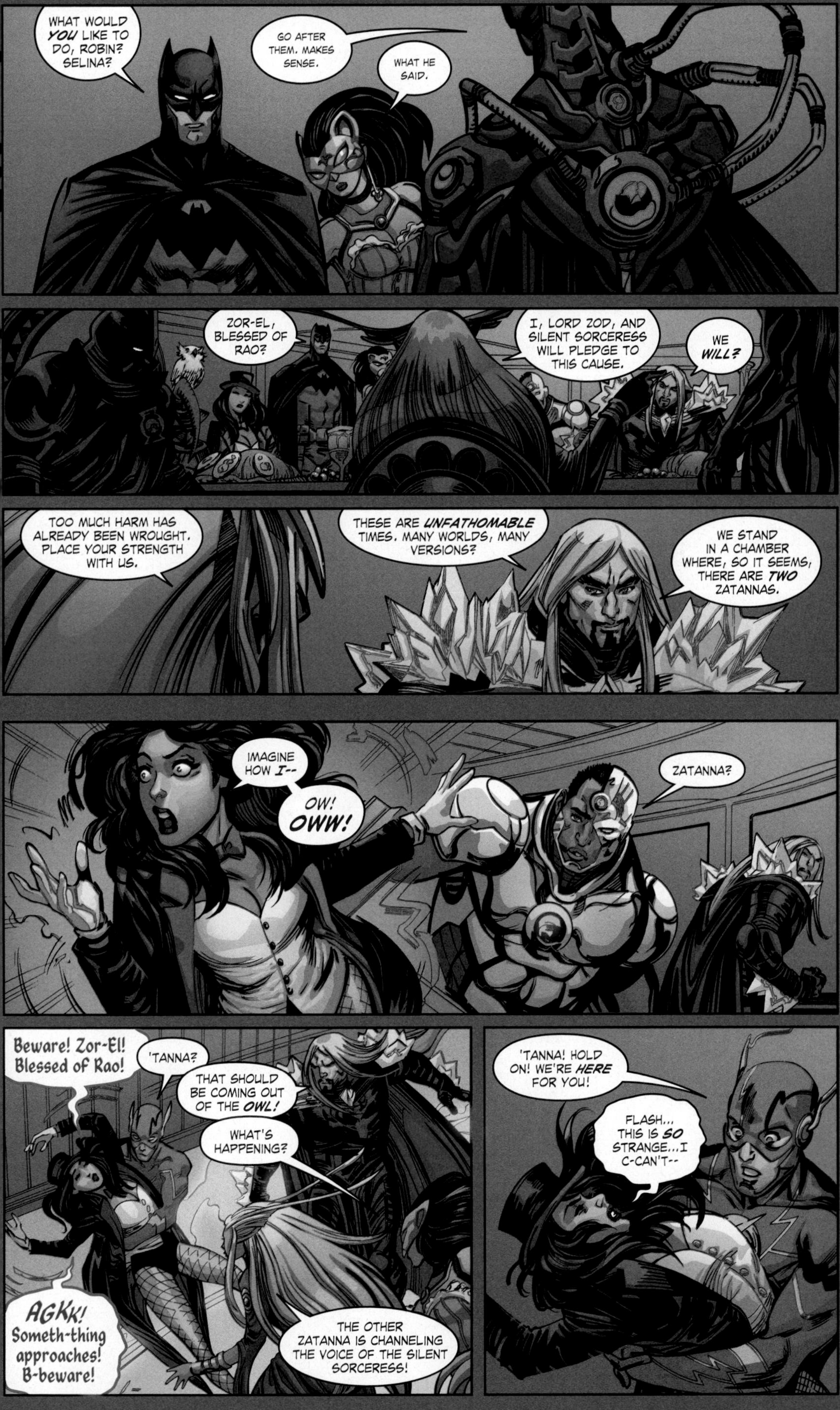
WHAT WOULD YOU LIKE TO DO, ROBIN? SELINA?
GO AFTER THEM. MAKES SENSE.
WHAT HE SAID.
ZOR-EL, BLESSED OF RAO?
I, LORD ZOD, AND SILENT SORCERESS WILL PLEDGE TO THIS CAUSE.
WE WILL?
TOO MUCH HARM HAS ALREADY BEEN WROUGHT. PLACE YOUR STRENGTH WITH US.
THESE ARE UNFATHOMABLE TIMES. MANY WORLDS, MANY VERSIONS?
WE STAND IN A CHAMBER WHERE, SO IT SEEMS, THERE ARE TWO ZATANNAS.
IMAGINE HOW I--
OW! OWW!
ZATANNA?
Beware! Zor-El! Blessed of Rao!
'TANNA?
THAT SHOULD BE COMING OUT OF THE OWL!
WHAT'S HAPPENING?
AGKK! Someth-thing approaches! B-beware!
THE OTHER ZATANNA IS CHANNELING THE VOICE OF THE SILENT SORCERESS!
'TANNA! HOLD ON! WE'RE HERE FOR YOU!
FLASH... THIS IS SO STRANGE...I C-CAN'T--

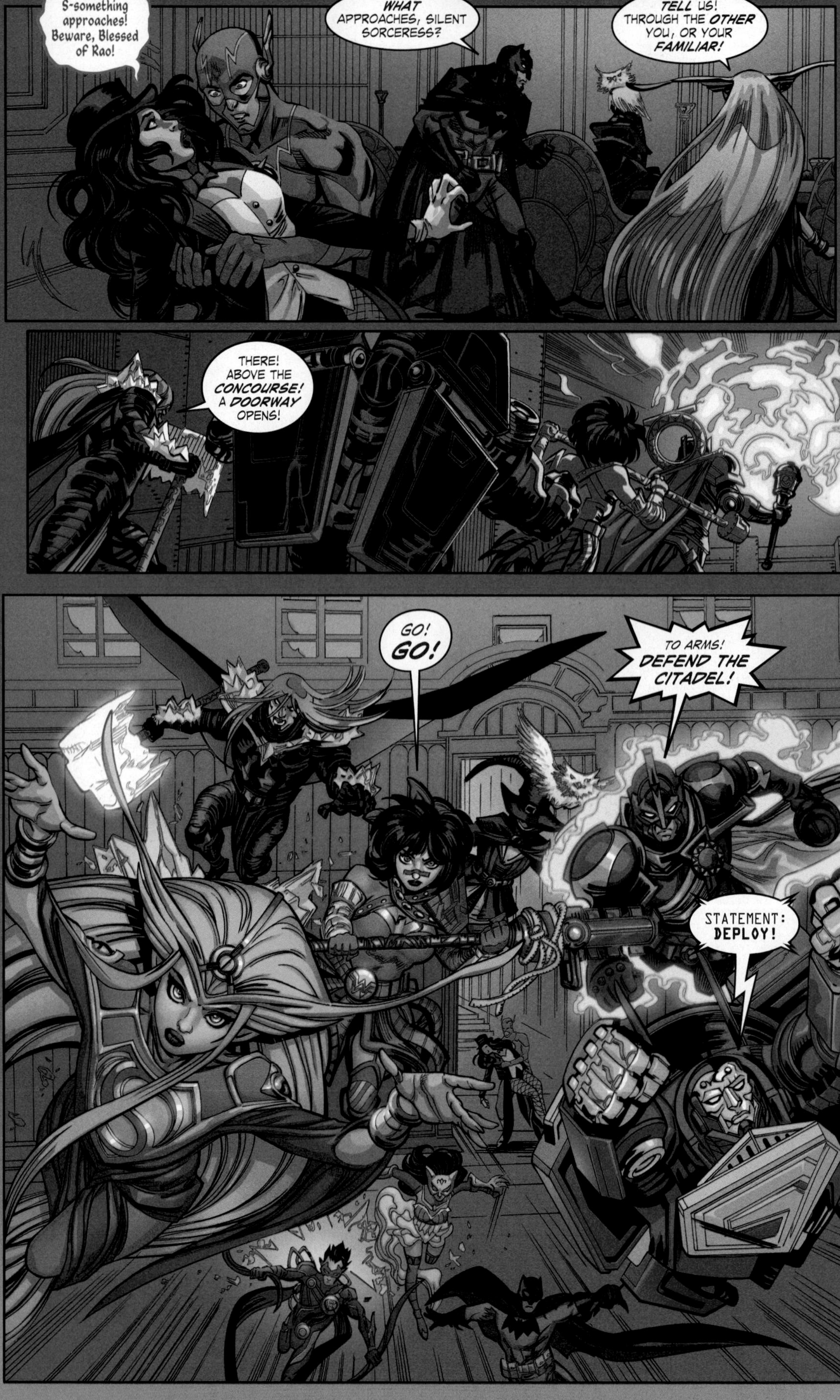
Beware! S-something approaches! Beware, Blessed of Rao!
WHAT APPROACHES, SILENT SORCERESS?
TELL US! THROUGH THE OTHER YOU, OR YOUR FAMILIAR!
THERE! ABOVE THE CONCOURSE! A DOORWAY OPENS!
GO! GO!
TO ARMS! DEFEND THE CITADEL!
STATEMENT: DEPLOY!

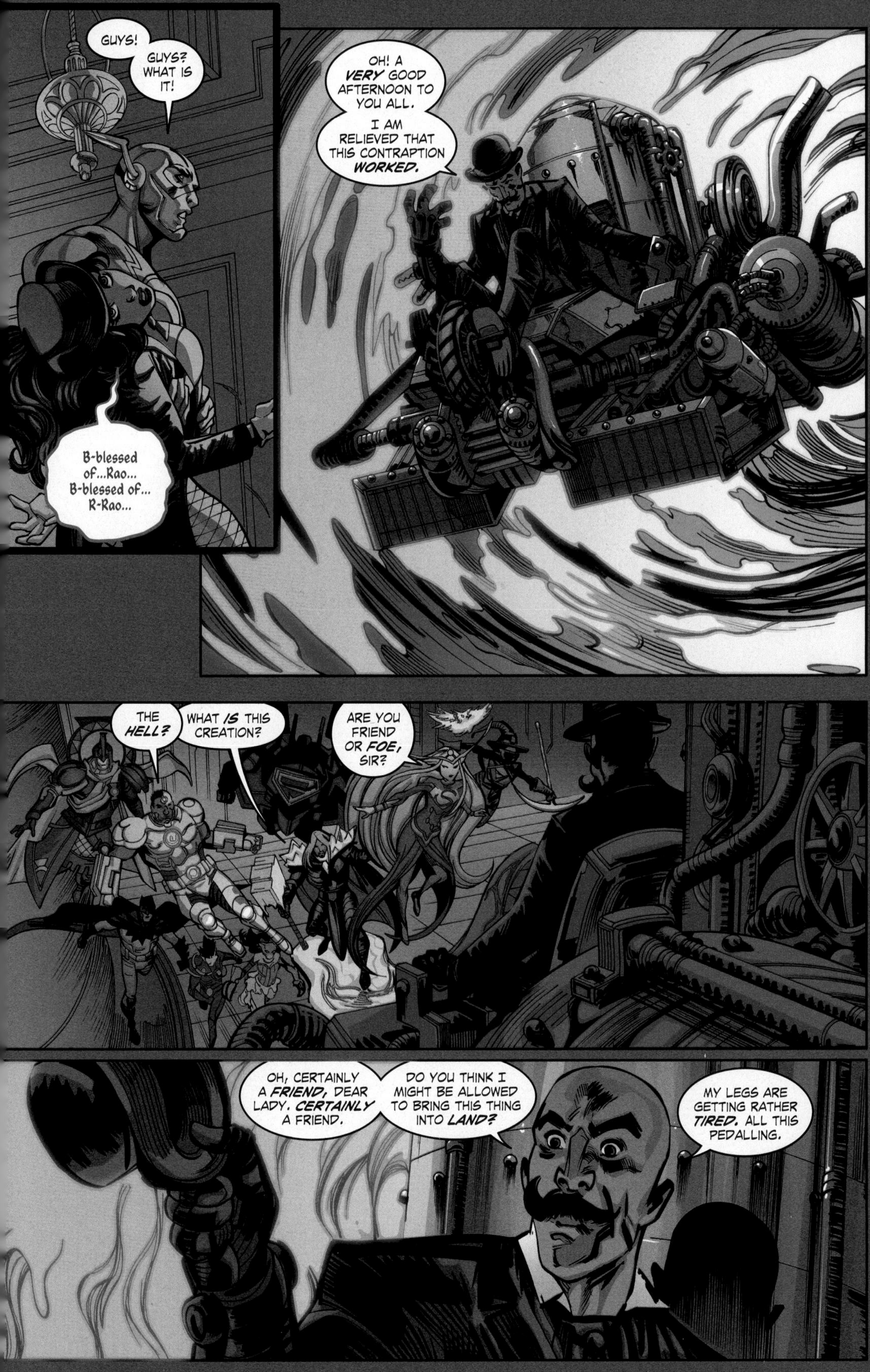
GUYS!
GUYS? WHAT IS IT!
B-blessed of...Rao... B-blessed of... R-Rao...
OH! A VERY GOOD AFTERNOON TO YOU ALL.
I AM RELIEVED THAT THIS CONTRAPTION WORKED.
THE HELL?
WHAT IS THIS CREATION?
ARE YOU FRIEND OR FOE, SIR?
OH, CERTAINLY A FRIEND, DEAR LADY. CERTAINLY A FRIEND.
DO YOU THINK I MIGHT BE ALLOWED TO BRING THIS THING INTO LAND?
MY LEGS ARE GETTING RATHER TIRED. ALL THIS PEDALLING.

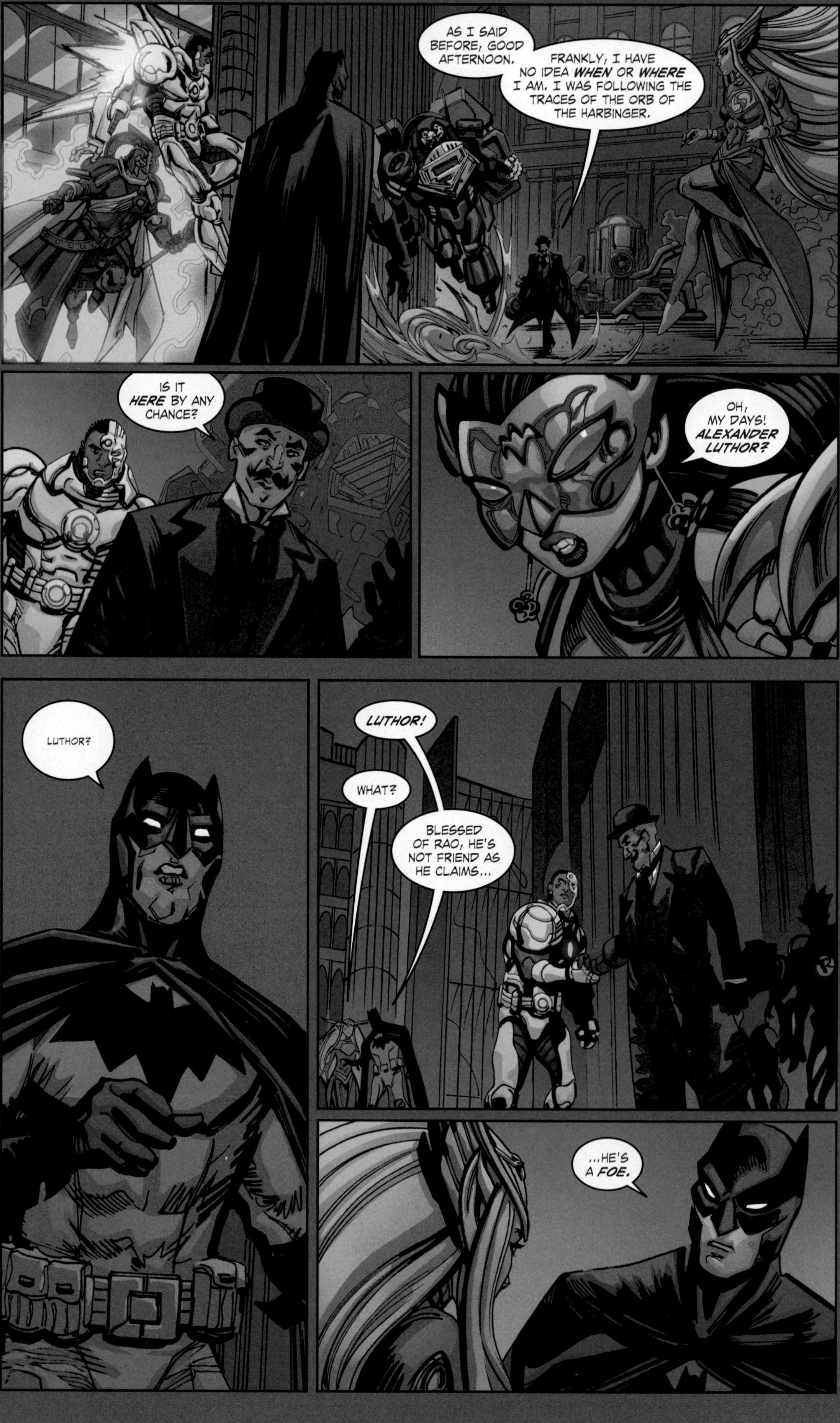
AS I SAID BEFORE, GOOD AFTERNOON.
FRANKLY, I HAVE NO IDEA WHEN OR WHERE I AM. I WAS FOLLOWING THE TRACES OF THE ORB OF THE HARBINGER.
IS IT HERE BY ANY CHANCE?
OH, MY DAYS! ALEXANDER LUTHOR?
LUTHOR?
LUTHOR!
WHAT?
BLESSED OF RAO, HE'S NOT FRIEND AS HE CLAIMS...
...HE'S A FOE.

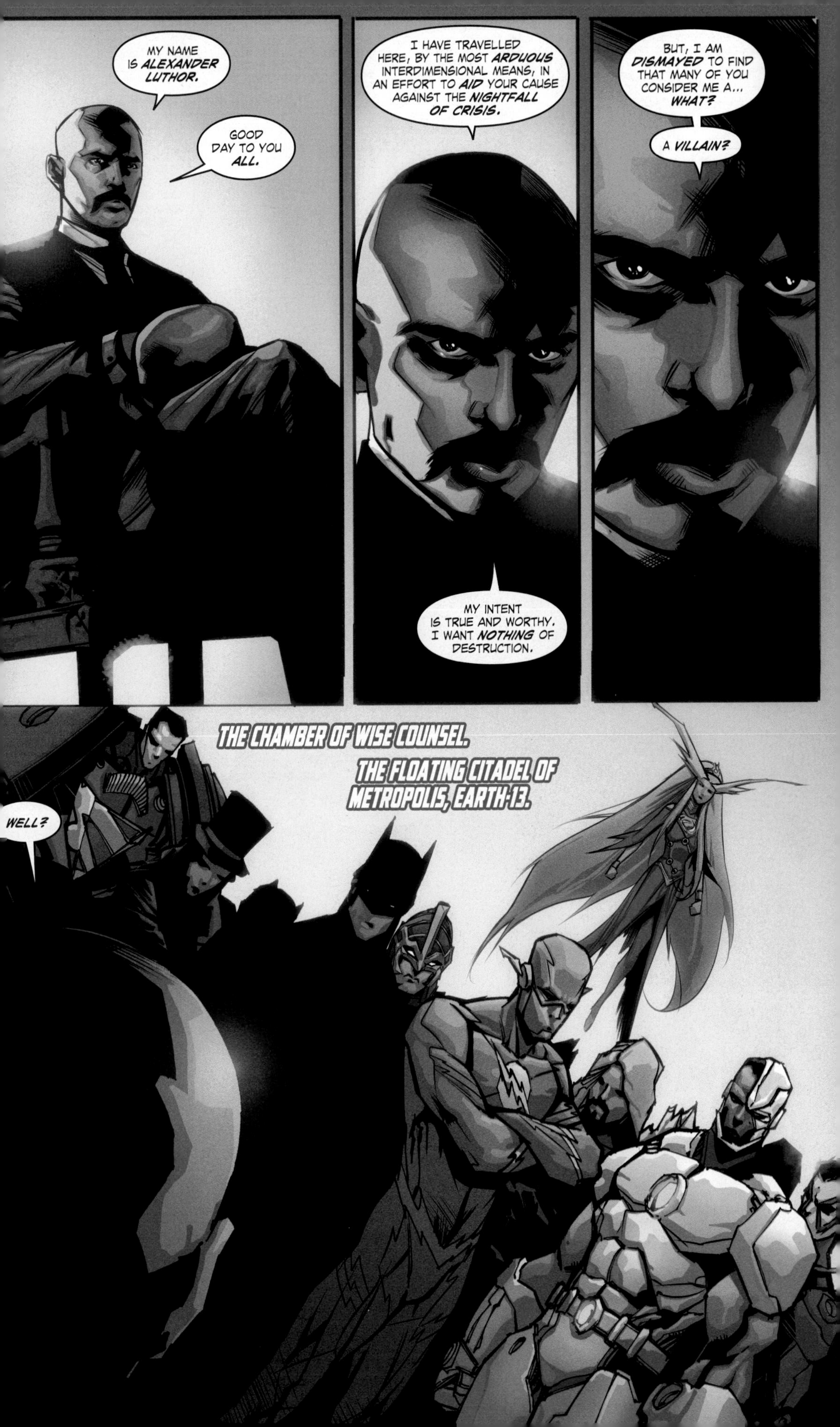
MY NAME IS ALEXANDER LUTHOR.
GOOD DAY TO YOU ALL.
I HAVE TRAVELLED HERE, BY THE MOST ARDUOUS INTERDIMENSIONAL MEANS, IN AN EFFORT TO AID YOUR CAUSE AGAINST THE NIGHTFALL OF CRISIS.
MY INTENT IS TRUE AND WORTHY. I WANT NOTHING OF DESTRUCTION.
BUT, I AM DISMAYED TO FIND THAT MANY OF YOU CONSIDER ME A... WHAT?
A VILLAIN?
THE CHAMBER OF WISE COUNSEL.
THE FLOATING CITADEL OF METROPOLIS, EARTH-13.
WELL?

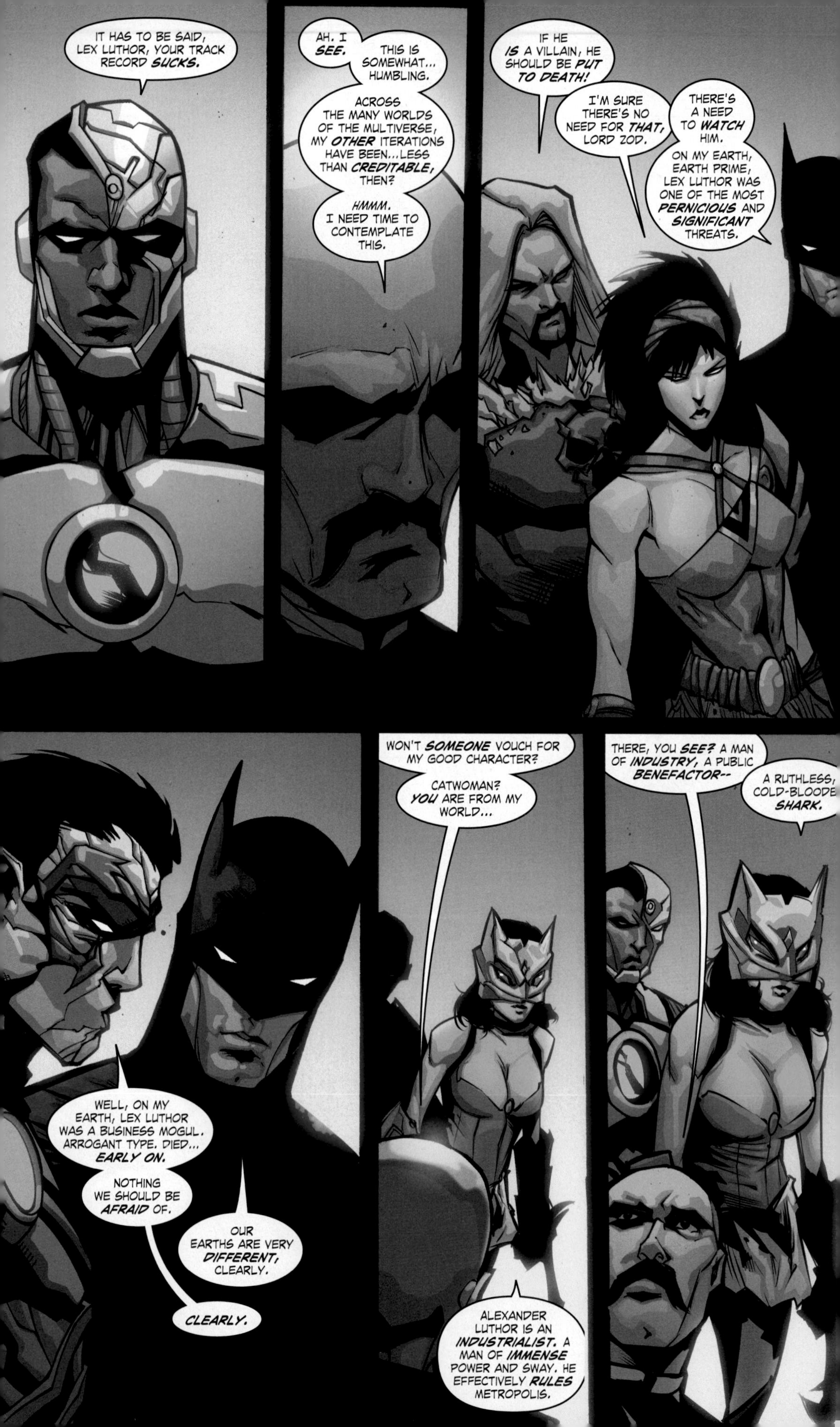

IT HAS TO BE SAID, LEX LUTHOR, YOUR TRACK RECORD SUCKS.
AH. I SEE.
THIS IS SOMEWHAT... HUMBLING.
ACROSS THE MANY WORLDS OF THE MULTIVERSE, MY OTHER ITERATIONS HAVE BEEN...LESS THAN CREDITABLE, THEN?
HMMM. I NEED TIME TO CONTEMPLATE THIS.
IF HE IS A VILLAIN, HE SHOULD BE PUT TO DEATH!
I'M SURE THERE'S NO NEED FOR THAT, LORD ZOD.
THERE'S A NEED TO WATCH HIM.
ON MY EARTH, EARTH PRIME, LEX LUTHOR WAS ONE OF THE MOST PERNICIOUS AND SIGNIFICANT THREATS.
WELL, ON MY EARTH, LEX LUTHOR WAS A BUSINESS MOGUL. ARROGANT TYPE. DIED... EARLY ON.
NOTHING WE SHOULD BE AFRAID OF.
OUR EARTHS ARE VERY DIFFERENT, CLEARLY.
CLEARLY.
WON'T SOMEONE VOUCH FOR MY GOOD CHARACTER?
CATWOMAN? YOU ARE FROM MY WORLD...
ALEXANDER LUTHOR IS AN INDUSTRIALIST. A MAN OF IMMENSE POWER AND SWAY. HE EFFECTIVELY RULES METROPOLIS.
THERE, YOU SEE? A MAN OF INDUSTRY, A PUBLIC BENEFACTOR--
A RUTHLESS, COLD-BLOODE
SHARK.

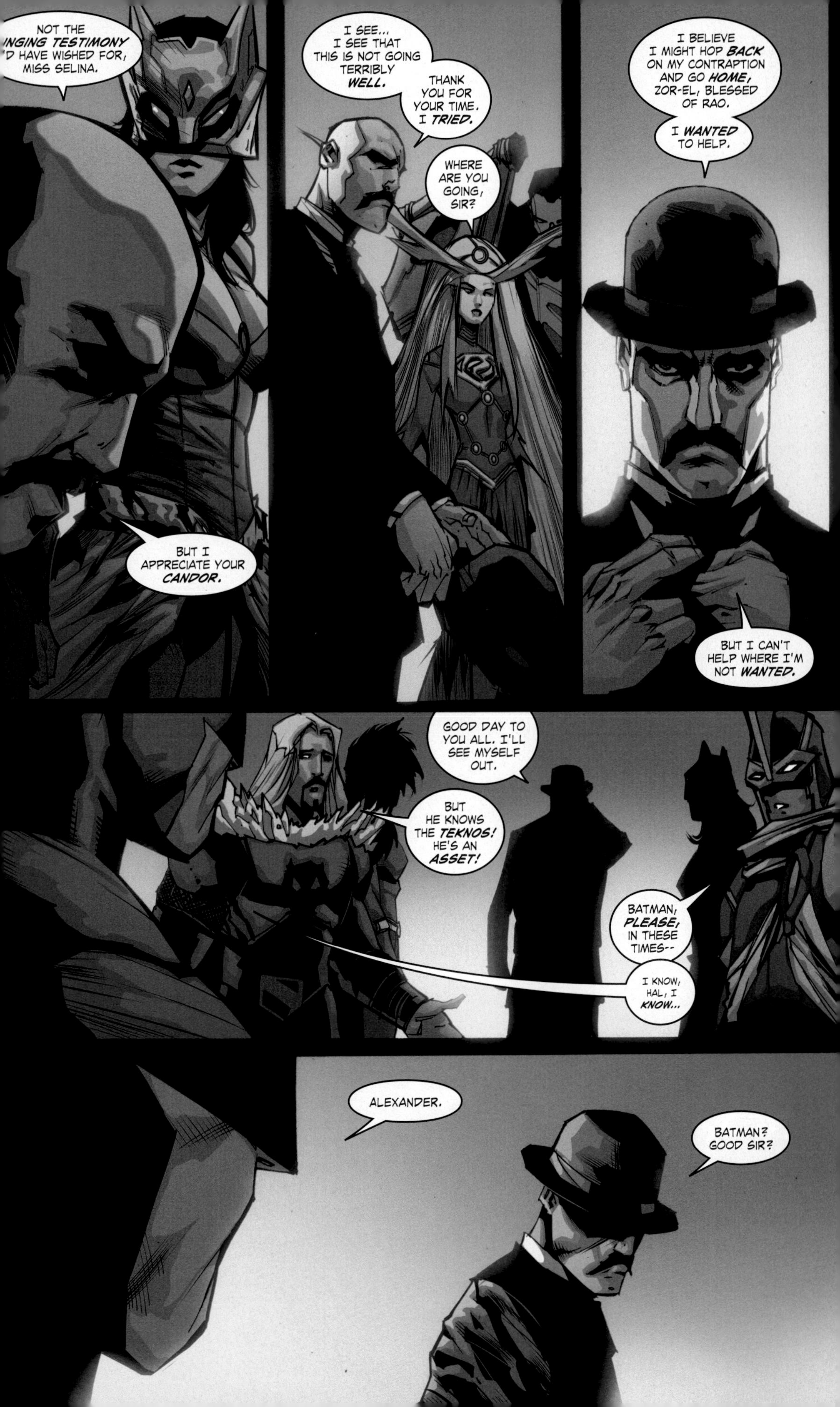

NOT THE INGING TESTIMONY 'D HAVE WISHED FOR, MISS SELINA.
BUT I APPRECIATE YOUR CANDOR.
I SEE... I SEE THAT THIS IS NOT GOING TERRIBLY WELL.
THANK YOU FOR YOUR TIME. I TRIED.
WHERE ARE YOU GOING, SIR?
I BELIEVE I MIGHT HOP BACK ON MY CONTRAPTION AND GO HOME, ZOR-EL, BLESSED OF RAO.
I WANTED TO HELP.
BUT I CAN'T HELP WHERE I'M NOT WANTED.
GOOD DAY TO YOU ALL. I'LL SEE MYSELF OUT.
BUT HE KNOWS THE TEKNOS! HE'S AN ASSET!
BATMAN, PLEASE, IN THESE TIMES--
I KNOW, HAL, I KNOW...
ALEXANDER.
BATMAN? GOOD SIR?

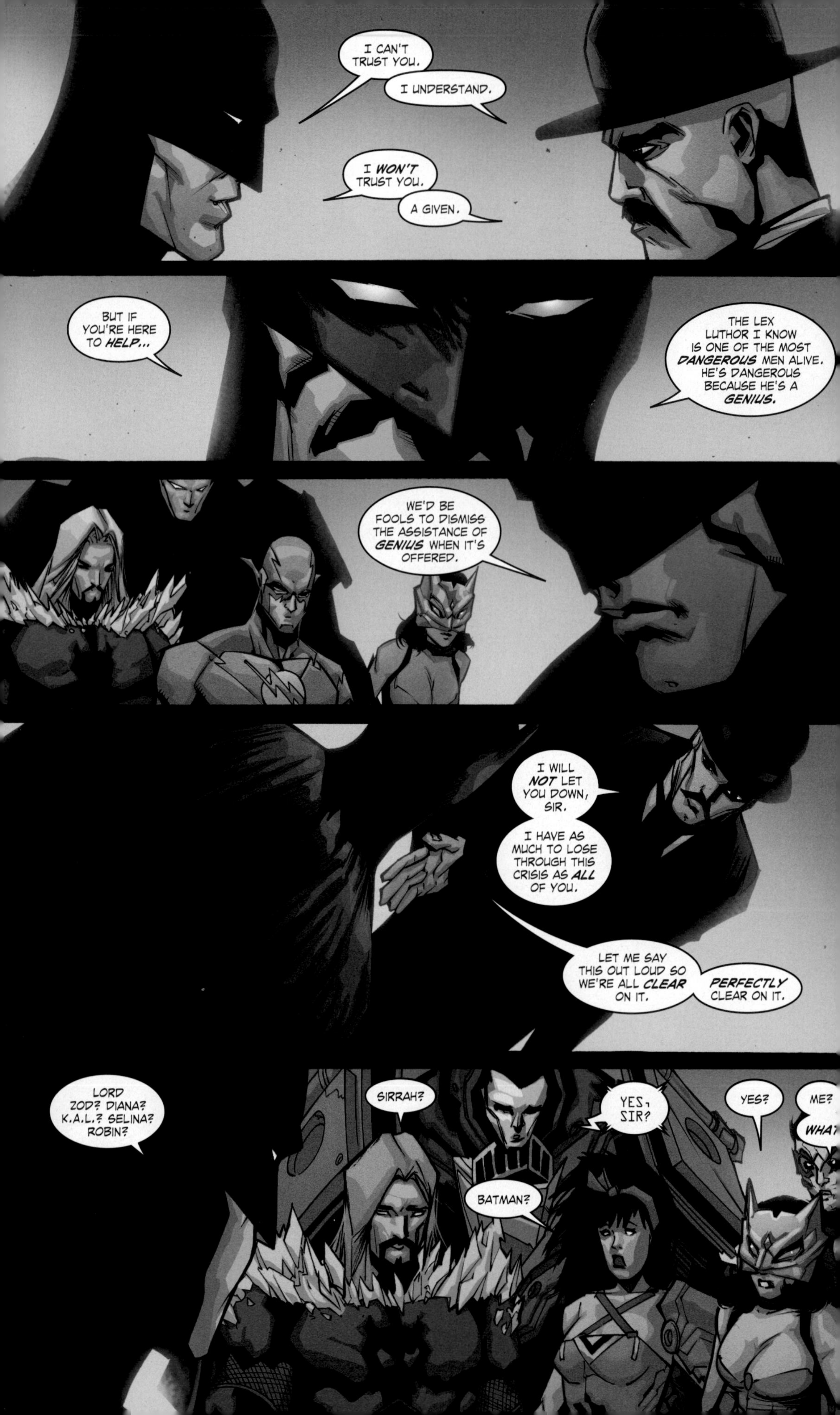
I CAN'T TRUST YOU.
I UNDERSTAND.
I *WON'T* TRUST YOU.
A GIVEN.
BUT IF YOU'RE HERE TO *HELP...*
THE LEX LUTHOR I KNOW IS ONE OF THE MOST *DANGEROUS* MEN ALIVE. HE'S DANGEROUS BECAUSE HE'S A *GENIUS.*
WE'D BE FOOLS TO DISMISS THE ASSISTANCE OF *GENIUS* WHEN IT'S OFFERED.
I WILL *NOT* LET YOU DOWN, SIR.
I HAVE AS MUCH TO LOSE THROUGH THIS CRISIS AS *ALL* OF YOU.
LET ME SAY THIS OUT LOUD SO WE'RE ALL *CLEAR* ON IT.
PERFECTLY CLEAR ON IT.
LORD ZOD? DIANA? K.A.L.? SELINA? ROBIN?
SIRRAH?
YES, SIR?
YES?
ME?
WHA
BATMAN?

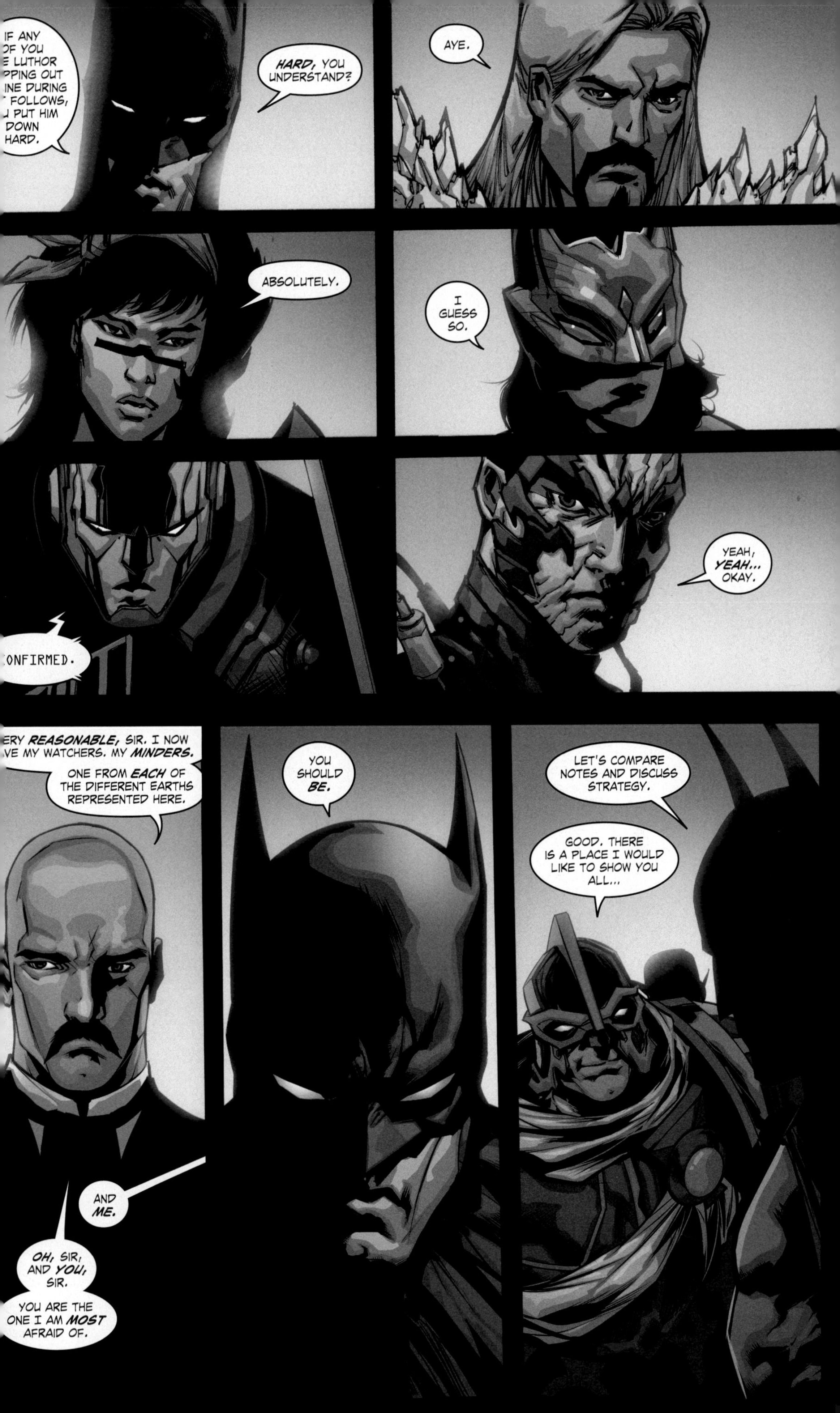
IF ANY
OF YOU
E LUTHOR
PPING OUT
INE DURING
T FOLLOWS,
U PUT HIM
DOWN
HARD.
HARD, YOU UNDERSTAND?
AYE.
ABSOLUTELY.
I GUESS SO.
ONFIRMED.
YEAH, YEAH... OKAY.
ERY REASONABLE, SIR. I NOW
VE MY WATCHERS. MY MINDERS.
ONE FROM EACH OF THE DIFFERENT EARTHS REPRESENTED HERE.
AND ME.
OH, SIR, AND YOU, SIR.
YOU ARE THE ONE I AM MOST AFRAID OF.
YOU SHOULD BE.
LET'S COMPARE NOTES AND DISCUSS STRATEGY.
GOOD. THERE IS A PLACE I WOULD LIKE TO SHOW YOU ALL...

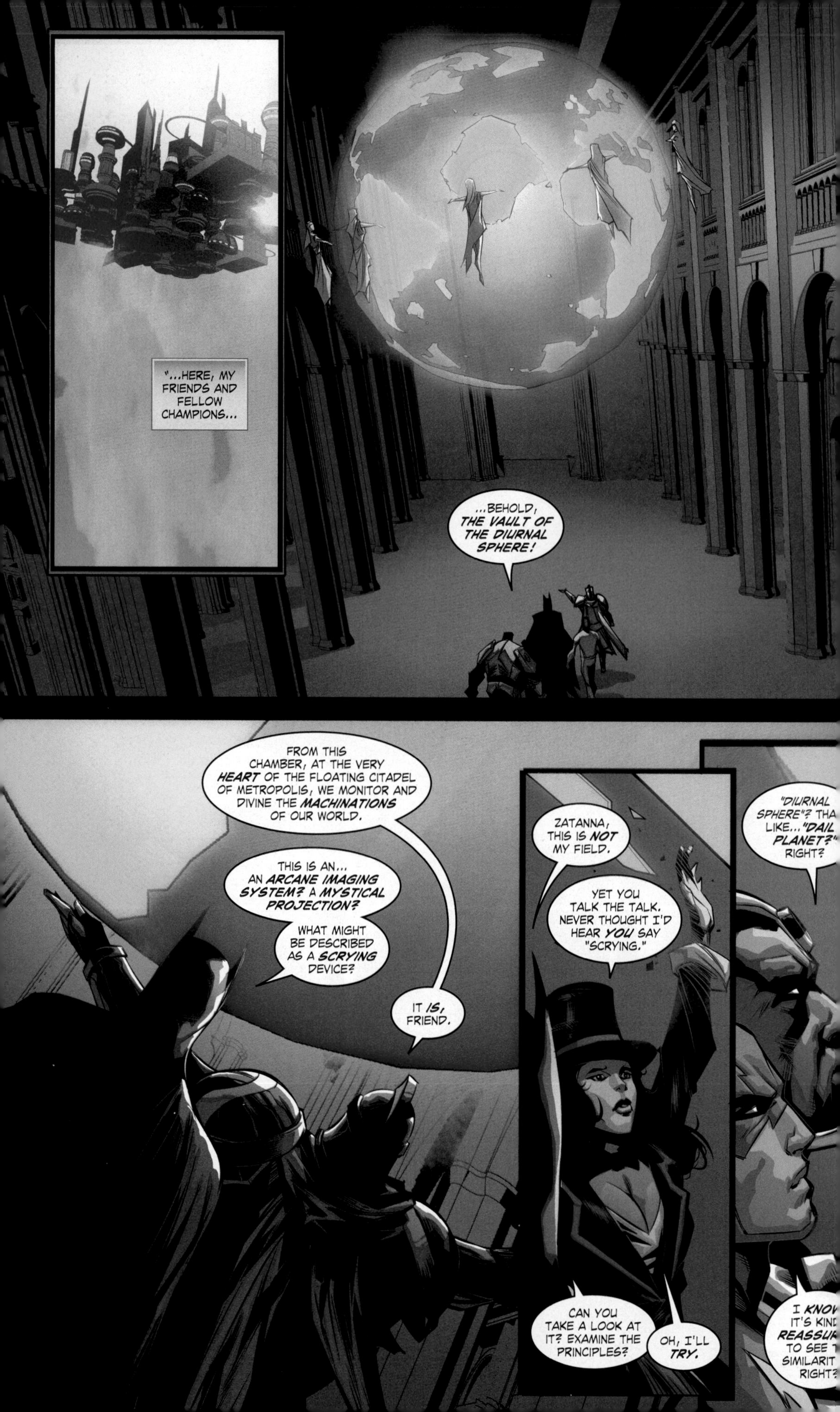
"...HERE, MY FRIENDS AND FELLOW CHAMPIONS...
...BEHOLD, THE VAULT OF THE DIURNAL SPHERE!
FROM THIS CHAMBER, AT THE VERY HEART OF THE FLOATING CITADEL OF METROPOLIS, WE MONITOR AND DIVINE THE MACHINATIONS OF OUR WORLD.
THIS IS AN... AN ARCANE IMAGING SYSTEM? A MYSTICAL PROJECTION?
WHAT MIGHT BE DESCRIBED AS A SCRYING DEVICE?
IT IS, FRIEND.
ZATANNA, THIS IS NOT MY FIELD.
YET YOU TALK THE TALK. NEVER THOUGHT I'D HEAR YOU SAY "SCRYING."
CAN YOU TAKE A LOOK AT IT? EXAMINE THE PRINCIPLES?
OH, I'LL TRY.

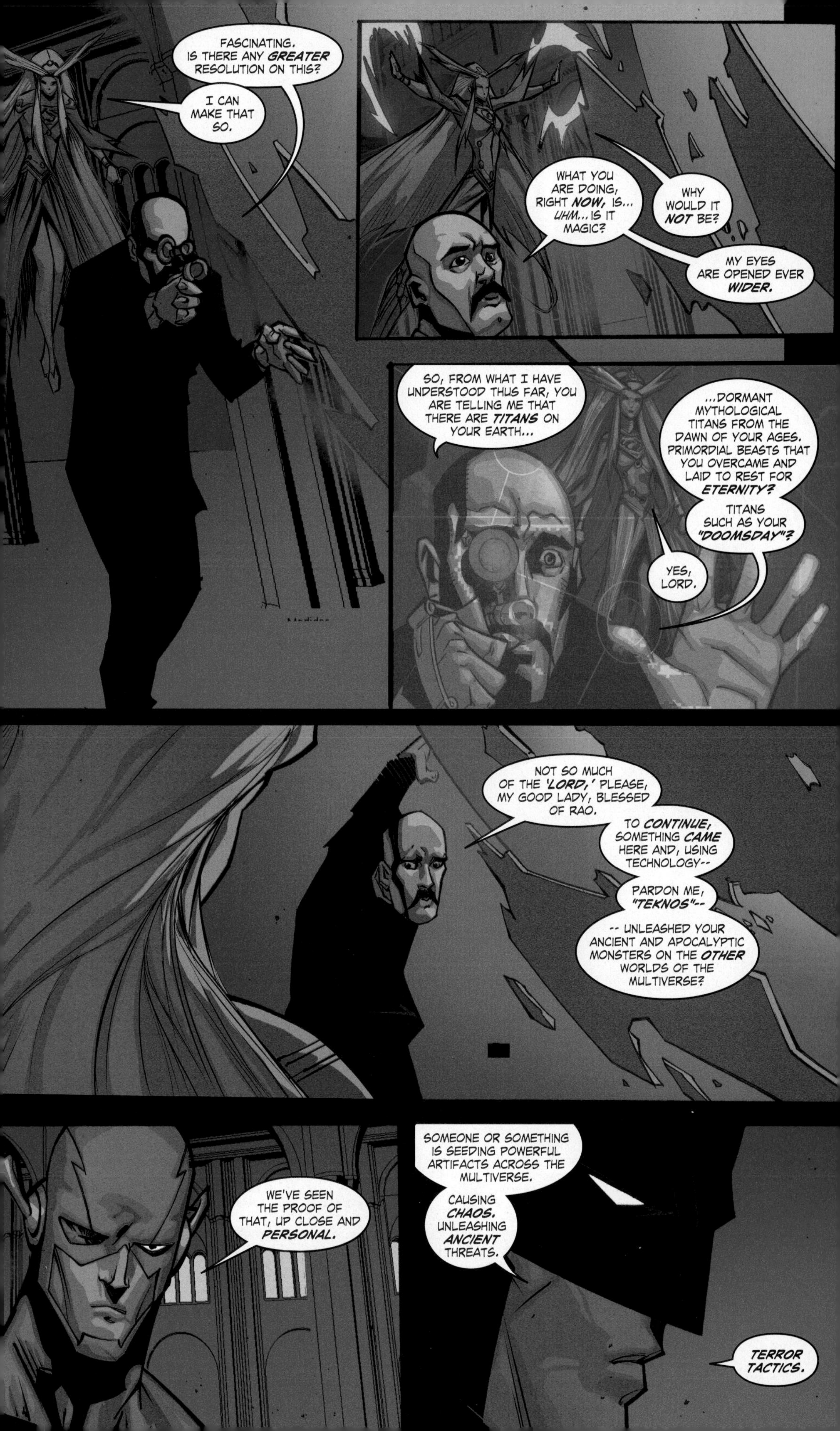
FASCINATING. IS THERE ANY GREATER RESOLUTION ON THIS?
I CAN MAKE THAT SO.
WHAT YOU ARE DOING, RIGHT NOW, IS... UHM... IS IT MAGIC?
WHY WOULD IT NOT BE?
MY EYES ARE OPENED EVER WIDER.
SO, FROM WHAT I HAVE UNDERSTOOD THUS FAR, YOU ARE TELLING ME THAT THERE ARE TITANS ON YOUR EARTH...
...DORMANT MYTHOLOGICAL TITANS FROM THE DAWN OF YOUR AGES. PRIMORDIAL BEASTS THAT YOU OVERCAME AND LAID TO REST FOR ETERNITY?
TITANS SUCH AS YOUR "DOOMSDAY"?
YES, LORD.
NOT SO MUCH OF THE 'LORD,' PLEASE, MY GOOD LADY, BLESSED OF RAO.
TO CONTINUE, SOMETHING CAME HERE AND, USING TECHNOLOGY--
PARDON ME, "TEKNOS"--
-- UNLEASHED YOUR ANCIENT AND APOCALYPTIC MONSTERS ON THE OTHER WORLDS OF THE MULTIVERSE?
WE'VE SEEN THE PROOF OF THAT, UP CLOSE AND PERSONAL.
SOMEONE OR SOMETHING IS SEEDING POWERFUL ARTIFACTS ACROSS THE MULTIVERSE.
CAUSING CHAOS. UNLEASHING ANCIENT THREATS.
TERROR TACTICS.

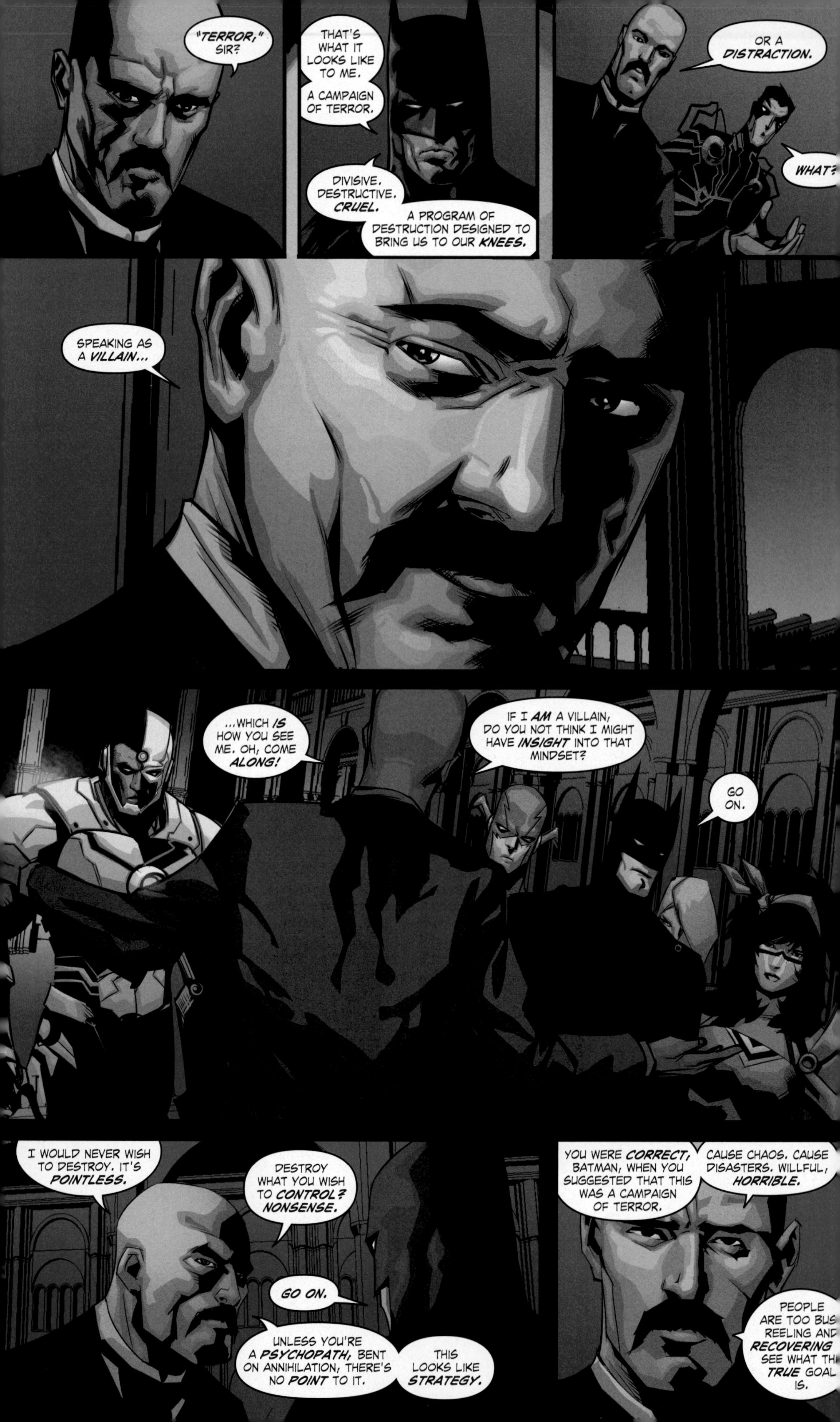
"TERROR," SIR?
THAT'S WHAT IT LOOKS LIKE TO ME.
A CAMPAIGN OF TERROR.
DIVISIVE. DESTRUCTIVE. CRUEL.
A PROGRAM OF DESTRUCTION DESIGNED TO BRING US TO OUR KNEES.
OR A DISTRACTION.
WHAT?
SPEAKING AS A VILLAIN...
...WHICH IS HOW YOU SEE ME. OH, COME ALONG!
IF I AM A VILLAIN, DO YOU NOT THINK I MIGHT HAVE INSIGHT INTO THAT MINDSET?
GO ON.
I WOULD NEVER WISH TO DESTROY. IT'S POINTLESS.
DESTROY WHAT YOU WISH TO CONTROL? NONSENSE.
GO ON.
UNLESS YOU'RE A PSYCHOPATH, BENT ON ANNIHILATION, THERE'S NO POINT TO IT.
THIS LOOKS LIKE STRATEGY.
YOU WERE CORRECT, BATMAN, WHEN YOU SUGGESTED THAT THIS WAS A CAMPAIGN OF TERROR.
CAUSE CHAOS. CAUSE DISASTERS. WILLFUL, HORRIBLE.
PEOPLE ARE TOO BUS REELING AND RECOVERING SEE WHAT TH TRUE GOAL IS.

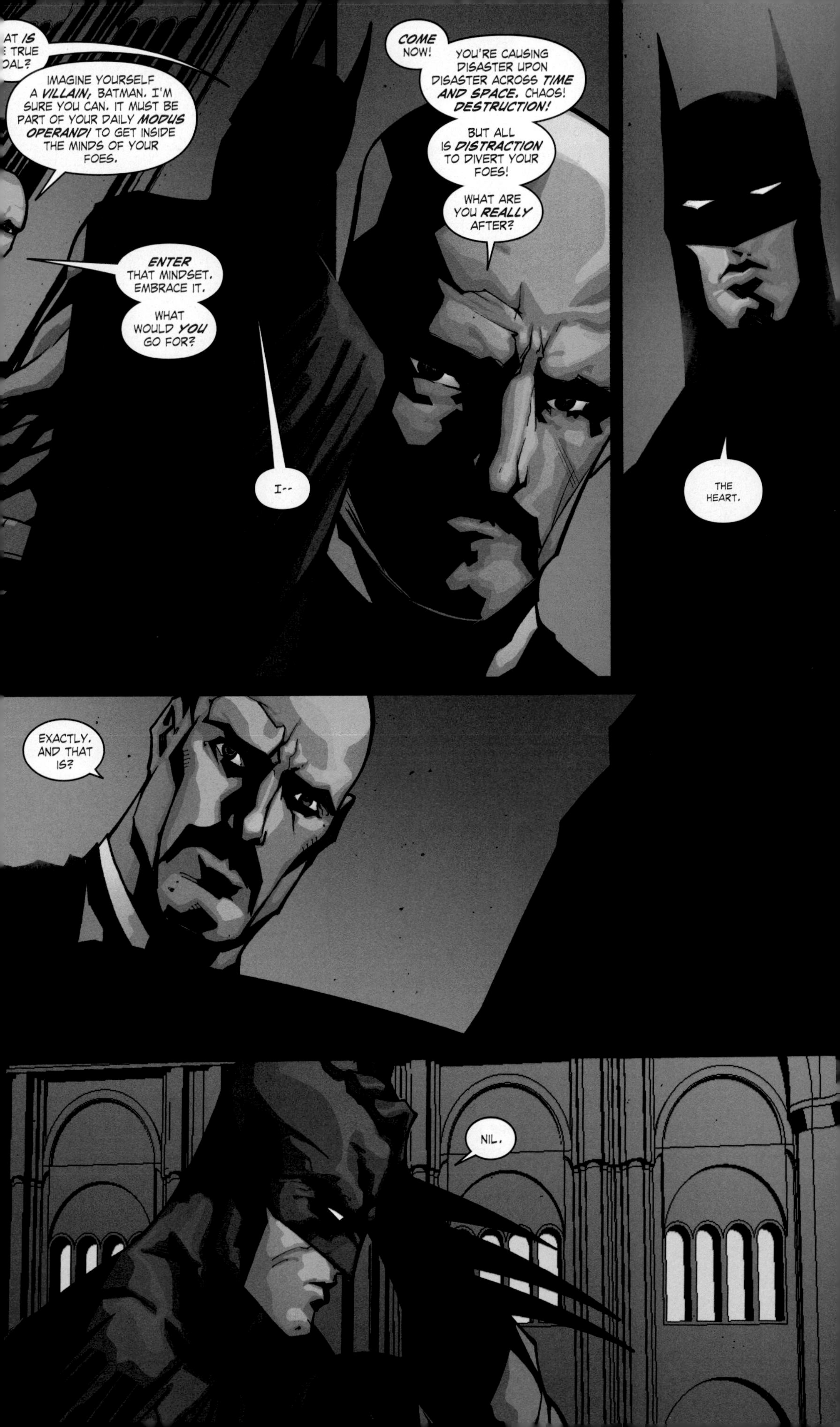
AT IS
TRUE
OAL?
IMAGINE YOURSELF A VILLAIN, BATMAN. I'M SURE YOU CAN. IT MUST BE PART OF YOUR DAILY MODUS OPERANDI TO GET INSIDE THE MINDS OF YOUR FOES.
ENTER THAT MINDSET. EMBRACE IT.
WHAT WOULD YOU GO FOR?
I--
COME NOW!
YOU'RE CAUSING DISASTER UPON DISASTER ACROSS TIME AND SPACE. CHAOS! DESTRUCTION!
BUT ALL IS DISTRACTION TO DIVERT YOUR FOES!
WHAT ARE YOU REALLY AFTER?
THE HEART.
EXACTLY. AND THAT IS?
NIL.

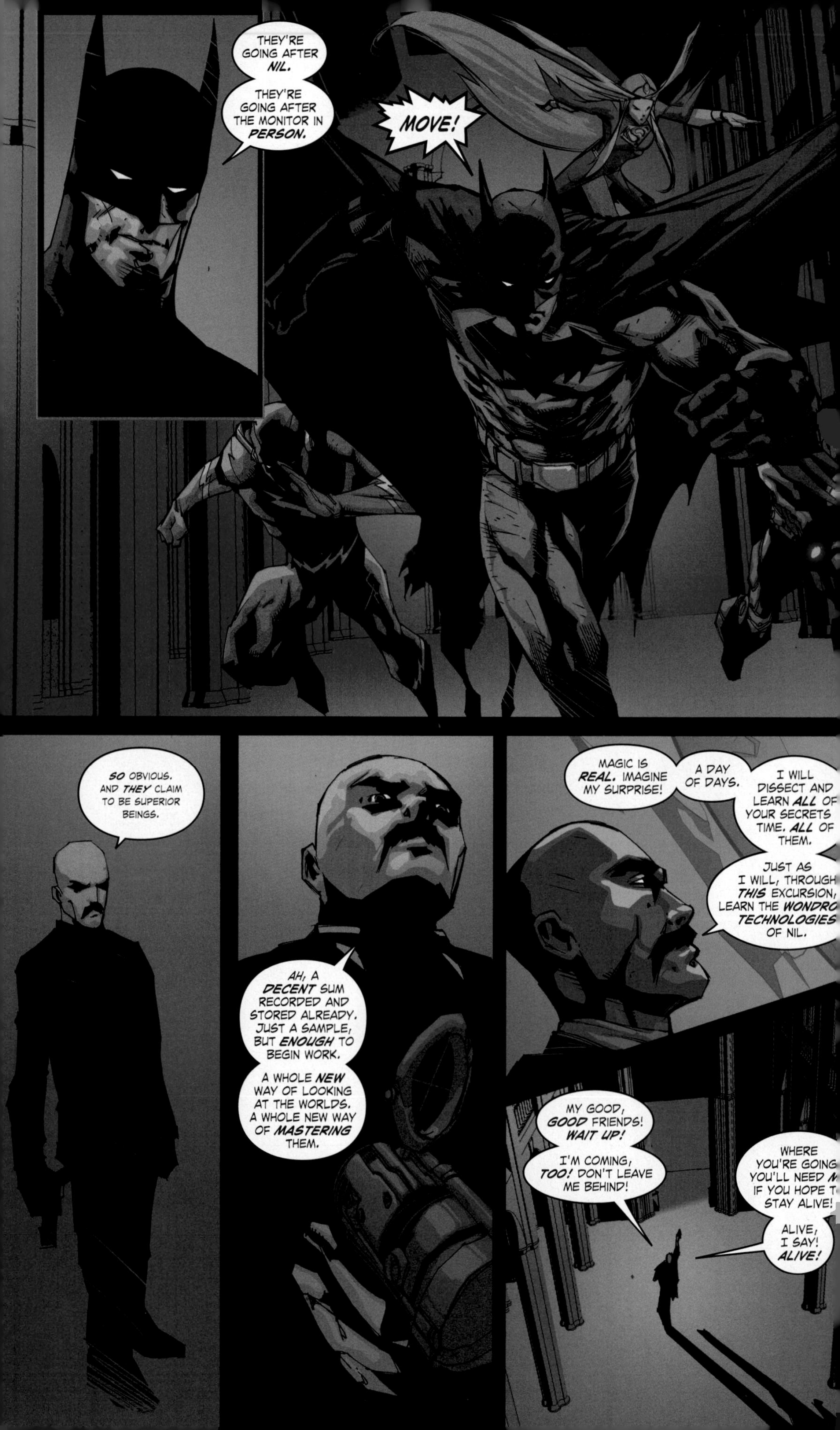

THEY'RE GOING AFTER NIL.
THEY'RE GOING AFTER THE MONITOR IN PERSON.
MOVE!
SO OBVIOUS. AND THEY CLAIM TO BE SUPERIOR BEINGS.
AH, A DECENT SUM RECORDED AND STORED ALREADY. JUST A SAMPLE, BUT ENOUGH TO BEGIN WORK.
A WHOLE NEW WAY OF LOOKING AT THE WORLDS. A WHOLE NEW WAY OF MASTERING THEM.
MAGIC IS REAL. IMAGINE MY SURPRISE!
A DAY OF DAYS.
I WILL DISSECT AND LEARN ALL OF YOUR SECRETS TIME. ALL OF THEM.
JUST AS I WILL, THROUGH THIS EXCURSION, LEARN THE WONDRO TECHNOLOGIES OF NIL.
MY GOOD, GOOD FRIENDS! WAIT UP!
I'M COMING, TOO! DON'T LEAVE ME BEHIND!
WHERE YOU'RE GOING YOU'LL NEED IF YOU HOPE T STAY ALIVE!
ALIVE, I SAY! ALIVE!

INFINITE CRISIS #1 variant cover by **Terry** and **Rachel Dodson**

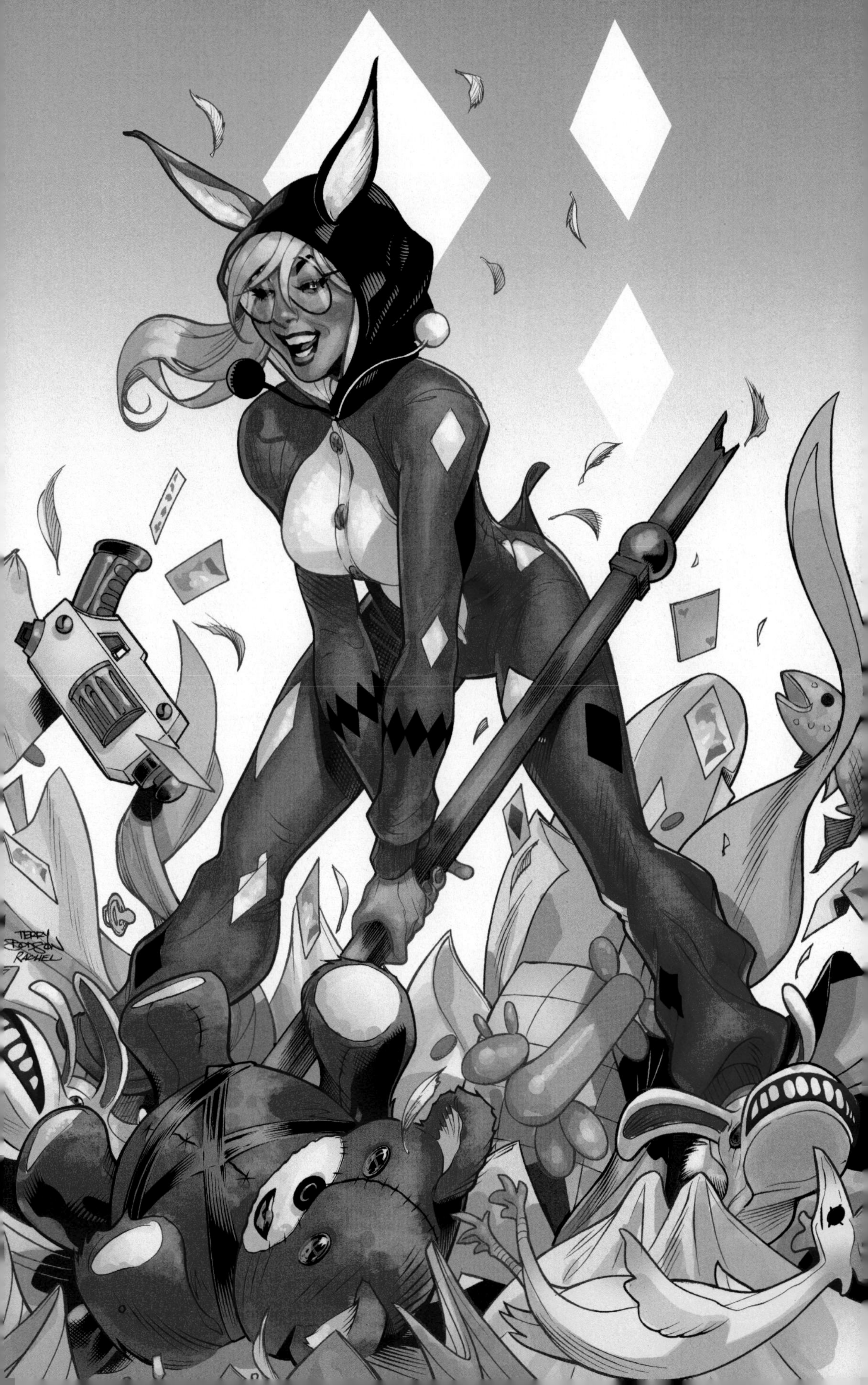

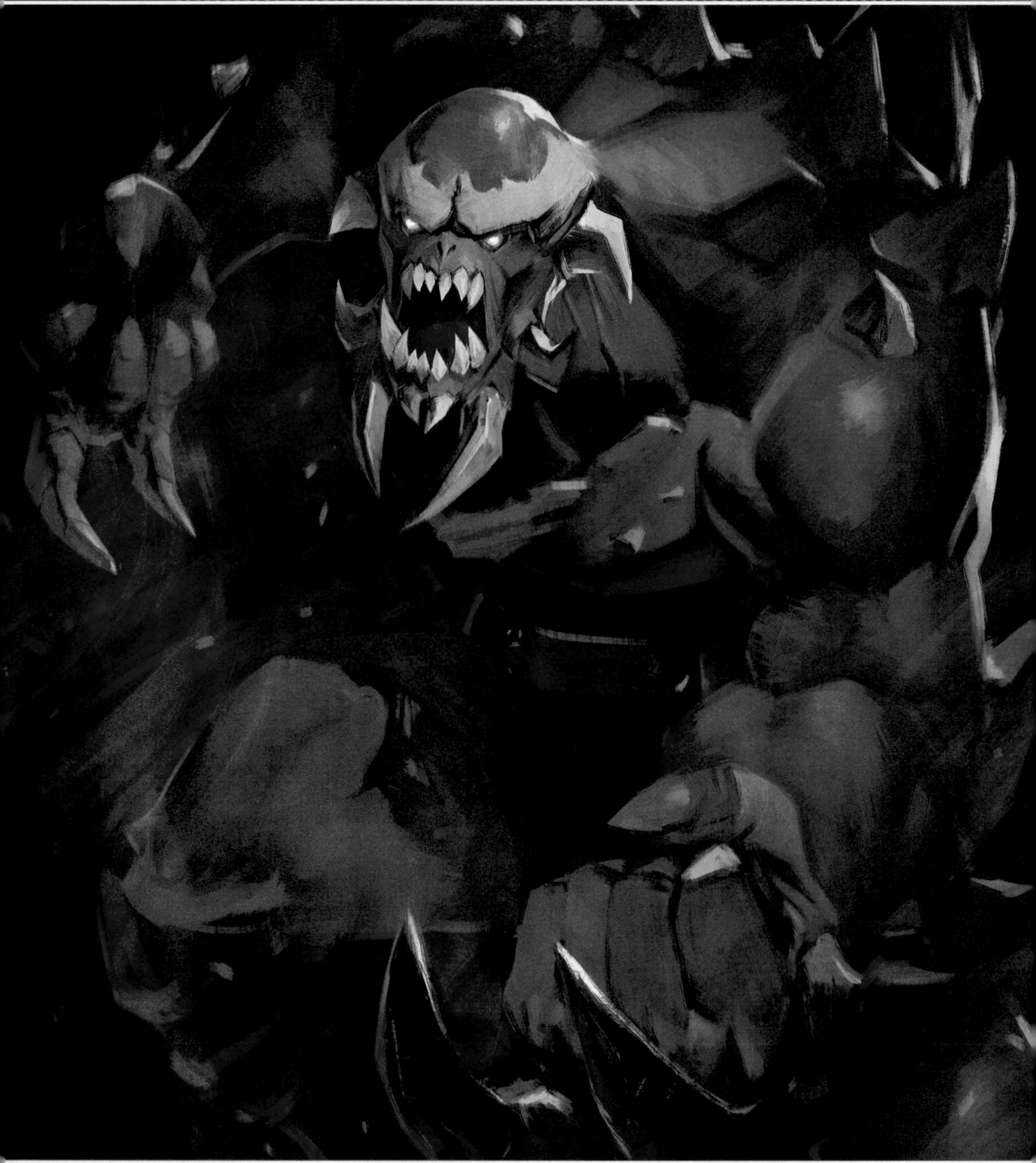

DOOMSDAY CHAMPION

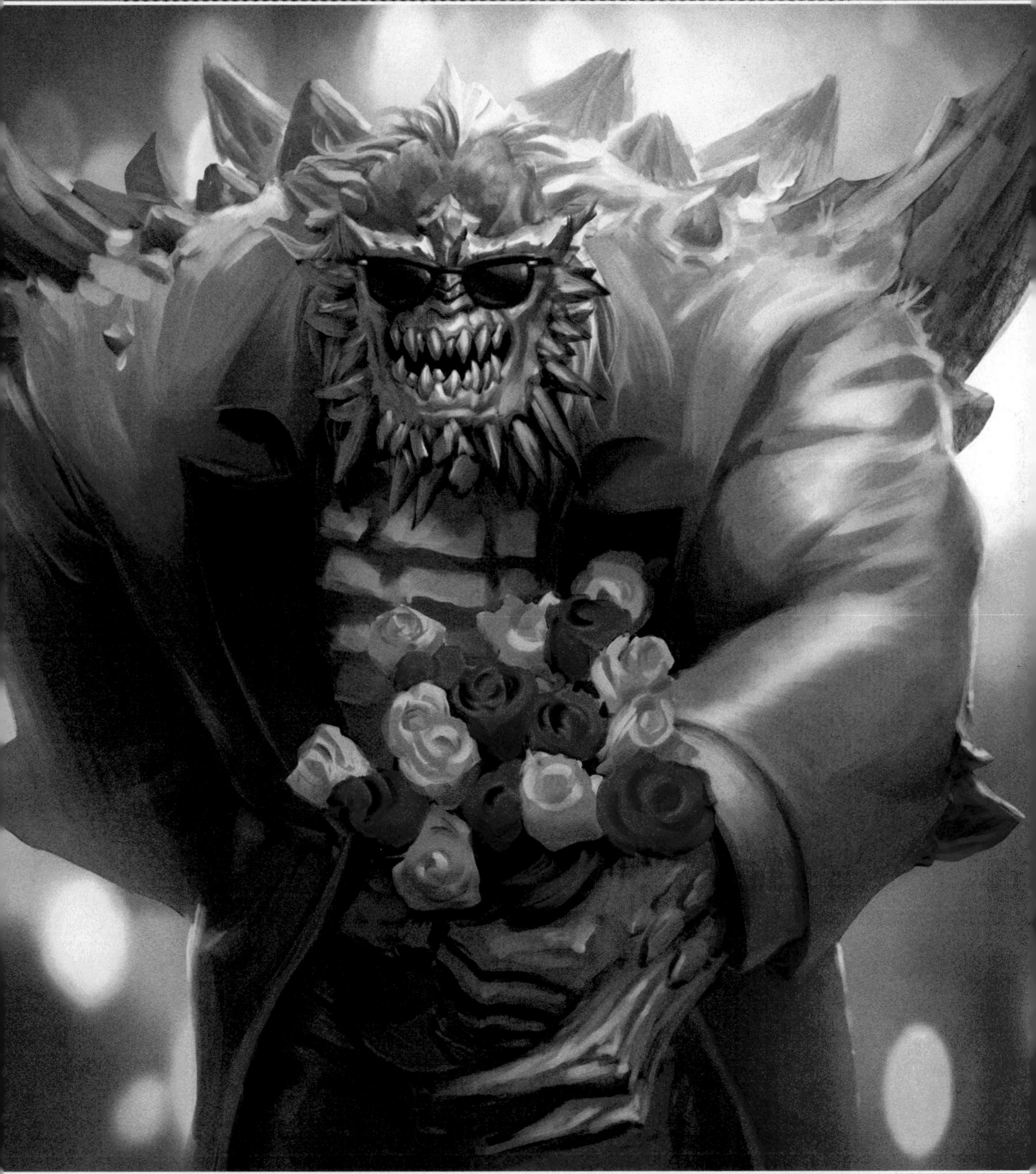

“FIRST DATE” COSTUME

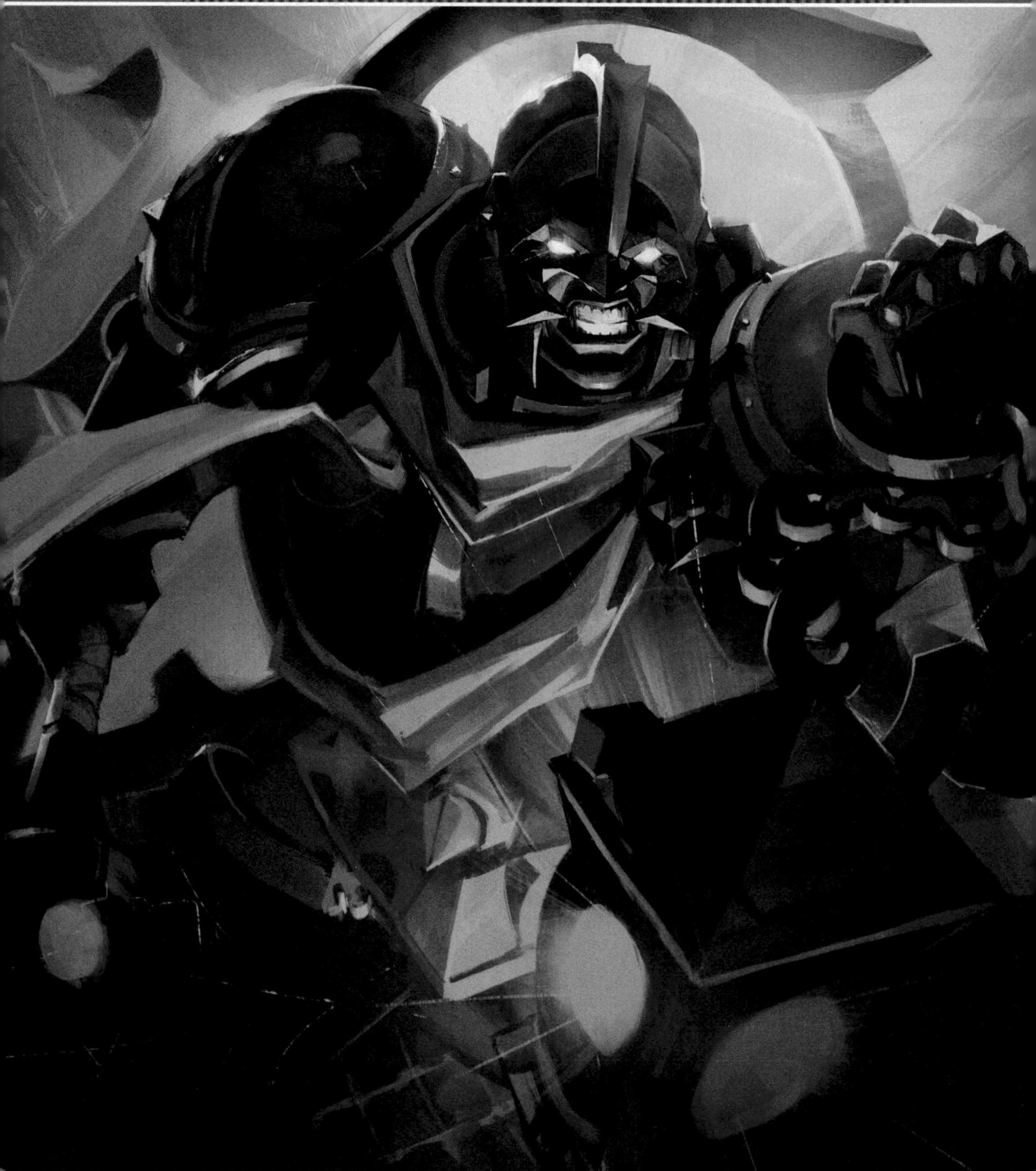

ARCANE GREEN LANTERN

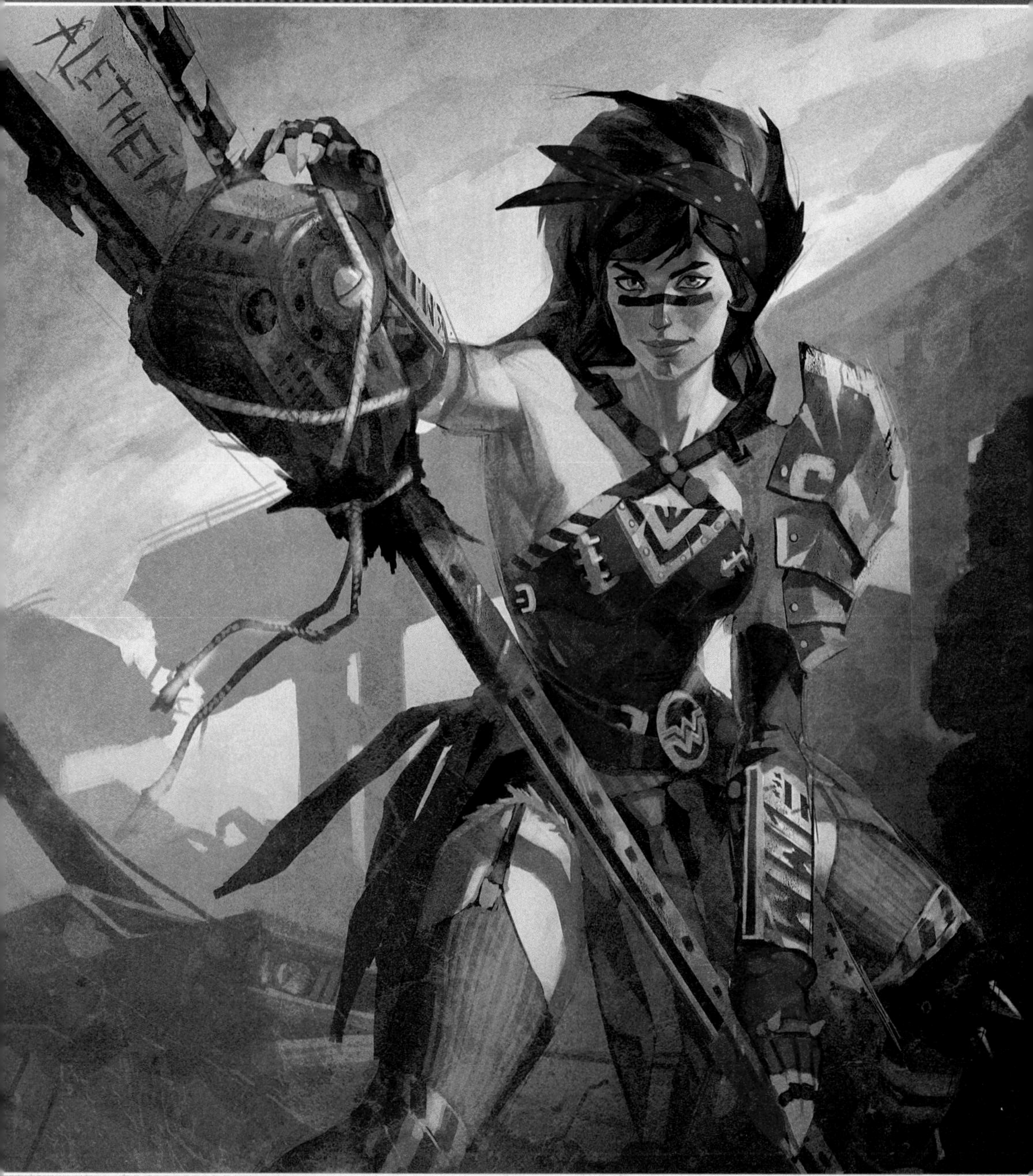
ALETHEIA

ATOMIC WONDER WOMAN

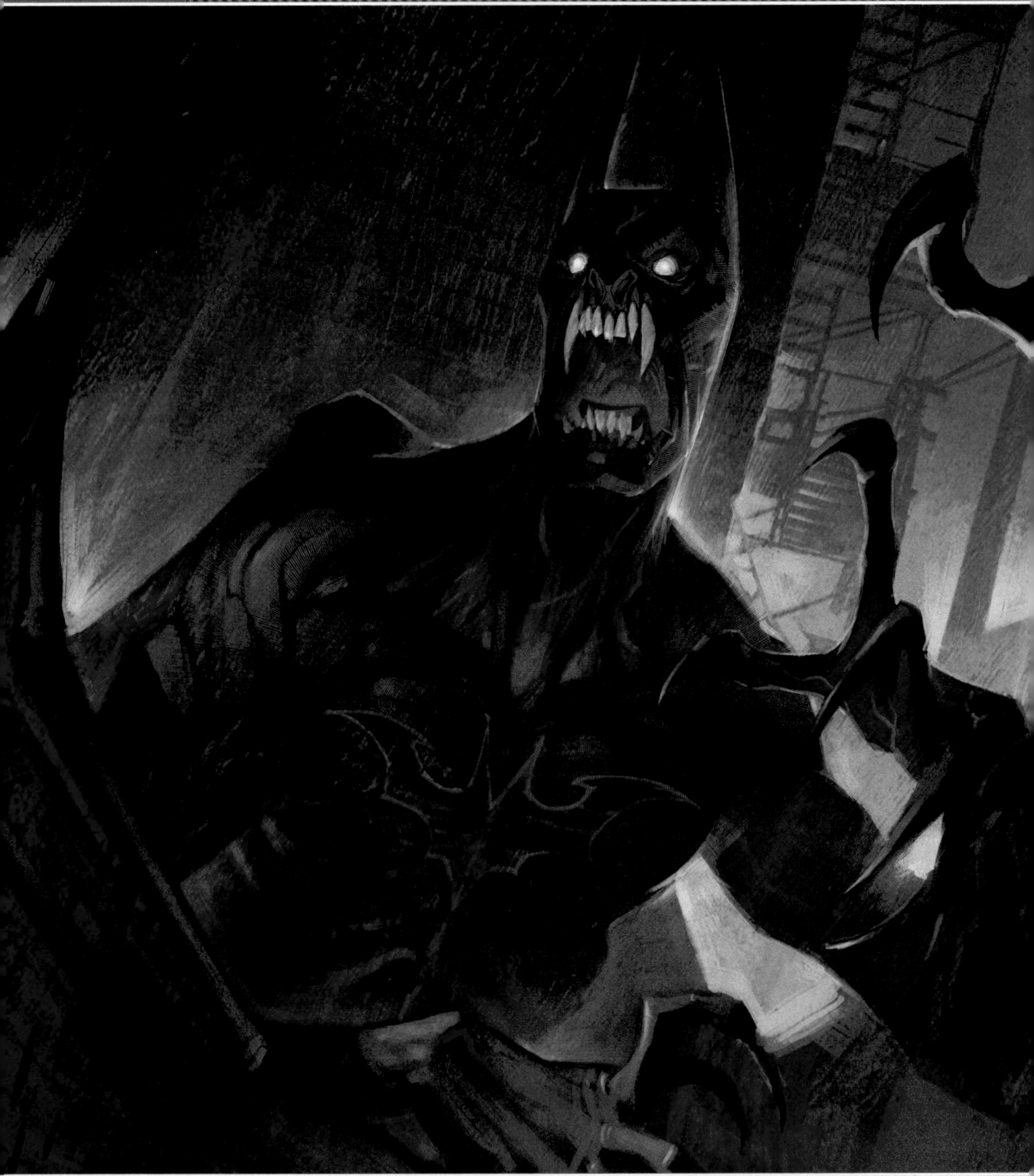

NIGHTMARE BATMAN

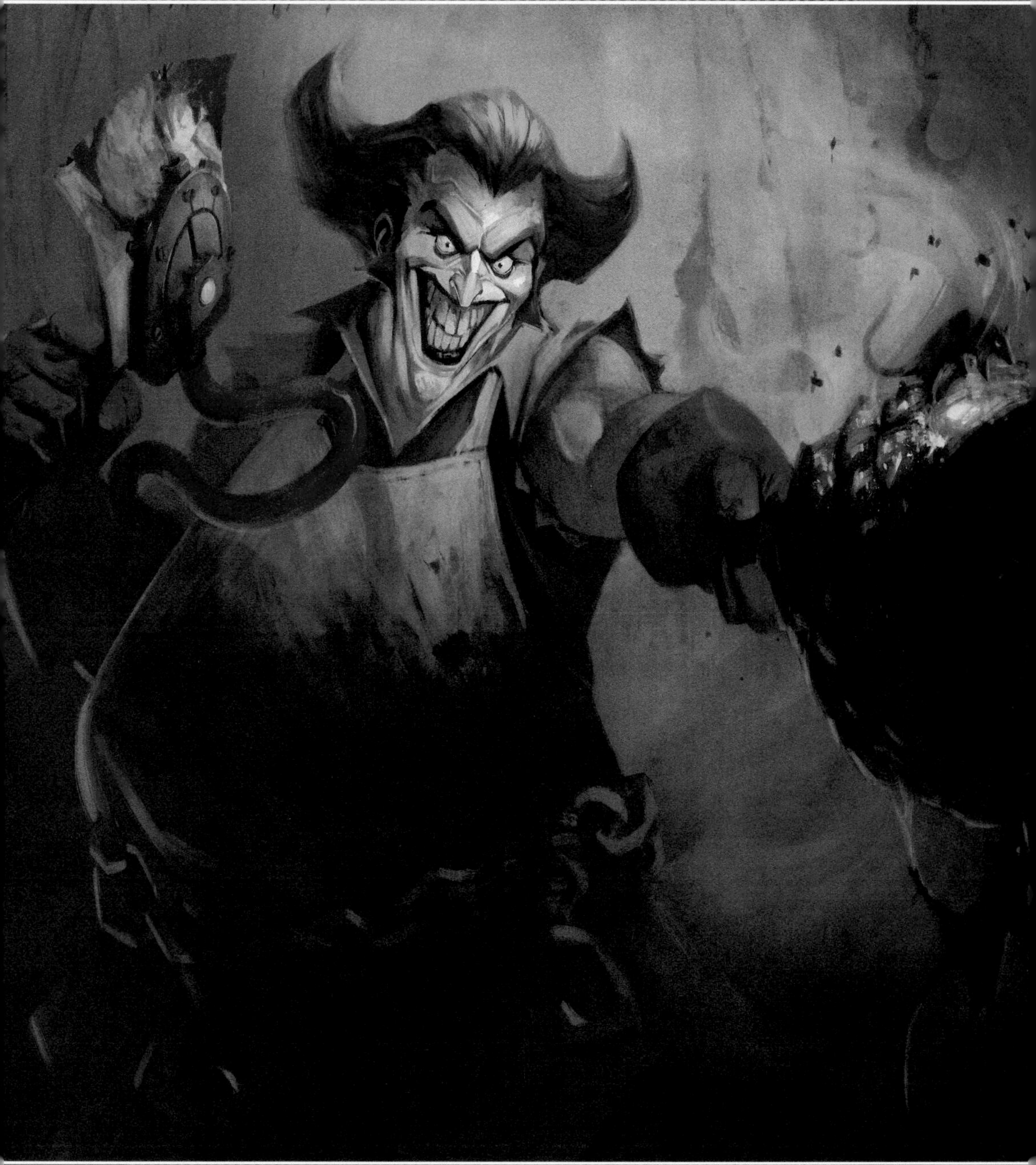

GASLIGHT JOKER

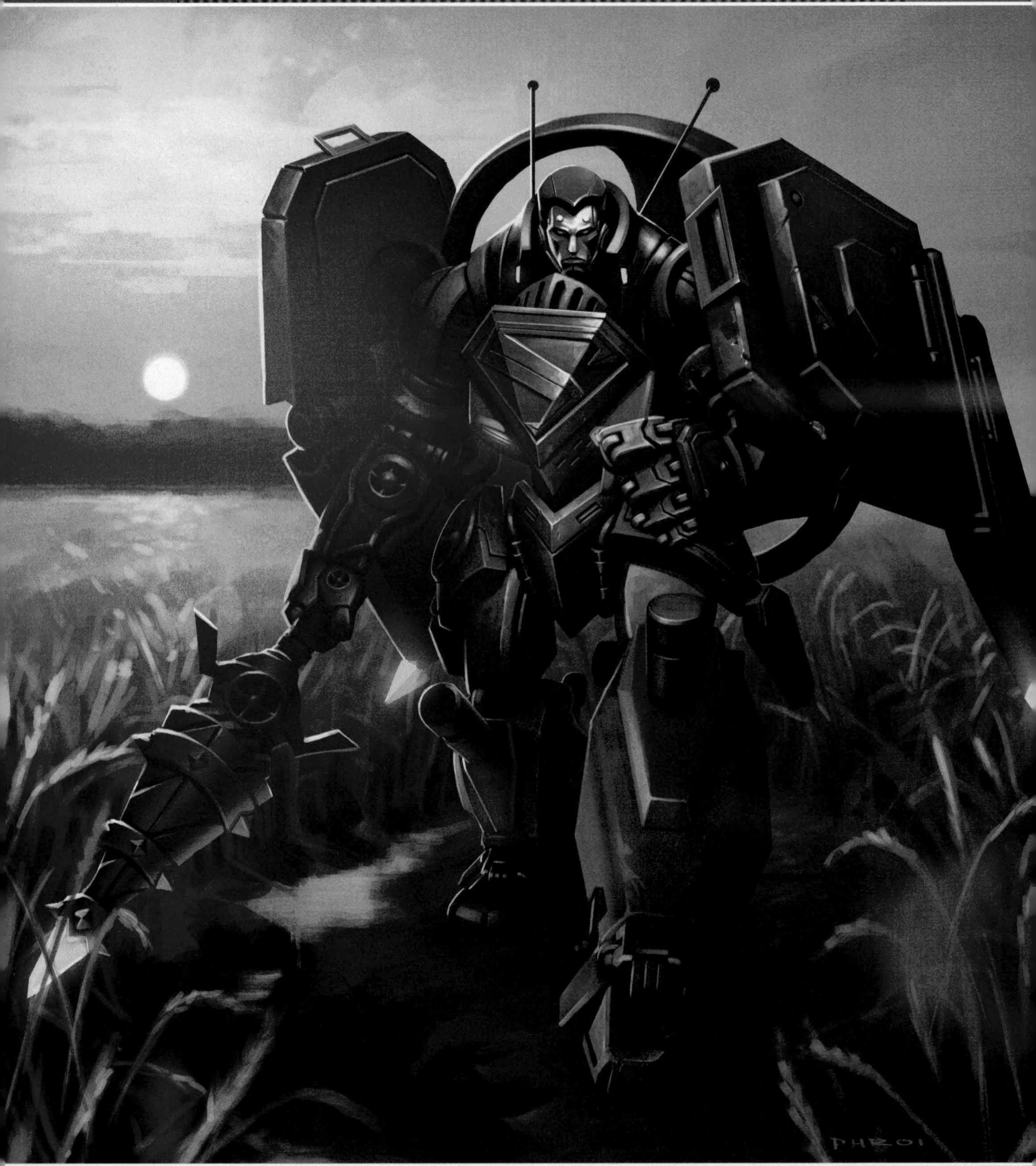
DHR01

MECHA SUPERMAN

ARCANE ZOD by Tom Derenick

ICE

FIRE

ATOMIC DOOMSDAY by Tom Derenick

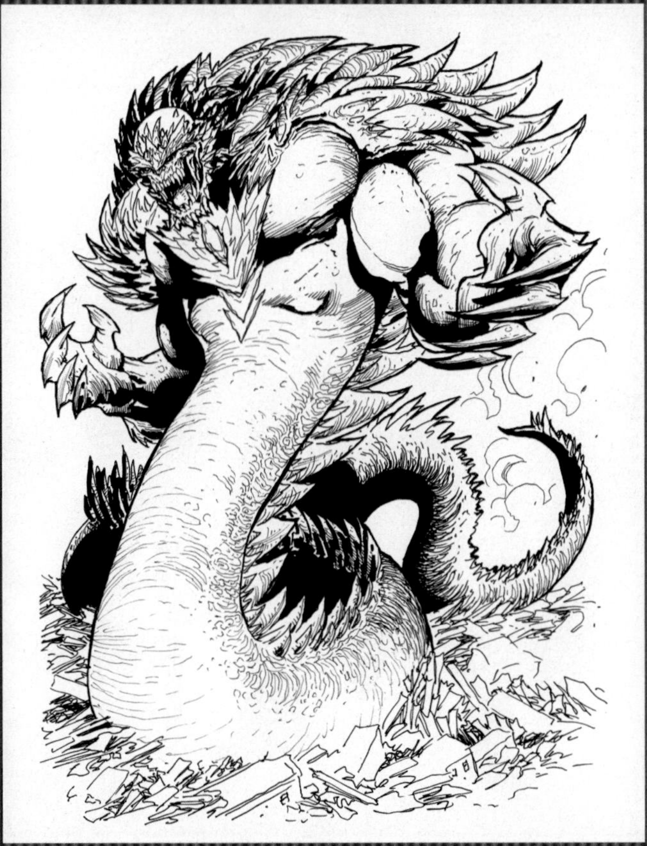

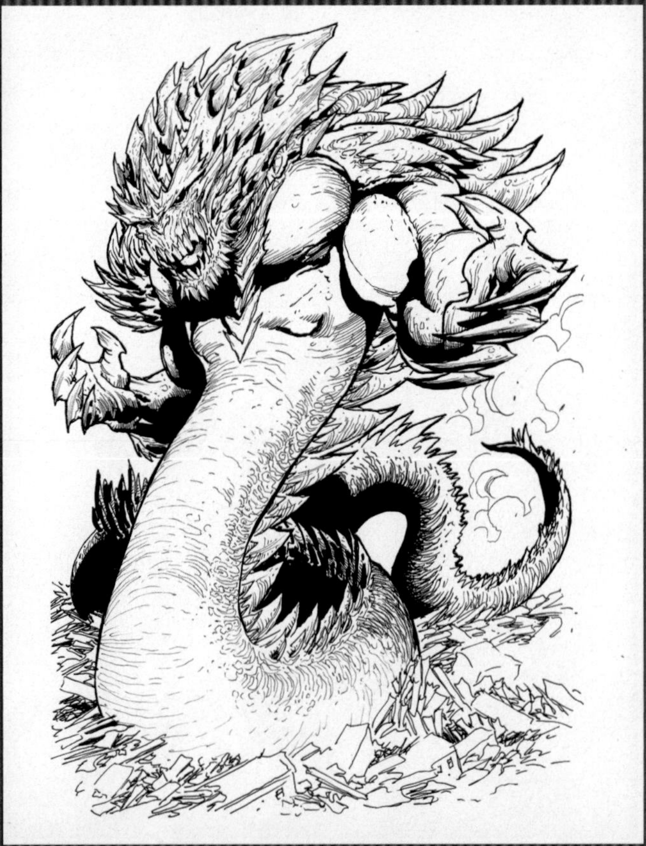

ATOMIC TWO-FACE by Jim Fletcher

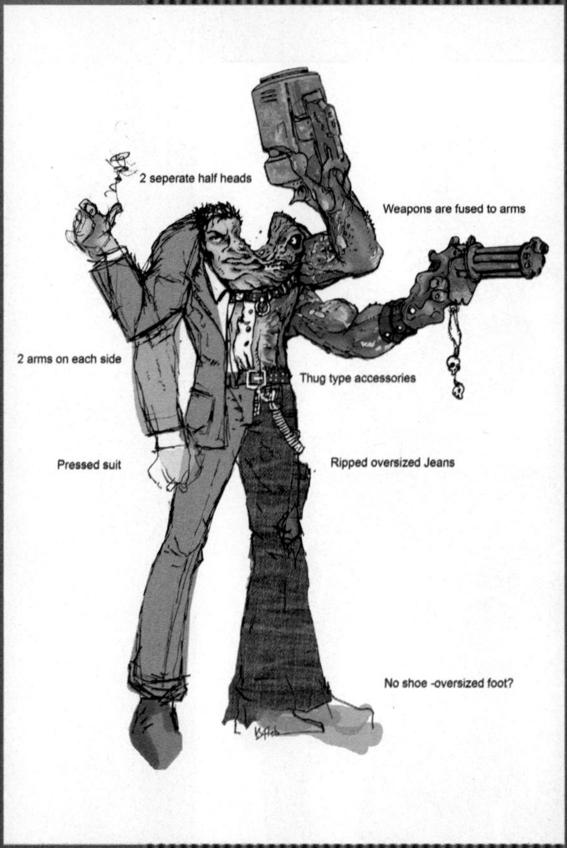
2 seperate half heads
Weapons are fused to arms
2 arms on each side
Thug type accessories
Pressed suit
Ripped oversized Jeans
No shoe -oversized foot?

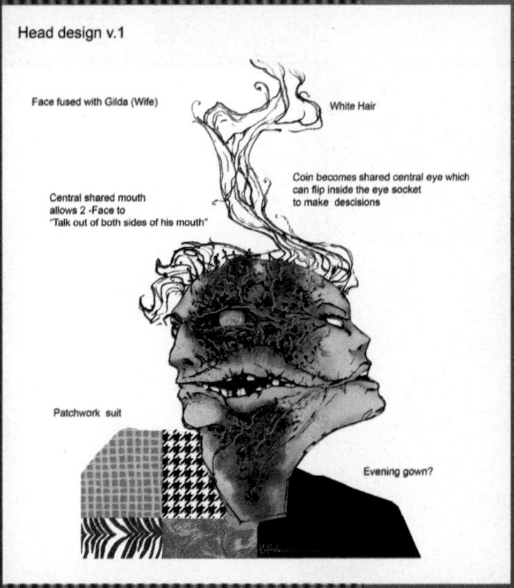
Head design v.1
Face fused with Gilda (Wife)
White Hair
Coin becomes shared central eye which can flip inside the eye socket to make descisions
Central shared mouth allows 2 -Face to "Talk out of both sides of his mouth"
Patchwork suit
Evening gown?

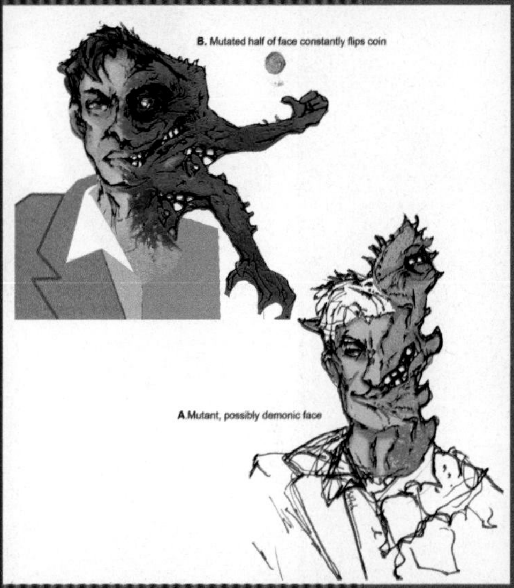
B. Mutated half of face constantly flips coin
A.Mutant, possibly demonic face

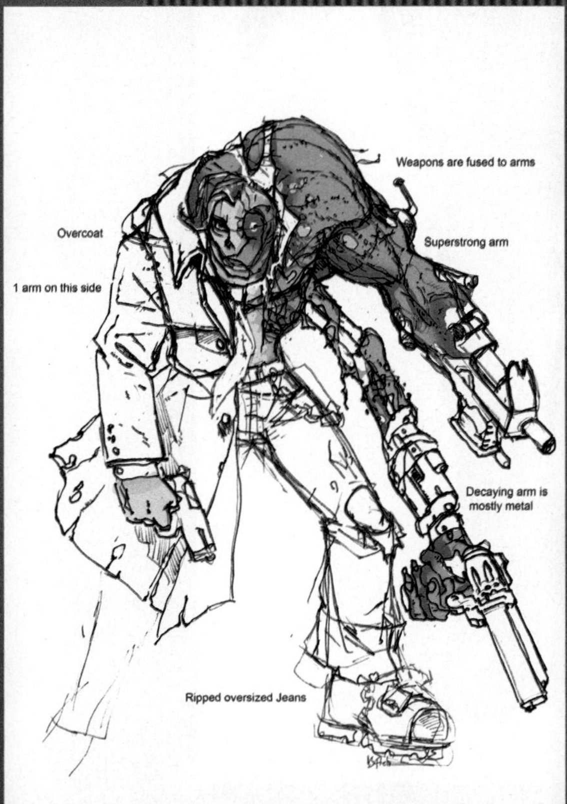
Weapons are fused to arms
Overcoat
Superstrong arm
1 arm on this side
Decaying arm is mostly metal
Ripped oversized Jeans

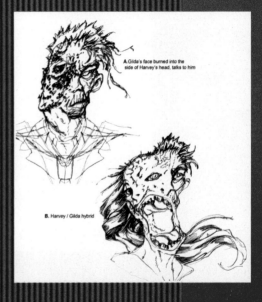

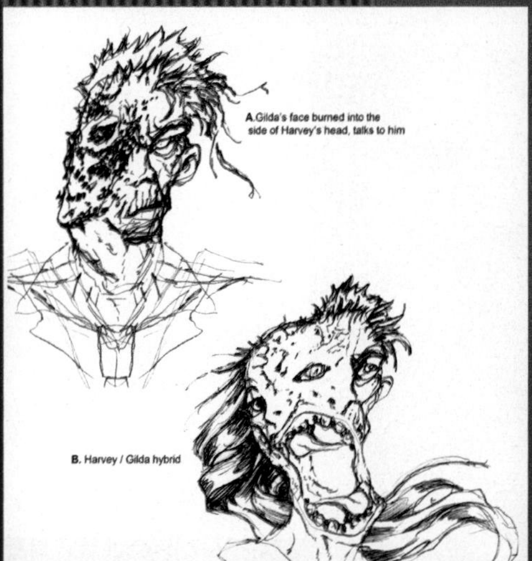
A.Gilda's face burned into the side of Harvey's head, talks to him
B. Harvey / Gilda hybrid

HARBINGER by Jim Fletcher

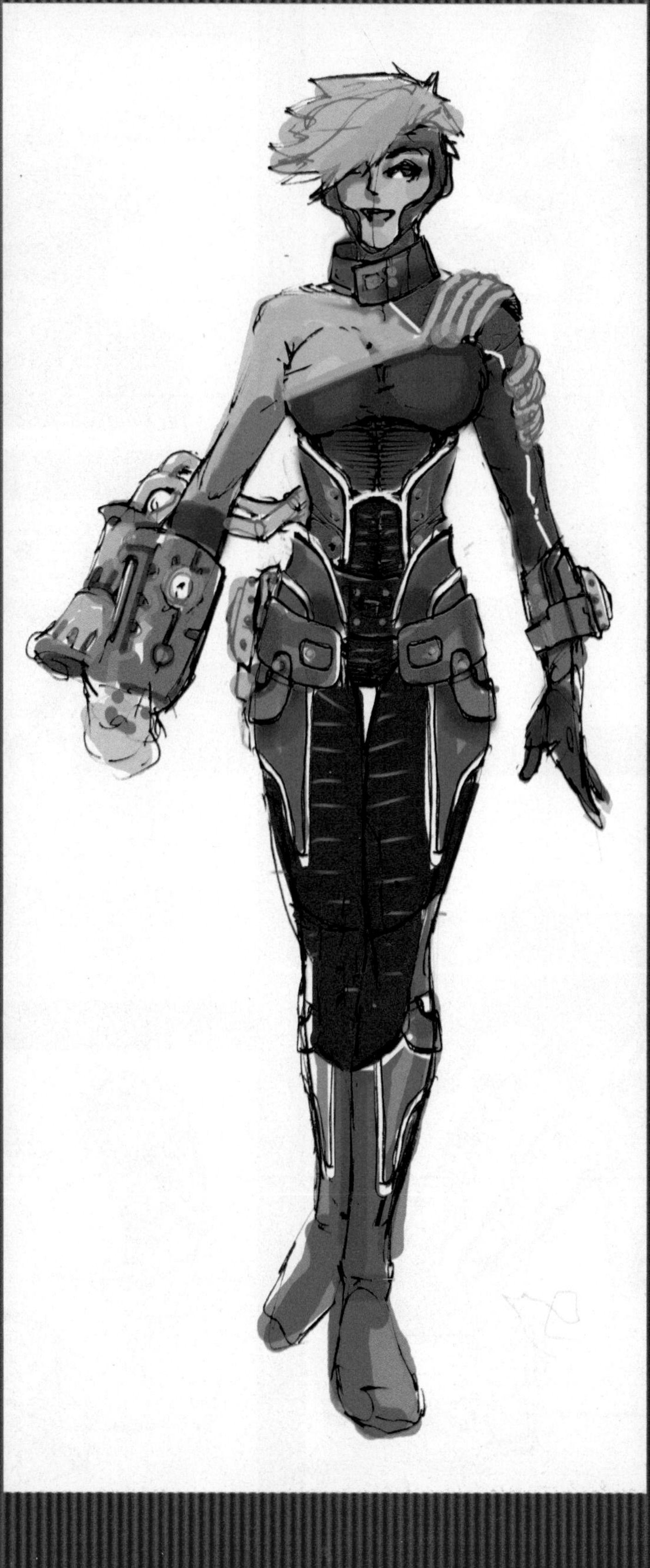